Time to RISE Up

Supporting Students' Mental Health in Schools

By Neil Moggan

TIME TO RISE UP

First published in 2024 by Scholary

The Dutch Barn, Bremhill Grove Farm, Chippenham, Wiltshire,
SN15 4LX, United Kingdom
Scholary is an imprint of Scholary Ltd

© 2024 Neil Moggan

All rights reserved. No part of this book may be reprinted or reproduced or utilised in any form or by electronic, mechanical, or other means, now known or hereafter invented, including photocopying and recording, or in any information storage or retrieval system, without permission in writing from the publishers.

British Library Cataloguing in Publication Data.
A catalogue record for this book is available from the British Library.

ISBN: 978-1-999909-2-8-4 (pbk)
ISBN: 978-1-999909-2-9-1 (hbk)

Foreword

Dr Liz Durden-Myers

This book is a much-needed exploration of student mental health, a subject of paramount importance in the landscape of education today. Arguably, the demands and expectations placed upon students are ever-increasing, and there arises an urgent need to create an environment that both nurtures academic success and prioritises the well-being of children and young people in our care.

There are many components of a successful education, but when distilled many would argue that as educators, we want our students to be happy, healthy, and successful, as children and as adults. Academic performance is but one lens through which a successful education can be observed and perhaps in education today this lens has become the dominant focus. Education can contribute to a much wider breadth of educational development goals including interpersonal relationships, emotional resilience, character, health and well-being and overall quality of life.

This book serves as a guide and a resource for educators navigating the intricate terrain of mental well-being within the context of education. It is a testament to the commitment we must all share in fostering a culture of empathy, understanding, and support within our educational environments.

Neil draws from a rich tapestry of research, practice, and professional insights, and presents a comprehensive roadmap for addressing the multifaceted aspects of student mental health. As we delve into these pages, we are confronted with the stark reality that mental health is not a luxury but a necessity. The pressures students face—from academic rigor to societal expectations—can cast a looming shadow over their emotional and psychological health. This book empowers readers with the knowledge and tools to dismantle the stigma surrounding mental health and encourage open conversations about our well-being.

Neil expertly takes the reader on a journey through this book to unravel the layers of student mental health and well-being, understanding the complexities that students grapple with daily, and how we as educators play a pivotal role in supporting those children and transforming their life chances.

Moreover, it emphasises the relationship between a positive state of well-being and academic success, challenging the archaic notion that mental health is a distraction from academic outcomes. Instead, it provides the sound rationale for positive mental health as the foundation upon which academic achievements can flourish, thus creating a positive feedback loop of success and well-being.

In an era where the world is increasingly interconnected and the pace of life is frenetic, the importance of mental health cannot be overstated. This book invites educators to become champions of mental health, equipping them with the knowledge to identify signs of distress and the skills to provide meaningful support.

This book encourages teachers to extend a hand—and is a stark reminder that seeking help is not a sign of weakness but a courageous step toward self-discovery and resilience. It helps teachers encourage students to embrace the concept of self-care, to prioritise their mental well-being amidst academic life, and to forge a path that leads not only to success in the classroom but also to a fulfilling and balanced life now and into adulthood.

In the spirit of collective responsibility, let this book be a catalyst for change, a call to action for all educationalists to become champions of mental health awareness and support. May it inspire a paradigm shift in how we perceive and prioritise the mental wellbeing of our students, ushering in an era where success is measured not only by academic achievements but also by the flourishing mental health and well-being of the individuals who grace our corridors and classrooms.

As we embark on this journey together, may the insights within these pages resonate with educators, parents, and students alike, fostering a community dedicated to nurturing happy, healthy, and successful children and young people equipped to navigate life's challenges.

Preface - Life Force

"Your purpose in life is to find your purpose and give your whole heart and soul to it."
Guatama Buddha

Why I wrote this book

As a teacher since 2004, I have been alarmed by the decline in students' mental health throughout the duration of my career. I became Head of Year in 2007, and I would support approximately 3 pupils from 160 per year group with mental health issues. Excuse me for generalising, but back then, these tended to be girls with anxiety and depression. Fast forward to now (2023), and it is often closer to 6 per class of 25, with both boys and girls being affected and younger and younger children being impacted. Intentional self-harm figures have gone through the roof, and our support services are overwhelmed with the level of need.

In my years teaching I have carried out many roles in schools and always wanted every child to make the most of their abilities so that they can lead a brilliant life. I have been a PE teacher, a form tutor, a head of year, a head of department, and a Director of Sport, Health & Relationships, Sex and Health Education (RSHE). I have taught thousands of children, some well, some not so well. I've had great successes and I've made a lot of mistakes.

Join me as I explore the reasons why in more detail and the creative ways schools have used to address this mental health epidemic. I hope this book encourages you to think, discuss and influence what we do in schools and how we can do our very best to give all our children the education they deserve and the life skills they need to live a long, healthy and happy life.

Key experiences

My life has been shaped by key personal and professional experiences that have resulted in caring passionately about early intervention programmes, trauma-informed practice and the link between physical activity and mental wellbeing to create a better future for our young people.

While we explore some of these, I want you to think about your own key experiences about mental health and wellbeing that impact your thinking on this subject.

In 2002, my father, a retired police officer, faced post-traumatic stress disorder (PTSD) after 25 years of service. Struggling with a sense of purpose, he found solace in a local running club. He embraced the club's camaraderie, engaging in marathons, triathlons, and more. This combination of physical activity and social bonds led him to triumph over PTSD and even represent England at 73, inspiring many in the process.

The first of many

In 2006, as a young teacher, personal challenges led me into isolation. Amidst a knee injury, unhealthy habits, relationship woes, and work pressures, I grappled with feelings of loneliness and concealed my struggles due to societal stigma. Despite seeking help from a GP, support was elusive, and the loss of a colleague on mental illness grounds underscored the need for better mental health awareness in education.

She was a lovely, caring lady, a brilliant, experienced teacher and leader, and a friend who gave so much to both our children and so many others, including myself. It has been heartbreaking to see how often this has happened in my teaching career, particularly with senior leaders who are crushed in an incredibly difficult and under-resourced situation. We have lost so many great teachers.

As I write, there is currently a recruitment and retention crisis in teaching. There are over 132,900 teachers in a Facebook support group for teachers planning to leave the classroom called 'Life After Teaching - Exit the classroom and thrive – Facebook group, 2023 and many initial teacher training courses are not getting the level of applicants required to fill the gap. Many teachers are battered and bruised from the impact and trauma of all the changes since lockdown, students' behaviour since Covid, feeling undervalued through lower pay in real terms and conditions, and the pressure of Ofsted and examination results.

Just like our Police, NHS workers and Fire officers, they deserve to be looked after better so that they can support society and give our young people the very best chance to be successful in the future. Unfortunately, I think teachers are being made to feel more disposable than ever in many places. Therefore, transforming staff wellbeing is an area I feel passionately about.

Finding my purpose

As a trainee teacher, my ambition was always to be a Director of Sport. I was inspired by my great friend/mentor/tennis opponent, Richard Stockings, and the incredible work he and his team had done to transform his sports college into a fantastic school through the power of Physical Education (PE). Like Richard, I wanted to create change for a whole school community through PE.

I achieved my ambition in the summer of 2014 when I secured my Director of Sport role at an Inner-City School that served one of the lowest socio-economic wards in Norwich. There was a 13-year life expectancy difference for our young people depending on what side of the main road outside of the school they were born on. When I first heard that statistic, the initial shock turned into anger, followed by a deep desire to take action to make a difference for these children.

Initially, we focused on reducing obesity and were recognised for our work by Sheffield Hallam University researchers who created a case study on us as one of the top 5 out of 250 schools with similar demographics. This case study was presented to the Department of Health & Social Care to inform the government's obesity strategy.

This programme and its recognition strengthened my resolve for wanting to focus on transforming the quality and quantity of our young people's lives.

One of the best academic frameworks I found for this is Swarbricks 8 Dimensions of Wellness (Swarbrick, M. 2006). I didn't just want to help our young people live longer, I wanted to give them the mental and social skills alongside the physical aspect so that they could not just survive but flourish. I also wanted to develop their financial literacy so they could develop the resources they needed in order for them and their future families to thrive.

Addressing the underlying causes

It dawned on me that for the previous 6 years since finding out about the 13-year life expectancy difference for my young people, I had been investing in ways to reduce that gap without improving the underlying factors that were causing this. A trauma Informed approach does this.

Therefore, I will continue to advocate for a trauma informed approach in our schools so that teachers can transform relationships to improve wellbeing, behaviour, engagement, attendance & progress in the short term and more importantly transform young people's life chances in the long term.

Feeling helpless

Another key experience occurred for me in Spring 2017. I vividly remember when three 12-year-old girls, Sarah, Phillipa and Amy, were brought in late to my gymnastics lesson. The teacher with them explained that the girls were really struggling with anxiety and asked if they could just sit out the lesson. This was the point that I realised just how far the average child's mental health had fallen since the start of my teaching career. It felt like I had been hit by a sledgehammer.

As a Director of Sport, I felt totally helpless that I had no strategies to support them and help them feel better. It fired me into action to research this area in more detail, so I didn't have to feel so helpless ever again.

Lockdown, time to think, and contrasting emotions

I appreciate that people had very different experiences of lockdown. For many it was incredibly challenging being boxed in with freedoms limited and opportunities to connect with loved ones curtailed and great trauma taking place. For others, it was a welcome chance to spend time with loved ones, take a break from the stresses of daily life and re-evaluate.

The first lockdown in the spring of 2020 was a chance for me to slow down and reflect, spend precious time with my young family, work with and invest in our key worker children and have time to research, plan and experiment with mental wellbeing strategies based on the mental fitness pyramid.

Our key worker children were lapping up the strategies I was experimenting with, and teaching was incredibly fun. I had access to the school fitness suite, and it was a chance to prioritise my own healthy habits around exercise, sleep, nutrition, hydration and mindfulness.

I was introduced to Trauma Informed Practice around this time through some excellent training through Beacon House where I first came across techniques such as the benefits of repetitive activities and pushing against heavy objects to regulate the amygdala.

A very different lockdown

The second lockdown in the winter of 2020/21 was the complete opposite. We lost an ex-student through intentional self-harm, it was devastating personally but even more so for his friends, family and the wider school community. He was a cheeky chappy who I had become more and more fond of as the years progressed, from first meeting him in lower school to regularly working out with him during after-school fitness club in his final year at our school.

I hadn't realised he was struggling with mental illness after he left school, and I was kicking myself. Why didn't I focus on mental wellbeing earlier so that he maybe could have benefitted. I was heartbroken for him, his friends and family and the wider community.

The fitness suite had been closed during this lockdown due to Covid restrictions. I was missing that opportunity to regulate my amygdala through weight training, the dark mornings and afternoons were not helping, and the hours and hours facing the computer screen throughout online learning did not suit me or my mental wellbeing.

Recovery

Schools returned and we worked incredibly hard as a team of teachers to make the school a fantastic place for our young people to attend every day to learn and recover from Covid.

Our early intervention programme was getting stronger every week as we found out what strategies worked with our different groups of children. We developed more and more innovative ways to implement an early intervention framework across the school. By now I had created the 'RISE Up' programme and I was supporting over 100 schools across the world in successfully implementing it.

The come down

As time progressed in a post Covid world, like many schools across the country, the pandemic had taken a significant toll on staff wellbeing. This was especially true for our staff team who had worked so tirelessly in incredibly challenging situations, the children we served, and our local community who were also grappling with the economic challenges that Covid had presented.

There was considerable instability and disruption resulting in the Academy changing Trust. Within the space of 12 months, we had lost our brilliant head teacher and his fantastic deputy, our chair of governors and approximately 50% of our staff. Any school in the world would have struggled with that amount of change, but particularly ours due to our local context. This level of change was starting to have a significant impact on the behaviour of many of our children who were crying out for some stability and love, having been through such a traumatic period.

For the first time in my teaching career, I was struggling to build the quality of the relationships I wanted with my young people, particularly with my most challenging children.

Hope

I had to find a solution as my current strategies just weren't working in my setting anymore. I enrolled onto the Diploma in Trauma and Mental Health-Informed Schools so I could deepen my knowledge of trauma informed practice to help young people to recover from trauma and particularly the impact of Covid for the children I taught.

That Autumn term in 2022 experimenting with Trauma Informed Practice was one of the most rewarding of my career as I became more emotionally available for my children and colleagues, I developed greater empathy and my relationships transformed with many of my most challenging young people to get the very best out of them despite the wider issues in the Academy.

Shaping philosophy

These key personal and professional experiences have shaped my philosophy and created a burning desire to champion early intervention programmes, trauma informed practice and the link between physical activity and mental wellbeing in our schools in a post lockdown world so that every young person and their teachers can benefit.

My journey in understanding children's mental wellbeing is deeply rooted in my multifaceted roles as a father, son, uncle, friend, and teacher. These connections have provided me with profound insights into the emotional intricacies that shape young minds. Through the lens of these relationships, I aim to approach the exploration of children's mental health within educational settings with a compassionate and empathetic perspective for all.

This unique blend of personal experiences, combined with my professional role as a teacher, forms the foundation of my writing. It drives me to uncover meaningful solutions that resonate on both a personal and societal level, with the ultimate goal of fostering a brighter and more nurturing environment for future generations.

Consider
How do your key personal and professional experiences impact your thoughts and feelings regarding mental health and wellbeing?

Looking ahead

In the initial segment of this book, we delve into the challenges surrounding children's mental health, examining school-related issues and delving into their origins, theories, and contexts.

Moving on to the second part, we pivot our focus to practical solutions for educators. By spotlighting early intervention programmes, we illuminate evidence-based approaches, best practices, real-world instances, and actionable recommendations.

Transitioning to the third section, we uncover the transformative potential of relationships and trauma-informed practices. Lastly, in the fourth part, we map out a pathway to progress, propelling us towards a brighter future for children's mental wellbeing.

A range of voices

Throughout our journey we will be brilliantly supported by mental health expert, Dr Catherine Wheatley, and a range of experts in their fields so that we can combine the evidence base with realistic practical application in schools.

We have also got a wide range of contributors to these important conversations, from children, parents, teachers and leaders. They are all part of our dynamic community determined to create a better future for our children. We hope you join us.

Navigating the path to empowering children's mental wellbeing

As you explore the pages of this book, our aim is to provide you with a comprehensive understanding of the challenges affecting children's mental health within educational systems.

By nurturing meaningful relationships and integrating these practices, you will be empowered to play a pivotal role in fostering the wellbeing of young minds, guiding them toward a promising way forward that holds the potential to reshape the educational landscape and empower future generations.

I am thrilled that you've chosen to engage with this book, and I sincerely hope you find our journey together to be enjoyable and enriching.

Preface References

- Life after teaching - Exit the classroom and thrive - Facebook group. (2023.). Available at: https://www.facebook.com/groups/LifeAfterTeachingExitTheClassroomAndThrive [Accessed 8 Jul. 2023].
- Swarbrick, M, (2006). A Wellness Approach. *Psychiatric Rehabilitation Journal*, pp.311–314.

Dedication

I would like to extend my heartfelt thanks to the following:

Dr. Liz Durden-Myers, for her invaluable guidance and support throughout this journey.

Dr. Catherine Wheatley, for her insightful contributions and all of our inspirational contributors, whose contributions enriched this book.

Will Swaithes, *Tracey Healey* and all the team at *PE Scholar*.

Janet Southgate, *Jonathan Richards*, and *Oscar Stelzar-Hiller*, for their invaluable assistance in researching and proofreading this book.

The thousands of young people I've had the privilege of teaching over the years, whose curiosity and enthusiasm fuelled my passion.

My colleagues, both past and present, who have been an integral part of this educational journey.

Finally, to *Katie*, *Charlotte* and *Jack*, your love, support, and patience mean the world to me.

Contents

Foreword III
Preface - Life Force IV
Why I wrote this book... V
Key experiences V
The first of many.. VI
Finding my purpose VII
Addressing the underlying causes.. VII
Feeling helpless... VIII
Lockdown, time to think, and contrasting emotions VIII
A very different lockdown.. IX
Recovery.. IX
The come down... X
Hope.. X
Shaping philosophy.. XI
Looking ahead.. XI
A range of voices... XII
Navigating the path to empowering children's mental wellbeing ... XII
Dedication XIII
Trigger warning XXIII

Part 1: What is the Problem?... 1
Chapter 1 Has there been a decline?...2
6 Wembley stadiums of children waiting for help 2
Self-Harm as a warning sign 4
Suicide prevention... 6
Professor Barry Carpenter's view 7
Eating disorder increase... 7
Decline in happiness 8
Understanding the alarming decline and outlining the key factors 10
Social media 10
The pandemic... 12
Family breakdown 13
Poverty, inequality, austerity and the cost of living crisis................. 14

CONTENTS

The Ukraine-Russia war 17
LGBTQ+ and mental health 17
Has our willingness to discuss mental health in schools contributed to a decline? 19
A crisis in mental health wait times for children 20
Academic pressures 21
Attendance in a post-lockdown world 22
Post lockdown behaviour 23
An education system in crisis? 25
Each child is unique 25
4 Influences on children's mental wellbeing 26
A call to take notice 27
Chapter summary 28
Critical questions 28
Additional insights 31

Chapter 2 - Imagine 38
Going upstream: addressing the root causes of children's mental health issues 38
Self-harm and storing up a problem 39
The U-turn 40
2050 mental illness hell 41
2050 mental health heaven 43
Time to decide 44
Lessons from the past: how a public health approach can help address children's mental health issues 46
Best practice for supporting children's mental health in schools 47
The importance of early support hubs for young people 50
The costs of mental health support in the UK 51
Chapter summary 54
Critical questions 55
Additional insights 56

Chapter 3 -
Should it be schools' responsibility to be the front line of mental health? 64
The role of a school 64
Reaching many 65
A moral responsibility? 66
Unhappy children cannot learn 67
Shaping wider society 67
The challenges for schools 68
Addressing these challenges 68
Schools looking after their staff 69
Inspectorates taking notice 70
Should it be the school's responsibility to be the front line of mental health? 71
What is the teacher's role in improving student wellbeing? 72
What can teachers do? 73
What can't teachers do? 74
Teachers: a mental health workforce? 74
The time challenge for teachers 77
Chapter summary *78*
Critical questions *79*
Additional insights *80*

Part 2: Early Intervention **85**
Chapter 4 - Identifying strugglers 86
Where are you today? 87
The mental health continuum 87
Using the mental health continuum 89
The mental health continuum check in 90
Reactive to proactive 91
The transformation of Adam: a teacher's journey 92
Recognising the stages for yourself 94
Putting on our own oxygen mask first 98
The myth of normal: nurturing teacher wellbeing 99
Concluding the chapter 101
Chapter summary *102*
Critical questions *102*

Chapter 5 - Reducing anxiety, raising aspirations 103
Nurturing Physical Literacy (Dr Liz Durden-Myers) 105
Building self-confidence 107
Positive affirmations 111
Catching glimmers 114
Self-kindness 116
Worries as a positive 120
Controlling the controllables and shrinking our worries 121
Creating a vision 127
Setting goals 129
Ikigai 132
The importance of the first step and moving forward 136
Perfectionism - a blessing and a curse 137
Measuring success 139
Chapter summary *141*
Critical questions *141*
Additional insights *143*

Chapter 6 - Building positive habits 147
The importance of sleep 151
Developing healthy sleep habits 152
Hydration habits 155
Nutrition habits 159
Practical tips for teachers 160
Balancing social media usage 162
Phone free schools 166
Top tips to help children balance their social media usage 167
Developing mindfulness 169
Practising gratitude 170
Body scanning 171
Journalling 173
Practising deep breathing 176
Chapter summary *178*
Critical question *179*
Additional inspiration *180*

Chapter 7 - Physical activity and the link with wellbeing ... 183
- A new challenge ... 185
- Repeaters ... 186
- Inclusive teams ... 187
- Stress busters ... 191
- Energisers ... 194
- The role of physical activity in building confidence ... 200
- *Chapter summary* ... 202
- *Critical questions* ... 202
- *Additional insights* ... 203

Chapter 8 - Getting your daily dose of happiness ... 206
- Feeling frustrated ... 206
- Feeling unmotivated ... 207
- Feeling unloved ... 209
- Pets as a secret weapon ... 209
- Feeling moody ... 212
- Feeling in pain ... 213
- Self-care menu ... 215
- Making learning stick for the long term ... 217
- *Chapter summary* ... 219
- *Critical questions* ... 219

Part 3: The Power of Relationships ... 221
Chapter 9 - The impact of trauma ... 222
- Schools falling apart post lockdown ... 222
- Becoming trauma informed ... 224
- What are adverse childhood experiences (ACEs)? ... 226
- What is affluent neglect? ... 228
- Toxic stress ... 228
- The ACE pathway ... 231
- What were the ACE questions? ... 232
- How does the ACE scoring system work? ... 233
- What about the impact of Adverse Childhood Experiences in schools? ... 233
- Understanding learned helplessness and its impact on children ... 234

Chapter summary *238*
Critical questions *239*
Additional insights *240*

Chapter 10 - Creating psychological safety 241
A story of hope 241
Professor Dan Hughes and the 4Cs 241
Protective factors 243
What are emotionally available adults? 245
What if that one person is you? 247
Coaching 248
Does each child you teach feel safe or under threat? 250
Fight/flight freeze vs calm, connected and safe 251
Face + voice + body = psychological safety 253
Watch your face 255
Psychological safety for your most challenging children 256
Investing in our most challenging young people 258
Low challenge? 259
Polyvagel theory in practice 259
Relationships are key 261
Chapter summary *262*
Critical questions *262*
Additional insights *263*

Chapter 11 - Connect before correct 280
Isn't this a book about mental health? 281
The need for punishment 284
A different world 285
Trauma taking its toll 286
Forgetting our basics 287
What if? 288
Hunting for solutions 288
Culling unnecessary rules 289
The Neurosequential model 291
The PACE model 293
Playfulness 294

Acceptance 295
Curiosity and empathy 296
Aren't trauma informed behaviour policies too wishy washy? 297
The motorway 298
Outcomes on individual students and class as a whole 299
Chapter summary *300*
Critical questions *301*
Additional insights *302*

Chapter 12 - Time to play 307
So where does play fit in? 308
Jaak Panksepp and balancing the 7 Systems Seesaw 310
Blocked trust 313
Emotional states become personality traits 314
The importance of play wrapped in care 315
Opportunities for schools 317
Play becomes healing 320
Recovery 321
The teenage brain 321
Mattering matters 322
The rollercoaster of recovery 323
Not all students will recover 324
Prioritising Self-Care 325
Bringing our colleagues along on the journey to trauma informed 326
Benefitting all 328
Chapter summary *329*
Critical questions *330*
Additional insights *331*

Part 4: Moving Forward Together 335

Chapter 13 - Creating whole school impact 336
Within PE 338
Where do wellbeing programmes fit in with the national curriculum? 340
Transforming outcomes 343
Within RSHE and personal development lessons 348
During form times 350
Social media content to improve the wellbeing of the whole school community 351
In school clubs 351
Sport sanctuaries 352
Student voice 353
Active play and active travel 353
Enrichment days 354
Staff wellbeing programmes 356
Cross curricular opportunities 357
Chapter summary 358
Critical questions 359
Additional insights 360

Chapter 14 - Creating cultural change, changing the narrative 373
Creating cultural change for children's mental wellbeing 373
A common language 375
Breaking the stigma: promoting open conversations and empathy 378
Using role models to break stigma 379
What do Ben Stokes, Simone Biles and Naomi Osaka all have in common? 381
Shifting perspectives and embracing a positive narrative 383
Chapter summary 386
Critical questions 386

Chapter 15 - Celebrating success 387
Mental health heroes 388
Sports awards evening 388
Success breeds motivation 388
Impact celebrating success has on our relationships 389
Celebrating our colleagues 391
Celebrating school success 393

Chapter summary *398*
Critical questions *399*

Chapter 16 - Time to RISE Up 400
Skills for the future 401
So what action do we need to take? 402
The secret formula for transformational teachers 402
Outstanding relationships 403
Early intervention strategies 405
Opportunities for physical activity and play 407
Everyone has a role to play to create this transformation 409
The benefits for our young people 418
Time to RISE Up together 419
Are you ready to RISE UP? 419
Chapter summary *420*
Critical questions *420*

Trigger warning

This book discusses sensitive and potentially upsetting topics such as self-harm, suicide, childhood trauma and mental health illnesses. Included below are a selection of helpline numbers and references to mental health services, meant to be of assistance in times of crisis for either yourself or someone close to you.

Mind
0300 123 3393
mind.org.uk
Offering help whenever you might need it through information, advice and local services.

Samaritans
116 123
samaritans.org
24-hour emotional support for anyone who needs to talk.

YoungMinds
0808 802 5544 *(parents helpline)*
85258 *(crisis messenger service, text YM)*
youngminds.org.uk
Committed to improving the mental health of babies, children and young people, including support for parents and carers.

Part 1:
What is the Problem?

Chapter 1 – Has there been a decline?

"In the middle of difficulty lies opportunity."
Albert Einstein

In this chapter we will explore the evidence base to see if my anecdotal experiences of a decline in the mental health of the children I teach in education, are reflected in wider society, and outline the scale of any potential problem. We will then explore a range of potential factors behind any decline and what the impact has been in schools.

6 Wembley stadiums of children waiting for help

At the 2023 Youth Sports Trust Conference, the keynote speaker was Dr Alex George, who is Youth Mental Health Ambassador to the Government. Dr Alex said we currently have the equivalent of 6 packed Wembley stadiums full of children waiting to be seen by mental health professionals in this country, with some waiting 2 years to be seen.

Like many of you reading this book, I have had the pleasure of taking minibuses full of kids to Wembley on school trips to watch England play. The scale of the stadium is impressive and it's certainly a challenge to get all your kids to and from the minibus without losing any among the throngs of the crowd. Now, times the capacity of Wembley by 6, and the numbers of young people struggling with mental illness without support seems staggering.

Each young person has a unique and sad story. Behind them is worried family, friends and teachers concerned for what the future holds for their loved one and are desperate to support them.

This book holds a special purpose for me: to potentially save lives. If just one teacher is inspired so that they can help a young person find solace, then the effort will be worth it. Our journey begins by looking at the facts and figures behind intentional self-harm and then we can work back from there.

We will start by looking at the evidence base through the eyes of Professor Louis Appleby, from his webinar for the Anna Freund Centre on July 2022 with Peter Fonagy, which looked at 'Is there a suicide crisis in young people?' Professor Louis Appleby leads the National Suicide Prevention Strategy for England so is incredibly well placed to explore this question. (Anna Freud National Centre for Children and Families, 2022)

The World Health Organization estimates that there are over 700,000 deaths by suicide per year worldwide, with about three-quarters of these deaths occurring in lower and middle-income countries. The lowest suicide rate on record in England was in 2007, with a rate of 9.0 per 100,000 population. However, the onset of the global recession resulted in a rise in suicide rates, which peaked five to six years later with an additional 700 deaths per year.

Based on the most recent data available from 2020, suicide rates vary significantly by sex, with males having a rate three times higher than females. The highest suicide rates in England are found among middle-aged men, particularly those in their 40s and 50s, driven by factors such as the economy and alcohol. In contrast, young people under 20 have the lowest suicide rates of any demographic group, about half the general population rate. However, suicide remains the most common cause of death in adolescents and adults up to the age of 35 in England, highlighting the urgent need for effective suicide prevention strategies across all age groups.

Looking at the data for suicide rates in young people, specifically those aged 15 to 19 in England and Wales, shows a steady rise since 2010. The rates for males and females combined are currently the highest seen in 20 years, while the rate for young girls is the highest seen in 40 years. There appears to be a slightly different pattern for girls, with a later onset to the rise and a steeper increase in recent years.

This is not unique to England. There are other countries that have seen a similar rise, they are other developed countries, and they tend to have a feature in common, and that feature is income inequality. Statistics coming out of the USA since 2011, according to the Centers for Disease Control and Prevention, demonstrate that incidents of self-harm for teenage girls have increased by 62 per cent in girls aged 15-19 and by an enormous 189 per cent for 10-14-year-olds, with similar increases for suicides. (The Social Dilemma, 2020)

These historically high rates are a cause for concern and highlight the need for effective suicide prevention strategies targeted towards young people. It is essential to understand the factors contributing to the increase in suicide rates among young people and work towards addressing them, to promote mental health and wellbeing in this population.

We have now established the evidence base that suicide rates for all young people is the highest it has been for 20 years and for young girls is the highest seen in 40 years. What about the data around self-harm though? Anecdotally, this appears to be a major issue in schools in a post lockdown world. Is self-harm an important issue that we need to consider as educators?

Self-Harm as a warning sign

According to Professor Lewis Appleby, self-harm is a significant issue that is closely related to suicide. Self-harm refers to intentional self-injury, regardless of the intent, and is a serious sign for the future. Approximately 50% of people who die by suicide have previously self-harmed, indicating a missed opportunity for intervention. Young people who self-harm may not always be treated as having a serious problem when they present at emergency departments, but evidence shows that self-harm has a major prognostic significance.

The risk of suicide is markedly increased, about 50-fold, in the year following an episode of self-harm. It is essential we recognise the significance of self-harm as a risk factor for suicide and to intervene appropriately to prevent further harm. (Anna Freud National Centre for Children and Families, 2022)

Professor Lewis Appleby and his team are actively monitoring self-harm rates across hospitals in Manchester, Derby, and Oxford in England. Their research indicates that self-harm is predominantly prevalent among young people, particularly females aged 15-19 years, and there is a very large peak. The concern is that this group of 15–19-year-old females is essentially demonstrating a longer-term suicide risk. Our concern for them should not be just on what they do on a particular day, but on what this might signify about their vulnerability long term. As a father, and a teacher who cares passionately about future generations, this worries me greatly.

There has also been an increase in the number of young people under 20 who are presenting to their general practitioners (GPs) due to self-harm. The data shows an abrupt rise in the number of girls aged 13 to 16 who are self-harming, indicating a possibility of moving down the age range. This trend highlights the need for effective and accessible support for young people struggling with self-harm.

The most common reason given for self-harm is to cope with emotions. This suggests a worrying trend towards normalising self-harm as a natural response to stress. As young people get older, having learned self-harm as a coping mechanism, they may carry this risk with them into higher suicide rate age groups, which could lead to a future increase in death by suicide.

Professor Lewis Appleby has cautioned against using the term "crisis" when referring to the current state of suicide and self-harm rates. However, he acknowledges that we are at a high point in these behaviours and that it should serve as a warning to all of us. It is clear that suicide and self-harm rates are increasing, particularly in young people, and that urgent action is needed to address this issue.

There has also been a surge in the number of young people presenting to A&E with self-inflicted injuries. According to a study by the Royal College of Psychiatrists, the number of children and young people admitted to hospital for self-harm increased by 50% during the pandemic. Timely care is vital but waiting times are growing and more under-18s are presenting at A&E for mental health issues. (The Royal College of Psychiatrists, 2022)

Within my school and many others there was a major increase in incidents of self-harm. Self-harm is often seen as a coping mechanism for dealing with emotional pain and trauma. It is a way for young people to exert control over their lives, even if only for a brief moment. During the pandemic, many young people turned to self-harm as a way of managing their feelings of distress and anxiety.

With what we are seeing in our schools at the moment around self-harm, this link worries me greatly for future years. The data suggests a growing problem that requires attention and intervention to address the underlying issues contributing to self-harm behaviours. We need effective support and treatment services to help individuals manage their mental health and reduce their risk of self-harm.

Suicide prevention

Professor Lewis Appleby found that suicide prevention cannot be limited to one factor. Suicide is influenced by a range of factors, including alcohol or drug use, academic pressures, physical health, bereavement, online risk, family factors, isolation, bullying, abuse, and experiences of being in care or identifying as LGBT+. These factors can act as antecedents to suicide in young people, with some being early traumatic experiences and others occurring in adolescence. (Anna Freud National Centre for Children and Families, 2022)

His study found that access to services specifically for children is key in suicide prevention. Furthermore, the study identified cumulative risk as a model for understanding how suicidal behaviour develops, with a combination of early life traumatic experiences and adversity in adolescence leading to an accumulation of risks, and a final straw event acting as the tipping point towards suicidal behaviour.

Professor Lewis Appleby emphasised the role of wider society in suicide prevention, particularly when societal values go wrong and people become disappointed, demoralised, and alienated. He suggested that society should reflect the values that young people seek, including diversity, inclusion, internationalism, protection for the environment, and abolishing inequalities. Young people want fair rent, real job prospects and opportunities, economic stability, a voice, and a vote that counts.

Suicide prevention statistics are not about one thing, and prevention starts with understanding the challenges of traumatic childhoods and the turbulence of adolescence. Suicide prevention ultimately takes us to creating a more hopeful future for young people.

Professor Barry Carpenter's view

At the 2022 Youth Sport Trust Conference in March, I had the pleasure of listening to Professor Barry Carpenter, the UK's first Professor in Mental Health in Education. He outlined findings regarding children's wellbeing, and it was depressingly stark. I have featured them here:

- In June 2020, 1 in 6 of all children had a mental health need, the true figure is likely to be much worse. One CAMHS provider in the Midlands has seen their typical waiting list go from 30 young people to 300 in just 6 months. The situation has deteriorated so much that some figures are not being released.
- Child psychologists reported seeing symptoms of Post-Traumatic Stress Disorder in children for the first time that are common with soldiers who have fought on the battlefield.
- In addition, there has been a 68% increase in young people with eating disorders since the pandemic started.
- Staff wellbeing data portrays an incredibly bleak picture at the moment as teachers struggle to process the trauma, they have also been through over the last 2 years.

In May 2023, we had 466,250 young people undergoing treatment or waiting to start care in CAMHS. This is the highest number on record, according to Young Minds. (Young Minds, 2023)

Eating disorder increase

Eating disorders are particularly dangerous as a mental illness, due to the significant physical, emotional, and psychological effects they can have on a person's health and wellbeing.

Hospital admissions for children and young people with eating disorders increased by 90% in the last five years. A stark rise of 128% has been seen in boys and young men — from 280 hospital admissions in 2015/16 to 637 in 2020/2021. (The Royal College of Psychiatrists, 2022)

In addition to the physical health effects, eating disorders can also have severe emotional and psychological impact on a person. Individuals with eating disorders often experience intense feelings of guilt, shame, and anxiety around food and their bodies, which can lead to depression, self-harm, and suicidal thoughts. Eating disorders are often accompanied by other mental health conditions such as anxiety, depression, and obsessive-compulsive disorder, which can further exacerbate the severity and complexity of the illness.

Decline in happiness

The Good Childhood Report, an annual publication by The Children's Society in the UK, has offered valuable insights into long-term trends in the wellbeing of children and young people over the past decade. While specific factors contributing to wellbeing may vary from year to year, some consistent trends have emerged:

One notable and concerning trend highlighted by the report is a consistent decline in children's reported levels of happiness or life satisfaction. This decline in overall well-being has raised questions about the underlying causes and how they may be addressed.

The report has frequently explored children's perceptions of their school experiences. It has consistently shown a decline in children's happiness with their experiences in schools, a significant finding considering the pivotal role that education plays in their lives.

Over the years, the report has provided data-driven insights into the wellbeing of children and young people. By tracking long-term trends, it offers valuable information for policymakers, educators, and researchers to better understand the evolving challenges and opportunities that impact the lives of children in the UK. (The Children's Society, 2022)

Figure 1:
Trends in children's (aged 10 to 15) happiness with different aspects of life, UK 2009-10 to 2019-20

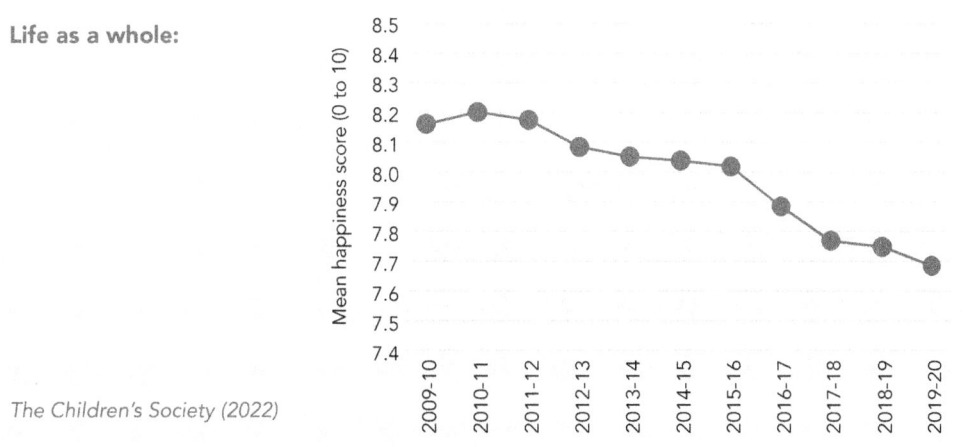

The Children's Society (2022)

TIME TO RISE UP

Similar trends have been seen in the annual Girls' Attitudes survey since 2009.

Figure 2:
Girls' Attitudes Survey

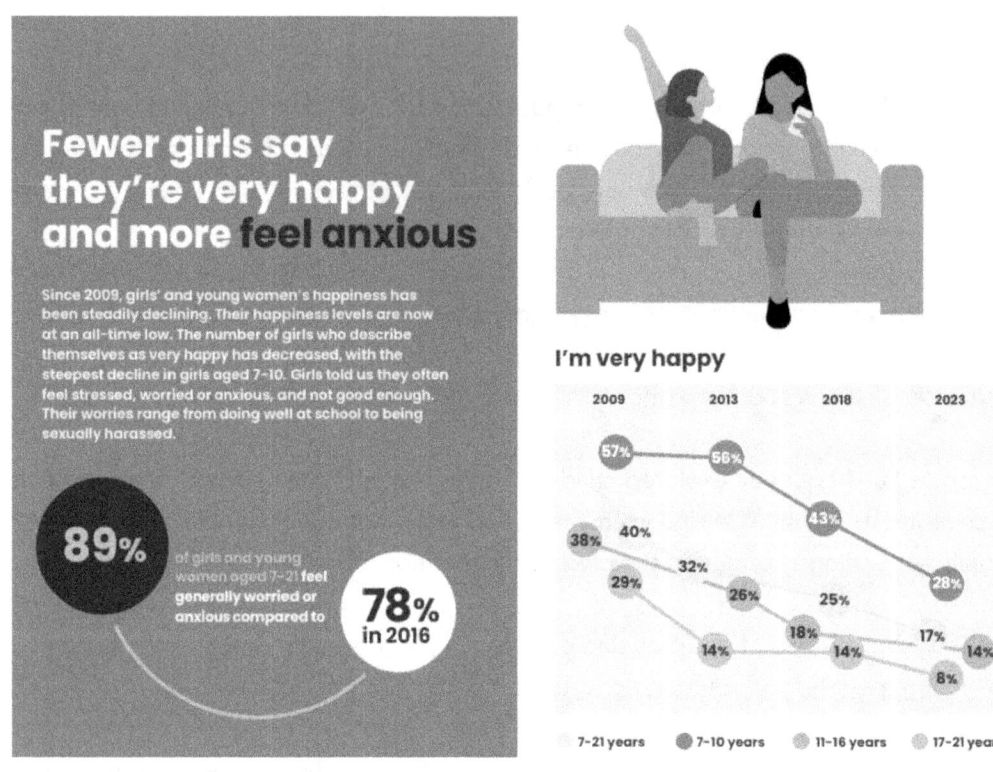

© Girl Guiding, 2023

It begs the question, are we letting our young people down?

Consider this…
- How does this data correlate with what you have seen in the duration of your teaching career?

Understanding the alarming decline and outlining the key factors

As we conclude this first part of the chapter, it's hard not to feel a sense of alarm about the state of children's mental health today. The narrative demands our attention and calls for meaningful action. In the face of rising suicide rates among young individuals and the distressing prevalence of self-harm, it becomes evident that we stand at a critical juncture, poised to shape the wellbeing of future generations.

Now we have established that the data proposes there has been a significant decline in the mental wellbeing of our young people, let's drill down to explore some of the factors behind it and how they have affected young people in schools.

In this section we will explore the role of social media, the Covid 19-pandemic, austerity measures since 2011, poverty and inequality, family breakdown, academic pressures, the War in Ukraine, and the cost-of-living crisis.

Social media

I want to start by exploring the role of social media. I remember being in my PE office when a trainee PE teacher introduced me to Facebook for the first time in 2007. Little did we know the impact social media was going to have on the way we, and young people live our lives.

Throughout my teaching career, I witnessed the growing importance of social media among young people, and anecdotally, it seemed to play a significant role in the decline of children's mental health.

In my teaching experience, it was not uncommon for 13-year-old girls to report spending over 13 hours a day on social media during weekdays and even longer on weekends.

Statistics from the U.S. since the availability of social media on mobile phones from 2011 show a significant increase in self-harm incidents for teenage girls, with a 62% increase in girls aged 15-19 and a 189% increase for 10–14-year-olds. The social psychologist and NYU professor Jonathan Haidt observed a 'gigantic increase' in depression and anxiety among young people, attributing it to the impact of social media on their sense of identity and self-worth, as well as their ability to connect with others. Similar patterns have been observed in England. (The Social Dilemma, 2020)

A report by The Wall Street Journal in September 2021 revealed that Facebook (now Meta), which owns Instagram, had conducted internal research showing the negative impact of the platform on the mental health of some teenagers, particularly teenage girls. However, Facebook chose not to disclose this information publicly until it was leaked to the media. These reports have ignited concerns about the impact of social media on children's mental health and have led to calls for more regulation and oversight of social media platforms. (Wells, Horwitz and Seetharaman, 2021)

A study conducted by Professor Lewis Appleby and peers found that about a quarter of young people who died by suicide had used the internet in ways related to suicide, particularly girls. Social media played a significant role in communicating suicidal intent, although searching for suicide methods was the most common online behaviour related to suicide. This has highlighted the need for regulation, such as the UK government's Online Safety Bill, to address the availability of unregulated information on suicide methods that has had fatal effects on distressed young people. (Anna Freud National Centre for Children and Families, 2022)

The increasing use of social media and computer games by children had a profound effect on their experiences in school. Many of us reported difficulties in getting children to participate in extracurricular activities. This combination of increased social media use and decreased physical activity negatively affected children's mental wellbeing.

Friendship issues became more prevalent, with children bringing external conflicts into school. Cyberbullying and sexting incidents increased, requiring more time from pastoral teams to resolve. Vulnerable children had little escape from bullying, and for some, the home was no longer a safe sanctuary. Research suggests that written comments can have a more significant impact on cyberbullying victims than verbal comments. Victims reported higher levels of stress, depression, isolation, and helplessness compared to victims of traditional bullying. Written comments can be saved and shared, leading to prolonged and widespread harm. The anonymity of the internet can result in more extreme and hurtful comments.

When I reflect back on our practices in schools and as teachers since the introduction of social media, I think many more schools would have reduced phone usage a lot earlier in schools and also spent more time educating parents on the dangers of social media.

While social media is a significant contributor to the decline in children's mental wellbeing, it is not the sole cause. It is also worth remembering that for some students it can be their only lifeline if they feel particularly isolated within school. I know this point was brilliantly articulated, by a student council to a fantastic headteacher, who was keen to rid his institution of children using phones during the school day.

Social media has though, been a significant contributor to the decline in children's mental wellbeing since 2011. We as teachers, parents and other professionals who work with children, need to be aware of these risks and provide guidance and support to help children navigate the online world in a healthy and safe way.

The pandemic

The COVID-19 pandemic left an enduring mark on children's mental health worldwide, described by the World Health Organisation Director-General as causing more "mass trauma" than World War II. A study estimated a 6% increase in adolescents with high depressive symptoms, underscoring the need for a comprehensive approach to address adolescent mental health. (www.youtube.com, 2022.)

Key impacts included:
- **Disruption of Routine:** School closures and lockdowns disrupted daily routines, causing stress and uncertainty.
- **Social Isolation:** Reduced social interactions and opportunities to play due to school closures increased loneliness, anxiety, and depression.
- **Family Stress:** Job losses, financial difficulties, health concerns, and loss of loved ones heightened family stress, affecting children.
- **Decreased Access to Mental Health Services:** Strain on resources made it harder for children to access the support they needed, compounded by remote learning.
- **Increased Screen Time:** Online learning and limited outdoor activities led to a significant increase in screen time.
- **Educational Stress:** Learning disruptions, exam uncertainty, and potential loss of opportunities added to stress.

Amidst this challenging landscape, specific narratives emerged, reflecting both the resilience and vulnerabilities of young minds.

As schools cautiously reopened their doors after the lockdowns, an unexpected challenge emerged – anxiety in PE changing rooms. A significant number of children reported feeling overwhelming anxiety when faced with changing in front of their peers. For some, this anxiety was so severe that it compelled them to avoid school altogether.

In response to this pressing issue, schools and mental health professionals rallied to provide support to these struggling children. Initiatives were launched to create safe spaces within changing rooms, where children could feel more at ease. Resources were developed to help parents and teachers address anxiety in children, offering strategies to navigate these difficult moments. Moreover, counselling and therapy services were made available for those in need. This issue highlighted the importance of understanding the unique struggles that children faced as they reintegrated into school life.

Reflecting on the COVID-19 pandemic, it was undoubtedly a challenging time for children and families alike. Yet, in the midst of adversity, it served as a profound wake-up call to many, shedding light on the urgent need to provide comprehensive mental health support and resources to young people.

The increased attention and awareness catalysed a redirection of resources towards addressing this already pressing issue. Funding for mental health services was bolstered such as 'Wellbeing in Education' grants, and initiatives aimed at promoting positive mental health in schools and communities gained traction.

Family breakdown

Family breakdown, a significant contributor to the decline in children's mental well-being since 2011, often inflicts more trauma on a child than the loss of a parent, as I was surprised to discover during my studies for my diploma in trauma-informed practice.

According to the Office for National Statistics, the number of children in single-parent households rose from 2.8 million in 1996 to 3.2 million in 2019. These children are more likely to experience emotional and behavioural issues, including anxiety, depression, and conduct disorders, along with difficulties in forming relationships and academic challenges.

Research by the Children's Society reveals that children experiencing family breakdown report lower levels of wellbeing compared to those in two-parent households. They are also at a higher risk of bullying, low self-esteem, and feelings of not belonging. (The Children's Society, 2022) Additionally, the Joseph Rowntree Foundation notes an increase in child poverty within single-parent households, rising from 36% in 2010 to 44% in 2019. Poverty can significantly impact a child's mental wellbeing, leading to heightened stress, anxiety, and depression.

Poverty, inequality, austerity and the cost of living crisis

Poverty and inequality have significantly contributed to the decline in children's mental wellbeing in the UK since 2010. Government austerity policies have resulted in substantial cuts to welfare benefits and public services, disproportionately affecting low-income families and children. These policies have led to increased poverty and income inequality, which, in turn, have had adverse impacts on children's mental health.

Research by the Child Poverty Action Group has shown that poverty is a major predictor of poor mental health in children, with children living in poverty more likely to experience mental health problems like anxiety and depression. Children from low-income families also have higher rates of behavioural problems and are more likely to experience traumatic life events, such as parental separation and domestic violence, with long-lasting effects on their mental wellbeing. (School staff in England on the impact of poverty on children and school life, 2023)

The impact of poverty and inequality on children's mental health is further exacerbated by the limited access to mental health services. The surge in demand has resulted in longer waiting times and reduced access to treatment, particularly affecting children from low-income families, who are less likely to have access to private healthcare or afford treatment costs.

Additionally, cuts to education and youth services have led to a lack of safe and supportive spaces for children to develop social and emotional skills. This lack of support can worsen existing mental health problems and lead to increased isolation and disengagement from education.

One contributing factor to the decline in children's mental wellbeing is the UK government's austerity measures. While austerity aimed to improve the economy, its negative impact on mental health has been well-documented. Education, in particular, bore the brunt of austerity. Between 2010 and 2019, schools in England experienced an 8% real-term budget cut, resulting in reduced resources, including mental health support services vital for children's wellbeing. (Institute for Fiscal Studies, 2019.)

These cuts have led to increased demand for mental health services among children. The number of children referred to specialist mental health services surged by 26% between 2015 and 2019, but the number receiving treatment significantly decreased. In 2018, the Children's Commissioner for England reported that only one in four children and young people with a diagnosable mental health condition received treatment. (Children's Commissioner for England, 2020.)

Early intervention and support are critical for children's mental health, but the government's austerity measures made it increasingly challenging for schools and mental health services to provide the necessary support. This left many children without the help they needed to cope with the stresses of modern-day life.

Real-time cuts to school budgets are a pressing concern for educators and parents alike. With reduced funding available, schools struggle to offer a curriculum suitable for their students' needs. Additionally, budget cuts hinder schools' ability to provide opportunities for clubs, trips, and experiences like activity weeks. These experiences are crucial for triggering the social engagement system in children, a fundamental aspect of their mental wellbeing.

Budget cuts also strain teachers and staff. With fewer colleagues to share responsibilities, staff members are stretched and many at risk of burnout, which can impact both staff and students' mental wellbeing. Prioritising children's mental wellbeing starts with adequately funding our schools.

Austerity policies have significantly impacted youth clubs. Cuts in local authority funding have led to the closure of over 600 youth clubs in England since 2012. This loss of safe 3rd spaces has resulted in increased boredom and potentially risky behaviour among young people. Youth clubs also provide opportunities for young people to find a sense of belonging and develop social and emotional skills, essential for mental wellbeing.

Without access to these clubs, young people may struggle to develop these skills and feel isolated from their communities. The decline of youth clubs is a noticeable shift from previous generations, highlighting the impact of austerity policies on the mental wellbeing of young people.

The cost of living crisis has had significant consequences for children's mental wellbeing in England. Families struggling to meet basic needs like housing, food, and utilities experience increased stress and anxiety among children. Financial stress leads to housing insecurity, food insecurity, limited access to essential services, parental stress, and social isolation. These factors collectively contribute to the decline in children's mental wellbeing.

Great Britain is one of the top 10 richest economies globally, yet 4.2 million children live in poverty, and many face inadequate housing and food insecurity. Life expectancy is declining, portraying a grim picture of the challenges faced by individuals across the nation.

Schools operate in this disheartening context, with attendance and behaviour concerns affecting even affluent areas. During a recent tour of a secondary school catchment area in Liverpool, I was accompanied by an exceptional PE teacher. As we drove, we passed a derelict house with no roof, and she revealed that 25 sets of families from her school squatted in similar conditions, only to come to school the next day. These children had no address listed on the school's Student Information Management system (SIMs).

This revelation deeply moved me, making me think of my own children and the stark contrast between their safe and comfortable home and the harsh reality faced by these vulnerable children. Encounters like these remind us of the immense challenges many children face beyond school walls. They underscore the dedication of teachers who work tirelessly to create nurturing and supportive environments for all students, even in the face of such adversity.

Such moments drive us to advocate for change, ensuring that every child, regardless of their circumstances, has access to a safe and stable living environment and the opportunity to thrive and reach their full potential.

The Ukraine-Russia war

The war in Ukraine has had a profound impact on the mental wellbeing of children both in Ukraine and in other parts of the world, including England. The fear and violence of war can have long-lasting effects on children's mental health, particularly when it is broadcast in the media. The constant images of destruction and violence can cause children to feel scared and anxious, even if they are far removed from the actual conflict.

Moreover, the possibility of nuclear weapons being used and the presence of Ukrainian refugees in UK schools brought the conflict closer to home. It certainly brought the conflict closer to me when a lovely Ukrainian boy joined one of my examination PE classes.

LGBTQ+ and mental health

Simon Scarborough is currently Head of PE at Crispin School. Simon is an Education Consultant for PE Scholar and is a former SENCO and Assistant Principal. Simon leads the way on embracing gender diversity and equity. Simon here will explore the impact of gender identity on mental health.

'In 2021, the LGBT+ young people's charity Just Like Us published a report called Growing up LGBT+ The impact of school, home and coronavirus on LGBT+ young people. Whilst it is well known that there have been large increases in the prevalence of mental health problems in young people since the Covid 19 pandemic, this report shines a light on how young people that identify as LGBTQ+ have been disproportionately affected.

Media reporting often focuses on the (perceived) challenges that the LGBTQ+ community (particularly transgender males) pose in society, rather than the challenges that the LGBTQ+ community themselves are facing in an increasingly polarised society.

Many young people that identify as LGBTQ+ live in households that do not accept them for who they are or worse, are abusive toward them or kick them out of the family home altogether. During the pandemic lockdowns, the support networks provided by friends and support groups were often cut off, increasing the sense of isolation and vulnerability. In schools, there may be little or no positive messaging about LGBTQ+ and / or schools may lack effective guidance on how to best support LGBTQ+ students.

"The research shows that LGBT+ young people today are still disproportionately facing bullying, lack of safety in school, more frequent tension at home and alarmingly poor mental health and wellbeing.

The pandemic has created additional challenges for LGBT+ young people who have been twice as likely to be lonely and worry daily about their mental health and much more likely than non-LGBT+ people to say their mental health has declined since it began.

There were significant differences across the sample of LGBT+ young people, with Black LGBT+ young people, disabled LGBT+ young people and LGBT+ young people who are eligible for free school meals most likely to have negative outcomes."

Here are just some key headline statistics from the Growing up LGBTQ+ report.
(Just Like Us, 2021)

- LGBT+ young people are twice as likely to contemplate suicide, and Black LGBT+ young people are three times more likely.
- LGBT+ young people are three times more likely to self-harm (31% have self-harmed, compared to 9% of non-LGBT+ young people) and experience drug or alcohol dependence (6% compared to 2% of non-LGBT+ young people).
- LGBT+ young people are twice as likely to have depression, anxiety and panic attacks as well as be lonely and worry about their mental health on a daily basis.

Has our willingness to discuss mental health in schools contributed to a decline?

I want to provide a balanced argument when exploring the factors behind the decline of children's mental wellbeing since 2011 and I was curious as to whether our willingness to break the stigma and discuss mental health/illness has contributed to the decline.

My research of the evidence base found the following. Mental health stigma is a significant issue in England, and children are not immune to it. The stigma surrounding mental health can prevent young people from seeking the support they need and can lead to feelings of shame and isolation (Saxena et al., 2019). However, the conversation around mental health has been changing in recent years, with increased willingness to discuss mental health in schools, workplaces, and communities.

There is some concern that discussions around mental health could contribute to an increase in anxiety and depression in some children. According to a study by Polanczyk et al. (2015), discussing mental health with children may increase anxiety levels temporarily. However, it is crucial to note that the benefits of open and honest discussions outweigh the potential risks.

Providing a safe and supportive environment where children can discuss their mental health concerns can help them feel heard, validated, and empowered to seek the support they need (McDaid et al., 2020).

While it is important to acknowledge the potential risks of discussing mental health, the benefits of creating a safe and supportive environment where children can discuss their mental health concerns, far outweigh the risks.

A crisis in mental health wait times for children

According to a survey conducted by Pulse and analysed by Young Minds, more than 80% of GPs claim that children are waiting too long for mental health support. However, just 2% of GPs say children and young people who need help are getting routine referrals within the government's four-week target. The research also warned that children were waiting twice as long as adults to access specialist support. (Buckland, 2022)

Most mental health problems start in childhood and adolescence, and support should be available as soon as possible to stop issues causing lasting harm. However, the survey found that waiting times for routine help stretched to three months on average, with a third reporting waits of more than a year.

The Commission on Young Lives has warned that the children's mental health system is not fit for purpose, with incidences of self-harm, attempted suicide, anxiety and behavioural difficulties having become more extreme since the pandemic. They are calling for the Government to establish a £1 billion post-Covid recovery fund to improve the quality and speed of services.

While the government has mandated a maximum four-week wait for children and young people to receive care, ranging from advice and support for them and their families, to specialist assessments and care plans, GPs have been swamped with record numbers of young people struggling with anxiety and depression after lockdowns. NHS statistics showed a record 90,789 referrals in March 2023, with growing alarm about the severe and long-term mental health problems that might develop.

Young Minds, which analysed the survey's findings, expressed concern about the situation, stating that "Young people are routinely failed, with severe consequences for their mental health, their futures and in many cases their basic safety. It makes no sense to have a system where young people have to wait for mental health support."

These findings are extremely worrying and further highlight the difficulties young people face when seeking help from NHS mental health services. While NHS staff are doing their best, without the right funding and support for services, the UK remains a long way from meeting targets for how quickly young people should be seen.

This paints a worrying picture of the treatment young people in need are receiving and a more pressing need to keep as many young people as we can to be in a state of mental wellbeing for as long as possible. With the delays in suitable treatments, young people are suffering from lost learning, and their education and future life chances can suffer greatly. It is also incredibly challenging for schools to support the young person without the specialist support required.

Academic pressures

Academic pressure has long been considered one of the primary causes of stress among students, and its effects on mental wellbeing cannot be overlooked. Since 2011, academic pressures have intensified, and research has shown a correlation between increased academic pressures and a decline in children's mental wellbeing.

According to a report by the Children's Society, the number of children who reported feeling unhappy with their lives increased from 14% in 2009 to 24% in 2018. The report suggested that one of the major contributing factors to this increase is academic pressure, with children feeling overwhelmed and stressed by the demands placed upon them by schools and exams. (Children's Commissioner for England, 2023.)

Moreover, a survey by the National Education Union found that 83% of teachers reported an increase in the number of students experiencing anxiety related to academic pressures, and 67% of teachers believed that these pressures had increased over the last two years. The survey also found that exam stress and pressure from schools were the two most significant causes of anxiety among students. Academic pressures can lead to a range of mental health issues, including anxiety, depression, and even suicidal thoughts. (Teacher wellbeing index 2019, 2019.)

I have spent time with a fantastic young lady in her early 20s who struggled significantly with her mental health at school and since. During our discussions it was extremely interesting to hear that sometimes teachers had unwittingly exacerbated her mental health problems by focusing too much on exam results, especially as a perfectionist high performing young person. This was an important piece of feedback for me to hear and reflect upon. As a subject leader determined to do well for my students and with the pressure of explaining results to my bosses each year, I was definitely guilty of this charge historically, and made me reflect on how I can do better at this in the future.

Attendance in a post-lockdown world

Since the start of the pandemic, attendance rates in schools across England have remained lower than before.

According to research by the FFT Datalab, a third of 15-year-olds have been persistently absent from classrooms in England during the school year 2022-23. It is important to recognise that absence is not always a matter of truancy, but may be due to factors such as illness, caring responsibilities, or mental health issues. (Adams and editor, 2023)

We also need to consider whether we are truly welcoming all children into our schools and creating schools where children feel psychologically safe and want to be there. Many schools and teachers do an incredible job of doing this, but I have witnessed some, that in the struggle to control behaviour, have tightened rules and reduced freedoms so much that they feel more like prisons than a place for young people to thrive in and develop a lifelong love of learning.

> **Consider this...**
> - What about your own classroom? If it was a ride at a theme park, would it have queues and queues of children wanting to come in or would there be a desolate corridor?

I am not saying we should be entertaining our students 100% of the time but we do need to consider the experience we are offering to all of our young people and whether they feel psychologically safe, supported, and able to contribute so that they want to attend school.

Post lockdown behaviour

Behaviours that challenge us are another symptom of the pandemic's impact on young people's mental health. The closure of schools and lack of social interaction has led to boredom, frustration, and a sense of disconnection from the world. Young people are acting out, engaging in risky behaviour, and struggling to control their emotions.

These behaviours are a cry for help. As a society and education system, we need to recognise the impact that the pandemic is having on young people's mental health and take action to provide the support they need.

These factors have combined to create many children who appear very different to their counterparts from 15 years ago. It is difficult to convey the difference many of us are experiencing on the ground on a day to day basis from children pre and post lockdown.

Geoff Barton, General Secretary of the Association of School and College Leaders (ASCL) summed up the situation brilliantly in this blog in April 2023.

'What we need to know is why behaviour is a significant issue. Last week, I met a seasoned veteran of headship. She's led several schools in different parts of the UK, and she said something that unnerved me: "Geoff," she said, "you have no idea how different young people are these days from when you were a head". Really, I wondered. Have young people actually changed?

So, earlier this week, I asked ASCL members to share their experiences of the behaviour of young people since the pandemic and whether standards had declined. My goodness. I wouldn't have expected the response I got – the sheer volume of responses or the bleak depiction of what they said.

Now, look, this is a difficult topic. The last thing we want to do is give the impression that pupils are running amok. Most young people are respectful, polite and abide by the rules with an understanding that those rules exist for the good of everybody in maintaining an environment that is safe and conducive to learning. Similarly, it has always been the case that the behaviour of some pupils is challenging for a variety of reasons, and managing those issues is part and parcel of school leadership. The issue here is whether poor behaviour is more prevalent and worse, why that might be the case, what impact this may have on institutions and individuals, and how it might be addressed.

Here's a sample of the messages received:
- *Since the pandemic behaviour is unrecognisable. It is manifesting itself in dysregulation on a scale never seen. Calm refusal to comply with basic expectations is regular now. Extreme anxiety. Many students do not see the logic that they have come to school and therefore need to go to lessons. Not coming to school at all is more common.*
- *An issue which was never a problem before, is pupils walking out of their classes for little reason and refusing to engage with teachers but just content to wander the corridors. Whilst the numbers are very small it is highly disruptive taking up hours of staff time.*
- *Social media is adding to the challenge with incidents happening outside of school which are then brought into school, and we just don't have the capacity to deal with them.*
- *Post covid we have seen a rise in the behaviour we previously did not have issues with. Basic compliance, non-attendance, defiance and a lack of respect has for a small core become the norm.*
- *The disruption to students' education has led to some of them losing all their 'filters' about how to behave or speak in a particular context. We have experienced vandalism of property, such as toilets, increase way beyond anything we had experienced before.*
- *A core group of pupils refuse to go to lessons, refuse to follow simple instructions and challenge sanctions on a daily basis; achieving compliance is an hourly struggle with these pupils who no longer respect what education has to offer and see schooling as optional.*

It is clear that behaviour has become more challenging since the pandemic, and that it is adding significantly to the pressures on school leaders and staff. Indeed, some respondents made the point that it is contributing to staff retention problems as a factor in teachers deciding to leave.

At a time when the education sector is already facing multiple pressures due to lack of sufficient funding, a recruitment and retention crisis, and the shrivelling of so many local support services outside of schools, these added difficulties contribute to the sense that schools are under-appreciated, under-resourced, and – frankly - under siege. Where we are now is completely unsustainable.'

(www.ascl.org.uk, 2023)

An education system in crisis?

The combination of all these various challenges facing our schools has led to an education system that is struggling to meet the needs of young people and their teachers. It is clear that teaching in many schools is much more challenging than it was before the pandemic. Without addressing these challenges, it will be difficult to provide an education that prepares young people for their future and nurtures their mental wellbeing.

As a society, we need to work towards improving as many of these factors as possible if we are to be in position to improve children's mental health. We can't keep pretending what worked in schools for the majority, works for many in a post lockdown world. We need to adapt to the conditions around us to create an education system that empowers teachers and our young people so that they can thrive in all aspects of their lives.

Each child is unique

It is crucial to understand that the decline in children's mental wellbeing since 2011 is not the result of any one factor or event. Instead, it is a complex and multifactorial issue that is influenced by a range of social, economic, and environmental factors. We need to consider these factors when analysing the decline, as they can vary in importance depending on the individual child and their circumstances.

Each child is unique and may have different coping mechanisms, social support systems, and personal strengths and weaknesses. As a result, some children may be more resilient to the risk factors that contribute to poor mental health, while others may be more vulnerable.

We also need to recognise that the impact of these factors can be cumulative, meaning that children who experience multiple risk factors are at a higher risk of developing mental health problems than those who experience only one. For example, a child living in poverty may also experience academic pressure, family breakdown, and limited access to mental health services, all of which can contribute to poor mental health outcomes.

Figure 3:

4 Influences on children's mental wellbeing

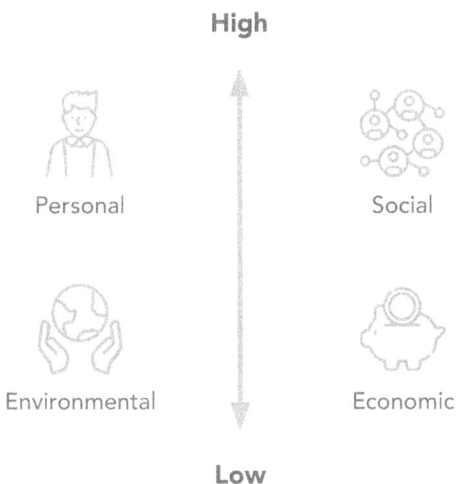

Understanding the relative importance of different factors and how they interact with one another, is essential for us as teachers and other professionals who work with children, to develop effective strategies for promoting mental health and wellbeing.

Consider this...
- Does your school monitor the mental wellbeing of your young people?
- If yes, what is your student voice saying about their mental wellbeing?
- If no, could you create a survey for your young people and share it on Google Classroom, so you have a clearer understanding of their current position to inform your strategy?
- What is your parent voice saying about their children's mental wellbeing?
- Is there any other school data you can use to evaluate their mental wellbeing?

A call to take notice

Looking closely at the data presented in this chapter, it's hard to ignore the decline in the mental wellbeing of our young people since 2011. This isn't just about numbers; it's a wakeup call that's echoing all around us, especially in the world of education. We can't sit idly by. We, as teachers, parents, and a society at large, need to rise up.

The factors behind this decline are complex, ranging from the influence of social media to the pressures of academics, from economic hardships to global events. It's time for all of us to pay attention and take action.

This is a reminder that we all have a part to play, beyond classrooms and textbooks. It's about creating a world where our young people's wellbeing is valued, their struggles understood, and their potential fully supported.

Chapter summary
- Suicide rates in in England and Wales for females aged 15 to 19 is the highest seen in 40 years.
- The pandemic has exacerbated mental health issues, with increased anxiousness and emotional difficulties observed.
- Eating disorders have become more prevalent among young people.
- Child referrals for mental health care have surged, with record highs and long waiting times for crucial support.
- Behind every statistic lies a unique, poignant story, as concerned families, friends, and teachers seek ways to provide vital support.
- Understanding children's mental health decline is vital for effective strategies in education and beyond.
- The decline is multifaceted, shaped by factors like social media's negative influence, cyberbullying's impact, and academic pressures.
- Poverty, inequality, and austerity measures exacerbate the issue, leading to urgent calls for support.
- The Covid-19 pandemic and global events highlight the need for comprehensive mental health approaches.

Critical questions

1. Rank what factors you believe have had the most significance on children's mental health in your setting.

2. What impact did Covid 19 have on the mental wellbeing of your young people?

3. How would you convince a headteacher/governor or sceptical colleague about the need for your school to improve the mental wellbeing provision of your young people within 2 minutes?

Chapter references

- Anna Freud National Centre for Children and Families (2022). 0:02 / 1:16:29.
- *Introduction Transformation Seminar with Professor Louis Appleby - Is there a suicide crisis in young people?* Available at: https://www.youtube.com/watch?v=cIFgkny9vYs [Accessed 29 Sep. 2023].
- The Social Dilemma. (2020). [Film]. Directed by Jeff Orlowski. United States: Exposure Labs.
- The Royal College of Psychiatrists (2022). *Hospital admissions for eating disorders increased by 84% in the last five years.* [online] The Royal College of Psychiatrists. Available at: https://www.rcpsych.ac.uk/news-and-features/latest-news/detail/2022/05/18/hospital-admissions-for-eating-disorders-increased-by-84-in-the-last-five-years [Accessed 29 Sep. 2023].
- Young Minds (2023). *Urgent referrals of children to emergency mental health services tripled.* [online] Young Minds. Available at: https://www.youngminds.org.uk/about-us/media-centre/press-releases/urgent-referrals-of-children-to-emergency-mental-health-services-tripled/#:~:text=The%20charity%20also%20found%20that,the%20highest%20number%20on-%20record. [Accessed 29 Sep. 2023].
- The Royal College of Psychiatrists (2022). *Hospital admissions for eating disorders increased by 84% in the last five years.* [online] The Royal College of Psychiatrists. Available at: https://www.rcpsych.ac.uk/news-and-features/latest-news/detail/2022/05/18/hospital-admissions-for-eating-disorders-increased-by-84-in-the-last-five-years [Accessed 29 Sep. 2023].
- The Children's Society (2022). *Good Childhood Report.* [online] The Children's Society. Available at: https://www.childrenssociety.org.uk/sites/default/files/2022-09/GCR-2022-Full-Report.pdf.
- Girl Guiding (2023). *Girls Attitudes Survey 2023.* [online] Girl Guiding. Available at: https://www.girlguiding.org.uk/globalassets/docs-and-resources/research-and-campaigns/girls-attitudes-summary.pdf [Accessed 14 Sep. 2023].
- Wells, G., Horwitz, J. and Seetharaman, D. (2021). Facebook Knows Instagram Is Toxic for Teen Girls, Company Documents Show. *Wall Street Journal.* [online] 14 Sep. Available at: https://www.wsj.com/articles/facebook-knows-instagram-is-toxic-for-teen-girls-company-documents-show-11631620739.
- www.youtube.com. (2022.). *Transformation Seminar: Professor Danny Dorling - When Will Life Return to Normal After the Pandemic.* [online] Available at: https://www.youtube.com/watch?v=cXx-9FehJa8 [Accessed 29 Sep. 2023].
- School staff in England on the impact of poverty on children and school life. (2023). Available at: https://cpag.org.uk/sites/default/files/files/policypost/Education_Anti-Poverty_Coalition_Report_2023.pdf [Accessed 29 Sep. 2023].

- Institute for Fiscal Studies. (2019.). *2019 annual report on education spending in England.* [online] Available at: https://ifs.org.uk/publications/2019-annual-report-education-spending-england.
- Children's Commissioner for England. (2020.). *The state of children's mental health services 2018/19.* [online] Available at: https://www.childrenscommissioner.gov.uk/resource/the-state-of-childrens-mental-health-services/.
- Just Like Us (2021). *Just Like Us releases Growing up LGBT+ report on bullying, schools and mental health.* [online] Just Like Us. Available at: https://www.justlikeus.org/blog/2021/11/25/research-report-growing-up-lgbt-bullying/.
- Saxena, S., Thornicroft, G., Knapp, M., & Whiteford, H. (2019). Resources for mental health: Scarcity, inequity, and inefficiency. The Lancet Psychiatry, 6(3), 169-181. https://doi.org/10.1016/S2215-0366(18)30572-6
- Polanczyk, G. V., Salum, G. A., Sugaya, L. S., Caye, A., & Rohde, L. A. (2015). Annual Research Review: A meta-analysis of the worldwide prevalence of mental disorders in children and adolescents. Journal of Child Psychology and Psychiatry, 56(3), 345-365. https://doi.org/10.1111/jcpp.12381
- McDaid, C., Kiasuwa, R., Keown, P., & Park, A.-L. (2020). How to create mentally healthy schools. BMJ, 370. https://doi.org/10.1136/bmj.m2815
- Buckland, D. (2022). *Crisis in wait times for children who need help.* [online] Express.co.uk. Available at: https://www.express.co.uk/news/uk/1648594/children-mental-health-support-nhs-gps-news-latest [Accessed 29 Sep. 2023].
- Children's Commissioner for England. (2023.). Children's mental health services 2021-2022. [online] Available at: https://www.childrenscommissioner.gov.uk/resource/29751/.
- Teacher Wellbeing Index 2019. (2019.). Available at: https://www.educationsupport.org.uk/media/b1qbtmzl/teacher_wellbeing_index_2019.pdf
- Adams, R. and editor, R.A.E. (2023). Third of 15-year-olds persistently absent from school in England since September. The Guardian. [online] 10 Feb. Available at: https://www.theguardian.com/education/2023/feb/10/third-of-15-year-olds-persistently-absent-school-england.
- www.ascl.org.uk. (2023). ASCL - *What we need to know is why behaviour is a significant issue.* [online] Available at: https://www.ascl.org.uk/News/Blog/April-2023/What-we-need-to-know-is-why-behaviour-is-a-signifi.
- Campbell, D. and Campbell, A. told to D. (2023). 'We are letting young people down': the secret psychiatrist on NHS mental health delays. The Guardian. [online] 9 Feb. Available at: https://www.theguardian.com/society/2023/feb/09/waiting-is-damaging-how-nhs-england-fails-young-mental-health-patients.

Additional insights

In an article in the Guardian, they reported that Children in mental health crisis spent more than 900,000 hours in A&E in England. A secret psychiatrist (Campbell and Campbell, 2023) wrote this powerful article about the current situation:

'We are letting young people down': the secret psychiatrist on NHS mental health delays'
In my role as an NHS psychiatrist, I work on wards in an inpatient unit, as an on-call doctor, and I also treat adults and children who have been referred to me by A&E staff because I'm also part of a liaison psychiatry service – a mental health team attached to an emergency department.

I see a fair number of under-18s who have presented in distress at A&E in a mental health crisis seeking support and have been brought in by their family, friends or an ambulance crew.

Some of these young people have a severe enduring mental illness, like a first episode or recurrence of psychosis, perhaps because they've not been taking their medication. A second group have committed self-harm or had suicidal thoughts or have tried to take their own life, and therefore may have severe injuries. They can be brought in from home, school or a public setting.

And a third group of emergency mental health presentations are young people with depression, low mood or behavioural challenges. In those cases, their diagnosis is often less clear. They're usually struggling because of a range of stresses they're facing, whether that's socially or educationally.

These young people are often desperate, and they all need help. But it's worrying that often they've not been able to access the help they need. Quite often a young person has been referred to NHS mental health services but then waited over a month or even over two months – and sometimes it can be many months – to see someone.
The trouble is that waiting is damaging. Those young people are very unwell to start with and their mental health gets worse while they're waiting. With mental health conditions, the longer you wait for care after first displaying symptoms, the harder you become to treat. While a young person is waiting for treatment, they can have difficulty establishing

and maintaining friendships, struggle at school and become more and more socially isolated. Their entire life chances can be blighted if their problems aren't treated urgently and properly.

Sometimes, not getting help for depression or an eating disorder, for example, worsens their mental health to the extent that their mental state is altered so much that they can do harm to themselves or to others because they feel they can't get the support they need. I see young people who have self-harmed by cutting themselves or tried to take their own life.

A&E is a difficult place for young people in a mental health crisis because emergency departments are busy, noisy places. Worryingly, the numbers of under-18s who end up there has been going up, in particular because of the pandemic. And the waiting times for mental health care outside hospitals seem to be getting worse.

These are very vulnerable young people whose health is fragile. Often, they're scared. They want to feel better, but they need someone to help them make sense of what's going on. It's the duty of NHS mental health services to give them help quickly so they start to recover. But that's where I feel that unfortunately we are falling short at the moment, by making them wait for care.

Waiting times for care are what worries me the most because these young people need timely care, so their condition doesn't get any worse. Mental healthcare for under-18s at the moment is clearly inadequate. As a country we are letting young people and their families down by having such inadequate mental health care. I'm not a parent. But if I had a child and were seeking mental health support for my son or daughter, I would be very worried.

Karl Pupé is a qualified classroom teacher with a decade's experience across the Primary, Secondary and Further Education sectors. Specialising in Behaviour Management, he worked as a Not in Education, Employment or Training (NEETs) Coordinator teaching students with severe Social, Emotional and Mental Health (SEMH) difficulties. He is the author of "The Action Hero Teacher: Classroom Management Made Simple" and has an additional perspective that we need to also consider:

Action hero teacher perspective:
Teaching Generation Z: the three key issues facing this 'crisis generation'
Educators, we are living in crazy times.

In our society, the old rules & protocols of how we live together are crumbling before our eyes. We are living through one of the most turbulent times in human history.

We are witnessing the death-throes of the Industrial Age as our world deals with consequences of the COVID19 pandemic & how it has radically changed our society overnight.

But the turbulence of 2020 allowed us to witness the sign of things to come: The Information Age. We stare in wonder & fear as the Internet 2.0 & Artificial Intelligence transform & shape our societies in ways that our ancestors could not imagine.

If you are an educator and you teach students between 8 and 23 years old (born 1997-2012), you are teaching Generation Z – the cohort that make up the bulk of our current students.

There are three characteristics unique to this group which are as follows:

1. They have mastered Digital Technology
COVID19 will be remembered as emergence of the Information Age & Generation Z are its first real citizens.

In a survey of 13-39 year-olds by youth marketing website 'YPulse', 72 per cent believed that 'hashtag activism' had the power to change the world, especially in light of the #BlackLivesMatter movement1.

Generation Z are the first ever human generation that do not know what life was like without the Internet. They are known as 'Digital Natives.'
Technology, especially social media, has given our students unprecedented opportunities to speak their minds - & have the World listen to them. The lines between the rulers & the

ruled are increasingly blurred & the Internet has democratised power & attention. In our classrooms, students are less afraid to question, debate, and in some cases, confront us about why things are the way that they are.

Educators can no longer rely on demanding obedience from our students. We must now use 'trust-based empathy'—dealing with our students based on mutual respect, shared values and the willingness to allow for curiosity and creativity in the classroom.

2. They are pessimistic about authority
According to Deloitte UK, when they interviewed older Gen 'Z'ers', a mere 12 per cent believed that the political and economic situation would change over the next 12 months2.

For many older Generation Z students, many of their defining moments were in the wake of the Great Recession, Government Austerity, & Brexit. This has made our young people more cynical & uncertain of the future.

Educators must move from merely giving lectures, but to become their coaches, showing them that education is still a gateway for a better future for themselves and the World.

We can no longer motivate them with the promise of a degree, a career pathway, and a steady job, but inspire them about how they can contribute to a better future for their communities and the causes they care about. As educators, we must learn to bridge our subjects to their interests moving from external signs of success to what appeals to their hearts and minds.

3. They expect companies and institutions to care
According to market research group Ipsos Mori, less than 30 per cent of students felt that the things they owned said much about their socio-economic status, compared to 42 per cent in 2011. The report revealed that: "Despite pressure of a harder economic context, there has been a cohort shift away from materialistic values."

In the UK, our students have witnessed the ever-widening inequality gap & damning discrimination based on gender, race & sexuality making these students more sensitive to issues around equality and fairness.

In 2021, after the death of George Floyd, students are more conscious than ever about how the companies and institutions that they interact with affect the world around them. Students support companies and institutions, not only for their product and services, but their stances on equality & fairness.

As educators, we must be willing to have the 'difficult conversations' with our students and learn to facilitate, wherever possible, the ability for them to explore these ideas and come up with solutions.

This does not mean that we give them carte blanche to say what they want, but with empathy, curiosity and respect to others, we must give them the chance to express their truths and lived experience, and how what they are learning can impact the world around them.

Generation Z believes that they live in a crisis generation, and they are actively looking at ways to make their world a tiny bit better. My advice is to give them that safe space to work on their ideas.

Sources

1. YPulse. 2020. This Is How Gen Z & Millennials Have Changed Activism. [ONLINE] Available at: https://www.ypulse.com/article/2020/07/14/this-is-how-gen-z-millennials-have-changed-activism/.
2. Deloitte. 2019. UK Millennials and Generation Z feel unsettled about the future. [ONLINE] Available at: https://www2.deloitte.com/uk/en/pages/press-releases/articles/millennials-and-generation-z-feel-unsettled-about-the-future.html.
3. Ipsos. 2018. Generation Z – Beyond Binary: new insights into the next generation. [ONLINE] Available at: https://www.ipsos.com/ipsos-mori/en-uk/generation-z-beyond-binary-new-insights-next-generation

The game has changed in teaching, and we need to move away from the traditional authoritarian method to a partnership with our young people if we all want to thrive.

Lockdown & Physical Education
David Savage (UEA PGCE Physical Education Subject Lead)

COVID-19 and the impact on teachers and pupils in PE
Physical Education (PE) is by nature a practical subject and one which more often than not requires teamwork or at the very least, being in the same space as others.

With the impact of COVID-19 forcing a change in schooling, lockdown learning required young people and educators alike to place themselves in front of a screen for several hours a day; this presents an obvious challenge, more than in other subject areas one might add. This is echoed by Tozer (2021) who suggests that those outside of the profession are unsure and unaware of the importance PE has on the nation's children.

Varea et al., (2020, p. 9) sum this up when they comment: "Covid-19 is affecting the delivery of PE, shifting to individual away from social, having limited physical contact, and shifting the role of the teacher…and how the pandemic produces fear and vulnerability. Such changes limit the ways teachers can teach and students can move through human and nonhuman bodies. This leads to a change on PE pedagogies…the shift away from direct instruction, feelings of dehumanisation, the role of space, families, and homes in producing learning." Therefore, it is suggested that whilst all classroom teachers have had to make significant changes to their pedagogy, teachers of PE have perhaps had the biggest challenge of all.

With the return to school and some normality returning, the impacts of COVID-19 can still be felt. PE teachers (n=40) in the region of East Anglia were contacted and asked about their PE provision and curriculum design. Whilst it would perhaps not be a surprise to know that schools often have and follow a different curriculum, it might be expected that during and shortly after a pandemic, these would align more closely with one another, especially given the guidance from various organisations (see NGB websites, DfE guidance, AfPE for further details). From the data gathered in this study, it would appear that teachers still had autonomy over their lessons and the freedom to deliver what they felt was appropriate for their pupils.

Perhaps unsurprisingly, it was highlighted that engagement was different to that of usual in-person PE lessons. Furthermore, different sub-groups also acted differently, such as High Prior Attainers (HPA's) seemingly less engaged than previously. Notwithstanding this, the rise in both cases of and discussions around mental health has also seen advocates stress the importance of regular physical activity as a 'de-stressor' and how this can be overcome through participation in PE lessons. It is suggested that understanding and maturity play a big part in acceptance of a situation.

It is also important to note the psychological impact this has had and is likely to have in the future on young people and both their attitude towards and participation in physical activity and sport. Whilst many pupils are likely to have been active during periods of lockdown, there are likely to have been as many who have been inactive, leading to a greater risk of adverse health conditions in later life. Notwithstanding this, many participants not only spoke about the physical impact of COVID-19 on pupils' wellbeing but highlighted the psychological and social aspects too.

Chapter 2 – Imagine

"There comes a point where we need to stop just pulling people out of the river. We need to go upstream and find out why they're falling in"
Desmond Tutu

In the preceding chapter, we delved into the data and factors that underlie the decline in children's mental health. Our exploration revealed a variety of influences, including social media, academic pressure, lockdown, and financial uncertainty, all playing a role in driving this concerning trend.

In the initial section of this chapter, we will contrast the potential outcomes of taking effective action now versus the consequences of inaction on what our world might look like. We will then conclude by investigating optimal approaches that schools can implement to bolster assistance for young people to save them from falling in the river later on. potential factors behind any decline and what the impact has been in schools.

Going upstream: addressing the root causes of children's mental health issues

As educators, we have a responsibility to support the mental health and wellbeing of our students. This means not only providing support and interventions for those who are struggling but also addressing the root causes of mental health issues.

The quote often attributed to Desmond Tutu, "There comes a point where we need to stop just pulling people out of the river. We need to go upstream and find out why they're falling in," highlights the importance of addressing the root causes of problems rather than just treating the symptoms.

When it comes to children's mental health, this means addressing the factors that contribute to the decline of their mental health, such as social media, academic pressure, family and home life, trauma, and financial instability. Rather than just providing support and interventions, we need to take a proactive approach and address these issues at their source.

For example, we can work to reduce academic pressure by creating a more balanced approach to education that emphasises not only academic achievement but also the development of social and emotional skills. We can work to address family and home life issues by providing resources, training and support for families who are struggling. We can work to address financial instability by advocating for policies and programmes that address poverty and inequality.

By taking a proactive approach and addressing the root causes of mental health issues, we can create a more positive and supportive environment for our students. We can help them develop the skills and resilience they need to navigate life's challenges and thrive both in and out of the classroom. As educators, we have a critical role to play in addressing the root causes of mental health issues and creating a better future for our children.

Self-harm and storing up a problem

Self-harm has become increasingly common among young people. While the reasons for self-harming are complex and can vary from person to person, a survey has shown that the most common reason for self-harm is to cope with emotions. According to Professor Lewis Appleby, this is particularly true among females, who are increasingly likely to use self-harm as a means of coping with their feelings.

Self-harm rates have increased across the board in females, but in particular in this youngest age group so that 20 percent of females under 25 are saying that at some time in their lives they have self-harmed. That is one in five! (Anna Freud National Centre for Children and Families, 2022)

This is a worrying trend because it suggests that young people are using self-harm as a positive coping strategy. This normalisation effect can make it seem like self-harm is a natural part of responding to stress, and this attitude could carry on into adulthood.

As young people age, they move up from relatively low suicide rates in their teens to higher suicide rates in their 30s and 40s. If they have learned to use self-harm as a positive coping strategy, this behaviour could lead to a surge in suicides in the future. This is particularly concerning because suicide prevention is a complex issue, and it is not always possible to predict who is at risk. However, we do know that self-harm is a key indicator.

It is essential to address the root causes of self-harm and to provide young people with effective coping strategies that do not involve self-harm. Schools can play a vital role in this by providing education on mental health, resilience, and coping strategies. It is crucial to teach young people that self-harm is not a healthy or effective way to cope with emotions, and there are other ways to manage stress and difficult feelings.

Mental health services also have a crucial role to play in providing effective support to young people who are struggling with their mental health. It is essential to provide timely interventions and to address the underlying issues that contribute to self-harm.

If we fail to address the root causes of self-harm and provide effective support to young people, we could be storing up a future problem of suicide and suicide prevention. We need to take action now to ensure that young people have access to the support they need and to prevent a surge in suicides in the future.

The U-turn

Unfortunately, though, England will now be the only UK country without either a dedicated mental health strategy or a commitment to creating such a plan.

In January 2023, leading mental health charities and social enterprises criticised the government's Major Conditions Strategy, stating that it betrays the government's promise to create a visionary new mental health plan in England. In Scotland for example, the "Choose Life" strategy is the national suicide prevention initiative. Wales has its suicide prevention strategy known as "Talk to Me 2", and In Northern Ireland, the "Protect Life" strategy is the government's approach to suicide prevention.

The charities' collective voice sends a strong message that to prevent poor mental health and support people with mental health problems in England, there must be a dedicated plan that shows the government is giving mental health the priority it deserves.

It is clear that there is a need for a comprehensive mental health plan in England, one that prioritises prevention and early intervention, and is not simply grouped with chronic health conditions. The government must commit to creating such a plan, providing sustained investment in high-quality mental health and social care services and preventative mental health interventions. This will be crucial in ensuring that young people receive the support they need to thrive, and that mental health is viewed as a crucial component of overall wellbeing.

2050 mental illness hell

From my experiences one of the groups that was most affected by lockdown were the children in Year 5 & 6 who started the pandemic in primary school and had no chance to say goodbye to their beloved teachers before starting secondary school with new teachers. Covid-19 systems in place at the time and facemasks made it difficult for many of these children to build good relationships with their new teachers and peers and discover how enjoyable secondary school can be. Subsequently many have been adversely affected in terms of behaviours that we find challenging and with finding a sense of belonging.

We also know that currently, the highest suicide rates in England are found among middle-aged men, particularly those in their 40s and 50s, driven by factors such as the economy and alcohol. This generation of young people will reach the age of 40 in 2050 so I decided to contrast what Mental Health Heaven and Hell might look like in society then.

Hell for mental illness in society in 2050 would be a world where mental health is still stigmatised and not given the attention it deserves. Mental health services would be underfunded, understaffed, and inaccessible to most people, leaving many people struggling in isolation and without the support they need.

In this world, mental illness would still be viewed as a sign of weakness or personal failing, rather than a legitimate health concern. People would be discouraged from seeking help or expressing their emotions, leading to a culture of silence and shame around mental health.

Schools and universities would lack the necessary resources and training to support young people's mental health, leading to a significant number of students dropping out of school or struggling to succeed academically. The lack of support would create a cycle of poor mental health and reduced life opportunities, with people experiencing difficulty in accessing education and employment. Artificial intelligence has now developed to a point where many low skilled jobs are replaced by robots leaving many people without a sense of purpose and value in the world and reliant on universal benefits.

Moreover, physical activity and social connection would be viewed as luxuries, rather than necessities, leading to a society of isolated and inactive individuals. Social isolation and loneliness would be common, leading to increased rates of depression, anxiety, and other mental illnesses.

In a society where mental health is neglected, suicide rates would skyrocket, and families, schools, and communities would be devastated by the impact, creating additional trauma for those left behind. Young people would feel trapped and hopeless, with limited access to the support they need to manage their mental health.

The impact of this neglect on families, schools, and communities would be immense. Families would suffer the loss of their loved ones, with many feeling powerless to help. Schools would struggle to support their students, with teachers feeling unprepared to manage the mental health challenges they face. Communities would feel the weight of the mental health crisis, with increased rates of crime, addiction, and homelessness.

The lack of investment in mental health would perpetuate a cycle of neglect and trauma, with the consequences of this neglect being felt for generations. Without proper support, young people would face significant obstacles in achieving their potential, with long-term consequences for their health, wellbeing, and life opportunities.

In this way, hell for mental health in society in 2050 would be a bleak and challenging world, with people struggling to access the support they need and facing a range of barriers to leading healthy, fulfilling lives.

2050 mental health heaven

In contrast to the bleak future described above, heaven for people in terms of mental health support would be a world where mental health is given the same importance as physical health. Mental health would be viewed as a vital component of overall wellbeing, and everyone would have access to a range of mental health services, support, and interventions.

In this world, schools would be equipped with highly trained mental health professionals who can provide early intervention and support to young people who may be struggling. All teachers would receive regular training on trauma informed practice and mental wellbeing, and mental health education would be integrated into the curriculum from an early age.

There would be a range of accessible and affordable mental health services available in every community, including open-access support hubs that provide flexible and early support for young people under 25. These services would be well-funded and well-staffed, with trained mental health professionals who can provide a range of interventions, including counselling, group therapy, and evidence-based treatments.

Technology would also play a vital role in mental health support, with virtual reality and other innovative tools being used to support young people with a range of mental health conditions. Apps and online platforms would provide accessible and confidential mental health support, and young people would have the option to access support remotely, if they preferred.

In addition to the mental health support services and interventions, in 2050, people across society would recognise the crucial role that physical activity can play in promoting positive mental wellbeing. There would be a greater emphasis on promoting physical activity as a tool to prevent mental health problems, improve mood and self-esteem, and reduce stress and anxiety.

Schools, colleges, and universities would prioritise physical activity, play and sports, and create programmes and environments that encourage young people to be active and engage in regular exercise. Moreover, there would be a greater emphasis on teams and events that bring people together, helping to build connected, supportive communities.

Social isolation and loneliness would be recognised as risk factors for mental health problems, and initiatives would be in place to promote social connection and community engagement. Events, community festivals, and other social gatherings would be widely available and accessible, and they would be promoted as opportunities for people to connect, feel loved and part of society.

In this way, young people in 2050, would benefit from a comprehensive mental health support system, where a range of interventions, services, and initiatives work together to promote positive mental wellbeing. They would be able to access the support they need, when they need it, and be supported to lead active, healthy, and fulfilling lives.

Overall, in 2050, mental health support for young people would be fully integrated into society, and young people would have access to a range of effective and affordable interventions and support services. This would help to promote positive mental health outcomes, prevent mental health issues from escalating, and ensure that all young people have the support they need to thrive.

Time to decide

It is crucial that society recognises the vital importance of investing in mental health and providing young people with the support they need to manage their mental health.

By prioritising mental health, we can reduce suicides and the devastating impact it has on families, schools, and communities, and create a future where all young people have access to the resources and support they need to lead healthy, fulfilling lives.

It is time for us and society to decide what sort of future we want for our young people and communities. The mental health crisis facing young people demands immediate attention, and we must act now to create a world where young people receive the support they need to thrive.

To create this world, we must first consider what provisions we want for our young people. We must prioritise mental health education, training, and support, providing young people with the skills, tools, and resources they need to manage their mental health.

Government, NHS, Schools, universities, charities and communities must work together to create a comprehensive mental health support system, ensuring that no young person falls through the cracks. It has to be a multi-agency non-politicised approach, and this has always been the challenge which we need to overcome together.

We must also consider what actions we want to see. We need to prioritise early intervention, providing support for young people before they start to struggle, rather than waiting until they are in crisis.

Furthermore, we must be prepared to make changes to create the world we want to see. This means challenging stigma and discrimination around mental health, prioritising funding for mental health services, and ensuring that mental health is integrated into all aspects of society.

Creating the world we want to see for our young people and communities will require a collective effort from all members of society. It will require investment, commitment, and creativity. But the rewards will be immense, with a society where all people have access to the resources and support they need to thrive, and where mental health is viewed as a crucial component of overall wellbeing.

In conclusion, it is time to decide what sort of future we want for our young people and communities.

Consider this...
- What do you want society to look like in 2050?

Lessons from the past: how a public health approach can help address children's mental health issues

If we assume that as a society we make the decision to prioritise mental health, let's now explore what lessons we can learn from the past in terms of a public health approach.

In the past, road traffic accidents were one of the leading causes of death for children in England. However, through a combination of public education campaigns, infrastructure changes, and legislative action, the number of road traffic accidents involving children has decreased significantly. This success story shows that a public health approach can be effective in reducing a significant health risk for children.

The "Think!" road safety campaign in the UK was launched in 2000 by the Department for Transport. This initiative has had a significant impact on reducing the number of road traffic accidents involving children. According to government statistics, the number of child deaths on UK roads has fallen by 75% since the introduction of the Think! campaign. (Department For Transport, 2020)

Today, we face a similar challenge with children's mental health. We need a similar approach to children's mental health to reduce death by intentional self-harm.

Just as with road traffic accidents, a public health approach to children's mental health would involve a range of interventions. These could include public education campaigns to raise awareness about mental health issues and reduce the stigma associated with seeking help, infrastructure changes to improve access to mental health services, and legislative action to address the root causes of mental health issues.

For example, schools could play a critical role in addressing children's mental health by providing education on mental health, resilience, and coping strategies. Mental health services could provide effective support to young people who are struggling with their mental health.

This support could include timely interventions and addressing the underlying issues that contribute to self-harm.

In addition to these interventions, we need to address the root causes of children's mental health issues, just as we did with road traffic accidents. This means looking at the social determinants of health, such as poverty, inequality, and social exclusion, and taking action to address these issues.

By taking a public health approach to children's mental health, we can create a more positive and supportive environment for our young people. We can help them develop the skills and resilience they need to navigate life's challenges and thrive both in and out of the classroom.

We can prevent the tragedy of intentional self-harm and reduce the number of young lives lost. We must act now to address this critical issue and ensure that our children have the support they need to live healthy and fulfilling lives.

Best practice for supporting children's mental health in schools

When it comes to physical health, we understand the importance of early intervention. We wouldn't wait for a child to become obese before offering support, nor would we make a teenager wait six months before treating a broken leg. Yet, with mental health, we tend to wait for problems to arise and then wait a bit longer before addressing them. This is a concerning trend that has serious consequences for our children's mental health and wellbeing.

It is critical that we recognise the urgency of early intervention for children's mental health. Waiting until a child is in crisis before providing support and interventions is not good enough. We need to take a proactive approach to mental health, just as we do with physical health, by identifying and addressing potential issues before they become problems.

Schools have a vital role to play in this process. Early intervention programmes, such as those that teach young people coping strategies and promote resilience, can help equip students with the tools they need to manage their mental health and wellbeing. By providing these programmes, schools can help students develop the skills they need to thrive both now and in the future. This is one of the ways we can go upstream and prevent young people from falling in the river.

In addition, schools can provide teachers with professional development opportunities and strategies to help them be more proactive in identifying potential mental health issues. By empowering teachers to recognise the signs of distress and intervene early, and providing opportunities for young people to let staff know when they are starting to struggle in a safe environment, we can prevent small problems from escalating into larger, more serious issues.

By taking a proactive approach to mental health, we can create a more positive and supportive environment for our students. We can help them develop the skills they need to manage their mental health and wellbeing, both now and in the future. As educators, it is our responsibility to prioritise the mental health and wellbeing of our young people and to recognise the urgency of early intervention in promoting positive outcomes.

In order to effectively support the mental health and wellbeing of our students, it is best practice for schools to embed a three-phase approach. This approach is designed to transform young people's wellbeing during these challenging times.

Figure 4:

3 Phase Mental Wellbeing Strategy For Schools

Early Intervention For All
Identify those who need support.
Teach Self care strategies to all (RISE Up).
Trauma informed front line.

Internal Specialist Support
Mental health support from trained counsellors.
External specialist support if required.
(MHST, Wellbeing Zone,
ELSA, Safeguarding)

External Specialist Support
For young people
in crisis.
(CAMHS)

© Future Action Limited, 2022

Phase 1 involves early intervention for all students. This includes identifying those who need additional support as soon as possible and teaching a toolbox of self-care strategies to all students. One example of a self-care strategy that can be taught to students is the RISE Up programme, which aims to build resilience and promote positive mental wellbeing in a range of cross-curricular ways. Frontline school staff should be trained to be trauma-aware to better support their students by integrating the 8 protective factors. We will focus on phase 1 in more detail in part 2 and 3 of this book.

Phase 2 involves providing internal specialist support in schools for students with mental health conditions. Trained counsellors can offer support to these students, and if required, schools can refer students to external specialist support. Examples of Phase 2 provision are: Mental Health Support Teams (MHST), Wellbeing Zones, Emotional Literacy Support Assistants (ELSA), and Safeguarding & Pastoral Teams. It is vital schools are supported to have this provision in place, so timely interventions are put in place to stop minor mental illnesses from escalating into more serious conditions.

In my school a Mental Health Support Team (MHST) was introduced to add capacity to the great work our internal specialist school counsellor and safeguarding team were already doing. MHSTs have three core functions: to deliver evidence-based interventions for mild-to-moderate mental health issues, support the senior mental health lead (where established) in each school or college, to introduce or develop a whole-school or college approach, and give timely advice to school and college staff, and liaise with external specialist services to help children and young people get the right support and stay in education.

By providing mental health support within schools, in a safe and familiar environment, MHSTs can help young people access support and interventions that can prevent problems from becoming more serious issues. MHSTs can also provide timely support to school and college staff, helping to keep children and young people in education and providing the necessary support to help them thrive. MHSTs represent an important step forward in providing mental health support to children and young people and ensuring that they have access to the support they need, where they need it most.

Phase 3 involves accessing external specialist support for those students who are in crisis. This support may include services provided by Children and Adolescent Mental Health Services (CAMHS).

It is important to note that while schools are generally good at phase 2, they often neglect phase 1 and accessing phase 3 can often lead to long delays due to the number of referrals CAMHS receive and the lack of capacity to support young people in crisis. By focusing on early intervention and equipping all students with self-care strategies, schools can create a more proactive and preventative approach to mental health support. We want to keep as many young people in phase 1 as possible and prevent them from slipping further down the inverted pyramid.

By embedding this three-phase approach into school policy and practice, we can create a more comprehensive and effective system of mental health support for our students. This will ensure that all students receive the support they need to thrive both now and in the future.

The importance of early support hubs for young people

Young Minds, the children's mental health charity, has been campaigning through their 'Fund the Hubs' initiative to create a network of early support hubs across the country. These hubs would provide young people with an additional safe place to go when they first start to struggle with their mental health.

An early support hub is a mental health and wellbeing hub that provides open access, flexible, early support for young people under 25 in their communities. Early support hubs already exist in some areas, and Young Minds wants to build on these successful examples with consistent, long-term funding.

I support this campaign as it creates additional safe places for young people to go to access early support. This approach could provide support for those young people who are starting to struggle and don't feel safe in school or able to talk to adults in that space. Early support hubs can reduce pressure on schools and reduce the number of young people who require more expensive services, such as CAMHS, later on.

The early support hubs are not only a cost-effective approach but also provide young people with the necessary tools and strategies they need to manage their mental health and wellbeing. With some creativity, this initiative could be extended to create replacement youth clubs that have disappeared over the years and frame mental health support to have a greater focus towards positive mental wellbeing to create more connected communities.

This would enable young people to access the support they need in a familiar and accessible environment, helping to promote positive mental wellbeing outcomes and prevent minor mental illnesses from escalating into more serious problems.

The costs of mental health support in the UK

Providing mental health support can be expensive, but the cost of not providing adequate support can be even greater. In the UK, the cost of Children and Adolescent Mental Health Services (CAMHS) treatment can vary significantly, with an average cost of £2,338 for a referral to a community CAMHS service and £61,000 for an admission to an in-patient CAMHS unit. (NHS, 2017.)

However, early intervention can be much cheaper to deliver and highly cost-effective. For example, the cost of delivering an emotional resilience programme in school is £5.08 per student, and the cost of delivering six counselling or group Cognitive behavioural therapy (CBT) sessions in a school is £229 per child. The Department of Health estimates that a targeted therapeutic intervention delivered in school costs about £229 but derives an average lifetime benefit of £7,252, representing a cost-benefit ratio of 32-1. Norfolk County Council is a great example of a council that has funded early intervention provision for schools in a cost effective manner.

Despite the government's prioritisation of mental health, there are still significant challenges in identifying and addressing mental health issues in a timely and effective manner. According to a report by the Children's Commissioner for England, the NHS is still failing to identify the number of children referred to CAMHS who don't receive treatment, how long children wait for a referral date to the beginning of treatment, how many children drop out of treatment, and whether treatment is effective.

While there are certainly financial costs associated with providing mental health support, the cost of not doing so can have serious long-term consequences for the mental health and wellbeing of children and young people.

By prioritising early intervention and investing in mental health support, we can create a more positive and supportive environment for our students, both now and in the future.

 **Chris Wright** is Head of Health & Wellbeing at the Youth Sport Trust. Here he wraps up this chapter on the need for us to all work together to create the best future we can for our children:

"Good health supports successful learning. Successful learners support health. Education and health are inseparable." (World Health Organisation)

Head teachers started telling us that the declining physical and mental health of young people is the biggest barrier to achievement, back in 2014. With the cuts across the education, sport and youth sectors we were predicting, back then, how austerity, changes in education policy and wider societal change were going to have a detrimental impact on the physical and mental health of children in the UK. I am sad to say those predictions have come true…and then some!

As a predominantly education-based charity we set about researching the pinch points in children's lives and where they were experiencing the 'cliff edge moments' around inactivity, mental health illness and the experiences or external factors that were exacerbating these issues.

The issue of declining health and wellbeing of children is such a massive and broad issue we had to be clear about where we could take positive action and what would help our 'customers' the most e.g. children and schools. We found that the key pinch points were as follows:

1. Early years transition into primary school: The loss of play from children's lives. This is the place where they build the foundations of physical, social, and emotional health through play and movement and we know by taking this away from a child impacts on their physical and mental health and neuro-development delay including speech and language.

2. Primary to secondary transition: The cliff-edge moment particularly in relation to physical activity, but also where we were seeing significant declines in children's mental health as their bodies and minds change, they leave the nurturing and 'safe' environment of primary school and have to navigate new friendships, environments, structures, and experiences.

3. Exam season: The repercussions of a high accountability stakes education system really taking its toll on adolescents. Young people are stressed, anxious, self-harming, absent and depressed as they are pressured from all angles to achieve certain grades at GCSE and are experiencing a journey through a test-intensive secondary school career.

We have seen significant impact over the last 6 years on issues of reducing inactivity and improving mental health, increasing children's social mobility and increasing achievement with programmes like Healthy Movers, Active in Mind and Change4Life Sports Clubs reaching over 250,000 children and young people. But what has really changed?

I would argue we have changed the lives of those children directly involved in our programmes, but as a children's charity with a mission of changing children's lives for good; there is a need to shift the focus to system change and societal perceptions.

Yes, we have hundreds of organisations with programmes and interventions that address the physical and mental health of children through sport and play, and yes we have policies and strategies that advocate for this. But what has really changed in children's lives which is having a detrimental effect on their physical and mental health and how do we stop the continued decline?

We need to work together as system partners to change the narrative…change the education system and what is important in children's lives, change their relationship with social media and the digital world, change the way we design spaces, transport and infrastructure and reclaim the place of play and sport in their lives and the lives of their families.

With the lingering stench of Covid, and now a cost-of-living crisis we are on the precipice of another pandemic; a children's health pandemic (www.who.int, 2022). But we have never had a more opportune moment to take positive action and demonstrate the power of sport and play to improve the health and wellbeing of all children and help them realise their potential.

Children only get one childhood! Let's create the happiest and healthiest children in the world!

Concluding this chapter, I resoundingly echo Chris's call for:

Firstly, the imperative of collaborative effort as system partners to redefine the narrative—reshaping the education system and reprioritising elements crucial in children's lives.

Secondly, the present juncture presents an unparalleled opportunity to enact positive change, elevating the wellbeing and potential of every child.

Lastly, let's unite to forge a world where children's happiness and health is prioritised to transform outcomes for us all. Let's go upstream and improve the system to stop so many young people falling in the river.

Chapter summary

- We need to go upstream and create a proactive approach in addressing the root causes of children's mental health issues. Educators have a critical role in creating a positive and supportive environment for students, developing their skills and resilience.
- Self-harm rates are increasing, particularly among young females, who use it as a positive coping strategy to deal with their emotions. If young people continue to view self-harm as a normal way to deal with stress and emotions, it could lead to a surge in suicides as they move into higher-risk age groups.
- To prevent this, it is essential to address the root causes of self-harm, provide young people with effective coping strategies, and ensure timely interventions through mental health services. Failure to do so could lead to a future problem of suicide and suicide prevention.
- There is a need for a comprehensive mental health plan in England, one that prioritises prevention and early intervention, and is not simply grouped with chronic health conditions. The government must commit to creating such a plan, providing sustained investment in high-quality mental health and social care services and preventative mental health interventions.
- Schools should embed a three-phase approach, including early intervention for all students, internal specialist support, and accessing external specialist support for those in crisis.
- Providing mental health support can be expensive, but the cost of not providing adequate support can be even greater. Early intervention can be much cheaper to deliver and highly cost-effective.

- To create a world where young people receive the support they need to thrive, the government, NHS, schools, universities, charities and communities must work together.
- We must prioritise mental health, invest in early intervention, and be prepared to make changes to create the world we want to see. By working together, we can create a future where mental health is a priority, and young people have the resources and support they need to lead healthy, fulfilling lives.

Critical questions

1. What mental health provision do you want for your children and the young people you teach?

2. What provision does your school already have in place?

3. What world do you want to live in, in 2050?

Chapter references

- Anna Freud National Centre for Children and Families (2022). 0:02 / 1:16:29. *Introduction Transformation Seminar with Professor Louis Appleby - Is there a suicide crisis in young people?* Available at: https://www.youtube.com/watch?v=clFgkny9vYs [Accessed 29 Sep. 2023].
- Department for Transport. (2020). THINK! Road safety. London: Her Majesty's Stationery Office.
- NHS. (2017) Benchmarking Mental Health. [online] Available at: https://static1.squarespace.com/static/58d8d0ffe4fcb5ad94cde63e/t/58ecf71de58c62adea37fa27/1491924766551/BenchmarkingMentalHealthCard2017FINAL.pdf
- www.who.int. (2022.). *Physical activity United Kingdom of Great Britain and Northern Ireland 2022 country profile.* [online] Available at: https://www.who.int/publications/m/item/physical-activity-gbr-2022-country-profile.

Additional insights

How we support children and young people's mental health in the UK

Sir Norman Lamb is a prominent advocate for mental health in the United Kingdom. He served as an MP for North Norfolk from 2001 to 2019 and held the position of Minister of State for Care and Support from 2012 to 2015. During his tenure, he worked tirelessly to raise awareness, reduce stigma, and improve mental health services. Sir Norman introduced important legislation such as the Mental Health Act 2007 and the Care Act 2014. His personal experiences and dedication have made him a leading figure in mental health advocacy, both within and outside of Parliament.

He remains actively engaged in mental health initiatives, collaborating with organisations and campaigns to promote mental health awareness and advocate for policy changes. His contributions have shaped mental health policy in the UK and have had a lasting impact on improving access to care and support for individuals with mental health conditions. Few people in this country are better placed to talk about this topic than Sir Norman.

'We are witnessing a disturbing increase in prevalence of mental health problems amongst children and young people. This trend predates the pandemic, but appears to have accelerated through periods of lockdown, which many young people found very hard to navigate. We do not fully understand all of the causes of this sharp increase in prevalence, but contributory factors may include the challenge of growing up in a highly complex world with multiple pressures both social and academic, pushing many young people into a state of anxiety. Social determinants of health, including poverty, clearly play a significant part. The explosion over the last 10 years of social media may well also contribute. Concerns about online bullying, pressure in relation to body image and the 24/7 ever present nature of social media will have an impact on the wellbeing of many young people. There is also a growing understanding of the clear correlation between bad things happening to children from the very start of life and the emergence of poor mental health and other negative impacts. Trauma, abuse, and neglect from early years is associated with an increased risk of poor mental health in teenage years and beyond. Given the impact of poverty, poor housing and stressed environments, prevalence of ill health is much higher amongst lower income families. Race also plays a disturbing part. Experience of racism is associated with an increased risk of mental ill health. Yet, probably

because of a lack of trust in services, young black boys are less likely to seek help early on but are then overrepresented in those detained under the Mental Health Act in a state of crisis.

With this as the backdrop, and with burgeoning demand, our children's mental health system seems broken and dysfunctional. High thresholds to even get onto the waiting list, accompanied by long waits for those who do manage, leave many families feeling helpless and in despair. So many staff in the CAMHS system work tirelessly and with true dedication but they work in a system that is desperately in need of reform. We all preach the principle of early intervention, yet in far too many cases, the first intervention comes at the latest possible moment, when a young person is in crisis. We have still failed to eradicate the cliff edge at 18 when children and young people's services are withdrawn and young people are told, in effect, to try their luck with adult services. This transition at 18 should have been scrapped long ago.

When a young person is turned away from a waiting list for a mental health trust because their illness is not serious enough, too often there is no alternative support available. This risks the young person deteriorating whilst they wait. Education is also impacted by delays in accessing help.

So the case for reform of a broken system faced with a rising tide of need is overwhelming. To help shape that reform, we should look around the world at countries which have recognised this need and acted. Countries like Australia, Canada and Sweden have all recognised the need to redesign the system to offer early intervention in a way which avoids over-pathologizing their need. Australia has established a service for young people called Headspace. Pioneered by Professor Pat McGorry, this service is there for young people to offer support at an early stage on any issue of teenage angst. In the UK, there is a network of something similar – Youth Information, Advice and Counselling Services (known as YIACS) which operates in a similar way, but their coverage is haphazard, depending on local funding. All of these countries have one thing in common. They have far shorter lengths of stay in their children and young people's inpatient units, compared to the UK. 10 or 11 days is a typical length of stay, compared to something approaching 70 days in England. I believe we often re-traumatise young people by sending them away from home to an environment which may well feel unsafe and may well not be particularly therapeutic. In Sweden, short stays in hospital involve a parent accompanying the child or teenager. How civilised is that?

CHAPTER 2 - ADDITIONAL INSIGHTS

Some positive steps have been taken in the UK. Increasingly, we are recognising the role of digital support for young people. The digital mental health company, Kooth, now has contracts with the NHS across most of England and in parts of both Scotland and Wales. This enables young people to access help via their mobile phones without having to sit on a waiting list for months. Valuable information to help young people understand what they might be experiencing is just a few clicks away and one-to-one sessions can be booked with a counsellor. All of this can be done anonymously, which can be important for a young person anxious about revealing how they are feeling.

Schools play a vital part in the happiness and wellbeing of children and young people. I am very attracted by the idea of a consistent measure of wellbeing for all children at school. This idea has been promoted by former Cabinet Secretary, Gus O'Donnell, and many others including David Gregson in Greater Manchester. A whole school approach to mental health and wellbeing is needed. We need to make schools more psychologically informed so that they understand better the challenges that children and young people face in their lives. Teachers need to have training on understanding mental distress and mental ill health as part of their core training to become teachers - to equip them to do an immensely challenging and complex job.

Our approach to behaviour also needs to be more sophisticated than in the past. To simply respond to bad behaviour by punishing the child often completely fails to understand that that child's behaviour may be driven by awful experiences that that child might have had at home or in their neighbourhood. I am a strong believer in the value of creating a disciplined and learning culture at school, but I strongly object to the approach of some in our education system who believe that the answer is to exclude from school (either formally or informally) the most difficult children, too often leaving them on the scrap heap. This might solve the problem for the school, but it creates a far greater one for society and utterly fails that young person. Amongst those permanently excluded from school, children with special needs, including mental ill health and autism, are significantly overrepresented. What sort of society is it which turns its back on children who are most in need of help and support?

Finally, we know that 50% of all adult mental ill health has emerged by the age of 14 and that about 75% of adult mental ill health has emerged by your early 20s. Yet we fail to invest sufficiently in supporting children and young people during these formative years. By international standards a low percentage of the total mental health budget goes to children and young people - and a tiny percentage of our total NHS spend. It makes sense to invest in these formative years, recognising that we have the potential for a very substantial return on our investment, both in giving young people the chance of a good life and in terms of their economic contribution to society. Conversely, the cost of neglect of these young people is incalculable.

Changes over time

Andy Mellor is the National Wellbeing Director for Schools Advisory Service and Strategic Lead for the Carnegie Centre of Excellence for Mental Health in Schools. Andy is incredibly well placed to put forward recommendations for what changes are required to transform our children's mental health.

"When I think back to my first year of teaching in 1988, I wonder whether, as teachers, we were aware of mental ill health and wellbeing as concepts? I'm not sure that we were. Decisions about additional support (the limited amount that there was) was predicated on an understanding that a child might have a special education need or some kind of barrier to learning. I'm sure looking back, that in those days, there were children diagnosed with behavioural or SEND needs where the roots of their behaviour or their difficulties lay in trauma and mental ill health. I'd like to think that in the vast majority of cases, referrals to behaviour or SEND provision is now predicated on a deeper understanding of the learner's need.

Now flip the coin and I do now wonder how many more learners are being supported because we now shine a far more educated light on learner need. This translates into significantly more diagnoses and intervention, but failure to consider the changing factors on the mental health of our learners over the last 30 years is to misrepresent the struggles that so many of our young people face.

Thirty years ago, there was no high stakes accountability, testing or inspection. Yes, we had exams, but they were clearly about the student doing well as we believed that these grades would help us on life's journey. Creating league tables and comparators to judge the "success" of schools inevitably builds pressure on staff and students. This pressure is *then compounded by an inspectorate which didn't exist in 1988 and which creates further pressure to be "outstanding" or at least "good."*

This pressure has shaped the whole topography of schools, what they are about and what they look like to the learner. As a result, personal development and the development of the whole learner including the "soft skills" which employers really value such as flexibility, resourcefulness, and lateral thinking, have been relegated to not measurable in league tables and success is defined by what is measured. Generations of learners leave schools as "failures" despite having skills and abilities in other areas that aren't measured, because of our centrally prescribed reductive approach.

As Einstein said, "If you judge a fish by its ability to climb a tree then it will spend its life thinking it is stupid."

So, learners have new pressures to deal with academically, but they also have greater social media pressures to deal with too. Social media didn't exist in 1988 and if bullying took place at school, then the bullied had respite when they went home, there was relative safety in their bedroom. Now social media permeates every aspect of a young person's life from never escaping the bullying to daily feeds of how "normal" people should look, behave and relate to each other. So much of this is inescapable and feeds peer pressure. The misogynistic social media characters feed boy's false information on how to treat women and girls, girls and young women are fed information on how they should look and present themselves socially.

So, when un-informed commentators suggest that this is a snowflake generation, it fails to consider all the above, and whilst schools can't do this work alone, there are things that they can do to change the game for young people.

Firstly, government needs to see the change that needs to take place and invest for the future of the country, not just the life of a parliament lest the blue side claims to have achieved success from the seeds the red side planted or vice versa.

This investment needs to support schools to create learner focused solutions which can be shared across the sector with far more visibility than currently is the case and replace the "evidence-based practice" where the evidence fits the prevailing political ideology.

Kerry Whitehouse at St Michael's High School is doing some outstanding work in supporting students to create resources that help parents to understand mental health and wellbeing and better support their children. Kerry has promoted this work but is the first to push her young people forward and they are truly a credit to themselves and their school. There is much about agency and student voice to be learnt from this school. Critically Kerry doesn't have a teaching commitment, so the school has found the resource to allow Kerry to devote her time solely to promoting this work.

Similarly, Lauren Howard has created an approach to peer-on-peer abuse which has engaged, motivated, and changed the lives of her students at Stour Valley Community School. Students are enabled and lead this work in school.

Michelle Bye-Gannon is doing some ground-breaking work in supporting the mental health of her male students. Now at the Chiltern Learning Trust, Michelle is getting young men talking about their mental health and creating a culture where doing so is supported and enabled.

These three examples show what can be done when teachers, who have time and resource, are freed to support the young people that they work with. As a country we need to invest in people like Michelle, Lauren, and Kerry, not at the detriment of teaching and learning but as recognition that our young people face newer and greater challenges to their mental health than young people have ever done outside of wartime.

As well as supporting the situation as we find it now, we also need a national conversation about whether the damage done by high stakes accountability and inspection is worth the damage it has created. There must be another way, but only by an open, honest conversation between people committed to change will we see this change."

A SENCO's view

Jenny Kitson-Cook *is a deputy head at an inner-city school in England. As a former SENCO, she is well placed to talk about best practice around mental health in state schools.*

'Over the last eleven years I have worked with a range of children from different demographic backgrounds, all of whom want to be successful in some shape or form, but more importantly want to be loved. Personally, the word love does not scare me in an educational context but does admittedly get some mixed reactions from some professionals based on the traditional definition of the word and the boundaries we set ourselves within that. I would even go as far to say that I much prefer the term child or children to that of students or pupils; to me the disassociated demeanour essentially stops 'the outside world of those that do not teach' treating the education of the children as one of the most influential journeys a person will ever take.

So, in my endeavour to treat every child as if they were my own, I try with all my might to ensure every decision in school for those I lead and for those I am surrounded by to always be as close to child centred as possible. But doesn't everybody? Not for me to answer, however I can write about some of the ways I have tried to be.

The best practice I ever watched, emulated and then refined was that of 'Team Around the Child' (TAC) meetings. While we all know time is precious, being overwhelmed and working in silos is the least constructive use of it. TAC meetings include the Head of Year, SENCO, Pastoral Managers (a.k.a Assistant Head of Year or Behaviour Team), the Head of Key Stage, Attendance Lead, Designated Safeguarding Leads, and the Deputy Headteacher.

Once a fortnight, for every year group, the children are discussed. No dilly dallying, no flapping, just directed conversations around progress and wellbeing. Within this method sits progress data, SEND data, professional reports, CPOMS logs, parental meetings or phone calls, form tutor discussions and much more, however it all pulls together to make sure each child is known. On top of this then sits Super TAC, with Senior Leadership and Senior members of the behaviour team to establish high level bespoke plans and accountability of those who show the most challenging behaviours. I truly believe that this investment in time has proven to be one of the most effective ways of identifying early intervention as professionally challenging conversations from all around the table look at every department contributing to a journey where a child might need more guidance and support.

Once needs are identified and interventions are put in place, often staff feel a sense of 'Whack-A-Mole'. Where one difficulty is being dealt with for one child, another three arise for someone else. This makes the pressures and challenges put on staff feel relentless, stressful and often exacerbated by a negative parental email. The only way I have found to lead the teams through the quicksand of increasingly growing SEND and behavioural needs is to be transparent. I work with the SENCO on plotting out the EHCP needs to ensure provision is adequately met, whilst picking up the group numbers with SEN Support children. Where a block of intervention has been started, conversation then grows around a concrete answer about when the child is going to start the next wave, even if it is annoyingly a term later. This then maps out across the school and while it may be perceived as frustrating, waiting for some sessions with the school therapy dog or an internal member of therapeutic staff has to be worth the wait. Boundaries in this climate are the key to survival, I stand by saying that schools cannot and should not be the fourth emergency service.

For those children who need external support services, they too are under-resourced and underfunded to be able to provide support for all those that need it. Thresholds to access services are higher than they have ever been, and I do not feel alone in becoming saddened and despondent about some children being missed. That said, we should all do our best with what we have, and I genuinely feel that is to be done through both early intervention and internal specialist support.

Try embracing the Emotion Coaching approach within the whole school CPD, be open to having a therapy dog in school and create internal meeting structures that, all in all, put love and education in the journey to trying our best.'

Chapter 3 - Should it be schools' responsibility to be the front line of mental health?

"Education is the most powerful weapon which you can use to change the world."
Nelson Mandela

As society has become more aware of the importance of mental health, there has been a growing debate about whether schools should take on the responsibility of being the front line of mental health support for children. This is a complex issue, as schools are already responsible for a wide range of duties. However, with the rise in mental health challenges among children, it is clear that schools have an important role to play in promoting children's mental wellbeing.

As such, the first part of the chapter will explore the question of whether it should be schools' responsibility to be the front line of mental health support for children. In the second part of the chapter we will explore whether it should be the teacher's role to improve student wellbeing.

The role of a school

Let's start with the role of a school. According to Hanushek, E. A. (1986), the role of a school is to provide education and instruction to students, with the goal of preparing them for future success.

Beyond academic instruction, schools also play a critical role in the social and emotional development of students. They provide opportunities for students to build relationships with peers, learn how to work in teams, and develop social skills.

In addition, schools serve as important community centres, bringing together students, families, and educators to support the growth and development of children. They may provide resources and support for families, such as counselling services, after-school programmes, and access to health care.

Overall, the role of a school is to provide a safe, supportive, and engaging environment where students can learn, grow, and thrive both academically and socially.

Three points stick out for me from Hanushek, when we are discussing the role of the school and mental health. If the goal is to prepare children for future success, then we need to give our young people the skills to navigate the modern world to protect their mental health and beyond that flourish. Too often, children's education is disrupted by mental illness that has been allowed to escalate, rather than children getting the support early enough. If schools play a critical role in the social and emotional development of students, then it is critical that we develop the skills our young people need. By preparing our young people properly, our students can learn, grow and thrive both academically and socially.

Paul Collin, inspirational headteacher at Bohunt Worthing, is certainly taking this approach: 'It's crucial, now more than ever to consider how schools and colleges are developing both the academic and the wellbeing of every young person. At Bohunt Worthing, we place a core emphasis on every child having the same opportunity in life. Being mentally fit, happy, energised and productive are key attributes that everyone can benefit from having.

We have introduced an Early Intervention Programme to ensure we are taking a proactive approach to these areas, working with all our young people to become the very best versions of themselves and achieve future successes.'

Reaching many

Schools are one of the few institutions that can offer a blanket service to nearly every child in the country. Unlike other mental health services, schools have the ability to reach a large number of children on a daily basis. This is particularly important, given that many children who experience mental health difficulties may not receive support from other services, either because they are not aware of the services available, or because they are unable to access them due to barriers such as cost or stigma.

One of the main advantages of schools promoting children's mental wellbeing is that they can offer support to nearly all children, regardless of their background, socioeconomic status, or geographic location. This means that children who may not have access to other mental health services can still receive support and guidance when they need it. In addition, schools are uniquely positioned to identify children who may be experiencing mental health difficulties, and intervene early, before problems become more severe.

Schools can help to destigmatise mental health issues by providing a safe and supportive environment where children can talk about their feelings and concerns. By integrating mental health education and support into the school curriculum, schools can help children to develop a positive attitude towards mental health and wellbeing. This can not only benefit children in the short term, but can also lead to positive long-term outcomes, including improved academic achievement, better social and emotional skills, and better overall health.

A moral responsibility?

As outlined in chapter 1, there has been an alarming rise in mental health challenges among children and young people in recent years, which has led many to argue that schools have a moral responsibility to take action and promote children's mental wellbeing.

Schools have a responsibility to create a culture that promotes mental health and wellbeing. This includes integrating mental health education and support into the curriculum, providing training for teachers and staff on identifying and supporting children with mental health difficulties, and creating partnerships with mental health professionals and community organisations.

While schools can play a critical role in promoting children's mental wellbeing, it is also essential to recognise that some of our school practices may contribute to the worsening of children's mental health. It is vital to hold up a mirror to our own practice and take a critical look at the policies and practices in our schools.

Schools may not be able to solve all of the challenges that contribute to mental health challenges, but they have a moral responsibility to do something to support and protect children's mental health. The consequences of not taking action are too high, and the impact on children's lives can be devastating. By taking action and promoting mental wellbeing, schools can help children to reach their full potential and thrive.

Unhappy children cannot learn

Research has shown that stress and negative emotions can have a significant impact on a child's ability to learn and retain information. Chronic stress can affect the development of the brain, specifically the prefrontal cortex, which is responsible for executive functions such as attention, memory, and decision-making. Stress can also impact the hippocampus, which is involved in the formation and retrieval of memories.

When children experience chronic stress or negative emotions, their brains release cortisol, a stress hormone that can interfere with the development of neural connections in the brain. This can result in a decrease in cognitive function and an impaired ability to learn and remember information.

Moreover, negative emotions and stress can also affect a child's motivation and engagement in the learning process. Children who are anxious or stressed may have difficulty focusing on tasks, lack interest in learning, and have reduced self-esteem, which can further hinder their academic performance.

Unhappy children cannot learn, which is a key reason why it makes sense for schools to prioritise children's mental wellbeing to ensure they can flourish academically. It is however, important to recognise that promoting positive mental health and wellbeing is not just about academic achievement; it is also about preparing children for life beyond school. By promoting mental wellbeing, schools can equip children with the skills and resilience they need to navigate the challenges of life and achieve their full potential.

Shaping wider society

By prioritising mental wellbeing in schools, schools can play an essential role in shaping wider communities and fostering a happier and more connected society. Schools can serve as a hub for promoting wellbeing for students and their families, as well as the wider community.

When schools prioritise wellbeing, they can create a ripple effect that extends beyond the school gates. Schools can help to create less devastated communities from the impact of intentional self-harm, and where people are better equipped to cope with the challenges of life. This can lead to a more connected society, where individuals and families feel supported and connected to each other.

In addition, when schools prioritise mental wellbeing, they can also contribute to the wider mental health agenda. Schools can help to reduce the stigma associated with mental health difficulties and create a more open and accepting society. This can lead to more people seeking help for mental health difficulties and receiving the support they need to thrive.

The challenges for schools

While there are many benefits to schools taking on the responsibility of promoting children's mental wellbeing, there are also challenges that must be addressed. One of the main challenges is the lack of resources and funding available to schools to provide comprehensive mental health support. Many schools are already stretched thin with limited resources, and adding the responsibility of promoting mental wellbeing can be a significant burden.

One of the most critical resources that schools need is funding. Schools require funding to provide mental health services to students, hire mental health professionals, provide training for teachers and staff, and establish partnerships with mental health professionals and community organisations. However, funding for mental health services in schools has been limited, and schools are often forced to rely on limited resources or external funding sources to provide mental health services.

Schools also require training and support for teachers and staff to identify and support children with mental health difficulties. Teachers and staff require specialised training to understand the signs and symptoms of mental health problems, to identify children who may be at risk, and to provide support and referrals to mental health professionals.

However, many teachers and staff may not have the necessary training or expertise to address these issues, which can lead to a lack of support for children who need it the most.

Addressing these challenges

To address these challenges schools can partner with mental health professionals and community organisations to provide comprehensive mental health services to students. By working together, schools, mental health professionals, and community organisations can provide a coordinated and effective approach to promoting children's mental wellbeing.

This can include offering mental health services on-site at schools, establishing referral systems to connect students with mental health professionals, and offering mental health education and support to students, teachers, and staff. I reiterate that this needs to be fully funded so schools have the workforce and expertise to deliver an effective service.

Moreover, schools can take advantage of technology and online resources to provide mental health services to students. Online therapy and counselling services, apps, and digital platforms can provide accessible and affordable mental health services to students, regardless of their location or socioeconomic background. Additionally, these resources can also be used to educate students, teachers, and staff about mental health issues and to provide support and guidance on how to manage and cope with mental health challenges.

Schools looking after their staff

Schools have a significant responsibility to promote the mental wellbeing of their students, but it is also important to recognise the importance of supporting the mental wellbeing of school staff. Research has shown that teachers and other school staff members are at increased risk of experiencing work-related stress, burnout, and mental health difficulties (Kyriacou, 2001; Rimm-Kaufman & Sawyer, 2004). Moreover, the COVID-19 pandemic has highlighted the need for schools to prioritise the mental wellbeing of their staff as they navigate unprecedented challenges.

One way that schools can support the mental wellbeing of their staff is by creating a supportive and inclusive work environment. This includes promoting open communication, providing opportunities for professional development and growth, and fostering positive relationships among staff members. Schools can also provide access to mental health resources and support for staff members, such as mental health counselling and supervision.

Schools can take steps to reduce work-related stress and burnout among staff members. This includes promoting work-life balance, providing adequate resources and support, and ensuring that staff members have a manageable workload. By taking action to support the mental wellbeing of their staff, schools can create a positive and supportive work environment that fosters staff wellbeing and promotes positive outcomes for students.

Furthermore, prioritising the mental wellbeing of school staff can have wider societal benefits. A positive and supportive work environment can contribute to improved job satisfaction and retention rates among staff members, which can ultimately lead to better outcomes for students.

When staff members feel valued and supported, they are more likely to provide high-quality teaching and support to their students.

Inspectorates taking notice

Promoting the wellbeing of young people has become a priority in both state and independent sector school inspectorates. This shift towards prioritising wellbeing in school inspections reflects growing recognition of the critical role that schools play in promoting positive mental health and well-being in young people.

In September 2019, Ofsted added personal development as a separate inspection category. This category evaluates how well schools are promoting the personal development of their students, including their physical and mental health, social skills, and attitudes towards learning. The addition of this category was a significant step towards recognising the importance of mental health and wellbeing in schools. Schools are now being held accountable for promoting positive mental health and wellbeing and are encouraged to prioritise the wellbeing of their students.

Similarly, the Independent Schools Inspectorate (ISI) launched a new inspection framework in September 2023. The framework includes significant changes, with pupil wellbeing and school leadership at the forefront of the inspection practice. The proposed changes were made in response to a fast-moving educational context and informed by reviews focusing on the safety and wellbeing of children.

The ISI's framework uses the definition of pupils' wellbeing in the Standards and Children Act 2004 as a guide, with thematic reports covering leadership and management, pupils' physical and mental health and emotional wellbeing, protection from harm and neglect, education, training, and recreation, contribution to society, and social and economic wellbeing. These changes in school inspections reflect a growing recognition of the importance of mental health and wellbeing in schools.

It would be remiss of me not to acknowledge the irony that Ofsted inspections often have a significant impact on the wellbeing of our senior leaders in schools. While these inspections are intended to assess the quality of education, they can inadvertently create additional stress and pressure for school leaders.

The high stakes nature of inspections, coupled with the fear of negative judgments and potential repercussions, can take a toll on the mental wellbeing of those in leadership positions. It is crucial that we recognise and address this irony, ensuring that the inspection process supports the overall wellbeing of our school leaders, allowing them to effectively lead and nurture a positive environment for both staff and students.

By fostering a culture that values mental health and prioritises supportive leadership practices, we can create a system where inspections promote growth and improvement without compromising the wellbeing of our senior leaders and teachers.

Should it be the school's responsibility to be the front line of mental health?

In conclusion, schools have a crucial role to play in promoting children's mental wellbeing. They are uniquely positioned to provide comprehensive mental health services to nearly every child in the country, helping to destigmatise mental health issues, identify children who may be experiencing difficulties, teach self-care tools and promote positive attitudes towards mental health and wellbeing.

However, schools must also take a critical look at their own practices and policies to ensure that they are not contributing to the worsening of children's mental health. Factors such as behavioural policies, academic pressure, bullying, social isolation, and lack of support can all play a role in the development of mental health difficulties in children, and schools must take steps to address these root causes.

Lack of resources and funding is a significant challenge for schools that want to promote children's mental wellbeing, but it is essential that they receive the necessary resources and support to provide comprehensive mental health services. This includes funding for mental health services, training and support for teachers and staff, and partnerships with mental health professionals and community organisations.

Schools also have a responsibility to support the mental wellbeing of their staff. Creating a supportive and inclusive work environment, promoting work-life balance, and providing access to mental health resources and support can all contribute to positive outcomes for young people.

Ultimately, promoting mental wellbeing is essential for academic success and preparing children for life beyond school. The shift towards prioritising wellbeing in school inspections reflects a growing recognition of the critical role that schools play in promoting positive mental health and wellbeing in young people.

By working together, schools can provide a coordinated and effective approach to promoting children's mental wellbeing, ensuring that all children receive the support and guidance they need to thrive now and long after they have left your care.

Consider this...
- What do you think? Should it be the school's responsibility to be the front line of mental health?
- In what ways does your school contribute to positive mental wellbeing for your young people and staff?
- In what way does your school contribute to negative mental health and illness for your young people and staff?

What is the teacher's role in improving student wellbeing?

In the second part of the chapter we will explore what is the teacher's role in improving student wellbeing.

It can be daunting to step away from our usual methods of teaching, but when we look at how many young people are suffering and the lengthy waiting times to receive specialist support from stretched and underfunded providers like Child and Adolescent Mental Health Services (CAMHS), then we as teachers can definitely play an important role.

What can teachers do?

The four key ways frontline teachers can help make a difference is to:
1. Cultivate fantastic relationships with their young people.
2. Help break the stigma associated with mental health.
3. Identify those who are struggling as early as possible.
4. Teach a toolkit of self-care strategies to empower young people to have the skillset to manage their own mental health in many cases now and long after they have left school.

As frontline teachers one of the most important roles we can play in transforming our students' mental wellbeing is by contributing to breaking the stigma around talking about mental health to change the narrative.

This is not always easy but one of the ways that has been most effective is talking about role models and their experiences of mental wellbeing/health/illness. This allows children to empathise and identify with the issues. We will discuss this in more detail in Chapter 15.

The average teacher has over 3500 interactions with children per day. That is a lot of opportunities to notice a difference in a young person and refer for early intervention. We are at the front line of this pandemic, and we can and do make a difference on a daily basis whether that is being the one constant in a young person's life or exploring ways to support them or bringing some light to their lives.

What if one of your interactions saved a child's life? What a legacy to leave!

After discovering the mental health continuum, I adapted the model so that I could find out where each member of the class is on the continuum within 2 minutes in a way that is anonymous to the rest of the group. This snapshot is an incredibly powerful tool to get a snapshot of where each member of your class is in that moment of time and enables follow up conversations so that the child feels firstly supported and noticed, and secondly whether they need to be referred to specialist counsellors within the school for additional support. We will explore this in more detail in Chapter 4.

With effective Continuous Professional Development teachers can give their young people a toolbox of self-care strategies so that children can own, manage, and build their mental wellbeing. This will enable them to be proactive about managing their own mental health, both now, and long after they have left school. We will explore this in more detail in Part 2.

Teachers are extremely well-placed to make a difference in these vitally important areas because of the quality of our relationships with young people. We can use these exceptional relationships to help them feel safe and open up about their mental health in a calm and supportive environment. By having these excellent role models bringing mental health front and centre of the conversation, we can break the stigma linked to mental health and enable our children to open up and feel listened to. We will explore relationships in more detail in Part 3.

What can't teachers do?

Whilst appreciating all that we can do as teachers to help our young people with their mental wellbeing, it is also important to acknowledge what we can't do so that everyone remains safe.

Doctor Catherine Wheatley will outline what our role is and isn't here:

Teachers: a mental health workforce?

'Today's teachers are frontline mental health workers: when young people are struggling, they are more likely to turn to a teacher than any other adult, and teachers are very often their only source of support [1].

The help and advice that teachers can offer has become more valuable than ever, thanks to the sharp rise in the number of young people reporting mental health concerns and the difficulty of accessing overstretched adolescent mental health services. Young people can wait years for an appointment with the Child and Adolescent Mental Health Service (CAMHS), but the support that they receive independently and directly in school can make a difference in many areas of their lives.

What's more, teaching staff have an unrivalled opportunity to positively impact young people: they can get to know their pupils, and they can very often identify those whose behaviour suggests they are experiencing a mental health problem (or are at risk of developing one). Perhaps unsurprisingly, the influence of individual teachers on pupils' mental health is as significant as their influence on academic test scores, according to research by the Centre for Economic Performance [2].

But although teachers are skilled professionals with a duty to promote student welfare, they are not trained clinicians or counselling psychologists, and they are not under a duty to identify mental health difficulties or disorders. Only appropriately trained professionals should attempt to make a diagnosis of a mental health problem, according to the Department for Education (DoE)'s safeguarding regulations [3].

Sometimes this line can feel blurred when staff have been empowered by mental health training and young people's distress is clear. So how can we best define teachers' roles in children and young people's mental healthcare – and what they can and can't do?

Promoting public health and acting as the first point of contact for young people when things go wrong are the two key approaches that teachers should follow, according to a report by the Royal Society of Medicine [4], which also argued that more funding should be made available to train and support staff who are already dealing with multiple responsibilities.

First, teachers should think of themselves as public health professionals, supporting population health by helping young people to stay healthy, protecting them from threats to their health and fulfilling their duty of care to enable all children to have the best outcomes. PE teachers have a particularly important part to play here, thanks to their role in promoting physical activity. Staff can also teach self-care strategies including sleep hygiene, healthy diet and self-care strategies for wellbeing where appropriate and in line with best practice.

In addition, they have a role in de-stigmatising mental distress by raising awareness of mental health and wellbeing. Simply nurturing young people is crucial: there is good evidence that when young people have a sense of being valued, and of belonging to the school community, there are positive outcomes across a range of health-risk behaviours including violence, substance misuse and disordered eating [5].

Second, teachers should think of themselves as primary care professionals and the initial access point for young people's mental health support. Staff are well-placed to observe young people day-to-day, and to identify those whose behaviour suggests they might be experiencing a mental health problem, or be at risk of developing one, according to the DoE's safeguarding regulations (3). They can offer general advice to young people and their families, and signpost to sources of help and support. In more severe cases, they can pass on information via the head teacher to social services or other authorities to ensure that support is escalated.

Adequate mental health awareness training to fulfil these functions is crucial, but not always available. As always, time and money are the key barriers when educating young people, promoting their positive development and providing them with frontline mental health services.'

It is not our job as teachers to diagnose mental health conditions, we have neither the time nor more importantly the expertise to do this. It is important we stay in our lane and recognise what our role is and what it isn't. This image clarifies what we can and can't do.

Figure 5:

Knowing our role

✖ We are not Psychologists

✖ We do not diagnose mental illness or trauma

✔ We are trauma informed and aware

✔ We are emotionally available

✔ We create psychological safety for all

✔ We create opportunities for children to regulate

✔ We teach children a toolbox of self-care strategies

The time challenge for teachers

Managing time will always be a constant balancing act due to the wide-ranging nature of teaching. There are always pressing priorities, deadlines to meet and something popping up that disrupts your day, but we have found that those teachers who have taken the interest and upskilled themselves with these important skills have reaped the benefits with happier, healthier young people who can then go on to thrive in a safe purposeful classroom and beyond.

In conclusion, our role in improving student wellbeing is undeniably significant. We have the power to be the light in the darkness, serving as positive role models and sources of support for our students. In the face of limited resources and stretched mental health services, we have the opportunity to make a real difference by cultivating relationships, breaking the stigma, identifying struggling students, and equipping young people with self-care strategies.

Through continuous professional development, we can acquire the tools and strategies to empower our students and create a safe and purposeful classroom environment. By incorporating fostering relationships, and deepening our understanding of mental health, we become transformative teachers who have the ability to positively impact the lives of our students.

Ultimately, by embracing our role in improving student wellbeing, we become agents of change, advocates for mental health, and champions for our students' overall development. Through our dedication and commitment, we can empower our students to navigate life's challenges, develop resilience, and lead fulfilling lives. This responsibility is one that should be embraced, treasured, and continuously pursued for the betterment of our students and the future generations they represent.

CHAPTER 3 - SHOULD IT BE SCHOOLS' RESPONSIBILITY TO BE THE FRONT LINE OF MENTAL HEALTH?

Chapter summary

- While schools may not be the only institution responsible for promoting children's mental wellbeing, they are uniquely positioned to provide a blanket service to nearly every child in the country.
- By providing comprehensive mental health services, schools can help to destigmatise mental health issues, identify children who may be experiencing difficulties, and promote positive attitudes towards mental health and wellbeing.
- By taking action on mental wellbeing, schools can shape their wider communities and foster a happier and more connected society.
- It is essential that schools receive the necessary resources and support to provide comprehensive mental health services.
- Schools have a responsibility to support the mental wellbeing of their staff which will ultimately contribute to positive outcomes for young people.
- Unhappy children can't learn, therefore promoting positive mental health and wellbeing is essential for academic success and preparing children for life beyond school.
- The shift towards prioritising wellbeing in school inspections reflects a growing recognition of the critical role that schools play in promoting positive mental health and wellbeing in young people. By working together, schools can provide a coordinated and effective approach to promoting children's mental wellbeing and ensure that all children receive the support and guidance they need to thrive.
- Teachers have a significant role in improving student wellbeing and can serve as positive role models and sources of support. By breaking the stigma, cultivating relationships, and equipping students with self-care strategies, we can make a real difference in student mental health.
- Continuous professional development helps us acquire the knowledge and skills to support student mental wellbeing effectively.
- By embracing our role in improving student wellbeing, we become agents of change and champions for students' overall development.

Critical questions

1. How confident do you feel in identifying those who are struggling?

2. Do you believe you can teach a tool kit of self-care strategies?

Chapter references

- Hanushek, E. A. (1986). The economics of schooling: Production and efficiency in public schools. Handbook of the Economics of Education.
- Kyriacou, C. (2001). Teacher Stress: Directions for future research. *Educational Review*, [online] 53(1), pp.27–35. DOI: https://doi.org/10.1080/00131910120033628.
- Rimm-Kaufman, S. E., & Sawyer, B. E. (2004). Primary-grade teachers' self-efficacy beliefs, attitudes toward teaching, and discipline and teaching practice priorities in relation to the "responsive classroom" approach. The Elementary School Journal, 104(4), 321-341. DOI: 10.1086/499194
- [1] NHS Digital. Mental health of children and young people in England, 2017. See https://files.digital.nhs.uk/3A/F08CA4/MHCYP%202017%20Service%20Use%20Tables.xlsx
- [2] Flèche S. Teacher quality, test scores and non-cognitive skills: evidence from primary school teachers in the UK. Seehttp://eprints.lse.ac.uk/83602/
- [3] Department for Education. Keeping Children Safe in Education, 2023. https://assets.publishing.service.gov.uk/government/uploads/system/uploads/attachment_data/file/1161273/Keeping_children_safe_in_education_2023_-_statutory_guidance_for_schools_and_colleges.pdf
- [4] Lowry, C. et al (2022). Teachers: the forgotten healthcare workforce. Journal of the Royal Society of Medicine. 115(4).https://doi.org/10.1177/01410768221085692
- [5] Lowry C, Stegeman I, Rauch F, Jani A. Modifying the school determinants of children's health. J R Soc Med. 2022; 115: 16–21.

Additional insights

Rob Connelly
Harleston Sancroft Academy

A great example of a school that is taking on responsibility for being on the frontline of mental health is Harleston Sancroft Academy, their fantastic headteacher, Rob Connelly, takes up the story:

'Teach who you are'… 'This is your School'… 'You create who we are'

'These are all things you will hear spoken across the Harleston Sancroft Community, empowering all members to experience a sense of belonging and ownership, contributing to positive mental health, knowing that they can influence and shape their experiences of what it is to be a part of our very special community; a community where children and adults are supported and encouraged to flourish in their daily lives… A place where everyone is celebrated.

The Harleston Sancroft Academy, an All Through School, is at the heart of the local community providing education, experiences and opportunities for children aged 3-16. As a school, deliberate actions highlight the importance of relationships; relationships are our cornerstone, reflecting the Church of England Vision for Education.

We educate for wisdom, knowledge, skills, hope and aspiration and it is these characteristics that underpin the decisions that are made daily, ensuring we create an environment that supports our school vision of 'Life in all Its Fullness' (John 10:10) - this is not to distract from academic rigour and excellence, it works as part of a symbiotic relationship where wellbeing, predicated on a secure base that provides availability, acceptance, sensitivity, cooperation and membership to all, enables people to 'be'. This independence and sense of true self, coupled with an interconnectedness and common purpose creates a climate where people witness true belonging.

Becoming an All-Through School in September 2022 was a conscious move to remove disconnect and promote common discourse and a consistent narrative that is shared and understood by all. Previous to this, as Executive Headteacher of a Primary and Secondary School in the same town, I would often see a lack of clarity around language, expectations, and purpose with many families working with both schools yet receiving a different message.

We see the school as the 'Heartbeat'; a vital, reliable organ, enabling the rhythms and routines of daily life to be carried out while responding to the strains, challenges and opportunities that are faced by all. We are constantly working hard to remove barriers, to provide opportunities through an excellent educational experience and a curriculum offer that is far broader than that which is solely planned for and experienced within the classroom.

The values that underpin our school are again a deliberate act and reflect the characteristics of what it is to be a 'good' citizen, one who can contribute to the wider world whilst developing a moral compass that will serve to replenish and enhance the health, wellbeing and sense of self-worth, shaping all generations and the communities within which we are a part of.

We do however have to be careful as in the current climate, many would question whether the idealistic approach, where education could be referred to as the universal panacea for all systemic issues and 'failings' is being asked too much - we currently operate within a system where accountability could be seen to override human flourishing in its truest sense. Why is it that schools are facing such challenges yet expected to provide resolutions whilst continuing to raise standards.

Flourishing starts from within, and it is vital that we enable adults to experience this, supporting young people, their families, and the wider community because people matter. Earlier this year, a parent shared with me the impact that our approach had had on her child and family, describing the school as a 'hope rope in a time of desperate darkness… where care, consideration and compassion has been absolutely empowering'.

Our school is full of learning, full of love, full of compassion and full of friendship.'

**Wellbeing and Mental Health within Secondary Schools -
A Headteacher's perspective**

Paul Collin is the inspirational headteacher at Bohunt Worthing School, in this section he shares his thoughts on the importance of wellbeing and mental health within secondary schools in a post lockdown education world.

Nurturing Social and Emotional Mental Health in the Aftermath of the Pandemic
'There are many buzzwords that have appeared over the years within Education, fads that come and go and educational processes and government initiatives that many of us that have been working in the industry for ten years or more will have likely seen beforehand, experienced and or used within the classroom. However, mental health and wellbeing is different. Due to the pandemic, it may have risen in profile over the last two years, increased in numbers, formal reports, and core topics of discussion, but it has always been with us.

Students are, after all human beings, mini adults, who require both learning, teaching, support, and of course nurture. Never has it been more important and more key within the education sector for wellbeing and mental health to be top of the agenda, so why has it taken a worldwide pandemic for us all to realise that?

Largely wellbeing is based on relationships, how one feels, how we connect and relate to one and another. Schools have so often been promoting academic over wellbeing and forced to hold both themselves and students to account for results via systems, judgments and inspections.

However, personal development is now sitting as a key fundamental on the inspection agenda and rightly so. It is the responsibility of everybody to ensure that all students, the generations of tomorrow, are raised on foundations that balance their intellect with their aspirations, dreams and their wellbeing.

The COVID-19 pandemic has significantly impacted the social and emotional wellbeing of our younger generation. Extended periods of isolation, disrupted routines, and heightened anxiety have left many students struggling with their mental health. As schools reopen and the education system adapts to the post-pandemic reality, it is crucial for headteachers and educators to address the social and emotional needs of students. In this chapter, we will explore effective strategies for schools and headteachers to support students' mental health and mitigate the long-term effects of the pandemic.

Cultivating a Safe and Supportive School Environment
Creating a safe and supportive school environment is the foundation for addressing social and emotional mental health needs. Headteachers should foster a positive school climate that encourages open communication, empathy, and inclusivity. This can be achieved through measures such as implementing anti-bullying policies, organising peer support programs, and providing mental health resources. By promoting a sense of belonging, students are more likely to feel comfortable seeking help and support when needed.

Integrating Social and Emotional Learning (SEL) Programs
Social and Emotional Learning (SEL) programs play a vital role in developing students' emotional intelligence, self-awareness, and interpersonal skills. Headteachers should prioritise the integration of SEL into the curriculum, ensuring that it is embedded across subjects and grade levels. These programs can teach students valuable skills such as self-regulation, empathy, conflict resolution, and responsible decision-making. By incorporating SEL, schools can empower students to navigate their emotions and develop healthier coping mechanisms. Programs such as those offered by Future Action, are great examples of these.

Establishing Student Support Systems
To address the diverse needs of students, headteachers should establish robust student support systems. This includes school counsellors, psychologists, and trained mental health professionals who can provide individualised support to students. By offering regular check-ins, counselling sessions, and intervention strategies, schools can identify and address mental health concerns early on. Additionally, partnering with external mental health organisations and local community resources can enhance the support network available to students.

Encouraging Peer-to-Peer Support
Peer support programs can be instrumental in helping students cope with the emotional aftermath of the pandemic. Headteachers should promote peer mentoring initiatives, where older students act as mentors to younger ones, fostering a sense of camaraderie and providing emotional support. Furthermore, creating student-led clubs and organizations

focused on mental health advocacy can empower students to address mental health stigma and promote a culture of understanding and acceptance.

Training and Supporting Educators
Headteachers must prioritise the wellbeing of their teaching staff. Providing professional development opportunities and training sessions on mental health literacy equips educators with the knowledge and skills needed to identify and support students' social and emotional needs. By fostering a culture of self-care and providing resources for teacher well-being, schools can ensure that educators are emotionally equipped to provide the necessary support to students.

The COVID-19 pandemic has highlighted the urgent need for schools and headteachers to prioritise social and emotional mental health. By cultivating a safe and supportive school environment, integrating SEL programs, establishing student support systems, encouraging peer-to-peer support, and training and supporting educators, schools can effectively address the social and emotional needs of students. By investing in the wellbeing of the younger generation, we can mitigate the long-term effects of the pandemic and foster a resilient and emotionally intelligent future society.'

Part 2:
Early Intervention

Chapter 4 – Identifying strugglers

"Be the person who shines a light on someone else's path, helping them to see the way forward when they've lost sight of their own strengths."
Unknown source

In the second part of this book I will outline some areas, techniques, and practices that we can introduce and encourage to create a supportive environment and give our young people a toolbox of self-care strategies to manage their own mental wellbeing now and long after they have left our settings.

In this chapter we are going to start by looking at identifying those young people who are struggling as early as possible so that they can get specialist support from trained mental health professionals.

As a teacher, it is essential to understand the importance of mental health in children. It is okay for children to not be okay, and it's important to shift the focus from mentally struggling to identifying where a child is, in that moment. Children's mental states can vary day-to-day depending on a wide range of factors, and it's important to recognise that some days may be harder than others.

One way to help children understand and be aware of their own mental health is to teach them to tune in to what their body is telling them. This can include things like changes in energy levels, mood, or appetite. By teaching children to pay attention to these signals, they can be more proactive in dealing with any mental health issues that may arise, and more open to support.

Creating a safe and supportive environment in the classroom is also crucial for children's mental wellbeing. Encourage open and honest discussions about mental health, and let children know that it is okay to talk about their feelings and concerns.

The mental health continuum

It's important for children to understand that their mental health can fluctuate depending on situations and circumstances, and that it's not always black and white. Teaching them about the mental health continuum, can help children to better understand where they are at any given moment, and take appropriate steps to improve their mental wellbeing.

Figure 6:

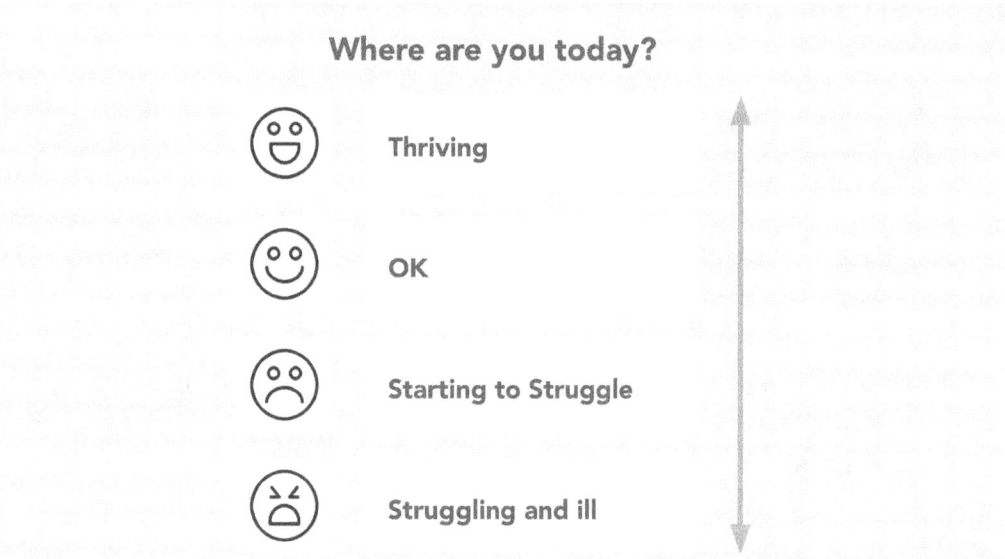

It can be helpful to give examples of what each stage on the continuum might look like in terms of thoughts, emotions, behaviours, and physical fitness. For example:

Thriving:
Thoughts: Positive and solution-focused, looking for opportunities and challenges.
Emotions: Confident, happy, and content.
Behaviours: Active and engaged in social activities, seeking out new experiences.
Physical Fitness: Engaged in regular exercise and taking care of physical health.

Feeling OK:
Thoughts: Neutral, not overly positive, or negative.
Emotions: Even-keeled, not experiencing extreme highs or lows.
Behaviours: Engaged in daily activities without difficulty.
Physical Fitness: Maintaining healthy habits, but not necessarily seeking out new activities.

Starting to Affect:
Thoughts: Negative and anxious, avoiding certain people or places.
Emotions: Anxious and stressed, experiencing more negative emotions.
Behaviours: Avoiding certain activities or social situations.
Physical Fitness: Neglecting regular exercise or healthy habits.

Struggling and Ill:
Thoughts: Negative and defeated, difficulty seeing solutions or hope.
Emotions: Depressed, helpless, and overwhelmed.
Behaviours: Withdrawing from social activities, avoiding people and situations.
Physical Fitness: Neglecting regular exercise and healthy habits, experiencing physical symptoms such as fatigue or pain.

It's important to note that everyone is different and will experience these stages in their own way. It's important that children learn to recognise their own signs, and practise self-care skills that will help them to improve their wellbeing.

It is worth noting that the mental health continuum is not a linear progression, but rather a fluctuation that can change from day to day or even hour to hour.

To help children understand this, it can be helpful to use real-life examples and scenarios. For instance, a child may start the day in a thriving state but an argument with a friend or a difficult maths test can move them to a state of starting to affect, but after getting a good night sleep and talking to a friend they are back to the thriving state.

Additionally, it's important to emphasise that there's no shame or judgement in any stage of the continuum. Mental health is not a destination, but rather a journey and it's important to know that it's possible to improve mental wellbeing.

We need to teach children various self-care strategies and coping mechanisms that they can use at each stage.

Using the mental health continuum

In our efforts to address the mental health needs of our young people, we discovered that many of them were struggling with their mental wellbeing but slipping through the cracks. This was particularly concerning given that mental health difficulties in childhood and adolescence can have long-lasting consequences and affect their overall development.

To tackle this challenge, I introduced the Mental Health Continuum to our staff. The continuum is a simple yet effective tool that helps identify young people who are struggling with their mental health but are not showing any obvious signs of distress. I first came across the mental health continuum on a podcast at the start of lockdown and I adapted the concept using my existing assessment for learning strategies. I wanted to create something that would work incredibly quickly with the 30 teenagers in my classroom and allow them to feedback anonymously to me, how they felt in that moment.

The tool provides staff with a structured approach to assess the mental health and wellbeing of children and enables you to be proactive in identifying any red flags or early warning signs.

As frontline teachers, we are in a privileged position of spending so much time with so many fantastic children and we are best positioned to provide that first piece of information to help trained professionals support those young people who need help the most.

The technique is in no way a diagnosis of mental ill-health, we are nowhere near qualified to do that as explained earlier in the book. This is merely the first step in identifying any children who may be struggling and referring them for additional exploration as early as possible before their problems escalate.

Try this:

The mental health continuum check in

Throughout this book there are strategies, tools and exercises you can try. Feel free to complete them or skim straight past. Some may be life changing for you, others may do nothing for you. My philosophy, when working with children and teachers is to encourage them to explore and find what strategies work for them.

With your class explain that everyone's mental health is on a continuum. At one end we are thriving and absolutely loving life, at the other end, we are really struggling to the point that we are seriously mentally ill. We are always at some point on this line. Some times in the day will be great and other times will be more of a struggle depending on your situation and circumstances.

In a moment we are going to close our eyes and bow our heads so no one else can see your answer apart from me, your teacher.

I will give you 4 options to choose from:
1. **Thriving**: You are loving life and looking forward to challenges.
2. **Ok**: Life is fine. You experience a few ups and downs but nothing you can't handle.
3. **Starting to affect**: You are starting to feel anxious about things and have started avoiding 1 or 2 people or places each day.
4. **Struggling and ill**: Your mental health is starting to have a major impact on you on a day to day basis. You might be withdrawing or avoiding 4 to 5 people or situations each day. If you feel like this you should ask your parent/carer to make an appointment to see your doctor.

Get young people to close their eyes and bow their heads. Once you are happy that all have their eyes closed, ask students to put their hands up for the category they are feeling in that moment when you call it out and then put their hand down when you move on to the next category. Go through the 4 categories fairly quickly mentioning if they are thriving, then if they are ok, if they are starting to struggle and then finally struggling and ill. Do not make a comment at any stage, this is a non-judgemental exercise.

Make a mental note of what students are communicating and identify any who you need to have a private 1-2-1 conversation to check in with.

Thank the class for sharing how they feel with you, ask them to open their eyes and return to learning and get on with your lesson.

As the lesson progresses and the class is working, take a moment to check in with those who are struggling and ill and starting to struggle.

This script might help….When we did the mental health continuum check in at the start of the lesson, I noticed that you put your hand up for struggling and ill, would you like to tell me more. I am here for you and happy to listen.

Depending on the child's response you may let them know about support in school or you may potentially notify your internal specialist counsellor, mental health support team or safeguarding team to keep them safe.

Reactive to proactive

The results of using the Mental Health Continuum have been truly remarkable. As students would walk into the class, I could normally pick up on visual cues that 3 children on average were clearly struggling in my classes.

By using the mental health continuum though, our staff were able to identify 3 additional pupils per class who were struggling with their mental health but going unnoticed. This has allowed us to direct these pupils to our school's social, emotional, and mental health counsellor for additional support and interventions as early as possible to stop problems from escalating, so that they are more likely to make a full recovery.

In addition to this, the Mental Health Continuum has also helped us identify 4 safeguarding issues that previously, had been missed. This has enabled us to put in place appropriate support for the children involved, ensuring that their safety and wellbeing is protected.

This process also helps you communicate to the whole class that you care about them and how they are feeling. It gives you a clear snapshot of where each young person is in that moment and informs your lesson planning so you can maximise outcomes.

It is incredibly quick to do. Once students are used to the process, it can take less than 2 minutes and the information gleaned is vital. It takes your school culture from reactive in identifying children who are struggling to proactive in one simple technique.

As I trialled this process with my classes post lockdown, I was constantly struck by how many children are walking around our schools struggling with their mental health, unwilling or unable to share their problems with adults who care about them. The numbers of children who were struggling and ill showed me that the mental health issues were twice as bad as I had originally thought.

There were many stories of hope though, and real satisfaction when I helped facilitate a child getting the expert support they needed to improve their life.

The transformation of Adam: a teacher's journey

I remember the first day I met Adam, an 11-year-old boy in my PE class. He was constantly late, disengaged, and often seemed to be in his own world. I found it difficult to connect with him and engage him in the lessons, despite my best efforts. I knew that he was struggling with Special Needs and was always in a state of disinterest. I was worried that I wasn't making an impact on him and that he wasn't getting the most out of his education.

A couple of struggling years later I introduced the Mental Health Continuum task to his class, where students would indicate their level of wellbeing on a simple scale. When I looked around the room, I noticed that Adam had his hand up for "struggling and ill." I knew I had to act.

During a quiet moment in the lesson, I approached Adam and asked if he would like to talk to me. He reluctantly agreed, and I could tell he was hesitant to open up. But as I listened, he shared a harrowing story with me. He told me that he was regularly being beaten up by his younger brother and that he often felt like ending his life. I thanked Adam for trusting me with such a vulnerable and difficult confession and assured him that I would get him the help he needed.

I immediately informed the safeguarding team and they spoke to Adam and his mother to ensure he was safe and getting the support he needed at home. Over the coming weeks, I made a point of regularly checking in with Adam, and our relationship began to grow. He started to open up more and was more engaged in the lessons. I could see that he was starting to feel supported and valued, and that made all the difference.

Adam's transformation was remarkable. He went from being a disengaged and disinterested young person to becoming one of our sports leaders and helping at events in our feeder primary schools. I was particularly proud of him when I heard that he had made an incredible impact on a young student with special needs at one of our feeder primary schools. It was a proud moment for both of us.

The journey with Adam taught me the power of making it as easy as possible for our children to have the opportunity to notify us that something isn't quite right, and then from there we can create the environment to give them the courage to communicate and open up about how they feel.

As the adult, we need to listen in a non-judgemental way, give empathic responses, and create connection. I learned that sometimes all a student needs is someone to show that they care. I am grateful to have been a part of Adam's journey and to have seen the impact that early identification, care, and support can have on a child's life.

The Mental Health Continuum has proved to be a valuable tool in our efforts to address the mental health needs of young people. By helping us identify those who are struggling with their mental health but slipping under the radar, we have been able to provide early support and interventions, helping to improve the mental health and wellbeing of our pupils.

I believe identifying those children who may be potentially struggling, as early as possible, and referring them to trained professionals should be an essential component of an early intervention mental wellbeing programme.

As a school you can decide how frequently you want to carry out the mental health continuum check in. Form time is an ideal place to make it part of your pastoral routine, but I would regularly use it in PE as it was so quick, and I found the information was vital for making sure I was attuned with where my class was on any given day. It also demonstrated to the class that I cared about them because I was bothered to ask them rather than just delivering my planned content and expecting them to lap it up with no regard for what was going on in their lives.

Recognising the stages for yourself

By recording them, you know how to recognise when you are struggling and what you will need to do to get back to your thriving stage or Ok stage. Everyone is unique and every one of your stages might look slightly different from the next person's.

Thoughts, emotions, behaviours, and physical fitness are all interconnected aspects of mental health, but they represent different dimensions of our wellbeing and contribute to our overall mental wellbeing in distinct ways. Here's a breakdown of each aspect:

Thoughts:
Our thoughts refer to the patterns of cognition, beliefs, perceptions, and internal dialogue that occur within our minds. They shape our understanding of ourselves, others, and the world around us. Thoughts play a significant role in mental health as they can influence our emotions and behaviours. Negative or distorted thoughts, such as self-criticism or catastrophic thinking, can contribute to feelings of anxiety or depression. On the other hand, positive and realistic thoughts can foster resilience, optimism, and a healthier mental state.

Emotions:
Emotions are subjective experiences that arise in response to our thoughts, perceptions, and external events. They are the feelings we experience, such as happiness, sadness, anger, fear, or joy. Emotions provide valuable information about our inner state and can influence our thoughts and behaviours. It is important to recognise and understand our emotions, as they can impact our mental wellbeing. Emotional regulation, which involves effectively managing and expressing emotions, is crucial for maintaining mental health.

Behaviours:
Behaviours refer to the actions we engage in, the choices we make, and the way we interact with the world. Our behaviours can be influenced by our thoughts and emotions. Engaging in healthy behaviours, such as practising self-care, maintaining social connections, seeking support, and engaging in positive coping strategies, can promote mental wellbeing. Conversely, engaging in harmful behaviours, such as substance abuse, social withdrawal, or avoidance, can negatively impact mental health. Behaviours are both a reflection of our mental state and a way to actively influence and improve it.

Physical Fitness:
Physical fitness encompasses our overall physical health, including factors such as exercise, nutrition, sleep, and general wellbeing. While physical fitness is often associated with our physical bodies, it also has a significant impact on our mental health. Regular exercise releases endorphins and improves mood, reduces stress and anxiety, promotes better sleep, and enhances overall cognitive function. Proper nutrition and adequate sleep also contribute to mental wellbeing by providing the body and brain with the necessary nutrients and restorative processes for optimal functioning.

It's important to recognise that these aspects of mental health are interconnected. Thoughts can influence emotions, which can, in turn, impact behaviours and physical wellbeing. Engaging in positive behaviours, such as exercise or practising positive thinking, can improve both emotional and physical wellbeing. Similarly, taking care of our physical fitness can positively influence our thoughts, emotions, and behaviours. Nurturing all these aspects in a holistic manner contributes to maintaining and enhancing mental health.

I will outline what my stages look like, so you have an example.

I know that when I am thriving my life looks like this:
Thoughts: I am kind to myself and search for challenges. I am grateful for all that I have and think positively to find solutions to my problems. I really want to help as many people as possible.
Emotions: I am so confident. I smile a lot and feel great.
Behaviour: I invest time in people & relationships. I get at least 7 hours sleep. I drink 3 litres of water a day. I eat more fruit and vegetables and less junk food. I laugh more.
Physical Fitness: I do weights or run and walk at least 10,000 steps a day and enjoy playing sport with my friends.

When I am OK:
Thoughts: I am calm and take a balanced approach to life. I focus on what is important and let go of things that are not important. I have a clear sense of purpose and direction and want to help people.
Emotions: I feel content and stable. I have a good balance between positive and negative emotions.
Behaviour: I maintain a pretty consistent sleep routine, eating habits and physical activity level. I communicate effectively and handle stress in a healthy way.

Physical Fitness: I maintain a moderate level of physical activity but am maybe not as consistent. I pay attention to my nutrition and hydration with the odd slip up.

When I am starting to be affected:
Thoughts: I become more negative, anxious, and stressed. I struggle to stay focused and have difficulty making decisions. I go in on myself and struggle to help others so much.
Emotions: I feel overwhelmed, frustrated, and sad. My emotions become more intense and frequent.
Behaviour: I start to neglect self-care activities such as sleep, nutrition, and physical activity. I may engage in unhealthy coping mechanisms such as binge eating.
Physical Fitness: I become more sedentary and may experience fatigue, and decreased energy levels.

When I am struggling and ill:
Thoughts: I am consumed by negative thoughts and feelings. I feel hopeless and helpless. I struggle to see the positive in anything. I look inward and don't have the capacity to help others.
Emotions: I feel extremely anxious, depressed, and irritable. My emotions are out of control, and I have a low mood.
Behaviour: I withdraw from nearly all social activities and struggle to complete everyday tasks. I neglect self-care activities such as sleep, nutrition, and physical activity.
Physical Fitness: I experience physical symptoms such as fatigue, and decreased energy levels. I may have difficulty sleeping and may have trouble concentrating. I rarely exercise.

When I start to struggle I know that it is time for me to work less, go to sleep earlier, prioritise some exercise, cut down on the junk food and caffeine, and spend some time investing in the relationships that matter to me, then the rest follows, and I start moving back up the continuum.

What about you? Could you notice any patterns in your thoughts, feelings, behaviours, and physical fitness to help develop your self-awareness?

Try this:

Recognising yourself in each stage

What are your thoughts, emotions, behaviour & physical fitness like for each stage? Write these down in this table. Start with the state of mind you find easiest to explain.

Thriving	OK	Starting to effect	Struggling and ill
Thoughts...	Thoughts...	Thoughts...	Thoughts...
Emotions...	Emotions...:	Emotions...	Emotions...
Behaviours...	Behaviours...	Behaviours...	Behaviours...
Physical fitness...	Physical fitness...	Physical fitness...	Physical fitness...

By recording them, you know now how to recognise when you are struggling and what you will need to do to get back to your thriving stage.

You may want to introduce this concept to your colleagues so that we can look out for our own wellbeing and help each other when we are struggling. Education is unnecessarily losing far too many high quality teachers and support staff due to poor staff wellbeing. Having strategies in place to support and recognise how we are feeling, and then understanding what we can do to feel better is one small aspect of a strong staff wellbeing offer.

Putting on our own oxygen mask first

As a teacher, it's easy to become so focused on helping our students that we forget to take care of ourselves. The job is never ending, there is always one more thing you can do to support student outcomes. But just as flight attendants instruct us to put on our own oxygen masks before helping others in an emergency, it's crucial for teachers to prioritise their own mental health if they want to effectively support their students.

Taking care of our own mental health allows us to show up for our students in the best way possible. It helps us stay calm, centred, and focused in the classroom, which in turn creates a safe and supportive environment for our students. It also sets a good example for our students, showing them that self-care is important and necessary for our overall wellbeing.

On the other hand, if we neglect our own mental health, it can be difficult to be there for our students in the way that they need us to be. It can also lead to burnout and compassion fatigue, both of which can have serious long-term consequences for our personal and professional lives.

So, how can we put our oxygen masks on first? There are many ways to prioritise our own mental health, and it can look different for everyone. Here are a few suggestions:

Take breaks when needed: Whether it's taking a walk outside, meditating, or simply taking a few deep breaths, it's important to give ourselves time to recharge throughout the day. I remember that when I first started at one of my schools, I was struck by constant knocking at the door and neediness from our young people. The days were so intense that I had to take 20 minutes a day to walk to the local shop and back just to give myself some space and some calmness so I could deal with the intensity for the rest of the day.

Prioritise self-care: Engage in activities that bring you joy and help you feel refreshed. Whether it's reading, playing an instrument, or going for a run, make time for the things that make you feel good.

Seek support: Whether it's talking to a colleague, a friend, or a mental health professional, don't hesitate to reach out for help if you need it. You don't have to go through it alone. In the current climate, I believe schools should be far more proactive in establishing support supervision for teachers in the same way counsellors receive supervision.

Putting our oxygen masks on first is crucial if we want to be the best support we can be for our students. By taking care of ourselves, we can create a positive and supportive learning environment for our students and set a good example for them to follow.

The myth of normal: nurturing teacher wellbeing

As I write this, there is a recruitment and retention issue for teachers, and we have to do far more to look after our brilliant teachers and senior leaders who give so much to our young people. They are human beings who we need to look after so they can help our young people flourish. They are not robots that we can push to the limit and then throw them on the scrap heap when they burn out.

The successful entrepreneur, Richard Branson, has a famous quote about looking after his employees so they can look after their customers. The quote is:

> *"Take care of your employees, and they'll take care of your business."*

In other words, Branson believes that if a company prioritises the wellbeing of its employees, they will be better equipped to provide top-notch service to their customers. This creates a virtuous cycle where happy employees lead to satisfied customers, which in turn leads to a successful business.

This philosophy should be applied to education as well. Schools who prioritise the mental health and wellbeing of their teachers will be better equipped to create a positive and supportive learning environment for their young people to flourish.

There are some schools that do this brilliantly and some that do this really poorly.

Where does your school sit on this staff wellbeing issue? I hope you are in a great setting that prioritises your wellbeing so you can take care of your students to the best of your ability. In the noble pursuit of guiding our students, it is often all too easy for us, as teachers, to overlook our own self-care and wellbeing.

For those embarking on their teaching careers, the landscape has evolved significantly. The advent of email access and virtual learning platforms like Google Classroom has unintentionally increased the demand on teachers, making us more accessible around the clock. Moreover, shrinking budgets and reduced support staff have added to the mounting challenges.

Regrettably, in some educational settings, there exists a pervasive myth that sacrificing one's own wellbeing is an inherent part of the teaching profession. However, I firmly disagree with this notion. I firmly believe that within the field of education, and among those who shape educational policies, there is a collective responsibility to prioritise and safeguard the wellbeing of teachers. By doing so, we enable them to better support the flourishing of our young people.

Recognising and challenging this myth of normal is essential. Teachers should not be expected to sacrifice their own mental, emotional, and physical health in pursuit of their vocation. Instead, it is imperative that we create environments that foster teacher wellbeing. This involves implementing supportive measures such as providing adequate resources, meaningful professional development, manageable workloads, and cultivating a culture that values self-care and work-life balance.

By valuing and nurturing teacher wellbeing, we not only enhance the quality of education but also set an example for our students. When we are equipped with the necessary tools and support to prioritise our own self-care, we are better able to create an environment that promotes student growth, resilience, and success.

As teachers, let us reject the notion that sacrificing our own wellbeing is an inherent expectation. Let us advocate for ourselves and for our colleagues, demanding the necessary support and resources to thrive in our profession. By addressing the myth of normal and collectively prioritising teacher wellbeing, we can foster a positive educational ecosystem that enables both teachers and students to flourish.

Concluding the chapter

In conclusion, this chapter emphasises the significance of recognising and addressing mental health, both in ourselves and the young people we interact with. By acknowledging that it's okay to not be okay, we create a space that fosters understanding and support. The mental health continuum technique provides a valuable snapshot of where children are on the mental health spectrum, enabling us to identify and provide timely assistance.

As front line teachers, we hold a privileged position in spending extensive face-to-face time with our students. This allows us to observe their wellbeing closely and identify any signs of distress or changes in mental health. By utilising the mental health continuum, we can gather crucial information to guide trained professionals in offering specialised support and interventions at the earliest possible stage, facilitating the potential for a full recovery.

Furthermore, we must recognise the importance of prioritising our own mental wellbeing. Just as we are instructed to put on our own oxygen masks first during a flight emergency, we need to take care of ourselves in order to effectively support others. By seeking support when needed, maintaining a healthy work-life balance, and practising self-care, we can ensure our own mental wellbeing and better serve our students.

In summary, by embracing the principles of the mental health continuum, and prioritising our own wellbeing, we can contribute to a positive and supportive learning environment for both ourselves and the young people we work with. Remember, it's okay to not be okay, and by seeking help and support, we can create a healthier and more empathetic educational community.

BOOK BONUS

Receive complimentary access to our taster 'RISE Up' online teacher training course so you can watch how to move your school from reactive to proactive when identifying children who are struggling with their mental health in 1 easy step.

https://bit.ly/RISEUPTASTER

Chapter summary
- It's ok to not be ok.
- Our mental health is on a continuum and will vary depending on our own personal situation and circumstances.
- The mental health continuum technique is an effective way of getting a snapshot of where your children are in that moment.
- As front line teachers we have a privileged position spending so much time face to face with our young people.
- The mental health continuum is vital for providing trained professionals with the first piece of information they need to provide specialist support to the young people who need it as early as possible so that they can make a full recovery.
- We need to put our own oxygen mask on first to protect our own mental wellbeing.

Critical questions

1. Can you recognise your unique thoughts, feelings, behaviours, and physical fitness for each of the 4 categories of the mental health continuum?

2. How confident do you feel delivering the mental health continuum task to your class?

3. What does the staff wellbeing offer look like in your setting? How could it be enhanced?

Chapter References
- Keyes CLM. The mental health continuum: from languishing to flourishing in life. J Health Soc Behav. 2002;43(2):207–22. [PubMed] [CrossRef]
- Branson, R. (2012). *Like a Virgin: Secrets They Won't Teach You at Business School.* London: Virgin Books.
- Keyes CLM. The mental health continuum: from languishing to flourishing in life. J Health Soc Behav. 2002;43(2):207–22. [PubMed] [CrossRef]

Chapter 5 - Reducing anxiety, raising aspirations

"Believe in yourself and all that you are. Know that there is something inside you that is greater than any obstacle."
Christian D. Larson

In this chapter we will look at how we can apply the mental fitness pyramid to build students' self-confidence and self-kindness, reduce anxiety and raise aspirations.

Mental fitness is a term that refers to the ability to take control of our thoughts and emotions, and to manage them in a way that promotes wellbeing. In this chapter, we will delve into the concept of mental fitness and explore how we can develop the skills to take control of our thoughts and emotions.

In order to maintain good mental fitness, we need to learn how to ask the right questions of ourselves in difficult moments. Instead of asking "Why can't I do this?" or "Why do I hate myself?", we should be asking "Where am I now?" and "What is my target for this moment?". By asking the right questions, we can gain insight into our thoughts and emotions and take control of them.

Another important aspect of mental fitness is resilience. Resilience is the ability to cope with challenges and bounce back from adversity. The ability to develop resilience is crucial in order to live a fulfilling life, no matter what challenges come our way.

I first came across the mental fitness pyramid during lockdown and started to experiment with how I could help my young people build their self-confidence and resilience when they were in a good place emotionally, rather than waiting for troubles to come along and totally rock them.

I wanted to reduce some of their anxiety by showing them how they could use their worries as a positive by creating a plan and taking action. I wanted to raise the aspirations of the children I taught and get them to think bigger about what they could achieve in their lives so they could live long, happy, and healthy lives.

The Mental Fitness Pyramid is a framework by Dorothea McCarthy (1964), that can help individuals understand and promote their mental wellbeing. Starting at the bottom and working our way up through the pyramid can help build and improve overall wellbeing.

At the base of the pyramid is 'Self-Confidence'. Building a foundation of self-belief by focusing on what we are great at can help us develop self-confidence, which is an essential building block of good mental health.

The next level is 'Self-kindness'. Being as kind to ourselves as we would be to our best friend can help build self-esteem. This can be achieved through self-compassion and understanding that mistakes are a normal part of life.

The next level is 'Worries as a positive'. We can reduce anxiety by creating a plan and taking action. By acknowledging our worries and creating a plan to address them, it can help us feel more in control and less anxious.

At the peak of the pyramid is 'Vision'. Visualising different aspects of our dream life can give us goals and raise our aspirations. By having a clear idea of what we want to achieve, we can set ourselves up for success and feel more fulfilled and purposeful.

Figure 7:

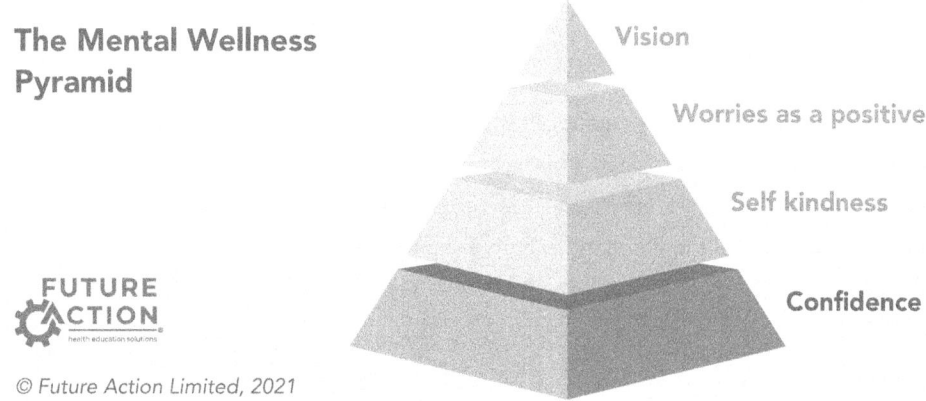

The Mental Wellness Pyramid

© Future Action Limited, 2021

Nurturing Physical Literacy (Dr Liz Durden-Myers)

As Neil has mentioned earlier, engagement in physical activity has benefits when improving health and wellbeing not to mention the potential therapeutic qualities it can offer. Physical literacy is a concept that is helping a multitude of contexts including schools, communities, leisure and sports settings reshape how they understand and approach the promotion of physical activity.

Physical literacy is defined by the International Physical Literacy Association as "the motivation, confidence, physical competence, knowledge and understanding to value and engage in physical activity for life" (IPLA, 2017). This definition and the one provided by Sport England (2023) both highlight the importance of confidence and how you feel towards physical activity as a key element in shaping participation in physical activity.

Confidence plays a pivotal role in engagement in physical activity, as both a catalyst and a reward for participation. Here's why confidence is so crucial:

1. **Initiating Action**

When someone is confident in their movement capability, it often gives them a secure sense of self-esteem and self-concept and reinforces their belief that being active and being capable of being active is attainable. Therefore, when opportunities arise to be physically active if you have a secure sense of self as being able to be active in a range of environments you are more likely to take up those opportunities.

2. **Overcoming Barriers**

Inevitably, challenges and obstacles arise whether it's a fear of failure, concerns about judgment, or physical limitations, confidence acts as a shield against these barriers. Confident individuals are more resilient in the face of setbacks, viewing challenges as opportunities for growth rather than reasons to give up.

3. **Sustaining Motivation**

Consistency is key to reaping the benefits of physical activity, and confidence plays a crucial role in sustaining motivation over the long term. When individuals feel confident in their abilities, they are more likely to persist in their efforts, even when progress is slow. Confidence, self-esteem and self-concept all help to fuel the fire of motivation, keeping individuals focused on their goals and committed engagement in physical activity even when it gets tough.

4. Enhancing Performance

Research has shown that individuals who approach physical activity with confidence are more likely to perform better. This phenomenon, known as the "confidence-performance loop," and it highlights the symbiotic relationship between belief and achievement (Lochbaum et. al, 2022). When individuals believe they can succeed, they often do, reinforcing their confidence in a positive feedback loop.

5. Boosting Self-Esteem and Self-Concept

Engaging in physical activity can have profound effects on self-esteem, and confidence plays a central role in this process. As individuals experience success and progress in their physical pursuits, their confidence grows, leading to a greater sense of self-worth, self-efficacy and self-concept. This boost in self-esteem extends beyond the realm of physical activity, permeating other areas of life and contributing to overall well-being.

6. Fostering Enjoyment

Finally, confidence enhances the enjoyment of physical activity, transforming what might otherwise feel like a chore into a source of pleasure and fulfilment. When individuals feel confident in their abilities, they are more likely to approach physical activity with enthusiasm and excitement, relishing the opportunity to move and challenge themselves, and be more intrinsically motivated while being active.

By nurturing confidence individuals can unlock the full potential of physical activity as a pathway to health, happiness, and fulfilment.

Building self-confidence

How many times have you taught a young person and you just couldn't get them to see the power and brilliance that they could use to change the world for the better? For me, the answer was far too many.

Confidence is an essential foundation for children as they navigate their formative years and develop into adults. Without confidence, children may struggle to believe in themselves and their abilities, making it difficult for them to set and achieve goals, make friends, and succeed in school and other areas of their lives.

Research has shown that children with high levels of confidence tend to have better social skills and are more resilient in the face of adversity. They also tend to perform better academically and are more likely to be successful in their chosen careers.

I wanted to build a foundation of self-confidence in the children I taught so would use the power of story to grab my children's attention using a character they knew and could relate to; it went along the lines of this:

'Once upon a time, there was a young and talented footballer. He had already accomplished many remarkable feats for someone so young, such as reducing child poverty during lockdown and increasing children's literacy through his story books. However, despite his successes, he faced many challenges along the way.

One of the most difficult moments for Marcus was when he missed a penalty in the Euros football final against Italy and was subsequently racially abused on social media. He also faced criticism in national newspapers for protecting his family's financial future by buying a number of houses, even though this was a smart thing to do, especially considering his family background and how they had escaped poverty.

If someone who has achieved as much in his young life as Marcus has, by helping others, has had to deal with that level of criticism, then all of us will face criticism at times and it is important that we can take it on the chin and still move forward.'

I wanted my children to develop a rock solid foundation of confidence so that it would help them deal with unwarranted criticism and negative comments and help them get through the tough times in the rollercoaster of life.

I wanted children to focus on building their confidence by reminding themselves of all their accomplishments using the reverse bucket list. I explained that they needed to remember that as individuals no one is better at being them in this world than they are, and that some people may dislike the very things that most people love about them.

I love what Marcus Rashford stands for and what he has achieved around child food poverty and children's literacy. He has achieved incredible feats already at such a young age yet even he gets heavily criticised. My children could really relate to him as they were from a similar background to him. I wanted to empower them and show that being born in a low socio-economic area does not define what they can go on to achieve.

This story of Marcus Rashford serves as a reminder to us all that building a foundation of confidence is essential for navigating the ups and downs of life. We can all benefit from having confidence to help us through the journey of life and deal with criticism when it comes our way.

I would get children to reflect on what they are good at, what they get praise for, and where they have had personal success before.

I would encourage children to look at all aspects of their lives to develop their sense of self rather than just being awesome at academia, a fantastic footballer or marvellous at music. I did this by breaking it down into different aspects, such as their hobbies, characteristics they possess, roles they play in life, and subjects at school.
It is important that a child's self-confidence is holistic so that if one skill falters they don't lose their whole sense of self.

For example, the gifted footballer in your school who is destined for a career as a superstar until they rupture their anterior cruciate ligament and don't know who they are anymore.

I have witnessed too many teenagers being released by professional football clubs and it absolutely destroys their self-confidence and desire to be physically active, so I collaborated with Improtech Soccer Elite Academies to give more young people the support they deserve around this area.

Improtech are helping develop young footballers within the education system. They offer an innovative, long-term development programme delivering the highest standards and top class training but with a greater focus on the mental wellbeing of the young people within their academies.

The children at my school love taking part in the programme and it is having a hugely positive influence on their mental wellbeing from being part of an inclusive team and being physically active as well as their progress in lessons across the school.

Former Sunderland & Manchester City striker and now Director of Improtech, Stephen Elliot, said "I have come across so many footballers who have either retired or lost their careers due to injury and have lost their own identity at the same time. At Improtech we feel it is vital to develop the whole person not just a footballer, so we are working with our coaches and partner schools to achieve this."

Try this:

Building confidence

We can create a strong foundation to our pyramid by asking ourselves these questions on a daily basis:

1. What are the things that you are good at?

2. Where have you had personal success before?

3. What do you get good feedback from other people about?

4. Break them down into 4 categories:
   - Hobbies e.g. Playing football
   - Characteristics e.g. Kind
   - Roles you play in life e.g. Great son
   - Subjects e.g. Art

Answer these questions to build a strong confidence foundation.

Why not tell your friends or colleagues what you admire about them to build their confidence and make their day!

Every group I ever teach the building confidence lesson, struggle to list what they are great at. I have delivered this session with groups of teachers, and they struggle even more. People are quick to focus on their weaknesses but not so fast to focus on their strengths. When this is the case I ask their friends to talk about what they admire about the person, or I will explain what I admire about them. You can see them visibly grow in confidence right before your eyes.

Positive affirmations

An affirmation is a powerful tool that can help you and your students overcome negative thoughts and set you up for a positive day ahead. An affirmation is a positive phrase that you repeat to yourself on a regular basis, it can be done silently or out loud. The benefits of using affirmations include getting rid of negative thoughts, setting yourself up with a positive mindset for the day, and feeling more in control.

Creating your own affirmation is simple, it can be tailored to your current state of mind, and it can change as your needs change. An example of an affirmation might be: 'I am going to have a brilliant day; I will smile and look for solutions to my problems.'

In my school, we guided students on how to create their own positive affirmations. We want to build a strong foundation of confidence that will help them navigate through the ups and downs of life. One of my students, Sam, in year 8 said this about the impact of the programme:

'My best subject has been PE because my mental health has gone from really low to the highest it has ever been. I've realised that I can turn my problems into solutions for my future. The RISE Up unit has helped me in many ways such as building my confidence and my self-esteem. Now my body knows that it can go further than I ever expected and my confidence about my mental health is higher than ever before.'

This is just one example of the positive impact that focusing on developing self-confidence can have on a person's life. I encourage you to try using these confidence tools for yourself and see the difference it can make.

Try this:

Positive affirmations

- Write an affirmation that would make you feel more positive about yourself and the day ahead each morning.
- Now say it to yourself each morning when you wake up or every couple of days, especially when you are feeling low to help you realise how special and unique you are.

One of my colleagues put this into practice with great results straight away.

"As a teacher, I had a short spell of waking up feeling fed up and annoyed each morning. I wasn't looking forward to going into school at all. I had previously attended some department training on the power of positive affirmations and decided to put it into practice.

I looked in the mirror and told myself, "I am going to have a great day." To my surprise, as soon as I put a smile on my face, I felt a shift in my mood and energy. I felt more positive and ready to tackle the day ahead.

When I arrived at school, I greeted my students with a smile and a positive attitude. My interactions with them were more engaging and enjoyable. I found myself more productive and focused during my lessons, and my students were more responsive and engaged in the learning process.

It was incredible to see the difference that simply deciding to have a great day made. I continued to practise positive affirmations every morning and noticed a significant improvement in my overall wellbeing, both in my personal and professional life."

 **Try this:**

The Reverse Bucket List

Depending on the group, I would sometimes use the reverse bucket list, particularly if I noticed many of the class were low in confidence.

A reverse bucket list is a list of things that you have already accomplished or experiences you have already had, rather than a list of things you hope to do or achieve in the future. It is a way of reflecting on and celebrating your past accomplishments and experiences.

Some people use the term "reverse bucket list" as a reminder that our lives are not defined by the things we still want to do but rather by the things we have already done. We tend to be forward-looking, setting goals and planning for the future, and forget the things we have accomplished in the past.

The reverse bucket list can be a way to remind ourselves of all the things we have already accomplished, and to be proud of the person we have become. It is also an opportunity to reflect on how these accomplishments have shaped us and brought us to where we are today.

The reverse bucket list can be a powerful tool for personal reflection and self-appreciation and can also serve as a reminder to celebrate our past successes as well as our future goals.

Catching glimmers

The idea of 'Catching Glimmers' offers a wonderful strategy to boost children's self-confidence as they navigate their way to new heights. This approach proves particularly effective in helping young individuals take that leap towards their next level of growth, whether it's facing an important exam, speaking confidently in public, or elevating their performance in competitive sports.

Glimmers represent those tiny moments of positivity that counteract negative triggers. They can stem from within, like personal achievements, or from external sources, like words of encouragement. These moments create a reassuring sense of safety in a child's mind, fostering their ability to adapt and persevere. By embracing these instances of brightness, kids can uplift their mood, bolster their mental wellbeing, and build resilience step by step.

The beauty of 'Catching Glimmers' lies in its simplicity—it's about noticing these small wins in everyday life. With consistent practice, children can accumulate these experiences, nurturing a growing confidence that empowers them to tackle life's challenges with a newfound sense of self-assuredness.

Let's consider a teenager who has been facing academic struggles. During an exam, they notice that they've answered the first three questions exceptionally well. This small achievement stands out amidst their overall challenges and begins to spark a glimmer of confidence. Similarly, imagine a young goalkeeper who moved up from the school team to County level. On their debut, despite initial nerves and some difficulties, they managed to make two solid saves and handled several crosses adeptly. These moments of success become their glimmers of progress.

Recognising each instance, whether it's a well-answered question or a successful save, gently nurtures their self-assurance, reminding them that even in the midst of challenges, they're making strides forward.

 **Try this:**

Glimmers of success

I've employed this technique during one-on-one discussions with young individuals who face challenges in specific performance situations. The following outline presents the fundamental questions I employ to develop their self-confidence and self-awareness:

1. **Identification:** "What are you struggling with?"

2. **Glimmers of Success:** "Did you feel 'good enough' at any time during your last performance?"

3. **Reflecting on Glimmers:** "Brilliant. What was the glimmer and what did it feel like? Were there any other glimmers? "

4. **Building on Glimmers:** "Fantastic. Hold on to that feeling. What would you like to do in your next performance to build on your glimmers?"

5. **Preparation Strategies:** "Great. What preparation do you need to make that outcome more likely?"

6. **Seeking Support:** "Do you need any help with that preparation?"

From there, we can create a plan to help the young person move forward with their challenge.

Self-kindness

"Be kind to yourself. It's hard to be happy when someone is mean to you all the time."
Christine Arylo

Self-kindness is an important aspect of a child's emotional and mental wellbeing. It refers to the ability to treat oneself with compassion and understanding, rather than with harsh judgement or criticism. Research has shown that self-kindness can have a positive impact on a child's self-esteem, self-worth, and resilience.

One study published in the journal, "Self and Identity" found that children who practised self-kindness had higher levels of self-compassion and self-esteem than those who did not (Neff, 2003). Another study, published in the "Journal of Child and Family Studies" found that self-kindness was positively associated with emotional regulation and wellbeing in children (Muris et al., 2018).

There are several ways that teachers, parents, and caregivers can help children develop self-kindness. One way is to model self-kindness ourselves. Children learn by example, and if they see the adults in their life treating themselves with kindness, they are more likely to do the same.

It is also important to teach children to be kind to themselves when they make mistakes or fail. Instead of criticising or punishing children for their mistakes, we can help children learn from them by encouraging them to reflect on what went wrong and how they can do better next time.

Self-kindness is essential for children's emotional and mental wellbeing. Parents and caregivers play a crucial role in helping children develop this trait by modelling self-kindness, encouraging self-compassion, and teaching children how to be kind to themselves when they make mistakes.

The inner voice, also known as self-talk, is the constant stream of thoughts and words that run through our minds. It can have a significant impact on our mental and emotional wellbeing, as well as our daily actions and decisions.

Unfortunately, many of us have developed an inner voice that is overly critical and negative, which can lead to feelings of low self-worth and self-doubt. It is the part of us that wants to sabotage our progress.

One way to start improving the relationship with our inner voice is to pay attention to how we speak to ourselves when we make a mistake. Often, we are much harsher with ourselves than we would be with others. We may berate ourselves, call ourselves names, and dwell on our mistakes for days.

Imagine how different our inner voice would be if we spoke to ourselves the way we would speak to our best friend. We would likely offer words of encouragement, remind ourselves that we are only human and make mistakes, and offer support and understanding.

To improve our relationship with our inner voice, we must work on reprogramming it to be more positive and supportive. This can be done by noticing when our inner voice is being negative and actively working to reframe our thoughts in a more positive light. For example, instead of saying "I can't do this" we could say "I can do this, I just need to try a different approach." or instead of saying "I am so stupid for making that mistake" we could say "Everyone makes mistakes, I will learn from this and do better next time."

Additionally, practising self-compassion can be a powerful tool in cultivating a more positive inner voice. Self-compassion involves treating ourselves with the same kindness and understanding that we would offer to a friend. It means acknowledging our own humanity and recognising that we are not perfect, but that we are worthy of love and respect, nonetheless.

To illustrate this point within lessons, I would ask children to think about the last time their friend came to them after making a mistake and what advice they gave to them. I then get them to think about what their inner voice would say to them if they made the same mistake. I would then get them to contrast the difference. I then explain that the most important relationship they will ever have will be with themselves as they are stuck with that person for the rest of their lives.

Sarah, a year 8 child, explains how this exercise helped her improve her self-kindness.
"I often struggled with being kind to myself, so I was keen to listen as my teacher asked us to think about the last time our friends came to us after making a mistake and to think

about the advice we gave to them. I thought about the time my friend fell over when she was trying to impress the boy she liked, she was so embarrassed.

Next, the teacher asked us to think about what our inner voice would say to us if we made the same mistake. I thought for a moment and realised the massive difference between the advice I gave to my friend that time and the thoughts I had towards myself when I did the same previously.

It was a real "a-ha" moment for me, and I nodded in agreement when Miss said that there was a major difference between the two.

From that day on, I made a conscious effort to be kinder to myself and to speak to myself with the same understanding I would offer to a friend.

I continued to do the exercise regularly and over time, I noticed a big improvement in my self-kindness and general happiness with myself."

By being mindful of how we speak to ourselves, and actively working to reframe negative thoughts and practise self-compassion, we can build a more positive and supportive inner voice that will serve us well throughout our lives.

This will be the most important relationship you will have as it will be with you every day for the rest of your life. Like any worthwhile relationship, we need to invest in it and put in the work to make it work as well as it can.

 **Try this:**

Reflecting on self-talk

The objective of this exercise is to help you understand the impact of your inner voice and encourage you to develop a more positive and supportive inner voice.

Instructions:
1. Begin by asking yourself to think about the last time you made a mistake.
2. Now imagine that a friend came to you with the same mistake and to think about what advice you would give your friend to make them feel better.
3. Now ask yourself to think about what your inner voice said to you when you made the same mistake.
4. Reflect on your answers. What do you notice?

This activity can be done regularly to help children become more aware of their inner voice and to encourage them to develop a more positive and supportive inner voice.

You can also flip this to what you said to yourself the last time you did something fantastically well.

1. Begin by taking a moment to remember a time when you achieved something truly wonderful.
2. Imagine a friend who has achieved a similar feat and think about the encouraging advice you would share with them.
3. Now, consider the thoughts that crossed your mind when you accomplished your impressive feat.
4. Reflect on your answers and see if you notice any interesting patterns or insights.

Worries as a positive

"Worrying is like a rocking chair, it gives you something to do, but it gets you nowhere."
Unknown

Worrying is a universal human experience that often accompanies uncertainty and challenges in life. It is a natural response to potential threats or negative outcomes, but excessive or chronic worrying becomes anxiety when it starts to significantly interfere with our daily life, functioning, and overall wellbeing. While worry is a normal and temporary response to stress or concerns, anxiety is characterised by persistent and excessive worry that is difficult to control.

It is important for children to learn how to use their worries in a positive way, as this can help them to develop coping skills, resilience, and a sense of control over their emotions. Children who are able to reframe their worries in a positive way are better able to cope with stress and anxiety.

It's important for us as teachers, parents, and caregivers to validate children's feelings and to provide a safe and supportive environment for them to share their worries. This can help children to feel heard and understood, and to develop a sense of trust in their caregivers. By providing a safe and supportive environment, we can help children develop the skills and confidence they need to use their worries in a positive way.

Figure 8:

The choice is yours

False	**F**	Face
Expectations	**E**	Everything
Appearing	**A**	And
Real	**R**	Rise

Fear is a powerful emotion that can have a significant impact on our students' lives. It can hold them back from pursuing their goals and dreams and keep them stuck in a state of anxiety and uncertainty. There have been so many brilliant young people who I have taught who have not gone on to achieve what they undoubtedly could have because they were so fearful of 'false expectations appearing real'. However, the way our young people choose to respond to fear can make all the difference in the world.

One approach to fear is to recognise that it is often based on false expectations. Our young people may imagine all sorts of negative outcomes and catastrophes that are unlikely to happen. By helping them recognise that their fears are often not grounded in reality, we can begin to help them and move forward with greater confidence.

Another approach is for our students to face their fears head-on and rise above them. This means taking a courageous and proactive stance, and actively working to overcome their fears. This can involve seeking out support and guidance, setting small achievable goals, and pushing themselves out of their comfort zones by presenting in front of their classmates or sitting that exam. By facing their fears and rising above them, they can gain a sense of empowerment and control over their lives and build their confidence further.

Ultimately, fear is a part of the human experience, and it is something that we will all encounter at some point in our lives. However, by showing young people that we have the power to choose how we respond to fear, we can learn to transform it from a negative force into a positive one. By either recognising the false expectations or facing it head-on and rising above it, we can take control of our lives and live with greater purpose, courage, and freedom.

Controlling the controllables and shrinking our worries

An important step in reducing anxiety is that we need to help young people recognise that there are some things within their control and some aspects of life that are outside of their control.

This means identifying the things in our lives that we have the power to change and taking action to improve them, while at the same time accepting and letting go of the things that we have no control over.

One of the most important things to understand is that we cannot control everything in our lives. There will always be circumstances, events and people that are beyond our control, such as natural disasters, accidents, and the actions of others such as Covid or the war in the Ukraine. However, we can start to control our own thoughts, actions, and reactions to these things.

By focusing on the controllables, we can take a proactive stance in our lives and make meaningful changes that will improve our wellbeing. This might involve setting goals and working towards them, developing healthy habits, or building stronger relationships with the people around us.

It is also important to understand that some things may be controllable in the long term, but not in the short term. For instance, a child may worry about their family's financial situation, but have little influence over it. However, as they transition into adulthood, they gain greater control over their own lives and can take steps to improve their circumstances. In such cases, it is important to focus on developing a resilient attitude and finding ways to cope with the things that are currently out of our control.

This is one way we acted as a PE department at the start of the first lockdown. We had a department meeting and recognised that it was a pretty daunting situation with a lack of information. We decided to focus on what we could control, which was how we could respond within school and help support our young people.

We allocated roles within the department to provide clarity on who would take the lead in various areas. I focused on the key worker children, three colleagues focused on creating and providing the online learning, and another colleague focused on social media content and providing enrichment activities to keep our community healthy and moving in a safe way. By having clarity and taking action we could focus our energies into something positive rather than worrying about a situation we had little control over.

When working with our key worker children at the start of lockdown, I wanted to create a psychological safe environment for my students, where they could focus on their lessons without the distractions of their worries and concerns and all the negative news in the media that was so unsettling for many. I came up with a simple yet powerful exercise: at the start of each lesson, the children would take a moment to think of five things they were grateful for.

I would begin by introducing the exercise to the class and model my top 5 reasons to be grateful at the start of each lesson. I explained that it was a way to signal to the children that it was time to compartmentalise their worries and focus on the lesson at hand. I wanted to remind them that it was a chance to realise that despite all their worries, there were also many great areas in our lives as well, which would help to shrink the enormity of the worry for many.

Each day, as the lesson began, I would remind them to take a moment to think of five things they were grateful for. Some children were grateful for their family, others for their friends, and some for their pets. Some were grateful for the beautiful weather, while others were grateful for the food school were providing for lunch. Many were grateful for school being open and for their teachers. This was the first time I had heard this in my entire teaching career and their positivity really rubbed off on me to create a fantastic environment for us all to work together to help them thrive in an incredibly difficult situation.

As the weeks went by, the children noticed a positive change in their attitude towards their lessons. They were more focused and engaged in the class, and they felt a sense of calm and contentment. They also realised that even though they had worries, they also had many things to be grateful for. As I walked into school over lockdown I couldn't wait to be with the children and support them, it was so enjoyable because of the positivity and the way we gave each other energy.

The gratitude exercise became a regular part of my lesson routines. I would use a soft tennis ball to pass to the speaker and children would take it in turns to share their number 1 reason to be grateful, out of their 5, with the rest of the class, while we listened respectfully. The children learned to appreciate the small things in life and to focus on the present moment.

This is an exercise I continue to do with my young family at dinner times and it also forms part of my daily journalling process to shrink my worries and be grateful for all the fantastic aspects of our lives.

Try this:

5 things you are grateful for

Write down 5 things you are grateful for right now:

1.

2.

3.

4.

5.

Like fear, worry is often seen as a negative emotion, something to be avoided at all costs. However, when used in the right way, worry can actually be a powerful tool for personal growth and positive change for both our young people and us as teachers.

One of the most effective ways to use worry as a positive force is to channel it into action. Instead of letting your worries consume you, take the time to think about what specific steps you can take to address the issues that are causing you to worry. This might involve making a plan, setting goals, or seeking out support from others. By turning your worries into action, you can transform them from a source of stress and anxiety into a source of motivation and inspiration.

Exam worries frequently create anxiety to rise in our young people. This case study shows how we can support our students by teaching them a technique so that they can use their worries as a positive.

Tia, a year 11 pupil, explains the approach that I supported her with

Tia's story
"I was struggling with anxiety when we returned after Christmas time because I was worried about how I would do in my exams this summer and how that would impact my future. Sir saw I was upset one lunch time and sat down to check I was ok. I let out how I was feeling panicky about my exams and my future, and it was stressing me out.

Firstly, he asked me what I could control about my exams, so I started talking about my preparation and how I hadn't done a lot of revision over the last few months.

My teacher said I had two choices. I could either fret and fear the future and get anxious about what was to come, or I could focus on creating a plan and taking action.

We then met after school the next day and we created a plan that included:
- Completing an audit of predicted grades in each subject to recognise how I was doing and what subjects I needed to focus on.
- We were to speak to my subject teachers to explain I was struggling and would like help.
- Trying my best in every single lesson and complete all homework set.
- Creating a revision schedule.
- Requesting & attending catch up sessions.
- Buddying up with a friend who enjoys the subject and could help me if I got stuck
- Visiting revision websites podcasts like GCSE POD or revision websites such as BBC Bitesize.
- Creating task cards, and taking part in low stakes mini quizzes with my friends to build in retrieval practice.
- Completing a new audit of predicted grades in each subject and celebrate the progress I make.

I started to focus on my preparation and by taking action I felt less anxious and more confident straight away. I started with small steps but as I could see myself progressing, my motivation increased, and I started to do more and more.

Sir then taught me about the power of three journalling to help me be grateful for all that I have, to build my confidence by focusing on what I had achieved that day, and to keep *me focused by setting my three wins for the next day. It's really helped me stay focused as I could see how much I was progressing each week.*

This whole process has really helped me feel less anxious and more confident about my upcoming exams. I have improved so much over the last few months and know that I've given myself the best chance to be successful in my exams.'

 Try this:

Creating a plan

Try this 'Creating a plan' exercise with a class or student who are struggling with worry.

1. What are the questions that are worrying you about the future?
2. Which are the ones within your control?
3. Mind map what you can do to solve your problem.
4. Ask yourself who can help you solve your challenge.
5. Complete a to-do list of tasks that will help you solve the problem.
6. As you complete each task, tick it off on your list, this will release dopamine which will keep you motivated.
7. Celebrate the gap and the gain. The gap is from where you were when you started to where you are now. The gain is all the new knowledge you have learnt to reach where you are now. Write this down on your reverse bucket list to keep building your confidence.*
8. Keep pushing forward to the next step.
9. Enjoy the journey.

*Source: Hardy, B. & Sullivan, D. (2021). The Gap and the Gain: Building Personal and Professional Growth. Hay House Business.

Creating a vision

"The future belongs to those who believe in the beauty of their dreams."
- Eleanor Roosevelt

In this section we are going to look at raising aspirations through creating a vision and why that is beneficial to a young person's mental wellbeing.

As a teacher for 19 years, one of the biggest challenges I have faced is helping children to believe in themselves and their potential. All too often, I have encountered children who undersell themselves and limit their own aspirations for the future or their families, who unintentionally do it for them. This can be a difficult obstacle to overcome, but it is important for the growth and development of some young people.

There are several reasons why children may limit their own aspirations. For some, it may be a lack of role models or exposure to different career paths. For others, it may be a lack of self-confidence or a belief that they are not capable of achieving success. Whatever the reason, it is important to understand that these limiting beliefs are not set in stone and can be changed.

One effective way to raise children's aspirations is to expose them to different role models and career paths. This can be done through field trips, guest speakers, and career days. By exposing children to different possibilities and showing them there are people who have succeeded in a variety of fields, they can begin to see that they too have the potential to achieve success.

Having a sense of purpose and taking action to achieve it can be a powerful tool for improving mental health. Research has shown that individuals who have a sense of purpose in life are less likely to experience symptoms of depression and anxiety and are more likely to report greater life satisfaction and wellbeing (Steger, 2009).

One study by Sheldon and Elliot (1999) found that individuals who had a clear sense of purpose in life had better mental health outcomes than those who did not. The study found that having a sense of purpose was associated with better self-esteem, greater life satisfaction, and less depression.

Another study by Wong (2011) found that individuals who had a sense of purpose in life were more likely to engage in self-care behaviours, such as exercise and healthy eating, which are important for maintaining good mental health.

It's important to note that finding a sense of purpose can take time and introspection, and it may change over the course of one's life. But once it's found, taking action towards it can be a powerful tool for improving mental health.

 Try this:

Discovering your life force

This tool is taken from the film 'Stutz' (2022) about counsellor Phil Stutz and his unique approach. Phil Stutz explains that if you are struggling for a sense of direction then you can always work on finding your life force. Your life force helps to drive you forward if you are feeling lost and helps you find what you are passionate about.

Think of a pyramid with 3 levels. At the bottom of the period is your relationship with your physical body. The second layer is your relationship with other people and the top layer is your relationship with yourself.

Firstly, get your body working more effectively by increasing your exercise, improving your diet, and increasing your sleep.

Secondly, take the initiative and reconnect with a friend face to face to develop that social connection. That person represents the whole human race, and it will impact you in a positive way by drawing you back into life.

Finally, the last challenge is to enhance your relationship with your unconscious self. You do this by journalling, so start writing and it will shine a mirror on your unconscious self. Things will come out that you didn't know that you knew. By working on your life force it is the first step in finding what you are passionate about if you feel lost.

It is a powerful tool when you have real clarity about what your purpose is.

Setting goals

Goals are a fundamental aspect of our lives. They give us direction, motivation, and purpose.

Setting goals and learning new skills can be a great way for children to:
- Meet new people
- Build self-esteem
- Feel a sense of achievement
- Give them a purpose
- Stay focused and help them understand how to best use their time
- Work hard

When we achieve a goal, we achieve it twice. The first time is in our minds, when we visualise what we want to achieve. The second time is in reality, when we go out and take action to make it happen.

The first step in achieving a goal is to visualise it in our minds. This is where we imagine what it would look like, feel like, and what we would be doing if we had already achieved the goal. This process helps us to build a mental image of what we want to achieve and to focus our minds on what we want to accomplish.

However, visualisation alone is not enough. It is only when we combine visualisation with action that we can turn our dreams into reality. Action is what transforms our visions into tangible outcomes.

When we set big goals, it's easy to get caught up in the end result and to forget about the joy and fulfilment that comes from the journey itself. But, by finding joy in the process, we can improve our overall wellbeing, reduce stress, and increase our chances of success.

When I reflect on my teaching career so far, the children who enjoyed revising for their exams often had great friendships, they created buddy groups, studied together, attended subject clinics, and often ate together. There was a real deep human connection there that made the process enjoyable rather than painful and led to great outcomes for these young people.

As teachers, it is important to consider how we can make the process as enjoyable as possible for our young people.

Consider this...
- How can you make working towards their goals as enjoyable as possible for your young people?

Having a clear goal can help children but we also know that not all children respond the same way to goal-setting activities. Some children may thrive with a clear goal in mind, while others may find it challenging and need more time to find their way in their own time.

In order to create a goal-setting culture that is inclusive and supportive of all students, it is important to be mindful of how we position these activities with our classes. This can be done by taking a flexible and individualised approach to goal setting.

For some students, it may be beneficial to set specific, measurable, and achievable goals. This can help to give them a clear sense of direction and purpose and can help them stay focused and motivated. For others, it may be more beneficial to allow them to explore their interests and passions in a more open-ended way, without the pressure of specific goals.

It's also crucial to provide support and guidance to students as they work towards their goals. This can be done through:
- Regular check-ins.
- Goal-setting workshops.
- Mentoring programmes.

By providing support and guidance, we can help students to overcome any obstacles or challenges they may face, and to stay motivated and on track.

Additionally, it's important to celebrate and acknowledge the progress and achievements of students, whether they are working towards a specific goal or exploring their interests. This can help to build their self-esteem, confidence, and motivation.

Creating a goal-setting culture that is inclusive and supportive of all students requires a balance of support and flexibility. By taking a flexible and individualised approach to goal setting, providing support and guidance, and celebrating progress and achievements, we can help all students to reach their full potential.

When we approach our goals with a fixed mindset, we believe that our abilities are set in stone, and we cannot change them. However, when we have a growth mindset, we believe that our abilities can be developed and improved through effort and learning. Therefore, it is important to be open to learning and trying new things, even if we may not succeed at first, as it is through these experiences that we can continue to grow and develop.

Intelligence, or cognitive ability, is a complex trait that is influenced by both genetic and environmental factors. Research has shown that genetics plays a significant role in determining a person's cognitive abilities.

According to a meta-analysis of twin studies, the heritability of intelligence is estimated to be around 50-75%. This means that about 50-75% of the variation in intelligence among individuals can be attributed to genetic differences. The remaining 25-50% of the variation in intelligence is thought to be influenced by environmental factors, such as access to education, nutrition, and social-economic status.

Some studies have shown that environmental factors, such as early childhood education, can have a significant impact on cognitive development and intelligence. For example, a meta-analysis of early childhood education interventions found that such programmes can have a moderate to large effect on cognitive development and academic achievement. Other environmental factors, such as nutrition and physical activity, have also been linked to cognitive development and intelligence.

It is also important to note that intelligence is not fixed and can change throughout a person's life. Through effortful learning and practice, people can improve their cognitive abilities and intelligence. This is the area that we can impact as educators and is the area I prefer to focus on with the children I teach.

By combining these approaches we can help young people to take their blinkers off, enjoy the big wide world out there, raise their aspirations and lead a life of purpose which should ultimately benefit their mental wellbeing.

Ikigai

The vast majority of young people I taught were lacking direction so I wanted to give them a tool that would tap into the areas that were most important. I compartmentalised different aspects of their futures and allowed them to focus on the areas that mattered most to them. I introduced the concept of Ikigai to some of my older groups.

The Japanese concept of ikigai, often translated as "a reason for being," has gained popularity in recent years as a way to understand and find purpose in one's life.

The origins of ikigai can be traced back to the Japanese island of Okinawa, which has been known for its large population of centenarians. Researchers studying the longevity of the Okinawans discovered that many of them attributed their long lives to having a sense of purpose or ikigai.

Ikigai is often represented by a Venn diagram with four circles: what you love, what you are good at, what the world needs, and what you can be paid for. The intersection of these four circles is where your ikigai lies. It is the sweet spot where your passions, skills, values, and potential for earning a living overlap.

Ikigai is a personal and unique concept and can be different for everyone. It can be found in a career, a hobby, a relationship, or even in small moments of everyday life. It's about finding what brings you joy, fulfilment and a sense of meaning.

Figure 9:

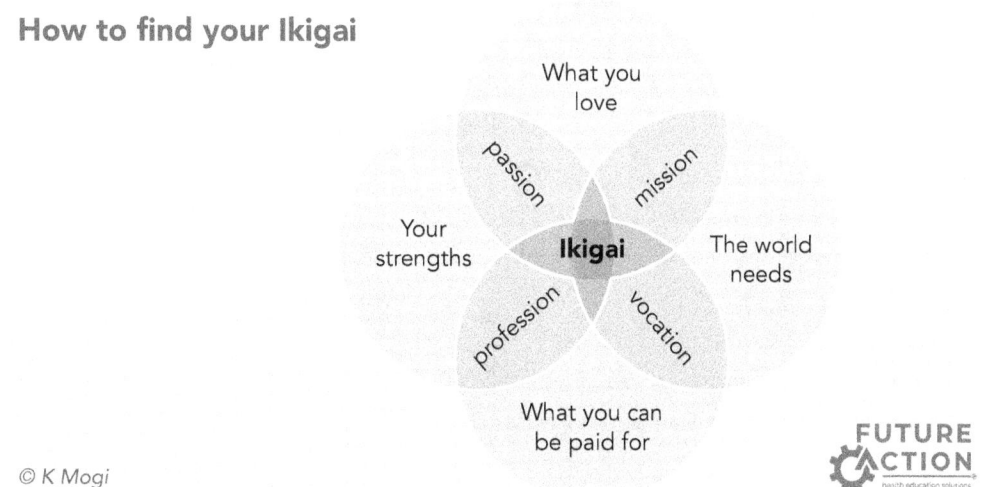

© K Mogi

 **Try this:**

Discovering your Ikigai

In order to discover your own ikigai, it can be helpful to break it down into a range of categories. By asking yourself the following questions, you can start to gain a better understanding of what it is that you truly want and value in life.

1. What do you want your ikigai to be when you are an adult?
   - What kind of work or career do you see yourself pursuing in the future?
   - What impact do you want to make in the world?
   - What causes or issues are important to you?

2. What will your health be like?
   - How do you want to take care of yourself physically and mentally?
   - What kind of lifestyle do you want to live?
   - What kind of diet and exercise do you want to maintain?

3. How do you want to be remembered by your friends and family?
   - What kind of person do you want to be known as?
   - What kind of memories do you want to create with your loved ones?

4. What will your family and relationships be like?
   - Who do you want to surround yourself with?
   - What kind of partner do you want to have?
   - What kind of parent do you want to be?

5. What hobbies do you want to excel at?
   - What kind of activities bring you joy and fulfilment?
   - What kind of skills or talents do you want to develop?

6. What will your dream house look like?
   - What kind of home do you want to live in in the future?
   - What kind of location do you want to live in?

7. Where do you want to live?
   - Where do you want to live in the future?
   - What kind of community do you want to be a part of?

By taking the time to reflect on these questions, you can start to gain a clearer understanding of what it is that you truly want and value in life, and what your ikigai may be.

Remember, this is a process, and it is normal for your answers to change over time and to not have answers to some of the questions. It can be useful to ask yourself these questions on a regular basis to revaluate your ikigai.

I would decide which questions I would show children depending on their ages, so that it was appropriate, and I would get children to spend some time to focus on the questions that mattered most to them.

Obviously, there are some big questions that many children would struggle to answer but it was the first step into tapping into the areas that they did care about and starting that journey towards a future in which they thrived and loved. The answers from children were compelling, there was a real range of responses which really helped some and others found it a waste of time.

A by product of this exercise was that it showed me what aspects of their life mattered most to them and helped me connect and build deeper relationships. Some children were much more interested in family life, some material objects, some their health or career.

Obviously, talking to children about their legacy can be quite a big ask for teenagers so I would use the power of story again and talk about how I would like them to remember me.

I told them that it was important to me that when they leave our school that they see me as someone who cared for them, who encouraged them to reach for their dreams, and who believed in them even when they had doubted themselves.

I would then ask them to imagine that they were shopping in Norwich City Centre in 30 years' time when they were in their 40s, and they bumped into me, who was now an old man. I would ask them to tell me how they were getting on.

After a few giggles as I'd mimic being an old age pensioner, walking slowly, all hunched up with a pretend walking stick, the students would then think for a moment and begin to jot down their thoughts. It encourages children to think about what they want their life to be like and what they may need to do to achieve that life.

It is also important to remember that it is ok for the child not to know all the answers of how they will do it yet. Many children will not know all the steps they need to take to achieve their goal. That's ok. Our role is to help them take the first steps towards that goal. The goal is to help them learn to think about how to achieve their goals and to take action. Their goals may or may not change as they mature but the key thing is to show them a process that they can apply throughout their lives whatever their goals.

Another important aspect of helping children achieve their goals is to remind them that they already have the resources they need to change. Children have the ability to learn and grow, especially when they have the support of their teachers, parents, and caregivers. It is so important that we encourage them to believe in themselves and their abilities. Some children even feel they need permission from the adults around them to go for the goals. My take on this was always it has to be someone, so why not you, strive for it and let's see how far you can go.

A real thrill of my teaching career has been seeing ex pupils Alfie Hewett (major Grand Slam wheelchair tennis Champion), Olivia Nicholls (International doubles tennis player) and Luke Hannant (professional footballer) take that attitude into their careers as professional sports performers.

It is important to remind children that the answers will come to them in time if they keep searching and taking steps towards their vision. Remind them that achieving their goals will take time and that it's important to keep working towards them. Encourage them to be patient and persistent.

The importance of the first step and moving forward

Taking the first step towards achieving a goal is often the most challenging, but it is also the most important. The famous quote "A journey of a thousand miles begins with a single step" (Lao Tzu) reminds us that every accomplishment, no matter how big or small, starts with that first step. Completing a 100 metre race or a marathon both start with that initial stride.

Research has shown that taking the first step towards a goal can have a powerful impact on motivation and self-efficacy. According to a study by Gollwitzer and Sheeran (2006), the mere act of formulating a plan to take action increases the likelihood of achieving a goal. This is because taking that first step activates the planning and execution stages of goal pursuit, which in turn increases motivation and self-efficacy.

It is important to note that the first step doesn't have to be a big one. It can be something small and manageable, such as making a to-do list or setting a deadline. The important thing is to take action and to get started.

The journey towards achieving our goals can often seem daunting and overwhelming for both us and the children we teach. However, it is important to remember that progress is not always made in giant leaps, but rather through small, consistent steps. This is particularly true when it comes to personal growth and self-improvement.

One of the most important aspects of keeping moving forward is to break down our goals into manageable chunks. This allows us to focus on the small steps we can take each day to make progress, rather than becoming overwhelmed by the end goal.

Another key aspect of taking small steps is to focus on progress, rather than perfection. We must be kind and patient with ourselves, and remember that progress is progress, no matter how small it may be. It is important to celebrate and acknowledge each small step we take, as it is these small steps that will ultimately lead us to our goal.

Kelly's story
'I've always been a perfectionist. Growing up, my parents always expected the best from me, and I always delivered. I was one of the top students in my class, and the leader of the school council. But as I entered high school, my perfectionism started to take a toll on my mental health.

It all started with a simple maths test. I had studied for hours and felt confident that I knew the material inside and out. But when I received my test back, I saw that I had missed one problem. Just one. But to me, that one mistake was a failure. I couldn't shake off the feeling that I wasn't good enough and that everyone else was better than me.

It didn't stop there. Every test, every paper, every presentation became a source of anxiety for me. I would spend hours upon hours studying and preparing, but no matter how well I did, I always found something to criticise about myself. My grades, which had always been straight A's, started to slip. I would stay up all night worrying about homework, and I would constantly miss school because I couldn't bring myself to face my friends and teachers.

My perfectionism also affected my relationships. I couldn't stand the thought of anyone seeing me as less than perfect, so I pushed people away. I stopped hanging out with my friends and stopped talking to my family. I was too afraid of them seeing my flaws and thinking less of me.

It wasn't until I was failing lots of classes, and my parents forced me to see a therapist that I realised how much my perfectionism was hurting me. I learned that it's okay to make mistakes and that no one is perfect. And slowly, I started to let go of my need to be perfect and my mental health started to improve. I started to reconnect with my friends and family, and I started to enjoy school again.

But it wasn't easy. It took a lot of hard work and self-reflection. And even now, I still struggle with my perfectionism at times. But I've learned that it's important to find a balance between setting high standards for yourself and also being able to accept your mistakes. And I hope that by sharing my story, it will help others who may be struggling with similar issues.'

Perfectionism - a blessing and a curse

Perfectionism can be both a positive and negative force in a child's life. On one hand, it can drive individuals to strive for excellence and achieve great success. On the other hand, it can lead to excessive self-criticism and a fear of failure, which can negatively impact their mental health.

One reason for the negative impact of perfectionism on mental health is that individuals who are perfectionistic tend to have high personal standards and are very critical of themselves, which can lead to feelings of inadequacy and low self-esteem. Additionally, perfectionists may have a fear of failure, which can lead to procrastination and a lack of motivation.

It's important for individuals to find a balance between setting high standards for themselves and also being able to accept their limitations and mistakes. In my experiences some of the most challenging mental health illnesses have mainly come from high achieving perfectionist students, all who have been girls.

As I spent time with Kelly recording her story, it was extremely interesting to hear that sometimes teachers had unwittingly exacerbated her mental health problems by focusing too much on exam results. Kelly was very clear that the teachers had not done this intentionally and appreciated that it was a hard balancing act but nevertheless teachers had made her mental health worse.

This was an important piece of feedback for me to hear and reflect upon. As a subject leader, determined to do well for my pupils and with the pressure of explaining results to my senior leaders each year, I was definitely guilty of this charge historically, and made me reflect on how I can do better at this in the future.

In my head I was directing the instructions to work harder to some lazier students who were not knuckling down, but the students who were hearing the message were the perfectionists and it was making their mental health worse when they were already flying in class and well on track to be successful.

In the aftermath of this, if I ever needed to speak to the class about work ethic I would then go round to my perfectionist students to reassure them on a one to one basis that the message was definitely not for them, and that they were doing amazingly well.

Consider this...
- Do you know who your perfectionists are in class?
- Do you need to have 1-2-1 conversation with them to reassure?

A brilliant set of exam results means very little for our young people if they are unable to operate in society through severe mental illness, so as educators we need to be mindful and take action to get the balance right.

 **Try this:**

A string of pearls

I love this exercise from Dr Philip Stutz from the film 'Stutz' regarding taking action to achieve our goals which encompasses perfectionism & self-kindness. It is called a string of pearls.

Imagine a string necklace and a separate group of pearls. Every time you take a step towards your goal, however big or small, add a pearl to the necklace. The key is to keep moving forward and adding the next pearl and then the next one and the next one to get to the place we want to get to.

Now, imagine on each pearl there is a tiny brown dot, that represents a piece of dog's mess. The imperfection is there to remind us that whatever we do there will always be something that we could have done differently, more successfully or added and that each pearl will be imperfect and that is ok. The most important thing is that you took action and became one step closer to where you want to be.

Measuring success

Many people are unhappy because of how they measure their progress. In their book the 'Gap & the Gain', Dan Sullivan & Benjamin Hardy explain that many of us have a goal or moving target that is often out of our reach. When we measure ourselves against that goal then we're in the 'Gap'. Although, when we measure ourselves against our previous selves, we're in the 'Gain'.

Many people aren't able to appreciate their progress because no matter how much they get done, they are usually measuring themselves against their ideals or goals.

By measuring your current self vs your former self it can make us feel good about ourselves, feel grateful, and feel like we are making progress even when times are tough, which in turn boosts motivation, confidence, and future success.

When a child is feeling down I use this activity with them to measure their gain rather than their gap.

 Try this:

The gap and the gain

1. Think about an area in your life where you have had some success.
2. Compare that success to where you were in your life two or three years prior to that.
3. What obstacles did you overcome in those previous years to get to that successful place?
4. What lessons can you take from that experience which will help you moving forward?

(Sullivan, 2021)

In summary, self-kindness and cultivating a positive inner voice are essential for children's emotional and mental wellbeing. Research shows that self-kindness is associated with higher levels of self-esteem, self-compassion, and emotional regulation in children. It is important to teach children to be kind to themselves when they make mistakes, fostering reflection and growth rather than self-criticism.

By nurturing self-kindness and fostering a positive inner voice, children can enhance their mental wellbeing and navigate life's challenges with greater resilience and self-acceptance. Investing in their relationship with themselves is a lifelong journey that will greatly impact their overall happiness and fulfilment.

Worries can be harnessed in positive ways for children's personal growth and development. Instead of allowing worries to consume and paralyse, teaching children to use worries as a positive force empowers them to navigate challenges, drive personal development, and embrace life's uncertainties with resilience and determination.

Chapter summary

- Be mindful of your inner voice and to try to reframe negative thoughts in a more positive light. Speak to yourself with the same kindness and understanding you would offer your friend.
- Fear can be debilitating for young people and create a lot of anxiety for them. We can use worries as a positive, by controlling the controllables, and creating a plan to reduce our anxiety about the future.
- Visualising big dreams can be important for some children to raise their aspirations.
- Small steps towards our goals is crucial to achieving them.
- By focusing on progress and having a growth mindset, we can keep moving forward and make progress towards our ultimate goal.
- We need to be mindful of pushing perfectionist students too hard so be mindful of getting the balance right.

Critical questions

1. Do you teach your young people how to build their self-confidence?.

2. Do you provide explicit physical activities with the focus on building confidence?

3. Do you currently teach your children about how they can develop their self-kindness?

4. Do you currently teach your children about how they can use their worries as a positive?

5. Are there any key worries that you have that you can turn into a positive?

6. Are you aware of your students who lack purpose or low aspirations?

7. Which activities would work best in your setting?

Chapter references

- McCarthy, D. (1964). Mental fitness. *American Psychologist*, 19(3), pp.201–202. doi:https://doi.org/10.1037/h0039771.
- Neff, K. D. (2003). Self-compassion: An alternative conceptualization of a healthy attitude toward oneself. Self and Identity, 2(2), 85-101.
- Muris, P., Meesters, C., & van der Bruggen, C. (2018). Self-kindness and well-being in children and adolescents: A meta-analysis. Journal of Child and Family Studies, 27(7), 2153-2166.
- Sheldon, K. M., & Elliot, A. J. (1999). Goal striving, need satisfaction, and longitudinal well-being: The self-concordance model. Journal of personality and social psychology, 76(3), 482.
- Steger, M. F. (2009). Meaning in life. In International Encyclopaedia of the Social Sciences (2nd ed.). Detroit: Macmillan Reference USA.
- Wong, P. T. P. (2011). The human quest for meaning: Theories, research, and applications (2nd ed.). Routledge.
- *Stutz*. (2022). United States: Netflix.
- Gollwitzer, P. M., & Sheeran, P. (2006). Implementation intentions and goal achievement: A meta-analysis of effects and processes. Advances in experimental social psychology, 38, 69-119.
- Sullivan, D. (2021). *Gap And The Gain*. S.L.: Hay House Business.
- IPLA (2017) Physical literacy definition. Accessed online: 19th April 2024 Available at: https://www.physical-literacy.org.uk/
- Lochbaum, M., Sherburn, M., Sisneros, C., Cooper, S., Lane, A. M., & Terry, P. C. (2022). Revisiting the self-confidence and sport performance relationship: a systematic review with meta-analysis. International Journal of Environmental Research and Public Health, 19(11), 6381.
- Sport England (2023) Physical Literacy Consensus Statement for England. Accessed online: 19th April 2024 Available at: https://www.sportengland.org/news-and-inspiration/physical-literacy-consensus-statement-england-published
- Mogi, K. (2017). *The Little Book of Ikigai: The Essential Japanese Way to Finding Your Purpose in Life*. London: Quercus.

Additional insights

Richard Stockings
Deputy Head at the Alice Smith School in Malaysia. In this case study, he explains how he has incorporated self-kindness into school wellbeing.

'I believe the work of Steve Peters and in particular the 'Chimp Paradox' has the potential to provide students with real tools and techniques that they can apply in all areas of their lives: managing examination stress; dealing with difficult friendships; standing up on stage and giving a talk; calming oneself in the pressure of a sporting contest. All these different aspects require us to stay calm and be present. Peters teaches us how to manage our thinking, how to manage our emotions and how to access the 'human' to do so even when under great stress and challenge.

The formal teaching of this material to students and teachers has had great value in an educational situation. Children can relate to 'the chimp' as the animal that needs exercising or distracting depending on the situation. Our ability to recognise when our thinking might hijack us and cause us to make poor decisions is a life skill.

At a time where student anxiety and depression is on the rise, mental health is important for us all. Helping students understand the brain and why it does what it does is enlightening for them. Creating real life scenarios and simulations where they can practise being in different modes from chimp, human and computer has been transformational in students' understanding of quite difficult concepts. This relatively simplistic concept has been understood and embraced by learners of all ages and testimonials from students confirm its value.

Staff have also benefited from such training and have reported on using this with their students and indeed colleagues when they feel they might be in challenging situations. Delivering this in conjunction with mindful breathing has been hugely helpful in creating a space, a moment of calm between stimulus and response. When we get triggered we are able to notice and breathe allowing the chimp to calm down and the human to be accessed.

Having bespoke wellbeing programs in schools allows professionals to give real ways of developing emotional regulation and managing one's emotions. It is the practice and repetition which establishes habit and ultimately brings the change that has been so worthwhile in exploring mind management techniques in my experience.'

Case Study
Megan Fergusson

Megan Fergusson is an inspirational young person who has combined a number of these strategies together to help her flourish despite adversity. Megan shares her story here:

My story
I was born into the world missing my lower left arm - this has only spurred me on throughout my life. Growing up as a young girl brought many challenges and hurdles along the way. However, if it wasn't for these I wouldn't be the person that I am today. My childhood growing up was sport, it was what has kept me going, kept me determined, kept me sane. This became very apparent when I wasn't able to play sports for 6 months. Breaking my ankle made me realize a lot of things, the importance of surrounding yourself with positivity and love, learning how to deal with stress in a healthy manner and continuing to be resilient. Finishing my schooling education as head of house alongside being a sports scholar has been a massive highlight which I will forever treasure. Being given the privilege of leading 70 girls to victory was something that I can't put into words.

Overcoming difficulties
Surround yourself with positive people, this is something that plays a significant role in the way in which people talk, present themselves, think and go about life. Being constantly around those who are miserable, complaining, and pessimistic will only give out negative energy and will gradually over time cause a knock on effect on those who they interact with.

It's all about your mindset. Having a 'can do' mindset will put you that much further above your competition when it comes to wanting to achieve something. Being in a negative frame of mind will only ever have a negative influence on your output. Whether this is work, performance, grades, the way in which you speak.

Communicating openly with those you trust. A worry or problem shared, is a problem

halved. Taking on too much stress/concern will only lead to an escalation of ….
Do the things you love. Reminding yourself on the things you can do and enjoy will release the feel good hormone dopamine which will improve our overall mental health.

Being told you can't do something, prove them wrong. This is something as an individual with a disability that I have strived to achieve over the years. Being a competitive individual that I am has only spurred me on to prove to not only those who didn't have faith in me from the beginning, but to those like myself that might be struggling to believe that even though they might be different to others around them, if you put your mind to something enough, anything is possible.

How do you build confidence?
Recognise what you are good at. By simply just reminding yourself of the things you are good at will immediately remind yourself of your self-worth.

Look for positives in negative situations. A lot of the time as humans when we are so caught up in a situation we find it hard to look for any positives. This is why often taking a step back, sleeping on it, writing a pros and cons list, or getting another's opinion can be of use. This therefore should hopefully give you a wider picture in a more rational state of mind.

By having a knock back the first time round, without fail has always given me more motivation and determination to get back up and go again. However, before being in this frame of mind it's important to allow yourself to be disappointed and upset. This is where after going through all the emotions, we are able to then get back up and prove our worth.

Give yourself targets. Having targets written down, stuck up or however you wish is something that once reached or ticked off only when achieved gives you that confidence boost of success. Having clear targets and goals will also increase motivation levels as you have a purpose.

How have you created a plan to reduce worries about the future?
Build a network on social media, reach out to people, and connect. Constantly building these connections throughout the years will only ever put yourself in a much stronger position compared to an awful lot of your competitors. The earlier you can start reaching

out to people, telling them what you are up to, your plans for the future etc the better. It gets your name out there, before you have even completed your education. This is vital as the demand and use of social media is only ever increasing rapidly and starting from a younger age, so get ahead of the game.

Individual research on what all the different opportunities/paths are when you know what sector you are keen to work in. This simply just allows you to have the full picture in not missing out on any possible opportunity.

Speak to those who have been there and done it, those that have had different experiences. Having the opportunity to speak to like-minded people who have been through the similar emotions, barriers, and thoughts that you yourself are going through or looking to go through will give you a little bit more confidence and preparation when having to make big decisions. Your connections will be very happy to share their journeys with you and from this information you can make calculated decisions. Of course, it's different for every individual but it is worthwhile and massively influential having all the facts.

Have a backup plan, don't put all your eggs in one basket. This is something that needs to most certainly be considered.

Ambitions for the future

My ambitions for the future consist of continuing to spread positivity in inclusiveness and awareness in our forever changing society. Haven recently signed a contract with the British para triathlon academy I am training full time with the goal of making the Great Britain team for the 2028 Los Angeles Paralympics. After my A levels I decided to take a gap year, working full time as a sports assistant at Daneshill Prep School for the year. September 2023 is when I then go and study at Cardiff Met, studying Physical Education, Sport Science and Coaching. After studying for 3 years and coming out with a degree I plan to go straight out into the working world. Working in a sports department within a school, continuing to grow and add to my experience and develop wider knowledge, with my end dream job being a director of sport. Through my teaching I hope to continue being an influential role model to all those around me and I look forward to giving all children out there the opportunities I experienced as a young girl who simply just loved playing sport.

Chapter 6 - Building positive habits

"We first make our habits, then our habits make us."
John Dryden

As a teacher, you have a unique opportunity to help your students develop the tools they need to succeed in life, both academically and personally. One of the most important ways you can promote your students' wellbeing is by helping them develop healthy habits. In this chapter, we'll explore how you can help your students cultivate habits that protect and enhance their mental health, with a focus in five key areas: sleep, nutrition, mindfulness, hydration, and managing social media use. We will cover exercise in chapter 7.

Sleep, nutrition, and hydration are all crucial for optimal physical health, but they also have a significant impact on mental health. In addition to these physical factors, mindfulness is another important tool for mental wellbeing. Finally, social media has become an important part of our students' lives, but it can also have negative impacts on mental health. By teaching your students how to manage their social media use, you can help them avoid some of the negative effects.

Throughout this chapter, we'll explore practical strategies for helping your students develop healthy habits in each of these areas. We'll provide tips and resources for incorporating exercise, sleep, nutrition, mindfulness, hydration, and healthy social media habits into your classroom and school culture. By making these habits a regular part of your students' lives, you can help them build a strong foundation for mental wellbeing that will serve them throughout their lives. With your help, your students can become healthier, happier, and better equipped to face the challenges of life.

>  **Consider this…**
> - Are your young people aware of what areas they should be focusing on to improve their mental wellbeing?

As teachers, it is important for us to understand how long it takes for a new habit to form to better guide and support our students. According to a study conducted by Phillippa Lally and colleagues (Lally et al., 2010) from the University College London, it takes an average of 66 days for a new habit to form. However, the length of time needed to establish a new habit varied widely among participants, ranging from 18 to 254 days.

It's worth noting that the amount of time it takes to form a new habit depends on a number of factors, including the complexity of the behaviour, the individual's personality and habits, and the consistency of the behaviour. Lally and her colleagues found that it was easier to form simple habits, such as drinking a glass of water with breakfast, than more complex habits, such as doing 50 sit-ups every morning.

You can help your students develop healthy habits by encouraging them to practise consistently over a period of time. It's important to note that forming a new habit may take longer than expected, so it's important to be patient and consistent in encouraging students to practise healthy behaviours. Regular check in's by form tutors and PE teachers can be incredibly powerful, in not only supporting young people as they improve their habits, but also in deepening the relationship by demonstrating that you remember what challenge they set themselves and showing that you care about them.

One way to encourage the development of healthy habits is by helping children track their progress. Tracking habits can be a fun and engaging way for young people to see their progress and stay motivated.

Here are some ways children can track their habits:
- Habit tracking journals
- Habit tracking apps
- Habit tracking charts
- Habit tracking stickers
- Habit tracking rewards

While tracking healthy habits can be an effective way to improve children's mental wellbeing, there are also potential downsides that we should be aware of.

Here are some of the potential downsides to creating and tracking healthy habits:
- Overemphasis on perfection
- Rigidity in routine
- Stress and anxiety
- Obsessive behaviour
- Lack of intrinsic motivation

It's important for us teachers to be aware of these potential downsides and to help students find a balance between tracking their habits and maintaining a healthy perspective. Encouraging our students to focus on the process of developing healthy habits, rather than just the end result, can help prevent some of these potential downsides. Additionally, emphasising the importance of self-compassion and self-care can help students maintain a healthy relationship with habit tracking and avoid the negative effects it can sometimes bring.

As always, it is about knowing our children, and helping them find a way forward that works for them. The quality of our individual relationships with each child is crucial to implementing this effectively.

Try this:

Habits audit

This quick habits audit will help you identify your healthy and unhealthy habits, so you have clarity on what you need to focus on to improve your wellbeing.

Ask yourself:
1. How much sleep are you getting on average per night?
2. How much exercise are you doing on a daily basis?
3. How much water are you drinking on a daily basis?
4. How much fruit & veg are you eating on a daily basis?
5. How much junk food are you eating on a daily basis?
6. How much time are you spending on social media?
7. Do you practise mindfulness?
8. Are you being kind to yourself with your thoughts?

Once you've scribbled down your answers, then reflect and record whether it is a good habit, satisfactory to you, or a poor habit. Recognise what you are doing well at and notice if there are any you would like to improve.

With most children and adults I do this with, they normally have some clear strengths and clear areas they can improve with some in the middle.

I find this is useful for myself to do as a stocktake every week, to check where I am and to refocus my efforts in the areas that I want to improve.

 **Consider this...**
- Do you guide your young people to improve and track their habits?

We will now focus on each of the five key areas and explore what we can do as teachers, to support our young people in developing healthy habits in these key areas.

The importance of sleep

Sleep is essential for our mental and physical health, and this is especially true for children and teenagers. As teachers, it is important to recognise the role of sleep in promoting student wellbeing and academic success. When children don't get enough sleep, they can experience a range of negative consequences, including difficulty concentrating, poor memory, and emotional dysregulation. These effects can translate into poor academic performance and behaviour problems in the classroom.

What is the link between wellbeing and Sleep?
Doctor Catherine Wheatley
Sleep is not a single state but a highly complex set of brain processes that support physical and mental functioning. Much remains a mystery about how sleep is related to learning and thinking, but getting enough, good-quality sleep is essential for healthy and effective functioning. Individual needs vary, but the NHS guidelines suggest that teens need 8-10 hours per night. Feeling tired is a good indication that we are not getting enough sleep.

Research from neuroscience has found that sleep regulates attention and supports the storage and consolidation of memories, promoting learning in school. At the same time, sleeping is 'down-time', a period of low stimulation when we can recover from daily mental stresses and physical strains. Studies have identified notable changes in core body processes during deep sleep that support heart and immune health and promote growth and repair. For example, blood flow to muscles increases during deep sleep, bringing oxygen and growth hormones.

With this in mind, it is not surprising that poor sleep is linked with negative wellbeing, including fatigue, poor concentration, lapses in memory and irritability. These problems can lead to low self-esteem and anxiety about coping with everyday life – which can often make sleep problems even worse. Good sleep hygiene – taking time to wind down at the end of the day, putting away screens well before bedtime, and keeping bedrooms cool and dark – can all help support good sleep.

Developing healthy sleep habits

Here are some habits that teachers can encourage in children to help them get a good night's sleep:

1. *Consistent sleep schedule:* Going to bed and waking up at the same time every day, even on weekends, can help regulate the body's internal clock and promote better sleep.
2. *Limiting screen time:* The blue light emitted by screens can disrupt the body's production of melatonin, a hormone that regulates sleep. Encourage children to limit their screen time in the evening, ideally turning off electronic devices at least 30 minutes before bedtime.
3. *Creating a relaxing bedtime routine*: A consistent bedtime routine, such as taking a warm bath or shower, reading a book, or listening to calming music, can signal to the body that it's time to sleep.
4. *Creating a comfortable sleep environment*: A comfortable, cool, and dark sleep environment can promote better sleep. Encourage children to use comfortable bedding, maintain a comfortable room temperature, and minimise noise and light disturbances.

 **Try this:**

Helping children choose how to improve their sleep habits

Share this table with your class and encourage them to select one strategy to try to enhance their sleep.

Guide to achieving healthy sleep	
Do	**Don't**
Read a book	Drink Caffeine
Relax before bed, try some breathing techniques or journalling.	Use electronics
Keep a consistent sleep schedule	Overeat before bed
Turn off the light & air the room	Drink alcohol
Try a sleep app such as www.calm.com	Overtrain before bed
Track your sleep using a wearable such as Fitbit, whoop, or an apple watch.	

By giving our young people choice over their strategy they are more likely to take ownership of it.

 **Consider this...**
- Are there any strategies that would enhance your own sleep habits?

Sleep Case Study: Sprowston Community Academy

Sprowston Community Academy is a large co-educational secondary school located in Norwich, Norfolk. Their inspirational 2nd in PE, Jonathan Richards, talks us through how we worked together to improve the sleep habits of their young people.

"At Sprowston we had an issue that is probably common with most teenagers, where many were feeling pretty tired during the school day, to the extent that for some students they felt it was affecting their ability to perform in lessons especially towards the end of the school day.

Some who felt they had low energy levels and were feeling tired frequently during the day, thought that it might be having a negative impact on their mood and mental health.

We thought that as the Physical Education Department, we could try to improve the situation by focusing on this area.

From the resources provided we spent most time working through the lessons on sleep and the importance of sleep with our young people and found that these could be easily incorporated within our existing PE curriculum.

Each lesson had a really clear focus and the students enjoyed taking part in the lessons because ultimately they could feel the powerful feedback the course was having on their day to-day lives by targeting small changes. The feedback from students was extremely positive.

A lovely moment when we realised the course was having an impact, was when a lad in Year 11 arrived at a PE lesson on Friday morning Period 1 on time for the first time in a long time, as normally he is a persistent latecomer to the lesson as he normally overslept. I thought I was seeing a ghost!!!!!!!

The lessons helped many students to re-evaluate their behaviour patterns around sleep and many have tried to reduce their 'screen time' at night and tried to have a consistent bedtime routine.

What also tied in really well with our work in PE was that some students were also aiming to increase their activity levels and reduce sugar intake to improve their sleep.

Quantitatively, there were improvements in perceived sleep quality, total sleep and also perceived energy levels in students at Sprowston during the programme. Students have also got a much better awareness of the importance of being kind to themselves and their bodies as a result.

We had some brilliant Student Feedback from our lessons, such as:
"Thanks for helping me to feel more alert and energised for school in the mornings in the lead up to my GCSE exams. Little steps have made a big impact". Dan, Year 11

"I started to think about how many hours of sleep I was getting and recognised I needed more" Ruby, Year 10.

"It was so easy to pick a meaningful target to use to improve my sleep. I shared my target with the rest of my family who copied the target". Alfie, Year 8'

Hydration habits

"Water is the driving force of all nature."
Leonardo da Vinci

Water is essential for life, and it plays a vital role in maintaining optimal health and wellbeing. Hydration is essential for all bodily functions, including regulating body temperature, aiding digestion, and transporting nutrients throughout the body. However, the role of hydration in mental wellbeing is often overlooked.

What is the link between wellbeing and Hydration?
Doctor Catherine Wheatley
Exercising without replacing lost fluid can lead to dehydration. The brain requires water to generate energy for thinking processes and hormone production, but our bodies lose water all the time through sweating, going to the loo and simply breathing.

While there is no clear and direct relationship between dehydration and wellbeing, drinking during daily activities is important for overall brain health: there is good evidence linking dehydration with brain fog, fatigue, low mood, and mental symptoms such as poor attention and memory.

Top tips for staying hydrated include sipping water throughout the day and eating your water in the form of fruit and vegetables.

It is important for teachers to encourage and support their students in drinking more. In this section, we will explore various ways how we can help young people to drink more and stay hydrated.

1. **Educate on the importance of hydration:** We can educate students on the importance of drinking enough water and staying hydrated. We can explain how water is essential for good health and wellbeing, and that even mild dehydration can negatively impact cognitive and physical performance. We can emphasise the importance of staying hydrated at all times but particularly during hot weather, physical activity, and periods of stress or illness.
2. **Make water accessible:** Leadership teams can ensure that water is accessible to students throughout the day. This can be done by providing enough water fountains in accessible places in schools or jugs of water in classrooms and encouraging students to bring reusable water bottles to school or even giving water bottles to students. It's important to make sure that students have regular opportunities to drink water, such as during breaks and lunchtime.
3. **Lead by example:** We can lead by example and make hydration a priority for ourselves. By regularly drinking water in front of our students, we can demonstrate the importance of staying hydrated and encourage our students to do the same.
4. **Encourage breaks for hydration:** We can encourage students to take breaks to drink water, particularly during physical activity or hot weather. Encouraging our students to take short water breaks can help them stay hydrated and alert, which can positively impact their wellbeing and academic performance.
5. **Incorporate water into classroom activities:** Teachers can incorporate water into classroom activities to encourage hydration. For example, they can provide opportunities for students to take water breaks during lessons or make water-related games and activities part of their teaching.
6. **Track water intake:** We can help students track their water intake, such as using a chart or log to record the amount of water they drink each day. This can help students become more aware of their hydration levels and encourage them to drink more water.

7. **Encourage children to keep water by their bedside:** Keeping a bottle of water by their bedside can help them start their day off right. As soon as they wake up, encourage them to take a few sips to kick-start their hydration for the day.
8. **Use a large water bottle:** A large water bottle can make it easier for children to track their water intake and ensure that they are drinking enough water throughout the day. Encourage them to fill it up at the start of the day and make it a goal to finish it by the end of the day.
9. **Take regular sips:** One of the most effective ways to stay hydrated is to take regular sips of water throughout the day. Try to encourage your students to take a sip every 10-15 minutes, even if they don't feel thirsty.
10. **Monitor urine colour:** Monitoring the colour of your urine can be a helpful way to assess your hydration levels. Clear or light-coloured urine typically indicates good hydration, while dark-coloured urine may indicate that you need to drink more water. By placing laminated Urine colour charts in each cubicle in your school it is an easy way to prompt young people and colleagues.
11. **Make hydration a habit:** By encouraging students to incorporate hydration into their daily routine, it can become a healthy habit that is easier to maintain. For example, you can make it a habit to drink water before or during meals.
12. **Flavoured water:** If your children find plain water boring, encourage them to try adding some flavour to it. Adding a slice of lemon or cucumber or trying flavoured water can add a refreshing taste to their water and make it more enjoyable to drink.

By promoting hydration, we can help support the overall wellbeing of our students. Encouraging and supporting young people to drink more water can have a positive impact on their physical and mental health, as well as their academic performance.

Try this:

Increasing your water consumption

1. How many litres of water per day do you drink at the moment?
2. Tick which strategy you would like to use to prompt an increase in the amount you drink:
   - Have a bottle of water by your bed so you can drink water as soon as you get up.
   - Have a large water bottle and fill it up at the start of the day.
   - Drink a glass of water at every meal time.
   - Monitor the colour of your urine when you go to the loo, the clearer it is, the more hydrated you are.
3. Take action.

This case study from my school in 2020 shows how we are developing our whole school culture around hydration. Our inspirational headteacher at the time, Paul Collin, wanted to improve the access to water to enhance outcomes for young people and staff.

Paul increased the number of water fountains around the school and placed them in areas that children could access during break and lunchtimes. He gave all children a school branded water bottle so they each had their own receptacle to drink from. He then amended the school rules around drinking within lessons (except in science labs), to make it as easy as possible for students and staff to stay hydrated.

To support this goal, I adapted a urine colour chart to meet our children's literacy needs, and our site staff laminated and displayed them in each loo across the school. We taught about the importance of hydration across the curriculum in a range of subjects such as in PE, Food technology, PSHE and Science. Teachers would act as role models drinking water in lessons and discussing strategies we used to increase our water intake.

Through implementing this strategy, we developed a culture where children were more aware of the importance of hydration and had easier access to staying hydrated. This approach contributed to successful applications for a number of whole school health awards.

Consider this...

- Do your children and colleagues understand the importance of hydration to their mental wellbeing?
- How could you improve your young people's ease of access to water in your setting?

Nutrition habits

"Let food be thy medicine and medicine be thy food."
Hippocrates

Food plays a crucial role in our physical health and wellbeing, but did you know that what we eat can also affect our mental health? In this section, we will explore the importance of food for mental wellbeing in more detail, including how certain nutrients can affect our mood and mental health, as well as practical tips for us teachers to support our children's nutritional needs.

What is the link between wellbeing and Diet?
Doctor Catherine Wheatley
Fruit and veg are just one portion of a mentally healthy diet. The relationship between what we eat and how we feel is highly complex, involving a range of biological pathways and mechanisms from hormone release to blood glucose and gut health.

To support all of these systems, it is better to consume a varied, balanced diet, including plenty of plants and avoiding unhealthy fats, than to focus on specific supplements that claim to improve brain health. In fact, only a small handful of supplements have been shown to improve cognitive function: for example, omega-3 fatty acids found in oily fish help build cell membranes in the brain.

Variety – including plenty of fibre and some fermented foods like yoghurt – is key to maintaining a healthy gut, which is important for the production of serotonin, responsible for mood regulation, and B vitamins, which support immune functions.

Foods such as chicken, avocados and bananas are all rich in a protein building block called tyrosine, which can boost the production of dopamine, the hormone or neurotransmitter that helps us feel pleasure. Choosing whole grains and brown rice and pasta over refined carbohydrates and sugar-heavy treats avoids the large fluctuations in blood glucose that are linked with mood swings.

How we eat is also important: sharing a relaxed meal with friends or family can improve mood, and using meals as a moment of mindfulness can support overall wellbeing.

Practical tips for teachers

In schools, there are many practical tips we can use to encourage children to consume these important nutrients. For example:

- Our canteens can offer a variety of foods: Offer a variety of nutrient-dense foods, including fatty fish, leafy greens, nuts, seeds, and whole grains.
- We can educate on the importance of nutrients: Teach children about the importance of these nutrients for mental wellbeing and explain how they can be found in different foods. This can be done in Food Technology, RSHE, PE or Science or in all four to really hammer home the point.
- Provide fortified foods: Provide fortified foods, such as milk and cereal, to help children get enough vitamin D. Breakfast clubs are a great opportunity to implement this.
- Offer healthy snacks: Offer healthy snacks that are rich in these nutrients, such as nuts, seeds, and fruit.
- Use school allotments to educate young people about the journey from field to fork and involve them by doing, this also incorporates biophilia. These allotments are frequently safe sanctuaries for children that boost their mental wellbeing.
- Provide cooking and nutrition classes: Providing cooking and nutrition classes can help children develop healthy habits and improve their understanding of nutrition.
- Consider the role of sweet treats as rewards. In moderation is fine but sometimes we go overboard, we can reward children in more creative ways.
- You may want to liaise with local convenience stores to create agreements to support each other. We worked with our local Tesco Express to reduce the sale of energy drinks and junk food in the morning before school, in return we had a staff presence in the store to reduce episodes of shoplifting.

 **Try this:**

Eating the rainbow every day

It is important to include lots of different colour fruits and vegetables in your diet. Can you try a food from every colour of the rainbow? Keep track of the colours you eat every day:

Day	Red	Orange	Yellow	Green	Blue / Purple	White
Monday						
Tuesday						
Wednesday						
Thursday						
Friday						
Saturday						
Sunday						

Questions:
1. How could you add more colour to your daily diet?
2. Create a meal that could include at least 3 of the rainbow colours.
3. Do you feel happier on the days that you eat all or most of the colours?
4. How do you feel on the days you do not eat many of the colours?
5. How much junk food do you eat at the moment?
6. Do you think reducing your junk food consumption will improve your mental health? Why?

> **Consider this...**
> - Do your children and colleagues understand the importance of nutrition to their mental wellbeing?
> - How could you enhance your school's culture around nutrition?

In conclusion, the link between diet and mental health is clear, and we have an important role to play in supporting the nutritional needs of the children we teach.

Balancing social media usage

"Technology is a useful servant but a dangerous master."
Christian Lous Lange

In today's digital age, it's impossible to avoid the impact of technology on children's lives. Social media and screen time have become integral parts of our daily routines, and it's important for us as teachers to understand the positive and negative effects of these technologies on children's mental wellbeing. While social media and screen time have their benefits, they also have the potential to harm children's mental health if used excessively or inappropriately.

What is the link between wellbeing and Social Media?
Doctor Catherine Wheatley

Controversy, speculation, and misinformation characterize the conversation about exactly how social media use is linked to wellbeing. Instagram, Snapchat, and other platforms are hard to avoid and provide essential news, information, and social connections to many millions of people. Yet evidence shows that some patterns of use are linked to depression, anxiety, low-self-esteem and decreased, delayed, and disrupted sleep.

Considering various distinct features of social media use can help demonstrate how it might impact wellbeing: these include the amount of daily engagement, the emotional connection that users have to their chosen platforms, and the type of content on offer. Evidence suggests that multi-tasking – such as doing homework while looking at a phone - or using two screens at the same time, and using devices near bed time, are more strongly linked to negative wellbeing than the number of minutes spent using social media. Deeper emotional connections to social media are also linked with worse outcomes. Platforms such as TikTok are designed to reinforce use: fewer 'likes', and fewer associated 'dopamine hits', are linked with anxiety and depression. This relationship can become especially clear when users are separated from their devices. Research has found that young people themselves are most worried about hacking, privacy, procrastination, bullying and less social engagement in person (Ecorys, 2020). More mindful use of social media may well be the key.

There are a number of positives of Social Media and Screen Time for young people such as:
- Helps to Build Relationships
- Provides Access to Information
- Boost Creativity
- Promotes Problem-Solving

We also know that there are a number of negatives of Social Media and Screen Time:
- Cyberbullying
- Disrupted Sleep
- Addiction
- Exposure to Inappropriate Content

One of the concerns about social media's impact on young people is that it may encourage them to compare themselves more against others. Social media platforms are designed to showcase the highlights of people's lives, which can create a distorted view of reality and lead to feelings of inadequacy or low self-esteem.

Research has found that social media use is positively correlated with social comparison among young people (Nesi and Prinstein, 2015). A study published in the Journal of Social and Clinical Psychology found that college students who used social media more frequently reported higher levels of social comparison, and that this was associated with increased feelings of depression and anxiety (Vogel et al., 2015). Similarly, a study published in Cyberpsychology, Behaviour, and Social Networking found that social comparison on Instagram was associated with lower self-esteem and increased feelings of depression (Fardouly et al., 2015).

We can help children develop a healthy relationship with social media by educating them about the potential risks of social comparison and encouraging them to develop a positive self-image.

I often use images such as these in my lessons to get young people to consider the meaning of the picture and how it relates to social media and comparison.

Figure 10:

I ask them how often they post something positive about their life when things have gone well compared to how often they post something negative about their life when things haven't gone well to emphasise that social media is a highlights reel the vast majority of the time, rather than real life.

I often use Cristiano Ronaldo as an example of someone who's achieved so much in football. However, if he were to compare himself to Lionel Messi, he might feel a bit disheartened. Living in a world of comparisons means we'll always come across those who've accomplished more or have things we wish we had. That's why I encourage children to focus on their personal progress instead. Comparing oneself only to their past self, aiming to be a better version of who they were yesterday, can lead to more positive and fulfilling growth.

We need to give our young people opportunities to build a foundation level of confidence in themselves which is not reliant on how many hearts their Instagram post achieves or how many views their Tik Tok video accumulates. We need to teach them to talk kindly to themselves rather than berating oneself when comparing themselves against the latest Instagram filtered photo.

By encouraging critical thinking and media literacy skills, we can help children develop a more realistic and balanced view of the world, which can contribute to positive mental wellbeing.

As teenagers navigate the challenges of adolescence, social media and screen time can play a significant role in their daily lives. While these technologies can offer a wealth of benefits, excessive or inappropriate use can also have negative effects on teenagers' mental wellbeing. Finding the right balance of social media and screen time for teenagers can be challenging, but it is essential for promoting positive mental health outcomes.

Our challenge as teachers is to help our young people get their balance of social media usage right. By getting the balance right, teenagers can develop healthy digital habits and minimise the negative effects of technology on their mental wellbeing. As teachers, it's important that we help young people to understand the ways in which social media companies generate revenue and the potential impact of these business models on their mental wellbeing. By educating children on the potential risks and benefits of social media use, we can help them develop healthy digital habits and make informed decisions about their online activities.

I then go on to explain to young people how it is very difficult for us as human beings to compete against these massive social media companies that are spending billions of dollars into the latest research and development to get us addicted to our screens.

Social media companies rely on revenue from advertisers to make a profit, and this has created an arms race for attention and time. Social media companies invest heavily in research and development to create engaging and addictive platforms that keep users glued to their screens. They use cutting-edge technology and data analysis to develop new features and algorithms that personalise the user experience and encourage users to spend more time on their platforms.

The cost of research and development in the social media industry is significant, with some companies spending billions of dollars each year on these efforts. For example, Facebook reported spending over $18 billion on research and development in 2020 alone (Facebook, 2021). This massive investment allows social media companies to create increasingly sophisticated algorithms and features, which can be used to keep users hooked on their platforms.

As teachers, it's important to understand the impact of social media companies' research and development on children's mental health. Educating children on how social media companies operate can help young people make informed decisions about their online activities.

Phone free schools

One way that schools can help promote healthy technology use among children is by creating phone-free zones within the school environment.

The benefits of phone free schools are:
- Reduced Distraction
- Improved Social Interaction
- Reduced Cyberbullying and Other Online Risks

It's important to encourage healthy technology use among our children, and phone-free zones within schools are one way to do so. Teachers can work with school administrators to establish phone-free zones in appropriate areas of the school, such as classrooms, cafeterias, and other common spaces. Additionally, teachers can educate children on the benefits of phone-free zones and promote healthy digital habits, such as using technology in moderation and taking regular breaks from screens.

As a teacher who has worked in schools where phones were permitted and then were not, I found that the environment where phones were not permitted was the best for student wellbeing and engagement. When our headteacher told us that he was going to ban mobile phones I thought that we were in for a major behavioural challenge with significant pushback from students.

The head carefully communicated the new rule to children, parents, and teachers so that everyone had plenty of time to ask questions and get their head around the new expectations. The implementation was superb, and children seemed more relaxed and engaged as if it was a relief to them that they did not have the distraction of their phone, and it appeared to allow them to be children again. Not only did children experience better mental wellbeing but engagement, behaviour and progress improved as well.

I am convinced that phones should be put away at the start of the school day until the end of the day to give our young people a safe space away from them. I always find teaching Year 8 students about balancing social media usage fascinating. It was not uncommon for over half of a class of girls to be on their phones for over 10 hours a day. They would be on their phones from the minute they woke up until they got to the school gate at the start of the day. They were not on their phones during the school day, but they would be straight on them the minute they were out of the school gate until they went to sleep that night.

Excuse me for generalising but the boys tended to be on social media a lot less, but they would play a lot more computer games. Again it wouldn't be uncommon for over half the boys per class to be using their screens for 8 hours a day. Over the last 10 years, I and many other colleagues found it harder to field school sports teams than earlier on in our careers. For the first time in our careers we were hearing reasons such as 'I want to go home and play Call of Duty Sir'. This is certainly a challenge that PE teachers will need to rise to more and more in the future, to make sure our extra-curricular programmes are meaningful and engage our young people, so that they are motivated to benefit from the power of inclusive teams.

Consider this...
- Is your school a phone free zone?
- What are your thoughts on phone free zones?

Top tips to help children balance their social media usage
- Educate young people about the potential risks of excessive social media and screen time use, such as the risk of addiction, cyberbullying, or exposure to inappropriate content. This can help them develop a healthy understanding of the role of technology in their lives.
- Turn off notifications, which can reduce the frequency and intensity of social media use.
- Set limits on social media use, such as setting a time limit or a daily usage goal.
- Taking regular breaks from social media and engaging in offline activities. We can encourage teenagers to leave their phones at home and engage in offline activities that promote positive mental health outcomes, such as exercise, socialising with friends and family face to face, or pursuing creative hobbies.

- Monitor young people's social media use and help them identify and avoid negative interactions such as cyberbullying, hate speech, or exposure to inappropriate content. A number of colleagues have reported to me about young men in their schools idolising people like Andrew Tate and their misogynistic views.

By implementing these strategies we can help children develop a healthy relationship with social media, reduce the potential negative impact on mental wellbeing, and promote positive outcomes, such as improved academic performance, increased self-esteem, and better relationships with peers.

Try this:

Reducing your social media usage

Here are a range of social media coping strategies to reduce your usage:
- Turn your notifications off.
- Decide the times that you are going to check your phone so that you are using your phone productively rather than doom scrolling.
- Go for a walk and leave your phone at home.
- Play sport with your friends.
- Read a book or paint a picture instead.
- Put your phone away where you can't reach it easily.
- Count how many times you reach for your phone in 20 minutes and then try and reduce the number each time.

Consider this...
- Which strategy do you think will work best for you? Go try it.

Developing mindfulness

"Mindfulness is a way of befriending ourselves and our experience."
Jon Kabat-Zinn

Mindfulness is a powerful tool for promoting positive mental wellbeing in children. It's a practice that has been around for thousands of years but has gained significant attention in recent years due to its potential benefits for mental and physical health.

At its core, mindfulness is the practice of being present and fully engaged in the present moment, without judgment or distraction. It involves bringing a focused and non-judgmental awareness to one's thoughts, feelings, and physical sensations. Through mindfulness, children can learn to cultivate a greater sense of self-awareness, regulate their emotions, and respond to stress in a more positive and effective way.

In this section, we'll explore what mindfulness is, how it works, and its potential benefits for children's mental wellbeing.

What is the link between wellbeing and Mindfulness?
Doctor Catherine Wheatley
Mindfulness is a way of paying attention to the present moment, using techniques such as meditation, yoga, and breathing. Practising mindfulness helps us become more aware of our thoughts and feelings so that, instead of being overwhelmed by them, we are more able to manage them. It does not work for everyone, and a 2022 trial involving hundreds of secondary schools concluded that universal mindfulness training for 11-14 year-olds did not improve mental health compared to what schools were already doing (Kuyken et al., 2022).

Nevertheless, there is growing evidence that for some individuals it can help reduce stress, anxiety and depression when practised regularly. Taking a minute to observe your breathing, paying attention to your food as you eat, or focusing on the sensation of walking, can all help bring a measure of calm to our day.

Practising gratitude

Practising gratitude involves intentionally focusing on, and appreciating the positive aspects of one's life, no matter how small or seemingly insignificant. Cultivating a gratitude practice can help children develop a more positive outlook, increase feelings of happiness and contentment, and reduce stress and anxiety.

I have talked about this strategy in detail in Chapter 5 - Shrinking our worries but I vividly remember this working particularly well on a Tuesday afternoon period 5 with my Year 9 taster exam PE group. Tuesdays were full on! Lessons all day, lunchtime clubs and with plenty of chaos going on, I always seemed to turn up flustered, but within 5 minutes all would be well with the world because of a simple activity.

I would ask the class to individually think about 5 separate things they were grateful for. To increase their thinking time, I would lead by example by saying 5 things that I was grateful for and then I would pass a low compression tennis ball around the room for each person to say the 1 most important thing they were grateful for. The class were trained to be silent and listen attentively to their class mates in a respectful manner. The whole exercise would take probably 5 minutes, but that time was worth investing for the benefits it would bring to the rest of the lesson in creating a great environment for our young people and myself to thrive in. Why not give it a try with your classes.

Here are some top tips for you to help your students practise gratitude:
- Practise gratitude in the moment: Encourage students to be mindful of the good things that happen throughout the day. When something positive happens, encourage them to take a moment to appreciate it and express gratitude.
- Use gratitude exercises: One simple exercise is the "gratitude jar," where students write down something they are grateful for each day and put it in a jar. At the end of the week or month, the class can read the notes together in form time and reflect on their blessings.
- Share gratitude with others: Encourage students to express gratitude to others. This could involve writing a thank you note, expressing appreciation in person, or performing a random act of kindness. When students share their gratitude with others, they not only reinforce their own positive emotions but also spread positivity to others.

Body scanning

Body scanning is a mindfulness technique that can be used to help children manage stress and anxiety, and improve their mental wellbeing (Burke, 2010). It involves focusing on each part of the body in turn, noticing any sensations or feelings, and gradually relaxing each area of the body. Body scanning can help children become more aware of their physical sensations and become more attuned to their bodies, which can help them feel more grounded and present.

Body scanning is generally considered a safe mindfulness technique, but there are some issues to be aware of. First, body scanning may not be appropriate for all children. Some children may find the process of paying attention to their physical sensations to be uncomfortable or anxiety-provoking. We should be mindful of students' needs and reactions and should provide alternative mindfulness techniques if needed.

Body scanning should not be used as a substitute for medical treatment or therapy. We should encourage students to seek additional support if they are experiencing significant mental health challenges.

When teaching body scanning as part of our recovery curriculum, after a rigorous circuit training lesson, it got a real mixed response from students, with some students loving it and others hating it.

This wellbeing programme was originally designed for teenage girls, but they tended to strongly dislike body scanning, if you excuse me for generalising. I don't know whether it was laying down on mats or the fact that they had a male teacher in me which affected their ability to feel psychologically safe. Either way, body scanning did not last long as part of their recovery curriculum.

The Year 8 boys, on the other hand, absolutely loved it and would pester me to do body scanning again and again after their circuit training lesson. When you think about a typical day for a year 8, there is lots of noise, energy, and physical contact with their peers, they tend to bounce around from lesson to lesson with very few opportunities for quiet moments to pause and reflect.

I wonder how the young people in your setting will find body scanning. Feel free to experiment and let me know how it goes, I would love to know.

Bobby's story

'My name is Bobby and I'm 13 years old. I love playing football and rugby and working out, but sometimes all that movement and noise can make my brain feel like it's going to explode. That's why I was really happy when my P.E. teacher introduced us to body scanning.

It happened after we finished a tough circuit training session. We had been running around, lifting weights, and doing all kinds of exercises for an hour, and I was feeling pretty exhausted. But then, our teacher told us to lie down on the mats and close our eyes.

At first, I thought it was weird. I mean, I'm used to being on the go all the time, and the idea of just lying still seemed kind of boring. But then, the teacher started talking us through the body scanning exercise. He told us to focus on each part of our body, one at a time, and notice any sensations or feelings.

As we went through the exercise, I started to feel more and more relaxed. I could feel the tension leaving my muscles, and I started to feel really peaceful and calm.

The best part of the body scanning exercise was that it gave me a chance to slow down. Normally, my mind is always racing, thinking about the next thing I have to do or worrying about something that happened in the past. But during the body scanning, I was able to focus on my breath and my body, and just be present.

It's became one of my favourite parts of my P.E. class. I love the way it makes me feel, and I know that it's good for my mental health too. Whenever I start to feel stressed or anxious, I remember the body scanning exercise and use it to calm myself down at home.'

Here are some tips and sources for teachers to help their students practise body scanning:
- *Find a comfortable position:* Encourage students to find a comfortable position to lie down, with their arms and legs uncrossed, and their eyes closed. They should try to find a position where they can relax and breathe comfortably.
- *Start at the feet and move up the body:* Ask students to bring their attention to their feet, noticing any sensations or feelings in this part of the body. They should focus on each area of the feet, including the toes, arches, and heels, and try to relax any tension in the muscles.

Journalling

Journalling is a simple yet powerful tool that can help improve children's mental wellbeing. It is the practice of regularly writing down one's thoughts, feelings, and experiences in a journal or diary. It can serve a number of purposes, such as helping children process and understand their emotions, setting and achieving personal goals, and tracking personal growth and development over time. Journalling can also be a creative outlet, allowing young people to express themselves through writing or other forms of self-expression. Many people find journalling to be a useful tool for stress management, self-discovery, and overall wellbeing.

To encourage students to practise journalling, we can incorporate it into classroom activities, provide prompts, and model journalling themselves. Journalling was ideal as a silent settler at the start of a lesson with certain groups. By making journalling a routine and creating a safe and supportive space for students to reflect on their experiences, we can help students develop self-awareness and improve their mental wellbeing.

 **Try this:**

The power of 3

The power of 3 is my favourite way to journal. I want a quick and efficient way to practise mindfulness and keep me on track to achieve my goals without writing and writing for hours on end. It matches my busy lifestyle, helps me appreciate all that I have in my life, and it is enjoyable to look back on from time to time to see how far I have come.

Write down 3 things you are grateful for today:

1.

2.

3.

Write down 3 ways you won today:

1.

2.

3.

Write down 3 ways you are going to win tomorrow:

1.

2.

3.

© (Sullivan, 2021)

I have subsequently added an area to write one word on the quality & quantity of my: Sleep, Diet & Exercise for that day so I can be mindful of the healthy habits that have the biggest impact on my mental wellbeing. It helps me to notice any patterns in my behaviour, keeps me balanced and prevents me from burning out.

Just like body scanning, I found students responded very differently to journalling. This time many girls loved having some time and space to reflect and write, whereas many boys didn't like it at all. Excuse me for generalising again, but that was my experiences in my school, I wonder how your students prefer to practise mindfulness.

Davina's story
Hi, my name is Davina and I'm 15 years old. I've been keeping a journal for a while now, and it's become an important part of my daily routine. At first, I wasn't sure what the point of journalling was. I mean, what could writing down my thoughts and feelings really do for me? But as I started to write more and more, I began to see the benefits.

For me, journalling is a chance to reflect on my day and process my thoughts and emotions. I can write about things that I'm excited about, things that are bothering me, or just random thoughts that pop into my head. Sometimes, just getting my thoughts down on paper can help me make sense of them.

One of the things I love about journalling is that it's completely private. I don't have to worry about what other people will think or say. It's just me and my journal. And that sense of privacy and safety allows me to be more honest with myself.

When I read back over my journal entries, I can see patterns in my thinking and behaviour that I might not have noticed otherwise.

Journalling is a chance to take a deep breath and slow down for a few minutes each day. It's a chance to be with myself and my thoughts without any distractions or pressures.

Journalling has helped me manage my emotions, understand myself better, and feel more grounded.

Here are some tips and research sources for teachers to help their students practice journalling:
- *Find a comfortable space:* Encourage students to find a quiet and comfortable space where they can focus on their journalling.
- *Use prompts:* Sometimes it can be difficult to know what to write about. We can provide prompts to help students get started. These prompts could be about emotions, experiences, goals, or reflections on their day.
- *Use positive psychology prompts:* Positive psychology prompts encourage students to focus on positive aspects of their life. For example, students could write about things they're grateful for, or positive experiences they've had recently.
- *Use gratitude prompts:* Encourage students to write down things they are grateful for.
- *Make it a routine:* Encourage students to make journalling a routine part of their day. This could involve setting aside time each day or week for journalling or incorporating it into classroom activities such as form time.

Practising deep breathing

Deep breathing is a simple yet effective technique that can help children manage stress and anxiety and improve their mental wellbeing. It involves taking slow, deep breaths, and focusing on the sensations of the breath moving in and out of the body.

Research has shown that deep breathing can be an effective technique for managing stress and anxiety. A study conducted by Li and colleagues (2015) found that deep breathing can help reduce symptoms of anxiety in children and adolescents. Another study by Zaccaro and Piarulli (2019) found that deep breathing can help improve attention and self-regulation in children.

I tended to incorporate deep breathing within the body scanning exercises I explained earlier but there are so many different methods of deep breathing that you can experiment with. I found that some students found it very calming whilst others could not see the benefit to it at all. Like all techniques in this book, it is for young people to experiment with what works best for them and discard the rest.

Here are some tips for you to help your students practise deep breathing:
- *Find a comfortable position:* Encourage students to find a comfortable position, either sitting or lying down, with their arms and legs uncrossed. They should try to find a position where they can relax and breathe comfortably.
- *Breathe deeply:* Instruct students to take slow, deep breaths, filling their lungs with air and then exhaling slowly. They should focus on the sensations of the breath moving in and out of the body.
- *Use guided meditations:* There are many guided meditations available online that teachers can use to help their students practise deep breathing.
- *Use counting:* Teachers can instruct students to count their breaths as a way to focus their attention and regulate their breathing. For example, students could count to three in their head as they inhale, hold their breath for four seconds, and then count to five as they exhale to reduce their heart rate.

Deep breathing is generally considered a safe technique for children, but there are some issues to be aware of. First, children who have certain medical conditions, such as asthma or heart disease, should consult with a healthcare provider before practising deep breathing. Second, children who have experienced trauma or have a history of anxiety may find deep breathing to be challenging or anxiety-provoking. Third, deep breathing should not be used as a substitute for medical treatment or therapy. We should encourage students to seek additional support if they are experiencing significant mental health challenges.

Consider this...
- Do you feel there is a place for mindfulness in schools?
- What different techniques would suit certain groups of young people in your setting?

Recent research has unveiled a captivating concept known as "Goldilocks Days." These are instances when different aspects of wellbeing align exceptionally well, creating a kind of sweet spot. These "Goldilocks Days" tend to occur when certain factors come together just right. For instance, approximately 11 hours of sleep, coupled with around 0.8 hours of daily screen time, contribute to these balanced days. (Duncan et al., 2023)

In wrapping up this chapter, it's clear that adopting healthy habits is crucial for promoting mental wellbeing in young people. With the knowledge and tools to prioritise their health, they are better equipped to navigate the complexities of life, embracing its challenges and joys with a sense of balance and mental wellbeing. As educators, we play a crucial role in empowering them to find this balance, fostering a generation that thrives both mentally and physically.

Chapter summary

- Small changes in habits can have a big impact on our lives. As a teacher, you can use these concepts to help your students develop healthy habits that promote mental wellbeing. It takes an average of 66 days for a new habit to form, and the length of time can vary depending on a number of factors. As a teacher, it's important to be patient and consistent in encouraging your students to develop healthy habits.
- Sleep is essential for our mental and physical health, and this is especially true for children and teenagers. During sleep, our body and brain undergo a series of critical functions that help us to maintain optimal health. Teenagers need between 8-10 hours of sleep each night to promote healthy brain development and cognitive function. We can develop a range of healthy habits or strategies to improve the quantity and quality of our sleep. By giving our young people choice over their strategy they are more likely to take ownership of it.
- Water is essential for life, and it plays a vital role in maintaining optimal health and wellbeing. Dehydration can impact mood, cognitive function, and behaviour. Teachers can play an important role in supporting children's mental wellbeing by promoting hydration and providing education on the importance of staying hydrated.
- Consuming a balanced diet that includes a variety of nutrient-dense foods is important for supporting mental wellbeing. Teachers can encourage children to consume these important nutrients by educating on their importance, and balanced meals at school.
- Social media and screen time can have both positive and negative effects on our children's mental wellbeing. As teachers, we can help children develop healthy digital habits by educating them on the potential risks of social media use, providing them with the tools and strategies they need to use social media in a healthy and balanced way, and creating a positive school culture that promotes healthy digital habits.
- Mindfulness is a powerful tool for promoting positive mental wellbeing in children. By cultivating a greater sense of self-awareness, emotional regulation, and resilience to stress, children can develop a greater sense of calm and wellbeing. As teachers, we can play a key role in promoting mindfulness in the classroom, and help children develop a powerful tool for promoting positive mental wellbeing.

Critical question

1. Do you teach your young people about the impact of habits?

2. Are there any habits that you would like to focus on for yourself?

3. Have you got an accurate idea of how often your young people are on social media?

4. How confident do you feel delivering a mindfulness lesson in your setting?

5. Whereabouts on your school curriculum would mindfulness lessons best fit?

Chapter references

- Lally, P., van Jaarsveld, C.H.M., Potts, H.W.W. and Wardle, J. (2010). How are habits formed: Modelling habit formation in the real world. *European Journal of Social Psychology*, [online] 40(6), pp.998–1009. doi:https://doi.org/10.1002/ejsp.674.
- Ecorys (2020). *Navigating the digital world: a synthesis of the evidence.* [online] Ecorys. Available at: https://www.ecorys.com/app/uploads/files/2020-09/navigating-the-digital-world%20(1).pdf [Accessed 1 Oct. 2023].
- Nesi, J. and Prinstein, M.J. (2015). Using Social Media for Social Comparison and Feedback-Seeking: Gender and Popularity Moderate Associations with Depressive Symptoms. *Journal of Abnormal Child Psychology*, [online] 43(8), pp.1427–1438. doi:https://doi.org/10.1007/s10802-015-0020-0.
- Vogel, E. A., Rose, J. P., Okdie, B. M., Eckles, K., & Franz, B. (2015). Who compares and despairs? The effect of social comparison orientation on social media use and its outcomes. Personality and Individual Differences, 86, 249-256.
- Fardouly, J., Diedrichs, P. C., Vartanian, L. R., & Halliwell, E. (2015). Social comparisons on social media: The impact of Facebook on young women's body image concerns and mood. Body Image, 13, 38-45.
- Facebook (2021). *Facebook Reports Fourth Quarter and Full Year 2020 Results.* [online] investor.fb.com. Available at: https://investor.fb.com/investor-news/press-release-details/2021/Facebook-Reports-Fourth-Quarter-and-Full-Year-2020-Results/default.aspx.

- Kuyken, W., Ball, S., Crane, C., Ganguli, P., Jones, B., Montero-Marin, J., Nuthall, E., Raja, A., Taylor, L., Tudor, K., Viner, R.M., Allwood, M., Aukland, L., Dunning, D., Casey, T., Dalrymple, N., De Wilde, K., Farley, E.-R., Harper, J. and Kappelmann, N. (2022). Effectiveness and cost-effectiveness of universal school-based mindfulness training compared with normal school provision in reducing risk of mental health problems and promoting well-being in adolescence: the MYRIAD cluster randomised controlled trial. *Evidence Based Mental Health*, 25(3), pp.99–109. doi:https://doi.org/10.1136/ebmental-2021-300396.
- Burke, C. A. (2010). Mindfulness-based approaches with children and adolescents: A preliminary review of current research in an emergent field. Journal of Child and Family Studies, 19(2), 133-144.
- Li, A. W., Goldsmith, C. A., & Potts, J. E. (2015). A randomised controlled trial of diaphragmatic breathing for asthma control. Journal of Asthma, 52(7), 707-713.
- Sullivan, D. (2021). *Gap And The Gain*. S.L.: Hay House Business.
- Zaccaro, A., & Piarulli, A. (2019). Breathing regulation and cognitive control: Empirical evidences, biological bases, and implications for healthy and pathological aging. Frontiers in psychology, 10, 2612.
- Duncan, M., Kuzik, N.C., Silva, D.A.S., Carson, V., Chaput, J.-P., Faulkner, G., Ferro, M.A., Turcotte-Tremblay, A.-M., Leatherdale, S.T., Patte, K. and Tremblay, M.S. (2023). Goldilocks Days for Adolescent Mental Health: Gender Differences in Optimal and Sub-optimal Movement Behaviours Combinations for Well-being, Anxiety and Depression. *Journal of Exercise, Movement, and Sport (SCAPPS refereed abstracts repository)*, [online] 54(1). Available at: https://scapps.org/jems/index.php/1/article/view/3117 [Accessed 1 Oct. 2023].

Additional inspiration

The power of light

Dr Shelley James
During the second lockdown, I was increasingly concerned about the amount of time our children were spending on screens combined with a lack of natural daylight as it was winter time. This combination was having a major impact on my own mental health, and I was worried what it was doing to the wellbeing of the children we taught. I reached out to Dr Shelley James, an international expert on light and wellbeing, TEDx and keynote speaker.

We partnered up to convince my headteacher to create learning opportunities for our young people away from a screen 1 day a fortnight to give their bodies a break during lockdown. Dr Shelley is going to give her unique take on the topic of light and the effect

It can have on our children's sleep & wellbeing:
"It's tough to be a teen today. Not only do they have to deal with the natural shifts in their hormones that can shift their sleep-wake cycle by up to two hours, but these brave young adults face unprecedented social and academic pressures, anxiety about climate change and breakdown of parent relationships. This perfect storm can leave them feeling depressed, distracted and deeply insecure.

There is growing evidence that light can help them to get the deep sleep they need to wake up feeling refreshed and ready to face whatever the day may bring. The same research also suggests that disrupting their body clock can have long-term consequences for their physical and mental development: increased alcohol and drug abuse, delayed puberty and metabolic disorders that lead to obesity and diabetes.

Their body clock needs a clear difference between bright 'wake-up' light during the day and complete darkness at night - and at least two hours without the blue 'wake-up' wavelengths that are like a cup of coffee for the brain. The problem is that most young people don't get enough bright light during the day. They spend their evenings online and often sleep in their room with screens and lights on.

Most remarkable young people I know are thoughtful and determined to make a difference in the world. They hate feeling groggy in the morning and suffer as much as their parents and teachers do when they see their friends feeling down or failing at school. And yet, I know from conversations with hundreds of teens around me that most of them have no idea that simple changes to their diet of light could make a world of difference.

Here is one proven way that you, as a parent or teacher, can help teens to recognise the value of sleep and make friends with their body clock. If they could get to bed when they wanted to and wake up naturally, there wouldn't be a problem. But staying up late and waking early for school means they're always running on empty.

Invite them to use a simple online sleepiness score to check how alert they feel at different times and in the evening.
(https://www.omnicalculator.com/health/epworth-sleepiness-scale).

Then invite them to try an experiment for a week: eat earlier, cut down on sugar and caffeine and switch off their screens and social media by 8 pm. Set them alternative homework that engages other sensory modalities and doesn't involve the computer:
- *Making a mind map.*
- *Reading from a book.*
- *Explaining the argument to someone else or practising the memory palace technique are all great alternatives to try.*
- *Make their bedroom completely dark or offer eye patches if the curtains and blinds don't do the trick.*
- *Charge phones in another room, use an alarm clock or invest in a dawn simulator for the wake-up call.*
- *Amber night lights plugged into the sockets will reassure those who are afraid of the dark without keeping their brains on high alert.*

Then in the morning, invite them to get outside, listen to a podcast or check their messages while walking around the block for 15 minutes - ideally more.

Finally, encourage them to get outside at lunchtime when their energy naturally falls - there's growing evidence that bright light is as good as a nap to energise and boost their mood.

They might feel groggy for the first couple of days but invite them to check in after a week: they might be surprised just how much brighter they feel.

(P.S. You might even be tempted to try some of these tips yourself!)"

Chapter 7 - Physical activity and the link with wellbeing

'Movement is medicine for the body and mind'
Dr. Kelly McGonigal, 2019

In this section, we will explore the role of physical activity in promoting children's mental wellbeing, how we can make learning this memorable for our young people and look at case studies from schools that have reaped the benefits of focusing on this area.

What is the link between wellbeing and exercise?
Doctor Catherine Wheatley
Exercise is one of the best medicines. Physical activity, and especially aerobic exercise, can successfully treat depression and improve self-esteem, which protects against the onset of mental health problems. More generally, it can improve feelings of wellbeing through a variety of biological, psychological, and environmental mechanisms.

Exercise that raises the breathing and heart rates increases the supply of oxygenated blood to the brain, stimulating the release of growth hormones and the creation of new brain cells and blood capillaries, and supporting new and healthy connections between neurons. Research has found that areas of the brain responsible for memory and attention can increase in volume after a programme of exercise, supporting learning and thinking skills and protecting brain health.

There is good evidence that exercising at moderate intensity is the best way to promote the release of endorphins, the body's natural pain and stress relievers and mood boosters, which are responsible for the 'runner's high'. Regular exercise can also promote stress resilience by optimising our physical responses to physical stressors, enabling us to better cope with the physical symptoms of psychological stress such as elevated heart rate and rapid breathing. The physical benefits of an active lifestyle, including cardiovascular fitness and weight management, can also be positive for self-esteem. Sleep may also be improved.

Learning new physical, social, and emotional skills through sport and physical activity, such as teamwork and perseverance, encourages feelings of mastery, which is also good for self-esteem. Being around other people who are part of your club or team, giving back to the community by coaching, refereeing, or encouraging friends to take part, and simply being outside in nature to for walking, cycling, or running, can all improve feelings of wellbeing.

The link between physical and mental wellbeing has been included in the statutory curriculum for Relationship, Sex and Health Education (RSHE) in English schools since September 2020.

The RSHE curriculum is compulsory for all state-funded primary schools and secondary schools in England, and it includes teaching on topics such as mental health, emotional wellbeing, and physical health.

The aim of including these topics in the curriculum is to help young people develop the knowledge, skills, and attitudes they need to maintain their physical and mental health, and to make informed choices about their wellbeing.

In researching this book I had the pleasure of interviewing one of the key decision makers, Josie Rayner-Wells, about the reasons why that decision was made. Following great work for the Norfolk Healthy Schools Team and the National Sex Education Bureau, Josie was working as a consultant for the Department of Education in remodelling the RSHE curriculum.

"By making the link between physical activity and mental wellbeing statutory in both primary and secondary RSHE curriculum, we are acknowledging the crucial role that Mental Health and Wellbeing plays in all aspects of a person's life. We know that Mental Health and Wellbeing is integral to reducing stigma and promoting wider health, and the evidence-based links to physical activity and brain chemicals make it even more imperative that we equip our young people with the tools to maintain a healthy body and mind." - Josie Rayner-Wells.

The Children & Social Work Act 2004 needed to be amended in 2017 to include a new duty on local authorities in England, to promote the educational achievement of looked after children and young people. As part of this duty, the amendment included a requirement to promote the physical and emotional wellbeing of these children, including the link between physical activity and mental wellbeing.

This means that local authorities are now responsible for ensuring that looked after children have access to opportunities to participate in physical activities and that they receive appropriate support to engage in these activities.

The amendment to the Children & Social Work Act 2004 reflects the growing recognition of the importance of promoting physical activity and mental wellbeing in children and young people, particularly those who may be more vulnerable or disadvantaged. By promoting physical activity and supporting mental wellbeing, it is hoped that looked after children will have a better chance of achieving their full potential and leading happy and healthy lives.

This is great news that the link has been recognised and that schools must deliver this education, but that creates new challenges (& opportunities) for teachers on the front line.

A new challenge

The Challenge for us as teachers is threefold:
1. How do we get young people to understand the key points in an engaging way so that they remember them now and long after they have left our care?
2. How do we motivate young people to develop physical activity habits without them feeling forced, judged, or getting bored?
3. How do we create opportunities and environments for children to get that regular physical activity?

We will explore the first 2 questions as the chapter continues and look at the 3rd question later on in the whole school impact chapter.

So, how do we get young people to understand the key points in an engaging way so that they remember the key points now and long after they have left our care?
Following whole school training on trauma informed practice in our recovery curriculum,

I was struck by the profound impact that deep breathing and resistance exercises can have on calming the amygdala and widening our window of tolerance. This inspired me to incorporate these techniques into our Physical Education recovery curriculum, using a memorable acronym to help children remember them long after they left school.

My goal was to create an acronym that was easy for everyone to remember, regardless of their age, abilities, or interests. I also wanted to involve as many activities as possible to give young people a range of options for promoting their mental wellbeing through physical activity. After much brainstorming and experimentation, I came up with the RISE acronym: Repeaters, Inclusive Teams, Stress Busters, and Energisers.
I will explore each category in more detail.

Repeaters

Repeaters are physical activities that are repeatable movements that trigger deep breathing, such as running, swimming, cycling, walking, and yoga. They help soothe the amygdala, which is responsible for our emotional response and whether we perceive that we are safe or in danger.

Practising these activities regularly can help children to feel calmer and more relaxed. It increases their "window of tolerance," which means it allows them to better manage their emotions and react more effectively in difficult situations by integrating the frontal lobe in their brain. Repeaters stabilise children's moods, helping them to feel more balanced emotionally and able to make more logical decisions.

Examples of repeaters activities include:
- **Running:** Simple, inexpensive, and effective way to boost mood, increase cardiovascular fitness, and reduce stress.
- **Swimming:** Provides a full-body workout and can be a great way to relieve stress, build endurance and improve flexibility.
- **Cycling:** A great way to get outside, boost mood, and improve cardiovascular fitness.
- **Walking:** A simple but effective way to boost mood and improve cardiovascular fitness, it also allows children to explore their environment and clear their minds.
- **Yoga:** Can be very beneficial for emotional wellbeing by providing a sense of relaxation and a way of dealing with stress.

This is by no means an exhaustive list, any activity that is repeatable, such as rowing, can be included.

Encourage children to try different repeater activities and find the ones that work best for them. By including repeater activities in their daily routine, children can improve their mental wellbeing and develop healthy habits that will benefit them in the long term.

Inclusive teams

There is a substantial body of research that suggests loneliness is strongly associated with poor mental wellbeing, including an increased risk of depression, anxiety, and other mental health problems. For example: A study by Cacioppo and colleagues (2006) found that loneliness was associated with increased activity in areas of the brain involved in the stress response, which can lead to negative emotions and poor mental health outcomes.

Creating a sense of belonging is essential for children's mental wellbeing because it helps them feel accepted, supported, and valued by the people around them. When children feel they belong, they are more likely to have positive self-esteem, feel safe and secure, and develop healthy relationships with others. Oxytocin is released and children feel loved.

Children who lack a sense of belonging may experience feelings of loneliness, isolation, and rejection, which can lead to anxiety, depression, and other mental health problems. They may also struggle with social skills and have difficulty forming meaningful connections with others.

On the other hand, when children feel a sense of belonging, they are more likely to participate in social activities, engage in positive behaviours, and feel motivated to learn and grow. They are also more likely to seek out help and support when they need it, which can be crucial for their mental health.

Inclusive teams, such as team sports, school productions, musical performances, chess clubs, or nature clubs, can provide children with that sense of belonging and social connection with their peers.

CHAPTER 7 - PHYSICAL ACTIVITY AND THE LINK WITH WELLBEING

Over the last 10 years or so, I have noticed, and many PE teachers have commented to me that it gets harder and harder to field school sports teams in line with the rise of social media and computer games.

As teachers we need to ensure that we help create inclusive cultures of all rather than just the star players as mattering matters to us all.

Examples of inclusive team activities include:
- **Any team sport:** Team sports like football, basketball, netball, and rugby can provide children with a sense of belonging and improve their physical and mental health.

Many schools offer a wide range of school sport fixtures so that their young people can benefit. Sprowston Academy and Bohunt Worthing are just 2 examples of hero PE departments up and down the country that create fantastic opportunities for their young people to develop their mental wellbeing through a comprehensive programme of fixtures.

James Panayi
Sprowston's Inspirational Head of PE and ex-Premier League footballer
"We have created a 3 tier system to try and engage as many students as possible. We want to give as many young people the social benefits of being part of a team and the pride of representing our school.

We have had more students play competitive football in the Autumn half term this year than ever before. This is often the first time they will be playing competitive sport. The third tier festivals have been great with a low stress format including self-refereeing and a reduced focus on the outcome.

It also provides a good opportunity for PE staff to mix, share experiences and network with teachers from other schools in a relaxed environment."

Back in spring, 2023, I was teaching a group of year eight girls who were beginner footballers, but also struggling with friendship issues amongst the class. There was significant social media usage amongst the group with some girls reporting being on their phone up to 11 hours a day. That is some effort when mobile phones are not permitted within the school during the school day.

Rather than follow a traditional skills base model of delivery that would have disengaged the girls, I used a sport education approach to reward students who helped create an inclusive environment for all to flourish.

As the lessons progressed I would add opportunities for the children to play fun games that would develop their skills such as queen of the ring to develop dribbling, but the main emphasis was helping the girls understand how football could develop their mental wellbeing and then being able to apply it.

I also partnered with Kate Reynolds at Belvedere Academy in Liverpool who applied inclusive teams in a brilliant way to their interform competitions to boost engagement.

Case Study
Belvedere Academy inclusive teams

The Belvedere Academy is an all-ability state funded girls' Academy secondary school in Liverpool and is part of the Girls' Day School Trust. Their brilliant Head of Physical Education, Kate Reynolds, talks us through their approach to inclusive teams:

'Like many schools, we run interform competitions for various different sports throughout the academic year. In the winter term this is usually netball and in the summer we do rounders. Historically, for netball, forms have selected the best 7 players to represent them and competed in a round robin. Forms are all mixed ability based on academic results, but naturally some forms have a larger number of students who have a greater sporting ability.

This year, after adopting the RISE Up principles within our lessons, we made some small tweaks which saw engagement rocket! Instead of the usual 7 students per form, we saw over 550 students from across years 7-11 take part. It was a fantastic week enjoyed by both staff and students.

Our intent was to promote our Interform netball competition as an Inclusive Team activity to try and increase our student engagement. We really wanted to make sure that the message of "it's the taking part that counts" really rang true with all pupils so that they felt that they belonged within our PE department and within our school.

Our Intended Learning Outcomes were:
- **Head:** To understand how to work together as a form to get the best out of each other's skills set, understanding how sport can be used as a social tool to increase mental wellbeing.
- **Heart:** To contribute to an enjoyable competition where everyone was included, and no-one felt left behind.
- **Hands:** To take part in the interform competition to the best of your ability.

We then focused on Implementation. In order to engage more students we dropped the idea of selecting the best 7 and told forms they could select as many students from their form as they liked, but everyone selected must play in at least two of the five fixtures they would play.

The emphasis was put onto the team captains (elected by the form) to decide who was playing in each fixture allowing a number of leaders to emerge. Forms were given time during PE lessons as well as the opportunity to come and practise their skills during our lunch time enrichment slots.

This meant that engagement in the netball enrichment increased too as forms took it upon themselves to try people in different positions to analyse their strengths and weaknesses and make informed decisions as to where each player would play, as they tried to predict who they would be marking in each fixture. Playing a round robin meant that each form would play against each other in a fair contest.

PE staff umpired and collected the scores, but the organisation of the teams was completely down to the students. This gave them a sense of ownership over their team and their competition.

In terms of impact, there was a friendly competitive buzz throughout school on the days running up to the event and the atmosphere on the week of the competitions was fantastic. Students created banners to show their form identity, created posters and wrote poems about the competition.

As this was an inclusive competition it captured students from across the whole school demographic; school team players, SEND students, EAL students, PP students, students whose attendance has been poor but who wanted to come to school to join in; everyone playing happily alongside each other, bonding over that sense of belonging to their form identity.

The competition also fell at the start of Ramadan and many of our Muslim students joined in too, some choosing to break their fast in order to compete effectively which is a very personal thing to do!

Giving pupils the option to take part or not and putting the emphasis on the development of life skills instead of simply playing to win meant that pupils felt psychologically safe when stepping up to play, knowing that they were in a fully supportive and inclusive environment. The team work, empathy, perseverance, and resilience on show was amazing to see.

We will be replicating the same set up again in the future when our rounders interform takes place in the summer. Already, students have asked if we can do more competitions of the same kind in dodgeball, football, bench ball and badminton; we will try and find time to do these too as we continue to use Inclusive teams and physical activity as a tool to drive up mental wellbeing within our school.'

Stress busters

Stress busters are physical activities that can relieve stress and tension in a safe and controlled way by releasing endorphins, a chemical that can make people feel good and reduce pain.

These activities can also help to increase children's confidence through the release of serotonin, a chemical that regulates mood and social behaviour. Engaging in stress busters can also improve self-esteem, reduce anxiety, and increase feelings of self-worth.

Examples of stress buster activities include:
- **Boxing:** Boxing can be a great way to relieve stress and tension by allowing children to physically express their emotions in a safe and controlled environment. I was initially reluctant to add a punching mannequin into the fitness suite, but some of the children kept asking, so I thought let's give it a try and see what happens. I was concerned that it may lead to fights in the school, but my fears were incorrect, and boxing training became a great addition as it gave children the chance to take out their stress and

frustration in a safe and controlled manner. It was great for engaging some students who were previously disengaged.
- **Weight training:** Weight training can be an effective way to relieve stress and tension, as well as build strength and self-esteem. We introduced a RISE Up club to give children the opportunity to push away their stress and frustration in a safe and controlled way. We deliberately cultivated a welcoming, inclusive environment for all and where our older students were encouraged to coach and support our younger students. Weight training became a great 3rd object to have deeper conversations with young people about their lives and how they were feeling whilst working out together. This approach was also extended to girls only clubs so we could help create psychological safety for as many young people as possible. This club became our second most popular club in total behind football and we would regularly have 30 children attend every lunchtime, leading to happier children and a calmer school in the afternoon.
- **Contact rugby:** Playing contact rugby allows children to expend energy and release pent-up emotions in a safe and controlled environment. With the current debate going on about safety in rugby, sometimes people are missing just what an inclusive sport it is. The beauty of rugby is that regardless of size and shape there is a position for everyone. Rugby has been a game changer for so many children I have taught in terms of helping young people find an outlet for their stress and anger and feel part of a welcoming team, often for the very first time in their life. Yes rugby is not for everyone, just like many other activities. However, if we give children the chance to choose then contact rugby can be great for some children's mental wellbeing.
- **Yoga:** By merging gentle physical movement, mindfulness, and controlled breathing, yoga provides a safe haven for introverts to unwind. Yoga becomes an emotional release, allowing introverts to channel inner tensions, anxieties, and pent-up thoughts within the confines of a peaceful practice.
- **Smashing a ball:** Activities like smashing a football, tennis ball, rounders or cricket ball can be a great way to relieve stress and tension and can be an outlet for children to release their emotions. Helping children release their anger and tension in a safe and controlled way is fantastic for supporting them to self-regulate and keep them within their window of tolerance.

When we push against a resistance we relieve stress and tension by releasing endorphins and increase our confidence through the release of serotonin. Smashing a football at a goal or a wall can help us achieve this.

Giving football crazy children an opportunity to have a kick around, take some shots and relieve stress in a PE lesson or as part of active play can be a great way to help young people self-regulate.

This method worked well one year in our school, where the year 11 group was particularly boy heavy. We used football as a vehicle to give the boys a regular break from revision, self-regulate and boost their motivation so they would give their all in their revision sessions. The outcomes were stunning with the boys performing half a grade higher than predicted on average in their GCSEs that summer.

Top tips:
- It's important to note that all these stress buster activities should be supervised and taught in a safe and controlled environment.
- Encourage your children to try different stress busters and find the ones that they prefer and work best for them.
- By including stress busters as part of their daily routine, children can learn to manage their stress and emotions in a healthy way.

Sammy's Story
My name is Sammy and I'm a 14-year-old boy. Growing up, I was often in trouble around school. I don't really know why, it just felt like something I couldn't control. My homelife wasn't particularly good either, which only added to the stress and frustration that I felt inside. It was like I had all this pent-up energy with no way to release it.

But then something happened that changed everything. When we went to high school, we were introduced to rugby. At first, I wasn't sure what to expect. I'd never played before, but I was eager to give it a try. We were taught how to tackle safely, and then we got to play a match.

From the very first moment, I loved it. It gave me such a buzz, being able to bundle each other, score tries, get all our stress out and not get in trouble. It was like the perfect outlet for all my pent-up energy. After playing rugby, I felt calmer and more relaxed. It really helped me keep out of trouble the rest of the day as I just felt calmer.

I started to get really into it, playing for the school and watching and learning more about rugby. I even joined my local club. At first, I was a bit nervous about joining, but everyone there was so welcoming. They looked out for me and made me feel like I belonged. Rugby has become my sport, and I can't imagine my life without it now.

Playing rugby has given me a sense of purpose and belonging that I never had before. It's given me an outlet for my energy, and a way to release all the stress and frustration that I feel inside. It's given me a community of people who care about me and support me. I never thought that a sport could have such an impact on my life, but it has.

Energisers

Energisers are physical activities that can boost energy levels by releasing dopamine and serotonin, chemicals that are associated with happiness and motivation.

Engaging in energising activities can make children feel happier, more motivated, and more confident. It can also increase their focus and productivity. These activities can provide children with a sense of accomplishment and satisfaction and can help them to improve their overall mood and energy levels.

Examples of Energiser activities include:
- **Circuit training:** Circuit training is a combination of cardio and strength training exercises that can boost energy levels and improve overall fitness.
- **Dance:** Dancing can be a great way to boost energy levels, improve coordination, and boost self-confidence.
- **High-Intensity Interval Training (HIIT) workouts:** HIIT is a type of workout that alternates short bursts of high-intensity activity with periods of rest. It can be an effective way to boost energy levels, increase cardiovascular fitness and burn calories.

I was speaking to a parent of a child who had enrolled in the Improtech Football Academy programme at his school. As part of the programme, each young person receives 10 hours of football coaching at school per week from an expert coach.

The parent said her son was incredibly happy each day and loved coming into school. This was a marked contrast to his primary school experience where every day was a challenge to get him out of the door and into school.

Mum said, 'Owen knows that he has got football every day to look forward to and the exercise energises him so that he feels calmer, happier, and more confident within his lessons in the wider school.'

Encourage children to try different Energiser activities and find the ones that work best for them.

By including Energiser activities in their daily routine, children can improve their mental wellbeing and develop healthy habits that will benefit them in the long term.

Danielle's story
Hey, my name's Danielle and I'm thirteen years old. Let me tell you about the power of the school dance show. The last couple of years have been a bit rubbish with Covid and missing out on lots of fun things.

A few months ago, we were offered the opportunity to dance in the Norwich School Sports Partnership dance show. I've always loved to dance, but I've never been taught to do it properly or perform in front of an audience. I was excited but also a bit nervous about the whole thing.

Our brilliant dance teacher Lisa trained us up. It was great to work with my friends, and we tried so hard. We were so motivated and engaged in it. Every time we practised, we got better and better. We had so much fun during rehearsals, and it felt great to be part of something special.

On the day of the show, we were all really nervous. We had practised so much, but we knew that anything could happen. We put on our costumes, did our hair and make-up, and went to the venue. When we stepped out onto the stage, the lights were bright, and the crowd was silent.

We started dancing, and I felt like I was in a dream. I couldn't believe we were doing it. It was like we were all in sync, moving as one. When the music stopped, we all held our breath. Then, suddenly, we got a huge round of applause from our friends and family. I can't describe how amazing it felt.

That show was a great experience for all of us. We learned that with practice and hard work, we could do anything we set our minds to. We also learned that we could count on each other and support each other no matter what. Now, I can't wait for next year's show. I know it's going to be even better, and I'm so excited to see what we can achieve as a team.

By incorporating the RISE acronym into our Physical Education & RSHE curriculum, we can provide children with a fun and engaging way to promote their mental wellbeing through physical activity. This can help to reduce the stigma around mental health and empower young people to take an active role in their own mental health and wellbeing.

How do we motivate young people to develop physical activity habits without them feeling forced, judged, or getting bored?

Film star Jonah Hill said in the documentary 'Stutz',
'When I was a kid, exercise and diet was framed to me as like, 'There's something wrong with how you look, But never once was exercise and diet propositioned to me in terms of mental health. I just wish that was presented to people differently."

Jonah Hill went on to share about how the shame he felt about being overweight—from within his family and from the world at large—often made him feel depressed, even when he became a Hollywood success.

"Having grown up overweight was something that sounds like not a big deal or like, 'Poor you,' or whatever—but for me personally, it intensely f—ked me up," Hill says.

As a teacher, it's important to understand the powerful impact exercise can have on children's mental health. There are so many forms of exercise that can benefit mental health, giving children a range of options to suit their individual needs.

One important step towards improving mental wellbeing is to aim for at least one physical activity each day. The more activities a child enjoys, the more likely their mental wellbeing will be in a good place.

Encourage children to try different activities within the different RISE categories, and to find the ones that work best for them. By understanding the many benefits that exercise can have on children's mental health, you can help to create an environment that encourages and supports physical activity.

This is so much easier to do for children who already love being active. The challenge becomes, how do we engage those children who are disengaged from Physical Education and activity due to previous bad experiences? The answer is to make young people feel as psychologically safe as possible.

A starting point could be to encourage your young people to dance to their favourite music in their bedroom or do some body weight exercises in their bedroom, like press ups, sit ups, squats, and lunges.

By taking away the audience, it takes away the threat of judgement and makes young people feel psychologically safer. The next step could be to go for a walk, jog, or bike ride with a friend, or do a fitness class online from the comfort of your lounge or go on a Geocaching adventure with a friend.

As their confidence develops they might join a gym or take an exercise class with a friend, join a sports team such as a netball or football team, or try a new activity such as joining a tennis club

It is not always easy to start being physically active if you lack confidence, so try to create a psychologically safe environment for your young people to take their first steps.

Case Study
Engaging disengaged students in PE using RISE activities
Intent

Post Covid, we had a group of year eight girls who were struggling with their mental health, friendships, and general confidence, and it was affecting their willingness to engage in their PE lessons.

Year 8 can be a tricky year anyway for some girls' engagement, as they go through puberty and start to recognise social pressures more and this was even more evident post lockdown.

We wanted this lesson to be the first step to re-engage the group in PE. We wanted to create a psychologically safe environment where the girls felt comfortable, and free to take part without feeling judged, under threat or worried about their performance. We also wanted to give our young people greater ownership over their PE lesson.

Learning objectives were as follows:
- **Head:** To understand the link between physical activity and mental wellbeing and to develop our self-kindness.
- **Hands:** To take part in a range of physical activities to boost mental wellbeing.
- **Heart:** To try our best and create a safe environment for everyone to thrive.

Implementation
The first thing we did was to meet and greet our young people in an ultra-positive way. We did this by using face, voice, and body to smile and welcome young people to the class. We high fived those students on entrance and made sure our voices were attuned and positive.

When introducing the lesson we stressed that the focus was purely on improving their mental wellbeing through being physically active rather than the girls being judged or assessed. We introduced the 4 RISE categories and how each category could benefit their mental wellbeing in a different way.

We gave students a range of physical activities from the RISE programme that we could offer in our sports hall and explained to the girls that we would create a carousel of activities that students could choose to take part in at their discretion.

After giving them a range of options, they voted for a circuit of skipping, a punchbag and small sided games of football and dodgeball.

We then explained how each activity would benefit their mental wellbeing. We encouraged the girls to demonstrate their leadership skills by creating their teams and making everyone feel welcome as and when they joined the activity. Skipping also enabled them to play skipping games they used to play in primary school to trigger their play system in a caring environment.

It was really important that we were as positive as possible with youngsters to create a classroom that was wrapped in care so that our children felt psychologically safe. As the girls took part in the activities that most appealed to them, we would go round and talk to them to show an interest in their lives and deepen the relationship. Investing in these relationships was critical if we were going to re-engage the group over the coming weeks and months.

Halfway through the lesson, we stopped the girls from their activities and did the self-kindness activity with them as explained in chapter 5 as we noticed an improved inner voice would help each of them.

The girls then returned to their preferred activity for the rest of the lesson. To exit the classroom we set the girls the 'exit ticket challenge' of telling us which 'RISE' Category of activity they had enjoyed the most, what specific activity they had completed and finally how the activity had improved their mental wellbeing.

We got some great responses from the girls showing they had taken a lot from the lesson. Keeley said 'My favourite activity was the stress buster through using the punchbag. It helped me get all my stress and frustration out and I feel a lot calmer now.'

Sarah said 'I preferred dodgeball which is an inclusive team game, I loved playing with my friends, and we had a lot of fun. It was nice to laugh with them and exercise together.'

Impact
The lesson proved to be a great first step in re-engaging the group within Physical Education. When analysing why the lesson was such a success, the girls gave us some brilliant feedback:

They really enjoyed the freedom to choose their activities, they loved the emphasis on prioritising relationships over performance and they thrived on the supportive, non-judgemental environment we created for them.

It gave us a blueprint on how to move forward with them so that they would love being physically active for life and understand how it can benefit their mental wellbeing.

In the weeks that followed, the girls would regularly ask for this style of lesson, so we incorporated more of this with additional self-care tools to help them improve their mental wellbeing and develop their engagement in Physical Education.

The role of physical activity in building confidence

Physical activity can play a crucial role in building confidence. The endorphins released during exercise can improve our mood and reduce feelings of stress and anxiety. Additionally, the sense of accomplishment that comes from pushing ourselves and achieving our fitness goals can also contribute to building confidence.

Exercises, such as weight training or circuit training can be fantastic for building our confidence. These types of exercises challenge our physical abilities and help us to develop strength and endurance. As we see ourselves getting stronger and achieving our fitness goals, our confidence in our own abilities increases.

We saw this in my school when I introduced the inclusive RISE Up fitness club, two lunchtimes a week, to give our children an opportunity to build their self-confidence through physical activity. Everyone in the school was welcome. I wanted to create a really welcoming atmosphere where no one felt judged and a culture where the youngsters coached each other and kept an eye out for each other to keep each other safe. I wanted to develop habits that they could then take out into the wider school and community and use long after they had left the school.

Charlie, a year 10 student takes up the story
"There was a group of boys, including me, who had lost interest in school and were struggling with our confidence following Covid. You could often found us hanging around on the streets, feeling a bit aimless and useless.

One day, the school decided to start a fitness Club. The club was open to all students, regardless of our backgrounds or abilities.

At first, I was a bit nervous to join the club. I didn't think I was good enough and didn't want to be judged by the others. But sir's encouragement and the promise of weight training equipment in the fitness suite eventually convinced me to give it a try.

I was surprised to find that I actually enjoyed the weight training exercises, even though It was tough. I wasn't competing against anyone else but myself, and I developed a sense of pride as I saw myself getting stronger and fitter.

As the weeks went by, I got more confident. I started to feel more in control of my body and my mind. I was also more motivated to attend school and to put my hand up more to answer questions.

I also started to make friends with other students. As my experience grew I was able to help show the younger students what to do. I was proud of my progress, and I was happy to show off my new muscles to my mates."

With time, numbers of students attending the club grew and grew so that it became our second most popular activity, behind football. We added girls only RISE Up club after school to create the most psychologically safe, least judgemental environment we could for our female students, and the fitness suite was open most lunchtimes to give our children the opportunity to build their confidence through exercise.

Combat sports such as boxing training or martial arts can also be great for developing confidence. These sports require discipline, focus, and determination, all of which can lead to increased self-esteem. Additionally, the physical and mental demands of these sports can help to build resilience and the ability to handle stress.

I was initially reluctant to add a punching mannequin into the fitness suite but some of the children kept asking for one, so I thought let's give it a try and see what happens. I was concerned that it may lead to fights in the school, but my fears were not correct at all, and boxing training became a great addition as it gave children the chance to take out their stress and frustration in a safe and controlled manner.

In conclusion, the RISE acronym is a simple and memorable way to incorporate techniques for promoting mental wellbeing through physical activity into our curriculum. By providing a range of activities that are inclusive, engaging, and effective, we can help children to develop positive habits for their mental and physical health that can last a lifetime.

Chapter summary
- Regular physical activity has been shown to have numerous benefits for mental health, including reducing symptoms of anxiety and depression, enhancing mood and self-esteem, and improving cognitive function.
- The RISE acronym is a simple but memorable way for teachers and children to remember 4 categories of physical activity that boost our mental wellbeing now and long after children have left our care.
- Repeaters are physical activities that are repeatable movements that trigger deep breathing, such as running, swimming, cycling, walking, and yoga, that can help soothe the amygdala, which is responsible for our emotional response and whether we perceive that we are safe or in danger.
- Inclusive teams are an important aspect of children's mental health, it's important to provide opportunities for children to be part of such groups and create a sense of belongingness, teamwork, and social connection among children.
- Stress busters are physical activities that can relieve stress and tension in a safe and controlled way by releasing endorphins.
- Energisers are physical activities that can boost energy levels by releasing dopamine and serotonin, chemicals that are associated with happiness and motivation.
- A number of young people struggle with low confidence when being physically active, so we need to find a way to make them feel psychologically safe to engage with physical activity.

Critical questions

1. Which physical activities help you most with your own mental wellbeing?

2. Do you explicitly teach the link between physical activity and mental wellbeing?

3. Can you provide opportunities for your young people to take part in a range of RISE activities to boost their mental wellbeing?

4. Are there any groups you teach that struggle to engage with physical activity? How could you reduce the threat level they feel within lessons?

Chapter references

- Cacioppo, J. T., Hawkley, L. C., Ernst, J. M., Burleson, M., Berntson, G. G., Nouriani, B., & Spiegel, D. (2006). Loneliness within a nomological net: An evolutionary perspective. Journal of Research in Personality, 40(6), 1054-1085.

Additional insights

Case Study
Charles Darwin Primary - Learning Happens From The Feet Up

Charles Darwin Primary School is based in the centre of Norwich and is part of the Inspiration Trust. It is one of the first primary schools I started working with as part of our collaboration with the brilliant team at Norwich School Sport Partnership.

In this case study, Charles Darwin's inspirational Head of PE, James Tuthill, talks us through their intent, implementation, and impact of the RISE Up programme in their setting.

Intent

'One of our targets for Physical Education, School Sport, Physical Activity (PESSPA) this year was to widen the scope for improving the wellbeing of our pupils. Following an introduction through our local Norwich School Sports Partnership I investigated the 'RISE Up' Early Intervention Mental Wellbeing programme.

We initially set out by completing the School Wellbeing Scorecard back in October 2022, achieving a score of 48%. This was useful as the suggestions offered gave us scope to enhance our school offer.

Our SEN and PE delivering staff completed the 'RISE Up' online teacher training and then set out our aim to provide the programme to our pupils.
Implementation:

Our next stage was to highlight appropriate pupils to access the programme. Through meeting the SENCo we noticed that we had a collection of young people, who have suffered childhood trauma and are less engaged in school and who were yet to receive support due to the strain of staffing.

We created a list of pupils who could then attend a purposeful active intervention to benefit their mental health and class engagement. They took part in two terms of intervention where the learning content of sessions around self-awareness, healthy habits, mental fitness and accessing the happiness chemicals were condensed to 15 minutes, to promote engagement followed by 30 minutes of active challenge through the RISE categories.

All of our pupils then accessed a Norwich School Sports Partnership event providing the pupils with an outlet for their positive relationship with physical activity and hosting a Day of Calm event with their staff which reinforced the importance of checking in on ourselves. We attended NSSP Pentathlon events and found they provided a perfect outlet of non-competitive active challenges for our young people who attended Bowling and Multi-Sport format events.

Impact
Following two terms of intervention, class teachers began to comment that they're seeing behavioural improvements which prompted measurement via the strengths and difficulties questionnaire (SDQ) comparison.

The SDQ questionnaire is a short behavioural screening questionnaire for children aged 3 to 16. The questionnaire is used to assess children's mental health and can be completed by children and young people themselves, by their parents or by their teachers.

Every single pupil involved in the 'RISE Up' intervention showed a marked improvement. Our SENCo highlighted that our 'RISE Up' programme had shown the most measurable impact of all interventions offered across the school with a string of noticeable positive impacts on previously concerning pupils.

These were some of the comments from our young people:
- "This is the best lesson ever" Year 5 pupil
- "My Ikigai involves people and food" Year 6 pupil
- In June 2023, I revisited the School Wellbeing Scorecard. Our comparative mark rose by 44% to 92% demonstrating how far we have come in improving the provision for the wellbeing of our young people.

TIME TO RISE UP

Pre Intervention:

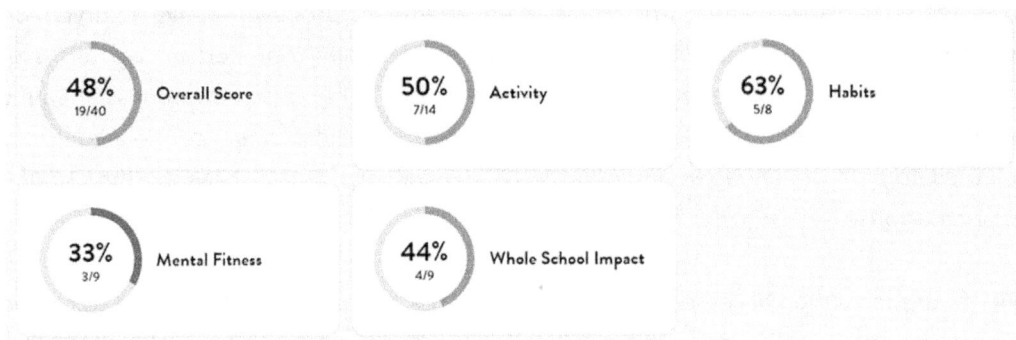

Post Intervention:

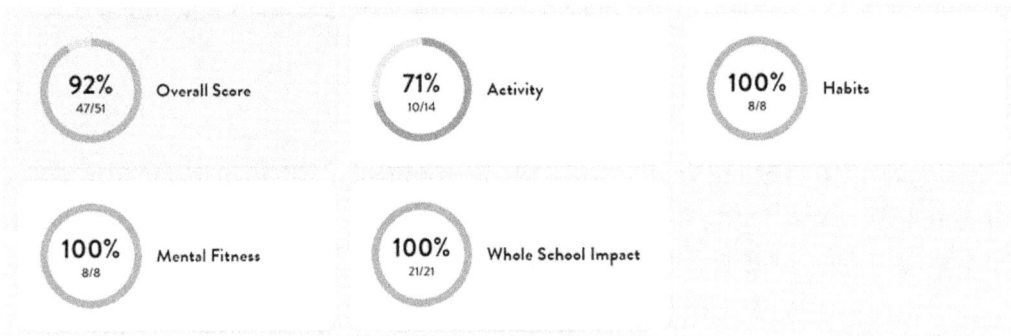

Moving forward

In the 2023/24 school year, we've planned to widen the impact of the 'RISE Up' content by attaching it to our 2 hours of PE across the school and continuing the Intervention group on a Monday morning to measure and contrast against attendance data.

Overall, the promotion of active learning and embracing Mike Kuczala's quote of "Learning happens from the feet up" has transformed our staff and pupils' outlook on learning, school, and their own lives.'

Chapter 8 - Getting your daily dose of happiness

"Happiness is not something ready-made. It comes from your own actions."
Dalai Lama XIV

Happiness is a state of mind that we all aspire to achieve. It is a feeling of contentment, satisfaction, and wellbeing that can uplift our spirits and make life worth living. But what causes happiness, and how can we cultivate it in our lives? The answer lies in the complex interplay of chemicals in our brain.

Studies have shown that happiness is not just a subjective experience, but a complex interplay of brain chemicals that create a state of wellbeing. In this chapter, we will delve into the ways in which we can harness the power of these happiness chemicals to improve our students' lives and our own.

Feeling frustrated

As a teacher, we have the privilege of working with young people and helping them navigate the challenges of growing up.

However, there have been times when I have felt frustrated and helpless in the face of their struggles. I would see young people who were feeling unloved, unmotivated, unconfident or in pain, and I would feel a deep sense of sadness and frustration that I didn't have any tools or strategies to help them feel a bit better. These young people needed something more, something that could help them develop resilience, feel loved, and be able to cope with the challenges they were facing.

It was then, that I started to research and educate myself on the different strategies and tools that could help these young people. Based on academic research, I created some lessons to help young people understand what the happiness chemicals are, how they help them and what activities they could take part in to trigger the release.

I saw how they were able to develop their confidence and motivation, stabilise their mood, and feel in less pain in the face of adversity. They were able to tap into their own inner strength and develop a sense of empowerment by taking action, which in turn helped them to lead happier, more fulfilling lives.

Feeling unmotivated

Dopamine is the chemical behind motivation and pleasure. It is a neurotransmitter, a chemical messenger in the brain that plays a critical role in our emotions, movements, and motivation. It's often referred to as the "feel-good" hormone, as it is released in response to pleasurable experiences and is associated with feelings of happiness, satisfaction, and reward.

Dopamine has many important functions in the brain and body. It helps regulate our moods and emotions, controls our movements, and plays a key role in our motivation and drive. When we engage in activities that trigger the release of dopamine, such as eating, or winning at a game, we experience a surge of pleasure and satisfaction. This reinforces the behaviour, making us more likely to repeat it in the future.

Dopamine is also involved in the brain's reward system, which encourages us to repeat behaviours that are beneficial for our survival and wellbeing. For example, when we eat a nutritious meal, our brain releases dopamine, which reinforces our behaviour and motivates us to seek out nutritious food in the future.

There are many activities that can trigger the release of dopamine in the brain. Some of the most common include:
1. **Exercise:** Regular exercise has been shown to increase the release of dopamine in the brain, which can improve mood and motivation.
2. **Eating:** Eating delicious food can release dopamine, which reinforces our behaviour and encourages us to seek out tasty food in the future.
3. **Social interaction:** Spending time with friends and loved ones can release dopamine, which reinforces social behaviour and helps us form strong relationships.

4. **Accomplishment:** Achieving a goal or accomplishment can trigger the release of dopamine, which reinforces our motivation and drive to succeed.
5. **Novelty and excitement:** Engaging in new and exciting activities can trigger the release of dopamine, which reinforces our behaviour and motivates us to seek out new experiences.

I created a self-care menu for young people to choose from to access Dopamine if they are feeling unmotivated. My top activities for helping children access Dopamine:
1. Complete an energiser workout
2. Do a self-care activity like painting your nails or having a relaxing bath.
3. Celebrate little wins like completing a to-do list
4. Complete a task like painting a picture or reading a book

While dopamine is essential for our wellbeing, excessive and prolonged exposure to it can have negative consequences, especially in children. One of the sources of excessive dopamine release is social media.

Social media platforms are designed to be addictive and trigger the release of dopamine in the brain through notifications, likes, and other forms of positive reinforcement. Children, who are still developing their brains and are more susceptible to addiction, are particularly vulnerable to the dangers of social media-induced dopamine. The overstimulation of dopamine in children can lead to an increased risk of depression, anxiety, and other mental health problems. It can also negatively impact attention span, memory, and overall cognitive development. As touched on earlier in chapter 6, we need to be so careful balancing our children's use of social media moving forward.

One of the other sources of excessive dopamine release is unhealthy food. Unhealthy foods, such as processed snacks, sugary drinks, and fast food, are high in fat, sugar, and salt. These ingredients trigger the release of dopamine in the brain and can lead to overeating and food addiction. Children, who are still developing their brains and taste preferences, are particularly vulnerable to the dangers of unhealthy food-induced dopamine.

Feeling unloved

Oxytocin is a hormone and neurotransmitter in the brain that plays a crucial role in social bonding, trust, and overall wellbeing. It is often referred to as the "love hormone" due to its ability to foster feelings of love, affection, and closeness in human relationships.

Oxytocin is released in response to a variety of positive social interactions and experiences, such as physical touch, intimacy, affection, and laughter. It also plays a role in maternal bonding and the birth process and is thought to contribute to the development of strong social bonds between mothers and their offspring.

Physical touch is one of the most effective ways to trigger the release of oxytocin. Hugs, handshakes, and other forms of physical affection can cause the hormone to be released, which in turn can help to strengthen bonds and reduce feelings of stress and anxiety. Engaging in physical activities, such as exercise and yoga, has also been shown to increase oxytocin levels.

In addition to its effects on social bonding, oxytocin has also been linked to a range of physical and mental health benefits. It has been shown to reduce anxiety and stress, alleviate pain, and improve sleep. Research has also suggested that it may play a role in reducing the risk of heart disease, enhancing the immune system, and improving overall cognitive function.

It is important to note that while oxytocin has many benefits, excessive or prolonged release of the hormone can have negative effects. For example, high levels of oxytocin can lead to increased feelings of anxiety and can have an adverse effect on the immune system.

Pets as a secret weapon

The bond between humans and their pets can have a significant impact on a child's overall wellbeing and happiness. One important hormone involved in this bond is oxytocin, it is released in response to positive social interactions and helps to create feelings of trust, affection, and security.

Studies have shown that spending time with pets, such as dogs or cats, can trigger the release of oxytocin in both humans and animals (Serrano, S.et al., 2017). For children, this can lead to increased feelings of comfort and attachment to their pet. This bond can be especially important for children who may be struggling with social or emotional issues, as pets can provide a non-judgemental source of comfort and support.

Playing with or petting a furry friend has been shown to increase oxytocin levels in both the pet and the human. Simple activities such as going for a walk with the family dog, cuddling with a cat, or playing with a pet can create positive social interactions that trigger the release of oxytocin.

Research has also found that children with pets exhibit lower levels of stress and anxiety and are better able to regulate their emotions (Stanton, A. & Levine, S. 2015). This is believed to be in part due to the release of oxytocin during positive interactions with their pet.

Having a pet can also provide children with a sense of responsibility and help to boost their self-esteem. Caring for a pet can teach children important life skills such as empathy, kindness, and patience.

I would often encourage interactions between children and their pets and stress the importance of taking them on walks. This increases the mental and physical health benefits, particularly for children who appeared unloved or struggled with feeling under threat and judged in PE so were not particularly physically active.

Therapy dogs are trained to provide emotional support and comfort to individuals who have experienced traumatic events. In recent years, dogs have been increasingly used in schools to support children who are struggling with emotional issues and behaviours that we find challenging. The idea behind using trauma dogs in schools is that the simple act of petting a dog or being near one can have a calming and therapeutic effect on students, leading to increased feelings of safety and wellbeing.

We were fortunate to have two therapy dogs at my school, Freddie & Bucky. They had a transformational impact on many of our young people, particularly those who were struggling the most. Richard is going to tell us what Freddie meant to him.

Richard's story
'Hi everyone, I'm Richard, I'm 15 and I want to share a story with you about a special dog that changed my life. His name was Freddie, and he was the therapy dog at my school.

I remember when I first saw him, I was a little nervous because I had never been around a big dog like him before. But, as soon as I stroked him, I felt this warm feeling in my chest, and I felt like we connected.

Every day, when I was feeling upset or just needed a break from class, I would go to see Freddie. He would calm me down just by being near me and I loved how he would wag his tail and give me lots of love. It was like he understood what I was going through.

One day, my teacher asked if I wanted to be responsible for taking care of Freddie before school. I was so excited and felt so honoured. I loved taking him for walks, playing with him and just spending time with him.

Having Freddie at school made such a big difference in my life. I felt like I had a friend who always had my back, no matter what. And I loved the responsibility of taking care of him. It made me feel important and like I was making a difference in someone else's life.

I will never forget Freddie and the impact he had on my life. I truly believe that every school should have a therapy dog like Freddie to help children feel loved and supported.'

By understanding the importance of oxytocin and encouraging activities that trigger its release, we can support children in developing strong emotional bonds, a positive self-image, and resilience in the face of challenges.

Top activities from my self-care menu for helping children who are feeling unloved include:
1. Play an inclusive team sport
2. Hug a family member
3. Listen to your favourite music which reminds you of happy times
4. Do something nice for someone else
5. Play with a pet such as a dog

Feeling moody

As teachers, we are often faced with the challenge of managing the moods of our teenage students. From stress and anxiety to irritability and frustration, teenagers can struggle with emotional regulation, leading to difficulties in the classroom.

But what if we could better understand the role that serotonin plays in promoting calm and regulating mood in our students? Serotonin is commonly referred to as the "feel-good hormone". It is believed to play a crucial role in regulating mood, appetite, and sleep. By understanding how this hormone functions and the activities that can trigger its release, we may be able to create a more positive and supportive learning environment for our students.

Serotonin is a type of chemical that acts as a neurotransmitter in the brain. When there is a sufficient amount of serotonin in the brain, it helps to promote feelings of happiness, satisfaction, and wellbeing. Low levels of serotonin, on the other hand, are linked to depression, anxiety, and other mood disorders.

There are several activities that can help boost serotonin levels, leading to improved mood and wellbeing. The first of these is exercise. Studies have shown that physical activity can increase the release of serotonin, making it an effective tool for improving mood (Harvard Health Publishing, n,d.). Light exposure, particularly sunlight, has also been linked to increased serotonin levels. This is why many people feel better during the summer months when there is more daylight.

Getting enough sleep is another important factor for boosting serotonin levels. Research has shown that sleep deprivation can decrease serotonin levels, making it more difficult to regulate mood (Psychology Today, 2021). Reducing stress is also key. Chronic stress has been linked to decreased serotonin levels, making it important to find healthy ways to manage stress in order to maintain good mental health.

Finally, diet plays an important role in regulating serotonin levels. Eating a healthy diet that is rich in tryptophan, an amino acid that is a key building block for serotonin, can help to increase serotonin levels.

Serotonin plays a vital role in children's health and wellbeing. By promoting a sense of calm, reducing stress and anxiety, and elevating mood, children who have balanced serotonin levels are more likely to be successful in their academic pursuits, as well as better equipped to handle the daily challenges of life.

We can play an important role in promoting healthy serotonin levels in children by incorporating activities and practices that boost serotonin, such as exercise, exposure to sunlight, healthy diets, and stress management techniques, into their daily routines. With a focus on promoting serotonin in children, schools can create a healthier, happier, and more productive learning environment for all students.

Top activities from my self-care menu for helping children who are feeling moody include:
1. Take part in a 'Repeater' exercise such as a run, swim, walk, yoga, or cycle
2. Meditate or complete some mindfulness activities
3. Get outside in the sunshine
4. Walk in nature

Feeling in pain

Endorphins are powerful neurotransmitters that play a crucial role in our overall wellbeing. They are often referred to as the body's natural painkillers and have a strong impact on our mood and emotions. Endorphins are released in response to various stimuli, including exercise, laughter, and even spicy foods.

Endorphins work by binding to specific receptors in the brain, blocking pain signals and reducing the sensation of pain. They also promote feelings of happiness, contentment, and even euphoria, making them an important part of our body's response to stress and pain.

One of the most well-known triggers of endorphin release is exercise. Physical activity, especially high-intensity workouts, has been shown to increase the release of endorphins, leading to a feeling of euphoria known as a "runner's high". Studies have shown that regular exercise can help to improve mood and reduce stress and anxiety (Harvard Health Publishing, 2021). In our recovery curriculum, circuit training played a major part to trigger the release of endorphins to boost the wellbeing of our young people.

Laughter is another powerful trigger for endorphin release. Research has shown that laughing triggers the release of endorphins, leading to a sense of calm and happiness (www.psychologytoday.com). This is why many people find humour to be an important tool for managing stress and anxiety. How can you find moments for you and your class to laugh together?

For our online lessons I would bring in my daughter's 'first joke book' and reel off the worst dad jokes to make our young people smile. My personal favourite was 'Why was the fish not very good at tennis? They didn't like to get too close to the net.' One year 9 student, Avi, soon started telling much funnier jokes to make his classmates laugh and it really deepened our relationship together and the class would look forward to his joke of the day at the start of each lesson.

Avi's story
"Yo, what's up guys? My name is Avi and I'm 14. So, during the lockdown, we had online classes and let me tell you, it was boring. But then, there was PE. Sir would tell the worst jokes ever, but somehow they would make us smile.

I started to get creative and came up with much funnier jokes. I'd share them during class, and it really lightened the mood. My mates were laughing and having a good time, and it made the classes so much more enjoyable. More and more of my classmates would login for our online lessons and look forward to the jokes section.

Classes can still be boring sometimes, but at least we have our jokes to keep us smiling and make the time go by faster. All you need is a good joke to bring a little joy into someone's day."

Finally, spicy foods are another trigger for endorphin release. Capsaicin, the compound responsible for the spiciness of chilli peppers, has been shown to stimulate the release of endorphins. Eating spicy foods can lead to feelings of euphoria and reduce pain and discomfort.

Top activities from my self-care menu for helping children who are feeling in-pain include:
1. Take part in a stress buster activity
2. Eat dark chocolate or chilli peppers
3. Laugh with friends
4. Watch a comedy

In conclusion, endorphins play an important role in our overall wellbeing and are involved in various physiological processes, including pain management and stress response. Engaging in activities that trigger endorphin release, such as exercise, laughter, and spicy foods, can help to improve mood and reduce stress and anxiety.

Self-care menu

Knowing that children will experience a variety of emotions throughout their daily lives and that those emotions have physical and chemical components, I created a self-care menu of activities tailored to the needs of a child.

When we recognise what we are struggling with the most, we can then plan a course of action to make us feel better. This menu was designed to help children identify how they were feeling and approach their emotional state from a positive perspective by being able to take some kind of action.

To begin, I outlined the four main happiness chemicals – dopamine, oxytocin, serotonin, and endorphins – and how these hormones impact our moods.

We would then complete a body scan. I would get the children to lie on their backs, close their eyes and take big, long deep breaths in for three seconds, hold it for four seconds, and then breathe out for five seconds. We would do a body scan where children would notice any physical sensations from their head down to their toes and then would focus on relaxing their whole bodies.

- I would then ask them to think about how they are feeling whether they are feeling motivated or unmotivated. I got them to give themselves a score out of 10, one for unmotivated 10 for super motivated. and ask them to remember their lowest score.
- They then gave themselves a score out of 10, whether they felt loved or unloved.
- I did the same for whether they felt confident or unconfident, and finally they did the same to whether they felt in pain or totally pain-free.
- I asked the students to remember their lowest score and we finished by having a stretch and slowly coming back up to return to their seat.

They would then select a task from the self-care menu to complete that evening for homework.

This activity was helpful for children to identify, not only what emotions they were struggling with, but also to take a proactive approach to self-care and practice. This empowered children to take control of their mental and emotional wellbeing by acknowledging how they were feeling in the present moment and taking responsibility for their emotions.

 **Try this:**

Self-care menu

Ask yourself:
- Are you feeling motivated or unmotivated?
- Are you feeling loved or unloved?
- Do you feel confident or not?
- Do you feel in pain?

Which one are you struggling with the most?
Select from the table below the aspect you struggled with the most, and then pick an activity from the menu to make you feel happier. Complete the activity you have chosen.

Unmotivated	Unloved	Low in confidence & mood	In pain
Complete an energiser workout	Do something nice for someone	Meditate or complete mindfulness activities	Laugh with friends
Do a self-care activity like painting your nails	Play a team sport	Take part in a 'Repeater' exercise such as a run, swim, walk, yoga, or cycle	Eat dark chocolate
Celebrate little wins like completing a to-do list	Listen to music		Watch a comedy
Complete a task like painting a picture or reading a book	Hug a family member	Get outside in the sunshine	Take part in a stress buster activity
Eat food (Preferably healthy treats)	Play with a pet such as a dog	Walk in nature	

Self-care Case Study

Eaton Hall Specialist Academy is one of the schools I worked in partnership with and is a residential special school catering for boys with social, emotional, and mental health difficulties with classes ranging from year 3 to year 11.

Their inspirational Head of PE, Mike Curry, will talk us through how they have used the self-care menu to support their most vulnerable children and their mental wellbeing.

'We found that accessing the 4 happiness chemicals really helped our staff to support our young people. Before we started our partnership, colleagues were aware that certain tools worked with certain children, but the programme clarified what worked well for specific situations.

We implemented the self-care menu in a wide range of areas in the school from one-to-one sessions with our young people, our care staff used the techniques in our residential settings, in PE & RSHE lessons, and in curriculum enhancement activities such as visiting Castle Acre to get our young people moving in nature. Immediately, the one-to-one sessions with our students became more structured as staff were able to use the knowledge gained to support our children.

Staff are now more confident in their delivery, which is relaxing children and helping to create a psychologically safe environment. A lot of relationships between staff and students have been strengthened as a result of our partnership. It has helped us improve our children's behaviour, their mental wellbeing, and supporting our most vulnerable children with SEND.'

Making learning stick for the long term

I wanted children to remember these concepts and strategies long after they had left my care, so I had to find a way to make the learning stick. I believe that we need to find ways to make it relevant, interesting, and enjoyable.

Using the DOSE acronym helped me do that. Dopamine, Oxytocin, Serotonin and Endorphins were quite challenging terminology for some of my young people but form a lovely acronym - DOSE! I would then talk to children about getting their daily DOSE of happiness and through repetition and referring to the self-care menu, learning began to stick.

I would use exit tickets so that children would have to tell me which happiness chemical they would trigger that night and what activity they were going to complete. It also gave me a lovely opportunity at the end of each lesson to connect, look deep into their eyes and give each young person some individual attention.

I wanted the young people to get hands-on and involve as many of their senses in their learning so that they were more likely to remember what they'd learned. The body scan was powerful for this as was getting the child to complete the actual activity. Sometimes, after doing it, we would take Freddie for a walk around the school field to trigger the release of oxytocin and make the children feel loved or create a space for children to complete their activity on the school field in the sunshine.

I would say next time you are feeling unloved or unmotivated try one of these activities. I'd try to find ways to make learning fun, such as telling stories about my friends that made me laugh, playing games or encouraging friendly competitions with classmates.

In conclusion, teaching children how to access the four happiness chemicals is a crucial aspect of their growth and development, not just for the present but for their future as well.

By equipping them with the tools to generate dopamine, serotonin, oxytocin, and endorphins, we are providing them with the ability to navigate life's challenges with resilience and positivity. This skill will not only benefit them in the short term but will also serve as a foundation for their long-term happiness and wellbeing.

As we come to the end of part 2, it is our responsibility to empower the next generation with the self-care tools they need to thrive. By prioritising their emotional health and wellbeing, we are setting them on a path towards a fulfilling and satisfying life.

Chapter summary
- There are 4 happiness chemicals: Dopamine, Oxytocin, Serotonin and Endorphins.
- Dopamine is great for motivation.
- Oxytocin makes us feel loved.
- Serotonin regulates our mood
- Endorphins mask our pain.
- Together they form the acronym Dose.
- Encourage your young people to get their daily DOSE of happiness.

Critical questions

1. Do you teach your children about the happiness chemicals?

2. What impact would the happiness chemicals have on your children and staff if we created environments at school that made it easier for us to access them?

Chapter references

- Serrano, S., Palma, A. I., & Sañudo, B. (2017). The Influence of Pets on Human Happiness and Health: A Review of the Recent Scientific Literature. International Journal of Environmental Research and Public Health, 14(8), 817. https://doi.org/10.3390/ijerph14080817
- Stanton, A. L., & Levine, S. (2015). Implementing a Pet Visitation Program to Increase Oxytocin and Reduce Cortisol. Journal of Child and Family Studies, 24(2), 355–365. https://doi.org/10.1007/s10826-014-9995-y
- Allen, K., Blascovich, J., Tomaka, J., & Kelsey, R. M. (1991). Presence of Human Friends and Pet Dogs as Moderators of Autonomic Responses to Stress in Women. Journal of Personality and Social Psychology, 61(4), 582–589. https://doi.org/10.1037/0022-3514.61.4.582
- Exercise and the brain: what happens to your brain when you exercise. (n.d.). Harvard Health Publishing. https://www.health.harvard.edu/mind-and-mood/exercise-and-the-brain-what-happens-to-your-brain-when-you-exercise
- Sleep Deprivation and Depression. (2021, November 3). Psychology Today. https://www.psychologytoday.com/us/blog/sleep-newzzz/202111/sleep-deprivation-and-depression
- Harvard Health Publishing (2021). *Endorphins: The brain's natural pain reliever.* [online] Harvard Health. Available at: https://www.health.harvard.edu/mind-and-mood/endorphins-the-brains-natural-pain-reliever.
- www.psychologytoday.com. (n.d.). The Science of Laughter | Psychology Today United Kingdom. [online] Available at: https://www.psychologytoday.com/gb/articles/200011/the-science-laughter [Accessed 30 Nov. 2022].

Part 3:
The Power of Relationships

Chapter 9 – The impact of trauma

"The quality of your life is the quality of your relationships"
Unknown source

In part 3 we are going to explore the importance of relationships and focus on trauma informed practice. Amongst one of the lowest points in my teaching career, I discovered an approach that was a gamechanger for both my young people I served and myself.

In this chapter we will explore the impact of Trauma on young people's mental wellbeing and progress in the classroom, and their life chances in the long term.

Schools falling apart post lockdown

As we returned to education in a post Covid world, there appeared a honeymoon moment post lockdowns where children and teachers were grateful to be back in their rightful place but as time progressed the impact of Covid started to take its toll.

Many senior leaders were exhausted from holding their schools together under extremely challenging situations. There was limited support from the central government, either communicating to them through the media, or releasing guidance documents late on a Sunday evening. They were then expected to answer questions and implement a few hours later. Many teachers were exhausted from the constant changes to school routines and trying to teach behind face masks. Lots of children didn't know whether they were coming or going with so many mixed messages over the Covid period and were starting to show signs of trauma. No one was getting out of this pandemic without being affected one way or the other.

Social media channels such as Twitter/X were awash with teachers across a whole range of subjects concerned about a decline in children's engagement and behaviour in the return to education.

Within my own school we were going through a period of significant change. We were changing trust, we had lost our inspirational headteacher, his brilliant deputy, and our chair of governors. Within 12 months, 50% of the staff body would change including over 90% of our senior leadership team. Any school in the country would struggle with that amount of transition, but our specific setting was reeling, and our children were understandably unsettled, with a vacuum in leadership in place at the time.

Within my own PE department, we had three members of the team off on long term maternity or paternity leave in the same year, and whilst personally I was delighted for my colleagues, it made maintaining standards incredibly difficult. Things were deteriorating fast with a new problem seemingly appearing on a daily basis. It felt like I was dealing with more problems in one year than I had in the previous 13 years combined of leading PE departments.

As leader of the department, I wanted to lead by example and maintain high standards and a sense of continuity for our young people, but the reality was very different. For the first time in my teaching career I was struggling to build the quality of the relationships I wanted with my young people, particularly with my most challenging children. By holding the line and following our school behavioural policies, all it was doing was pushing children further and further away from me.

I had never been more committed to transforming the chances of the young people I taught but I was doing the opposite. Children were questioning rules that I'd had in place for the previous 18 years with no challenge at all. For the first time in my teaching career I felt like I couldn't teach anymore, I felt a failure and a fraud, I wasn't supporting my colleagues, and I was miserable. My own personal wellbeing was a mess. It was utterly devastating seeing all the hard work we had put in over the previous 6 years, to transform the school for our young people and local community, just crash and burn around me and not be able to do anything about it.

Becoming trauma informed

I had to find a solution as my current strategies just weren't working in my setting anymore. I wanted to deepen my knowledge of trauma informed practice to help young people to recover from trauma and particularly the impact of Covid for the children I taught. So I enrolled onto the Diploma in Trauma and Mental Health-Informed Schools through Trauma Informed Schools UK.

Before starting to look at the strategies that made a difference, we need to develop an understanding of what trauma informed practice is and what we are trying to prevent.

So, what does being trauma aware mean? According to Lisa Cherry (2023), "A trauma aware approach seeks to provide an environment that means that when we are vulnerable, the environment we are in will aid recovery and healing and not add to it."

I had to ask myself some pretty challenging questions during the summer term, about whether I was aiding recovery or making things worse. My answers were not pretty. I was definitely retraumatising some of the children by not looking beyond the surface behaviour and that was incredibly difficult to face up to, but that was the reality and I had to own that to move forward.

What does being trauma informed mean?
According to the Serious Mental Illness adviser (2020), being trauma-informed means we recognise 3 pillars to it:

1. **Recognise** the prevalence of adverse childhood experiences (ACEs) / trauma among all people.
2. Recognise that many behaviours and symptoms are the **Result** of traumatic experiences.
3. Recognise that being treated with **Respect** and kindness – and being empowered with choices – are key in helping people recover from traumatic experiences.

Figure 11:

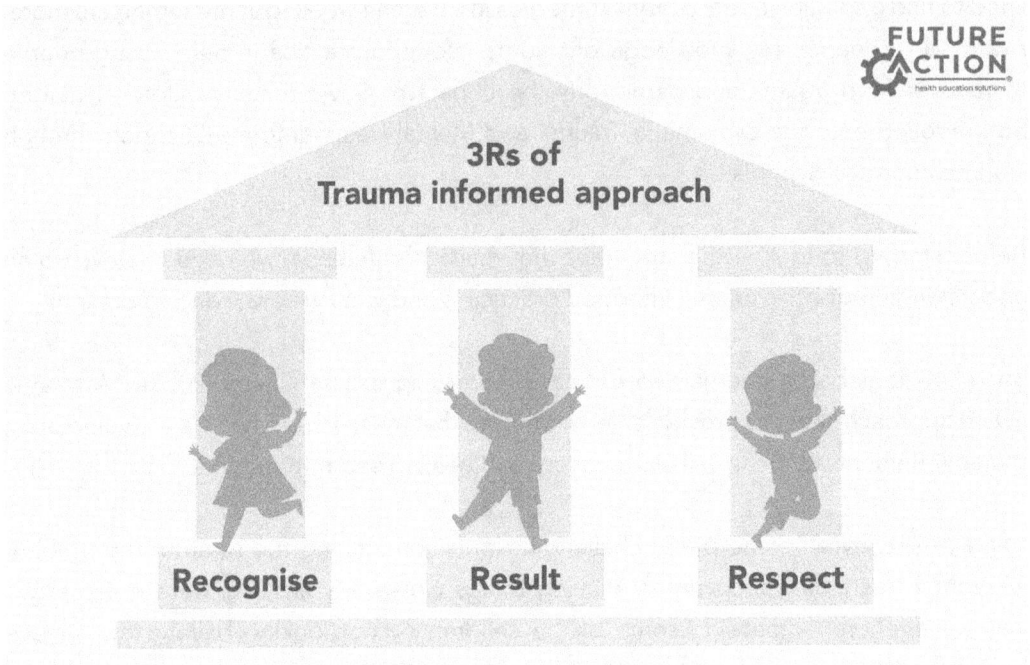

Consider this...

On a scale of 1-10 (1 being strongly disagree, 10 being strongly agree), how much do you agree with number 2 - We recognise that many behaviours and symptoms are the result of traumatic experiences?

What are adverse childhood experiences (ACEs)?

Trauma occurs when children are exposed to events or situations that overwhelm their ability to cope with what they have just experienced.

Figure 12:

Adverse childhood experiences

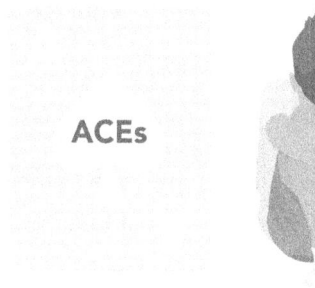

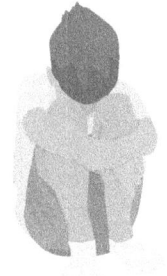

Trauma occurs when children are exposed to events or situations that overwhelm their ability to cope with what they have just experienced.

These can range from Big 'T' Traumas such as:
- Child physical abuse
- Child sexual abuse
- Child emotional abuse
- Emotional neglect
- Physical neglect
- Mentally ill person in the home
- Drug addicted or alcoholic family member
- Witnessing domestic violence
- Loss of a parent to death or abandonment by parental divorce
- Incarceration of family member

To small 'T' traumas such as:
- Moving house
- Birth of a new sibling
- Failing at an exam
- Friendship issues
- Illness/injury
- Loss of opportunity

The key thing to remember is that all of us process trauma differently so what might have a significant impact on one person may not have such an impact on another.

Numerous ACE studies have shown that about 1 in 2 of us have experienced at least 1 adverse childhood experience. Just think about that - about half of every class you teach have experienced at least 1 adverse childhood experience. If you throw in the impact of Covid and the loss experienced there then the actual reality is a lot higher.

One thing that startled me as I completed the trauma informed diploma was the damage caused by parental separation, which was frequently impacting young people, as much as losing a parent.

We had a child join our school from Ukraine who had to leave their country due to the war with Russia. Can you imagine the loss of friends, family, your home and what that must be like to deal with as a teenager? On the surface it looked like they were dealing with the situation incredibly well, but we do need to be mindful of what these young people are going through and how we can support them effectively. We also have Russian children in our schools, and we need to be mindful about how they are being affected by the narrative in the media.

In a post Covid education world in my setting, our children were struggling with intergenerational trauma, the impact of Covid, school trauma through the school being dysfunctional at this point and any other traumas they had experienced on top of this. It was a potent mix which created some incredibly challenging situations and behaviours as children struggled to cope with what life was throwing at them.

In conversations with some overseas colleagues in International Schools at this time, it was apparent that some of their children were struggling with affluent neglect. It was not uncommon for children to be stuck in different countries to their parents and/or being stuck in front of a computer all day with little face to face human interaction and emotional support.

What is affluent neglect?

The term "affluent neglect" is often used to describe a situation where wealthy or affluent parents fail to provide their children with emotional support, guidance, and attention, despite providing them with material comforts and financial security.

Affluent neglect can manifest in different ways, such as parents being too busy with their careers or social activities to spend quality time with their children, delegating child-rearing responsibilities to nannies or other caretakers, or prioritising material possessions over the emotional needs of their children.

Affluent neglect can be confusing and damaging for children because it sends mixed messages about what is truly important in life. On one hand, children may be provided with material comforts and financial security, which can create the impression that their parents care for them and want to provide for their needs. However, at the same time, these children may be lacking in emotional support, guidance, and attention from their parents, which can create feelings of loneliness, resentment, guilt, grief, and low self-esteem.

As teachers, it's important for us to be aware of the potential impact of all forms of neglect on children's mental wellbeing. By working together as a community, we can help to ensure that all children, regardless of their socio-economic background, have the emotional support they need to thrive and succeed in life.

Toxic stress

So what does happen to children when they struggle to cope with what life has thrown at them? When our body perceives that we are in danger it releases cortisol and adrenaline to keep us safe. These chemicals are great, for example, if we are crossing the road and we see a lorry flying towards us and they help us get out of the way. However, prolonged exposure can lead to physical illness, mental illness, and early death.

Figure 13:

Toxic Stress

Our body releases cortisol and adrenaline when it feels in danger.

Prolonged exposure can lead to physical illness, mental illness and early death.

The ACEs Study

The Adverse Childhood Experiences (ACE) studies are a series of ground-breaking investigations that have explored the relationship between childhood trauma and health outcomes later in life. The first ACE study was conducted in 1998 by Dr. Vincent Felitti and Dr. Robert Anda from the Centers for Disease Control and Prevention (CDC), along with other collaborators. The study involved over 17,000 participants from the Kaiser Permanente health maintenance organisation in San Diego, California.

The ACE study was a significant departure from traditional medical research, which had largely focused on individual risk factors for health outcomes. Instead, the ACE study looked at the impact of childhood experiences, specifically the presence of abuse, neglect, and household dysfunction, on health outcomes later in life. The study found that individuals who had experienced ACEs had a significantly higher risk of negative health outcomes, including mental health problems, substance abuse, chronic disease, and early mortality.

Following the success of the original ACE study, a number of follow-up studies were conducted to expand upon the findings. One such study was the ACE-II study, which was conducted between 2004 and 2005 and included a new sample of participants from five states across the U.S. The study aimed to replicate the original ACE study findings and expand upon them by exploring additional health outcomes.

Another study that built on the original ACE study was the "Clarifying the ACEs" study, which was conducted in 2013. This study aimed to clarify the definitions and categories of ACEs used in the original study. The researchers found that certain types of childhood experiences, such as emotional abuse and neglect, had a greater impact on health outcomes than others.

There have been several studies completed in the UK that have explored the impact of adverse childhood experiences (ACEs) on health and wellbeing.

One of the most notable studies in the UK is the "Scottish Adverse Childhood Experiences (ACE) Study", which was conducted in 2015. This study surveyed over 8,000 adults in Scotland and found that ACEs were common, with 49% of participants reporting at least one ACE. The study also found a strong link between ACEs and poor health outcomes, including mental health problems, substance abuse, and chronic disease.

Another study in the UK is the "Welsh ACE Study", which was conducted in 2018. This study surveyed over 2,000 adults in Wales and found that 44% of participants had experienced at least one ACE. The study found that ACEs were linked to a range of negative outcomes, including poor mental health, risky health behaviours, and lower educational attainment.

In addition, there have been a number of smaller studies conducted in the UK that have explored the impact of ACEs on specific populations or health outcomes. Overall, these studies suggest that ACEs are a significant public health issue in the UK and highlight the need for early intervention and prevention efforts to mitigate the impact of childhood trauma on health and wellbeing.

The ACE studies have also explored the potential intergenerational impact of childhood trauma. The "Intergenerational Impact of ACEs" study, conducted in 2019, found that parents who had experienced ACEs were more likely to have children who also experienced ACEs, highlighting the need for early intervention and prevention efforts.

Overall, the ACE studies have had a significant impact on our understanding of the impact of childhood experiences on health and wellbeing. They have highlighted the importance of early intervention and prevention efforts to address childhood trauma and promote resilience in individuals who have experienced ACEs.

The ACE pathway

The Adverse Childhood Experiences (ACE) pathway is a theoretical framework that explains how childhood trauma can lead to negative health outcomes later in life. The ACE pathway begins with conception and encompasses the prenatal period, childhood, and adulthood. It includes multiple factors that interact and impact health outcomes, including genetics, epigenetics, environmental exposures, and social determinants of health.

Figure 14:

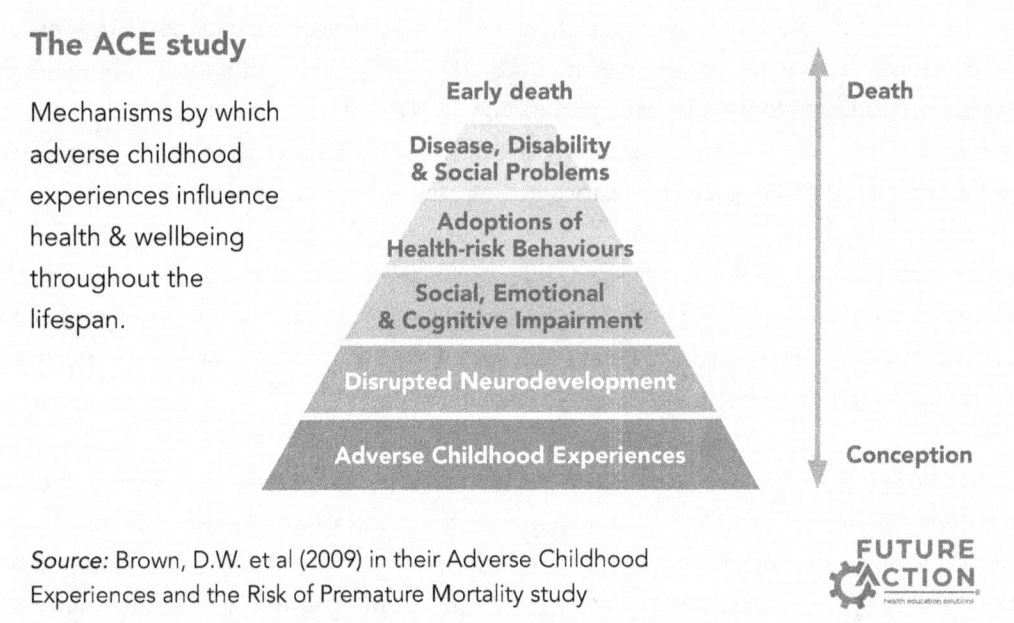

Source: Brown, D.W. et al (2009) in their Adverse Childhood Experiences and the Risk of Premature Mortality study

During the prenatal period, exposure to adverse experiences such as maternal stress, substance abuse, and malnutrition can impact foetal development and increase the risk of negative health outcomes later in life. For example, maternal stress during pregnancy has been linked to a higher risk of behavioural problems, anxiety, and depression in children.

In childhood, exposure to ACEs such as abuse, neglect, and household dysfunction can impact physical and emotional development and increase the risk of negative health outcomes later in life. ACEs can trigger the body's stress response system, leading to chronic stress and inflammation, which can damage the body's systems and increase the risk of chronic disease. Childhood trauma has been linked to a higher risk of mental health problems, substance abuse, chronic disease, and early mortality.

In adulthood, the impact of ACEs can continue to impact health outcomes. Adults who have experienced childhood trauma may be at higher risk of negative health behaviours, such as smoking, substance abuse, and unhealthy eating habits, which can increase the risk of chronic disease and early mortality.

The ACE pathway also includes the impact of social determinants of health, such as poverty, racism, and social inequality, which can exacerbate the impact of ACEs and increase the risk of negative health outcomes. For example, individuals who have experienced childhood trauma and live in poverty may have limited access to healthcare, healthy food, and safe living conditions, which can increase the risk of chronic disease and early mortality.

Overall, the ACE pathway highlights the complex and multifaceted nature of childhood trauma and its impact on health outcomes later in life. By understanding the ACE pathway, we can better understand the importance of early intervention and prevention efforts to address childhood trauma and promote resilience in individuals who have experienced ACEs.

What were the ACE questions?

In the Original ACE study, participants were asked whether they experienced the following before the age of 18:

Personal:
- Emotional abuse - humiliated/sworn at/put down/insulted.
- Emotional neglect - feeling unspecial/not important/not loved/not supported.
- Physical abuse - push/grab/slap/throw things at you.
- Sexual abuse.

Related to other family members:
- A family member suffering from depression or mental illness.
- Loss of a parent or parental separation/divorce.
- A family member being addicted to drugs or alcohol.
- Witnessing domestic violence.
- A family member in jail.

More recent ACE studies ask more questions.

How does the ACE scoring system work?

Each type of trauma counts as one 'ACE'. The study found that as the number of ACEs increase so does the likelihood of the child suffering from:

Learning difficulties, poor educational attainment, low attendance, exhibiting violent behaviour or being given a diagnosis of ADHD.

In 2015, a study by Fuller-Thomson and Lewis, of 700 8 year olds found that if a child had 3ACEs or more they were:
- 3 times as likely to experience academic failure
- 5 times as likely to have attendance problems
- 6 times as likely to have behavioural problems

From children that had 4ACEs or more, over 50 of them had learning problems. When we compare a child with 4ACEs or more to a child with no ACEs, then they are 32 times more likely to have behavioural problems.

Once we have detected threat, we are hardwired to perceive more threat and this can lead to a downward cycle of mistrust and poor behaviour, between child and teacher, unless steps are taken to rectify and improve the relationship.

What about the impact of Adverse Childhood Experiences in schools?

Adverse Childhood Experiences (ACEs) can have a significant impact on children's mental health and academic performance in a school setting. Here is some data and sources that demonstrate the impact of ACEs on children in a school setting:

- A study of over 8,000 adults in Scotland found that individuals who experienced four or more ACEs were nearly three times more likely to have poor mental health in adulthood (Bellis et al., 2014).
- A study of over 200,000 students in California found that students who experienced ACEs had lower academic performance, attendance, and graduation rates compared to students who did not experience ACEs (Murphy et al., 2014).

- A study of over 1,000 children in the U.S. found that those who had experienced ACEs had a significantly higher risk of being diagnosed with a mental health disorder (Flaherty et al., 2013).

As teachers, it is important we are aware of the impact of ACEs on children's mental health and wellbeing.

Understanding learned helplessness and its impact on children

Award-winning author Dr. Mine Conkbayir (2022) highlights that childhood trauma often leads to a state of learned helplessness in survivors. This psychological phenomenon manifests through various characteristics that can significantly affect an individual's mindset and behaviour.

Figure 15:

Learned Helplessness

Childhood trauma typically gives rise in survivors to:

- Feeling useless
- Wondering what's the point
- No one cares
- Low motivation
- Low self-confidence
- Low / no expectations of success
- Difficulty with persisting
- Not asking for help
- Ascribing a lack of success to a lack of ability
- Ascribing success to factors beyond their control, such as luck

© Dr Mine Conkbayir

Some common characteristics of learned helplessness include feelings of uselessness, questioning the purpose of actions, a belief that no one cares, low motivation, diminished self-confidence, having low or no expectations of success, difficulty with persistence, reluctance to ask for help, attributing lack of success to personal inability, and attributing success to external factors like luck.

You may have encountered or observed similar behaviours in children and wondered why some of them appear disengaged or unmotivated. Understanding learned helplessness is crucial to avoid misjudgement and labelling.

Children who have experienced an abusive childhood with limited control or escape options suffer profound consequences. Their healthy brain development and functioning are impaired, which significantly impacts self-regulation, behaviour, and learning processes. The effects of learned helplessness can be pervasive and hinder a child's overall wellbeing and academic progress.

By familiarising ourselves with the concept of learned helplessness and recognising its potential signs, we can provide a more empathetic and supportive environment for children who have experienced trauma. Through understanding and appropriate interventions, we can help them regain a sense of agency, rebuild their self-confidence, and foster their resilience.

Consider this...

Assessing your school's position on the Trauma Spectrum

As teachers, it is essential to evaluate and reflect on our school's approach to trauma and its impact on students. Jennifer L. Walton-Fisette, a professor of Physical Education and Sport Pedagogy at Kent State University, refers to Souers and Hall's (2019) "Spectrum of Trauma Savvy Practices" as a tool for educators to identify where they currently stand on the trauma spectrum based on their beliefs, philosophies, and teaching practices.

Take a moment to consider where your school falls on the Trauma Spectrum by ranking your school within the following categories:

1. Trauma-inducing
This describes a setting that not only lacks safety but actively creates an unsafe environment for both students and adults. In this category, practices and policies may unknowingly contribute to re-traumatisation or disregard the impact of trauma.

2. Trauma-indifferent
This category represents a setting that does not take childhood trauma into consideration when developing policies and practices. The school may lack awareness or understanding of the effects of trauma on students and may not prioritise trauma-informed approaches.

3. Trauma-informed
This category signifies a setting where stakeholders have gained knowledge about childhood trauma and are familiar with related strategies. The school acknowledges the impact of trauma and works towards implementing practices that promote safety, understanding, and support for students.

> **4. Trauma-invested**
> This category reflects a setting where stakeholders actively apply their knowledge and work collaboratively to enhance safety and support across the board. The school community has made a conscious commitment to trauma-informed practices and consistently integrates them into their policies, curriculum, and interactions.
>
> Now, take some time to reflect on your own school's practices and beliefs. Rank where you believe your school currently stands on the trauma spectrum.
>
> Engaging in this activity will allow you to gain insight into your school's current position and serve as a starting point for further discussions and actions to promote trauma-informed practices.
>
> Remember, this is an opportunity for growth and improvement as you strive to create a safe, supportive, and inclusive environment for all students.

By prioritising trauma-informed practices and addressing the underlying issues that contribute to learned helplessness, we can empower children to overcome adversity and cultivate a positive educational experience that promotes their overall growth and development.

Overall, these studies demonstrate the impact of ACEs on children's mental health and academic performance in a school setting.

I hope this data makes you stop and reflect on what you and your school are doing to support your young people. A combination of this data, and what I was witnessing in my own school meant that there was no turning back for me, my old approach had to go.

Chapter summary

- In the aftermath of lockdowns, schools struggled massively with attendance, behaviour, engagement, and wellbeing of young people.
- A trauma aware approach seeks to provide an environment that means that when we are vulnerable, the environment we are in will aid recovery and healing and not add to it.
- Trauma informed means recognising: the prevalence of adverse childhood experiences (ACEs) / trauma among all people; that many behaviours and symptoms are the result of traumatic experiences; that being treated with respect and kindness – and being empowered with choices – are key in helping people recover from traumatic experiences.
- Trauma occurs when children are exposed to events or situations that overwhelm their ability to cope with what they have just experienced.
- Trauma can be caused by a wide range of factors both big and small. Each individual processes trauma differently.
- Research completed by Brown, D.W. et al (2009) in their Adverse Childhood Experiences and the Risk of Premature Mortality study found that ACEs are a leading determinant of the most common forms of physical illness such as cancer, diabetes and heart attacks, mental illness such as depression and anxiety, and early death in the western world.
- As the number of ACEs increase, so does the chance of your young people struggling with disrupted neurodevelopment impairing their social, emotional, and cognitive functions. This manifests itself in learning difficulties, weak attainment, low attendance, violent behaviour, being given a diagnosis of ADHD and being disengaged.

Critical questions

1. Does any of the data from the ACE Studies surprise you?

2. What are your thoughts on the ACE pathway from conception to early death?

3. Do you recognise any of your young people in your school on that pathway?

4. What did you notice about behaviour and engagement in the years after lockdown in your setting?

5. Does your school create an environment that supports healing or hinders it and retraumatises children?

Chapter references

- Cherry, L. (2023, July 28). Being Trauma Aware. [Blog post]. Retrieved from https://www.lisacherry.co.uk/being-trauma-aware/
- SMI Adviser (2020). What Does It Mean to Be Trauma-Informed? SMI Adviser. https://smiadviser.org/knowledge_post/what-does-it-mean-to-be-trauma-informed#:~:text=Being%20Trauma%2Dinformed%20means%20to,the%20result%20of%20traumatic%20experiences
- Felitti, V. J., Anda, R. F., Nordenberg, D., Williamson, D. F., Spitz, A. M., Edwards, V., ... & Marks, J. S. (1998). Relationship of childhood abuse and household dysfunction to many of the leading causes of death in adults: The Adverse Childhood Experiences (ACE) study. American Journal of Preventive Medicine, 14(4), 245-258. https://doi.org/10.1016/S0749-3797(98)00017-8
- Brown, D.W., Anda, R.F., Tiemeier,H., Felitti,V., Edwards, V..J., Croft, J.B., and Giles, W.H. (2009) Adverse Childhood Experiences and the Risk of Premature Mortality. AM J Prev Med 37
- Bellis, M. A., Hughes, K., Leckenby, N., Perkins, C., & Lowey, H. (2014). National household survey of adverse childhood experiences and their relationship with resilience to health-harming behaviours in England. BMC Medicine, 12(1), 72.
- Bellis, M. A., Lowey, H., Leckenby, N., Hughes, K., & Harrison, D. (2019). Adverse childhood experiences: retrospective study to determine their impact on adult health behaviours and health outcomes in a UK population. Journal of Public Health, 41(3), e243-e250. (Scotland)

- Brown, D.W., Anda, R.F., Tiemeier,H., Felitti,V., Edwards, V..J., Croft, J.B., and Giles, W.H. (2009) Adverse Childhood Experiences and the Risk of Premature Mortality. AM J Prev Med 37, 389-396
- Fuller-Thomson, E and Lewis D (2015) The relationship between early adversities and attention deficit/hyperactivity disorder, Child Abuse & Neglect, Volume 47 Sept 2015 Pages 94-101
- Flaherty, E. G., Thompson, R., Dubowitz, H., Harvey, E. M., English, D. J., Proctor, L. J., ... & Runyan, D. K. (2013). Adverse childhood experiences and child health in early adolescence. JAMA Pediatrics, 167(7), 614-621. https://doi.org/10.1001/jamapediatrics.2013.22
- Murphy, S. A., Johnson, R. E., Lohan, E. M., & Lohrbach, S. (2014). The association between adverse childhood experiences and absenteeism among an urban population of middle and high school students in California. Child Abuse & Neglect, 38(10), 1638-1643. https://doi.org/10.1016/j.chiabu.2014.03.017
- Conkbayir, M. (2022). The Neuroscience of the Developing Child. Taylor & Francis.
- Walton-Fisette, J. L. (2020). Considering trauma-savvy practices in school health and physical education. Journal of School Health, 91(9), 10.

Chapter 10 – Creating psychological safety

"One feels safe in the midst of danger, when one has a sense of trust."
Lao Tzu

A story of hope

The Adverse Childhood Experiences (ACEs) studies have shown that individuals who experience ACEs are at a higher risk for negative health outcomes later in life. However, it is important to note that not all individuals who experience ACEs develop negative health outcomes. Research shows that a range of protective factors before the age of 18, can help interrupt the cycle from childhood adversity to early death. (Felitti et al 1998)

The studies identified a number of protective factors that can mitigate the negative effects of ACEs, such as supportive relationships with caregivers or other adults, positive coping strategies, and access to mental health services.

While the ACE studies have demonstrated a clear link between childhood trauma and negative health outcomes, the presence of protective factors and the individual's ability to cope with adversity can play a significant role in determining their overall health outcomes.

Interventions by **emotionally available adults** before the age of 18, can interrupt the trajectory from childhood adversity to challenging behaviour, learning difficulties, long term mental, physical and societal ill-health.

Under 18s can recover from trauma if they are helped to make sense of their story by an emotionally available adult.

Professor Dan Hughes and the 4Cs

Dan Hughes is a clinical psychologist and author who specialises in the treatment of children who have experienced trauma and attachment difficulties. He has developed a therapeutic model called Dyadic Developmental Psychotherapy (DDP), which emphasises the importance of creating a secure attachment between children and their caregivers as a means of healing from trauma.

As part of his approach, Hughes (2011) has identified four key components, which he calls the "4Cs," that are essential for children to make sense of their story to aid recovery from trauma. A child's story needs to be **Coherent, Consistent, Comprehensive and Congruent**.

Young people need to make sense of their story to aid recovery from childhood trauma for several important reasons:

1. **Integration of experiences:** Childhood trauma can disrupt a young person's sense of self and their understanding of the world. Making sense of their story involves integrating fragmented or confusing experiences into a coherent narrative. It allows them to understand how their past experiences have shaped their present emotions, thoughts, and behaviours.

2. **Empowerment and agency:** By making sense of their story, young people can gain a sense of control and agency over their own lives. It helps them recognise that they are not defined solely by their traumatic experiences and that they have the power to shape their future. Understanding their story can empower them to make positive choices, set goals, and overcome challenges.

3. **Emotional regulation:** Childhood trauma often leaves young people with unresolved emotions and intense reactions triggered by reminders or similar situations. Making sense of their story enables them to identify and understand the emotional responses associated with their trauma. It provides an opportunity to develop healthy coping mechanisms, regulate emotions, and manage stress more effectively.

4. **Meaning-making and closure:** Understanding their story helps young people find meaning and purpose in their experiences. It allows them to explore questions like "Why did this happen to me?" and "What can I learn from this?" Making sense of their trauma can lead to a sense of closure and provide a framework for moving forward in their healing journey.

5. **Self-Compassion and Acceptance:** Trauma can often lead to feelings of shame, self-blame, or a distorted self-image. Making sense of their story involves developing self-compassion and accepting themselves as survivors rather than victims. It encourages young people to challenge self-judgement and develop a more compassionate and forgiving attitude towards themselves.

6. **Building Resilience:** Making sense of their story is an essential step in building resilience. It helps young people develop a coherent narrative of their lives, which can serve as a source of strength and resilience in the face of future challenges.

Understanding their story can foster a sense of identity, self-worth, and belief in their ability to overcome adversity. Now as teachers, it is not our role to provide all of those things, but it does give us hope that traumatised children may recover with the right support from specialist counsellors and caregivers. Our role as frontline teachers is to provide an environment that means when our children are vulnerable, the environment they are in will aid recovery and healing and not add to it.

I was fortunate to attend a masterclass with Dan Hughes in London, in October 2022, and the man is an absolute genius when it comes to helping young people heal. If you take nothing from this book, please look into his work and how it can help you support your most challenging young people. We will be looking at more of his work later on in this book.

Protective factors

The ACE studies identified a number of protective factors that can mitigate the negative effects of ACEs, so what are they?

Protective factors for a young person include:
1. I believe my mum or dad loved me.
2. When I was small other people helped my parents take care of me & seemed to love me.
3. Someone in my family enjoyed playing with me and I enjoyed it too.
4. Family, friends, or neighbours talked about making our lives better.
5. When I was a child there were people who helped me feel better when I was sad or worried.

6. When I felt bad I could almost always find someone I could trust to talk to.
7. There are people I can count on now.
8. Someone in my childhood believed in me.

It is very difficult for teachers to provide the first 4 protective factors, but I believe that teachers can absolutely provide the final 4 protective factors:
- When I was a child there were people who helped me feel better when I was sad or worried.
- When I felt bad I could almost always find someone I could trust to talk to.
- There are people I can count on now.
- Someone in my childhood believed in me.

There are so many brilliant teachers and pastoral teams who do this work day in day out to support their young people.

One emotionally available adult can make all the difference for a young person who has suffered from trauma and that one person can often be found in our classrooms.

When we implement a trauma informed approach successfully, we trigger the social engagement system and start to work together as a class rather than in a battle against each other to win.

Enjoyment returns to the classroom for both children and us as teachers. Children become more engaged, behaviour issues melt away and children start to fly and make progress. The more we are triggering the social engagement system, the more the relationships deepen and the safer our young people feel with us.

Longer term, this gives us the opportunity to show we care and to communicate protective factors, leading to trust that can break the ACE cycle and show children there is a different story ahead for them.

The good news is that we can train teachers to become more emotionally available to our young people and that not only benefits them greatly, but also benefits us and our own wellbeing.

What are emotionally available adults?

Emotionally available adults are those who are able to be present and attuned to their own emotions and the emotions of others. They are able to respond to the emotional needs of children in a supportive and empathetic way.

The emotionally available adult shows empathy and acknowledges the child's feelings and reactions. Emotionally available adults understand that each child experiences events differently, and they respect and accept each child's individual emotional responses.

To better understand how the child is accepting the event, emotionally available adults use several techniques, including:

- **Active listening:** Emotionally available adults actively listen to the child's verbal and nonverbal communication, without interrupting or judging. This helps the child feel heard and validated.
- **Reflection:** Emotionally available adults reflect back to the child what they are hearing and seeing, using statements like "I understand that you feel upset," or "I see that you are feeling sad." This shows the child that their feelings are being acknowledged and taken seriously.
- **Validation:** Emotionally available adults validate the child's emotional response, even if they don't necessarily agree with it. This means acknowledging that the child's feelings are real and understandable given their perspective and experiences.
- **Support:** Emotionally available adults provide support and reassurance to the child, letting them know that they are not alone and that they have someone who cares about them.

By accepting how the child is processing the event, emotionally available adults can create a safe and supportive environment that promotes positive mental health and emotional wellbeing. This helps children feel seen, heard, and understood, and helps them develop the resilience and coping skills needed to navigate difficult events and emotions.

Case Study
Ian Wright & the Importance of Emotionally Available Adults

Let's take a look at the story of television and radio personality and former professional footballer, Ian Wright, and the influence his teacher, Mr Pigden, had on him and his life chances.

There is a beautiful video clip where Ian Wright unexpectedly comes face to face with the teacher who changed his life. Someone had previously told Ian that Mr Pigden had died, but from the clip we can see how emotional Ian gets and the huge impact Mr Pigden had on his life.

If you get a chance watch the clip, it lasts under 2 minutes, but it is difficult to watch without shedding a tear, it is so powerful. (www.youtube.com, 2010)

Ian explained:
'The first real positive male role model I had in my life was Mr Pigden. He changed my life by recognising that when I was stood outside that classroom, for being naughty, that I needed more, and he gave it to me.

He would sit me down and talk to me. You know when I would get what he would call the heebie-jeebies. I would get angry from being like this to full on rage. He would sit me down and talk to me and explain to me how to communicate. I was like a little Tarzan or something.

He took me out of the class. He literally taught me to read and write properly himself and then turned me into a monitor, so I would go round with the school register and would collect them up, I would be the milk monitor guy, I'd take messages to the teachers and then once he realised I could play football and everything.

He started to teach me to play football and how you have to pass to other people and why you have to pass to people, why you have to communicate nicely and why you have to give other people encouragement.

I realised how much of an effect that man had on my life and how important it is to have a positive male figure in your life.'

I wonder how Ian Wright's future would have played out if Mr Pigden had not intervened when he did.

As a young boy, Ian unfortunately suffered from a number of ACEs such as physical abuse from his stepfather, an alcoholic family member, emotional neglect, and parental separation.

Ian was starting to demonstrate the impact of ACEs with his behaviour in primary school and that was when Mr Pigden started to intervene to change Ian's life for the better.

For Ian Wright, Mr Pigden 'gave me some self-worth, he made me feel that I was important. He gave me a feeling that I had some use. I don't know why I didn't tell Mr Pigden about what was going on at home but just having his encouragement really helped.'

Often, as teachers we do not know what is going on outside of school in our students' lives, but we do know that so many of our young people are currently struggling in school with their wellbeing, attendance, engagement, and behaviour in a post Covid education world.

The good news is that as teachers, we can become more emotionally available to our young people through greater awareness and staff training, and that not only benefits them greatly, but also benefits our own wellbeing.

What if that one person is you?

What if you had a similar impact on one or more of your young people currently in your care? What a legacy to leave and what a gift to give to someone.

In researching this book, I was fortunate enough to have coffee with a brilliant headteacher, Rob Connelly, whose stated aim was to be Mr Pigden for his young people. His philosophy is rooted in love and care for his children, staff, and families, as he outlines in additional insights in Chapter 3.

There are many inspirational leaders and teachers up and down the country, like Rob, doing this on a daily basis but we need more. We need an army of leaders and teachers to invest in and adopt Trauma-Informed Practice in our schools, to break the cycle and change the endings of our children's stories. We need more leaders and teachers to be brave enough to lead with love.

When I reflect on my teaching towards the end of the academic year, I was not as emotionally available as I should have been for a number of reasons and that was having a negative impact on the young people I was teaching.

Simply by becoming more emotionally available, my relationships with my young people were transformed leading to a whole range of benefits for both myself, but more importantly the children I serve.

To start the new school year in the Autumn term, I made a commitment that I would be more emotionally available to my young people and colleagues. It didn't matter if I didn't have solutions, the important factor was to listen, really listen. Not in a 'listen for 2 minutes and my brain starts thinking about potential solutions' way or wondering about the list of a thousand other things to do. I tried to forget about the challenges I was facing behind the scenes and really started to take a keen interest in how my young people and colleagues were doing, and it had a transformational impact.

I looked out for children who I could see were clearly struggling and I made a point of asking how they were and listening to them and providing empathic responses. It was really powerful and led to me starting to use breaktimes to coach some of these young people to help get them back on track and thriving again.

Coaching

I spent 6 weeks coaching Mitchell, every Monday and Friday breaktime, after noticing him struggle with his confidence and anger on the football pitch during school matches. He also had behaviour issues around school. In Mitchell's own words you will hear about the transformational power of listening, and showing empathy:

'I was lacking in everything, my behaviour went extremely bad, I felt worse as a person, and nothing was going right for me, and I was slowly letting myself down without even knowing it. Even in football I would just get angry really quick and lose my temper and stress all the time. I didn't have the bestest of games, I thought I wasn't good enough. I wasn't scoring as much, and I felt very low to the point I didn't know what to do. Goals

weren't coming, I had issues, I started being lazy, I had a negative mindset and had no motivation to keep going at all, I just wanted to give up and thought there was no point in even trying anymore

The frustration was horrible, every day I would always get frustrated over the smallest of things which I never did before, I wasn't happy I was down, stressed and frustrated all the time. I tried to improve every day after I realised I need to change for good. I set unrealistic goals, I thought in 1 day I would improve massively and feel good about myself, but I was very wrong. And me having that hunger made me frustrated as I just wanted to be the best version of myself, but I thought it would happen short term. This was absolutely unrealistic, and I didn't even realise at the time.

What I liked about coaching was that you listened and understood me. It felt amazing to have someone to speak to and listen. I felt so low and didn't want to be here in the summer, everything was going wrong, and my family situation was poor. I used to go up to my roof and think about ending it, I'd never do it, but I was lost. Coaching has changed everything for me.

The moment I realised it was working was when I started being calm, my behaviour and my attitude was a lot better. I started being on time and not getting consequences in school which felt amazing. But the moment that stuck with me most was training on a Friday, but before that, I had practised all alone just shooting into an empty goal and gradually gaining confidence and being consistent near the goal. But on this Friday training everything went right, I was scoring loads, dribbled well, and created so many chances and I remember everyone saying "he's back" because before my downfall I had been scoring all the time.

Then the next day we had a quarter final cup game we won 4-2 I scored 2 and got 2 assists. I couldn't believe it. I was happier than ever; I was back to scoring and on the pitch I was smiling even when I missed a chance because I knew I would score my next one that's the mentality I have "I will score". All throughout the game. Ever since that game I have scored at least 1 goal every single game and the streak continues.

My problem is 90% solved, of course everyone still has some sort of problem in their lives. Life looks a lot better now looking at it. I actually have motivation and I get up in the morning and do what I need to do. Life is like a blessing once you realise it's full of *worth, all you need to do is just stay happy, motivated, and consistent and everything will be amazing. But most important of all is having that POSITIVE mindset. It can change a whole person's life around; it most certainly changed my life. I love every single day of life now; I rarely feel sad and thrive through every day as I should do. The difference is crazy, a couple of months ago some days I didn't even want to be here anymore, now I'm just glad I'm still here and doing what I do best because it is what I am meant to do and is what I will always do.'*

All Mitchell needed was someone to listen to him. There is huge potential for schools to use coaching models to support our young people to help them flourish.

Does each child you teach feel safe or under threat?

Figure 16:

All of us as human beings have a need to feel safe and be safe. Our amygdala is constantly looking for cues around us to check that we are safe.

This is no different for our children within our classrooms. When they do not feel safe they cannot learn, as an over stimulated amygdala prevents the brain from being integrated.

The integration of the brain enhances various aspects of our children's development, including their capacity for learning and focus, emotional and social intelligence, impulse control, stress regulation, empathy, reflection, and problem-solving abilities.

All key skills if we want our children to thrive in education and beyond.

TIME TO RISE UP

 **Consider this...**

Does each child you teach feel SAFE or UNDER THREAT?

As teachers we can protect our young people and help them feel psychologically safe through our body language and increasing our safety cues. When we do this we trigger their social engagement system leading (over time) to happier children who are more capable of learning.

Fight/flight freeze vs calm, connected and safe

According to Polyvagel theory, when their social defence system is triggered, our children go into fight/flight response which can lead to rage, anger, irritation, frustration or panic, fear, and anxiety and this is where many of us have seen an increase in behaviours that challenge us in our classrooms since Covid.

Figure 17:

Triggering the social defence system

Fight

Can lead to:
- Rage
- Anger
- Irritation
- Frustration

Flight

Can lead to:
- Panic
- Fear
- Anxiety

Fright

May demonstrate:
- Dissociation
- Numbness
- Depression
- Raised pain threshold
- Helplessness
- Shame
- Shut-down
- Hopelessness
- Feeling trapped

If they go past the fight/flight response into the freeze response they may demonstrate dissociation, numbness, depression, raised pain threshold, helplessness, shame, shutdown, hopelessness, and feeling trapped.

Sadly, I am sure many of us teachers can think of a few children who we have taught since lockdown with these characteristics.

Children who have suffered from trauma in the past are more susceptible to perceiving trauma/danger even if they aren't in danger. Sometimes, even the simplest, non-threatening instruction can be perceived as a threat to their safety and an opportunity for conflict.

For the first time in my teaching career, I had children challenging me on why they had to answer the register 'Yes sir'. I was pulling my hair out with frustration at the situation, I had never been so committed to improving mental wellbeing but all I was doing was making the situation worse! As teachers we need to be so mindful of unintentional signals we are sending out to our children.

Teenagers are more sensitive to facial expressions due to brain development, making them hyper-vigilant to facial expressions. They are wired to look for psychological safety cues from their environment, including their teachers. Creating a safe and containing learning environment is crucial to promoting positive mental health and educational outcomes for young people.

There is a correlation between learning difficulties and trauma, which can be exacerbated as the child gets older. For example, teenage girls with autism may struggle to maintain their "mask" as academic pressure and puberty become more pronounced, which may lead to self-harm and school avoidance. Creating a safe and supportive environment for these students is critical to their wellbeing and academic success.

When teachers are able to co-regulate with their students and create a socially engaged state, students are more likely to remain curious, make better decisions, and think more clearly. Without psychological safety cues, the social defence system can kick in, making even the simplest instruction feel like a threat to the student and leading to fight or flight responses.

Creating a safe and containing learning environment is critical to promoting mental wellbeing and educational outcomes for our young people. By providing psychological safety cues, and understanding the unique challenges faced by young people, we can create an environment that supports the growth and development of our students.

We want our students to be calm and connected, settled, grounded, curious and open to new ways, compassionate, mindful and being in the present. To achieve this we need to trigger their social engagement system in order that all our young people feel psychologically safe, so how do we do that?

Face + voice + body = psychological safety

Our face, voice and body are of utmost importance when sending the right signals to create psychological safety in our classrooms.

Meeting and greeting our students on entry at the start of the lesson becomes crucial. Welcoming our students with a smile, a fist bump or high 5 and a friendly question or comment to let them know that you see them and notice them is transformational.

Figure 18:

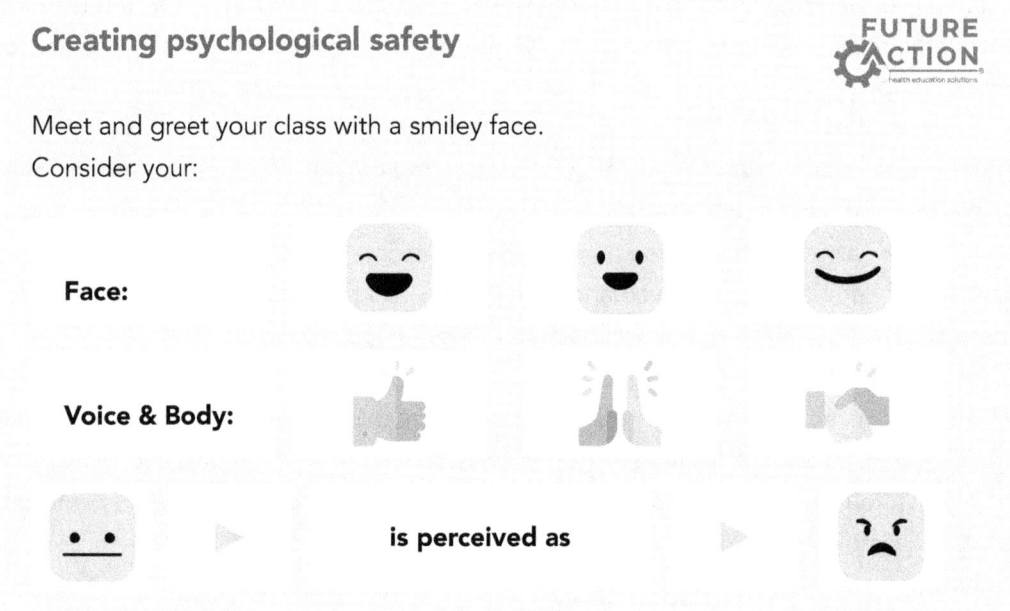

In the panic and uncertainty of teaching in a post lockdown world, many of us became fearful of human touch and for many teachers this has led to greater distance in our relationships with our students.

If you are struggling with getting your relationships back to pre-pandemic levels try a positive meet and greet.

I now say morning or afternoon and the child's name in the register to continue to create that culture of psychological safety.

Every interaction is an intervention, and you never know I may have been the only person that week to welcome them to a classroom. The meet and greet has now been part of my start of lesson routines for a considerable period of time but I was getting it all wrong in the summer term.

I fist bumped and high-fived more children in those 3 months than the rest of my life combined and this simple technique was transformational.

I now fist bump or high 5 on entry, exit, during lessons and when I walk around school a simple smile and a thumbs up reassures young people that they are psychologically safe with me.

Consider this...
It is important to stay authentic to yourself but consider what would work for you so you can increase the psychological safety cues to your young people.

Watch your face

One of the most impactful lessons I have learnt is that children who have suffered trauma in the past perceive a neutral face as someone who is angry.

We all know that the pressures of teaching can be high with the relentless workload, pressure to achieve exam results, Ofsted judgements, and the desire from every teacher to help young people thrive. Therefore, I appreciate that it is not always the first thing on your mind to walk around school smiling but children pick up on it and are making judgements about your mood.

The summer term was incredibly difficult for me personally. There was a lot of instability and disruption in my school, I was highly stressed and barely smiled all term. No wonder this was triggering my children's social defence system leading to further conflict, creating additional stress and we just couldn't break the cycle until I changed.

The knowledge of the impact of a neutral face on the social defence system led me to try to walk around the school smiling like a Cheshire cat. The response was incredibly positive from our children.

It sounds crazy but on my walk to and from school over those months I practised smiling! I smiled at pets, nothing in particular or at strangers.

People must have thought I was a massive weirdo if they walked past me, but I want to trigger people's social engagement system to reassure them that they are psychologically safe with me.

I even encouraged my year 9 exam group to remind me to smile during lessons. We would have a joke about it when the smile slipped, and the cheeky chappies would remind me. It created a lovely atmosphere in the class and one in which they all started to flourish.

 **Try this:**

Psychological safety checklist

As your lesson progresses it is worth going through a quick checklist to keep that feeling of psychological safety.

1. Be mindful of your face – are you still smiling?
2. Are you still engaged?
3. Are you emotionally available to your children?
4. Is your voice in tune with the needs of the class?
5. Are you within your window of tolerance and regulated?
6. Is your body language open and non-threatening?

In the last week of that term we had a visit from Ofsted. I was teaching 5 lessons that day, meeting one of the inspectors and trying to sort out cover for an absent colleague at the last minute.

My stress levels were higher than at any point that term. Some of my children started to misbehave, the challenge and defiance from the summer term was back! In my mind I was angry and thinking 'not today of all days to mess around' but I had to quickly take a step back and notice that I wasn't as regulated as normal, my face, voice and body language had dropped. I quickly responded to get the outcomes I wanted.

Psychological safety for your most challenging children

Often the kids who need the most love will ask for it in the most unloving of ways. For your most needy young people who might be struggling to access the classroom, ask them where they feel is safest and that will help them build trust in your relationship.

Bear in mind that this is a long term journey and sitting at the back in silence may be the first step they need to move forwards to better outcomes for you both. Often as teachers we do not know what is going on in our children's lives behind the scenes and just turning up for school in the first place might be a massive win in itself for that young person.

John's journey

I am really proud of one of my students in Year 9, called John, who struggles massively with shame, dissociation, and rage. He was frequently being removed from lessons for his behaviour in the wider school and is one of those children who you really worry about.

Monday morning, John arrived in my class in a very wobbly way intent on getting sent out of the lesson. By simply asking him in a calm and quiet tone where he felt psychologically safe in my classroom and reassuring him that I would not be asking him any questions that lesson, it was the first step to his recovery.

He made huge strides in just two months, he became engaged in his learning, we worked out together in the fitness suite to push away his stress and anger and he even smiled! When John said 'I have used muscles I never knew I had sir and I feel so much calmer' it gave me that special buzz that lets you know you are in the right job.

I was on duty and John was truanting refusing to enter his science lesson. I asked him where he would feel psychologically safe in the class and after some quick negotiations with his science teacher we got him back in the room.

I asked John about how science was going later that term, while we were working out. I was delighted when he told me 'I sit in my normal place now sir, it's been going much better and I'm not getting sent out anymore'.

When we invest in our most challenging relationships as teachers, it not only benefits everyone else in the class, but it could also break the cycle of trauma, the associated illnesses and early death of a young person. If we can make our young people feel psychologically safe we can help them to thrive and enable them to achieve their undoubted potential.

Investing in our most challenging young people

Think about your favourite teacher when you were at school. What did they know about your life outside of school? I bet the answer is quite a lot.

My favourite teacher knew my mum and my older sisters, he knew how much I loved football and PE, he knew my favourite team, and he knew that I liked to have fun in lessons, and I could be a lazy bugger if he didn't push me, and that boundaries worked well for me.

Now think about the child who you are struggling the most with. What do you know about their life outside of school? How much time have you invested into finding out about their life outside school? What do you know about their story? And their passions and interests? Are there any staff who have a great relationship with this child, who can help you fill in the gap if the child does not want to tell you yet because they don't trust you?

Start taking an interest in them and their lives outside school. Ask them questions about their interests and listen closely and ask follow up questions. Show them that you are human and not the robot teacher that they probably think you are.

As teachers, we innately do this with those children who we naturally bond with, but what if we did this with our most challenging young people, so we can look deeper than the surface poor behaviour from a scared child, who is struggling to cope with life.

 **Try this:**

Investing in your most challenging child

1. Pick a child who you are struggling with their behaviour at the moment.
2. What do you know about their life outside of school?
3. Who can you speak to who gets on well with the child?
4. What information can they give you to help strengthen or reset the relationship?
5. Ask the young person questions about their interests. Listen carefully and ask follow up questions.

Low challenge?

One of the criticisms of creating psychological safety is that it means that we can no longer present challenge to young people. That is not the case at all. We need to create psychological safety first and then challenge. If we do that, people feel safe enough to rise to the occasion and take the challenge on. If we don't create psychological safety and just challenge, then people feel overwhelmed by what is asked of them and go into social defence.

One of the criticisms of young people, I often hear, in a post lockdown education world, is that they are flaky, and they have less resilience. There have certainly been times when my students have not met the standard I was looking for. On reflection, most times I had not done enough to create psychological safety for the level of challenge I had then posed to my young people.

Therefore, it is important that we increase our psychological safety cues before we challenge. There may well be more psychological safety cues than pre Covid, but as Eddie Jones says in his book 'Leadership', neither way is better, it's just different and we have to adapt to the conditions we are facing. By doing this, we create the conditions for young people to thrive in.

Polyvagel theory in practice

On my journey of learning about Polyvagel theory, I was delighted to find out how we can use psychological safety to optimise performance for all our children in sporting situations such as making the jump from junior to adult sport or to representative level, performing in exams or school shows, and in pressurised situations after our children leave our care. It means that trauma-informed practice is relevant to all young people we teach if we want them to flourish, regardless of whether they have suffered from childhood trauma.

Michael Allison has developed 'The Play Zone', a science-backed approach to optimise resilience and performance based on Polyvagal Theory. Michael works with many people including International top 10 tennis professionals to optimise their performance as an executive coach. Michael explains 'The Play Zone' in more detail here:

'Polyvagal Theory, by Stephen W. Porges Ph.D., explains the evolutionary changes in the autonomic nervous system that occurred in our transition from asocial reptiles to social

mammals. Although we retain the same primitive neurophysiological reactions to threat, as social mammals we have a unique capacity to detect features of safety and welcome in the environment and people around us, which adaptively dampens defences, calms physiology, and fosters co-regulatory relationships with others.

As a subconscious surveillance system, our autonomic nervous system is constantly monitoring and regulating our physiology in different ways depending on whether we interpret the current conditions as safe, dangerous or life threatening. These physiological shifts (i.e. heart rate, breathing, metabolic output, etc.) are reflected in how we feel, and directly influence how we experience the world and interact with others.

The Play Zone is my unique application of Polyvagal Theory to optimize resilience and performance through our physiology. It originated in my work with professional athletes as an approach to manage emotions, improve focus, and enhance performance in the high stakes world of competition. Traditional sports psychology focuses on top-down strategies to manage performance anxiety without appreciating the underlying physiology driving how we feel, and the tremendous impact this has on our ability to perform. Whether we feel nervous, tight, and afraid of making a mistake, or relaxed, focused and confidently in control, is more than setting an intention or shifting our mindset. Between our potential and our performance is how we feel, which resides in our physiology.

When in our Play Zone, we experience a feeling of relaxed focus, calm energy, and a confident connection to what we are doing and who we are doing it with. In the heat of competition, when in our Play Zone, we are able to play when everyone else attacks, defends and protects.

When we press too hard, tighten up, or fold under pressure, it's not that we aren't good enough, but rather we are in a threat-oriented physiological state that doesn't support our intentions and highest potential. Essentially, every core component of performance, including reaction time, technique, speed of movement, problem solving, concentration, creativity and even our confidence, is dependent upon, and dynamically changes, as our physiology adaptively shifts in response to the challenges we are facing.

When we understand this, we have an opportunity to meet our body where it is, without shame, blame or criticism. When we take the stage and feel nervous, we don't try to make it go away, repress what we are feeling, or pretend we are in control. Instead, we relate to what we are feeling with kindness, patience, and compassion. We stay on our own side. We look for a friendly face or listen for a reassuring voice. We open our posture, relax our shoulders, soften our gaze, sigh, or slow down our exhales. We become skilful at recognizing our physiological shifts, and we build inner resources, strategies, trusting relationships, and ways of relating to our bodily reactions that help to realign our physiology to support our intentions, resilience, and performance. And then we see what happens...'

© Copyright 2023. All Rights Reserved. Michael R Allison www.theplayzone.com

Relationships are key

Trauma itself does not necessarily have a significant impact on the mental health of a young person. Research shows that if the young person has an emotionally available adult to help them make sense of the world, then they can be protected from the impact of their trauma.

Without an emotionally available adult, toxic stress persists. The increased and consistent release of cortisol and adrenaline contribute toward mental and physical illness in adulthood.

Therefore, we need this generation of young people to each have access to at least one available adult, particularly within the school environment, where they spend the majority of their days. Young people are more anxious since Covid and many of their windows of tolerance has narrowed. It is crucial that we increase their windows as much as possible so young people can access their integrated brain.

We need to create as many emotionally available adults as possible in our schools so that every young person can find their emotionally available adult who they can connect with. Those schools that invest in these will reap the rewards by placing the student/teacher relationship at the absolute heart of their school.

Therefore, relationships have become even more important than ever before. If we get these right then everything else falls into place, engagement, wellbeing, attendance, behaviour, progress, and attainment enabling young people, us as teachers and schools to succeed together.

We are in the business of people; children are at the heart of what we do. We need to intentionally connect with our young people and enable all of them to feel psychologically safe, supported, and able to contribute.

Chapter summary

- There is hope, young people under 18 can recover from the effects of trauma.
- There are 8 protective factors that minimise the impact of trauma.
- Emotionally available adults who listen without judgement, demonstrate empathy, and help young people make sense of their story are key to healing.
- We need to put our oxygen mask on first to protect us from blocked care.
- Creating a safe and containing learning environment is critical to promoting positive mental health and educational outcomes for young people. By promoting emotional literacy, providing psychological safety cues, and understanding the unique challenges faced by young people, educators can create an environment that supports the growth and development of their students.
- Our face, voice and body are crucial for developing psychological safety.
- We need to invest in our most challenging young people and increase our psychological safety cues so that they can thrive.
- Psychological safety does not mean low challenge.

Critical questions

1. What does your face - voice - body communicate to children at the moment?

2. How can you increase your psychological safety cues in your classroom and around school?

3. Do you have any opportunities to implement a coaching model in your setting?

4. Do your colleagues receive training on being emotionally available to their young people and how to create psychological safety cues?

Chapter references

- Hughes, D.A. (2011). Attachment-focused family therapy workbook. New York: W.W. Norton.
- www.youtube.com. (2010). Ian Wright gets a big shock! [online] Available at: https://www.youtube.com/watch?v=omPdemwaNzQ [Accessed 2 Oct. 2023].

Additional insights

Case Study
Psychological safety

The Belvedere Academy is an all-ability state funded girls' Academy secondary school in Liverpool. I am delighted to work in partnership with their team as part of our 'Liverpool RISE Up' Trauma Informed PE programme. Their brilliant Head of Physical Education, Kate Reynolds, talks us through their approach:

'The start of our Year 11 PE lessons probably look the same as many schools up and down the country. We stand in the corridor leading to the changing rooms with a smile on our faces to meet and greet the students. One by one they pass by until the usual crowd stop and say "Miss, I've forgotten my kit!".

Now, we as teachers know just as much as they do that this kit has not been "forgotten" as it is now nearly December and this particular group of students have been without kit since the start of the year, giving various excuses ranging from the believable to the ridiculous! "We're moving house, and I've packed it away, I left it on the bus, I thought it was in my locker, but I've looked and it's not there!"

So here comes the reassuring smile and the teacher's response, "Don't worry, you can borrow some."

BANG.

Before you know it you're at war against the screeches of "eeeeeeeey I'm not wearing that, it doesn't fit, it's not been washed, it stinks!" No one is in a winning situation. "You're not joining in if you're not in kit."

"Fine I won't join in."
"Well I'm not doing it either then" cry three more pupils from the class.
Especially in girl's PE we can find ourselves in a vicious circle getting nowhere, with nobody getting anything positive out of the situation. This is when we decided to use the RISE Up programme as a tool to guide the students back into PE.

Intent
To get these girls into a psychological safe space to find out what the barrier really was that was stopping them from engaging in PE. To then break down that barrier together so that PE became meaningful and enjoyable again.

Creating psychological safety
On their next PE lesson the students were met outside the changing room as normal with those who didn't have kit being asked nicely to go and wait in the old fitness suite.

This was presented as a place where they could be as honest as they liked and would be free from judgement. Students felt like they could open up and be honest. They were then shown the first series of slides from the Rise Up Programme.

Intended learning outcomes:
Head: *To understand what the RISE up wellbeing programme is.*
Heart: *To contribute to a safe environment for everyone in the class to discuss mental health, to try your best and listen to everyone's contributions in silence.*
Hands: *To take part in a practical session*

After outlining to the students why their curriculum was designed the way it was, and the importance of wearing appropriate clothing in order to take part safely, they were asked "What is it that we can do to help you to take part in physical activity safely when in school?"

We discussed the options available to them and found out they liked the curriculum as there were always options. We discussed the PE kit and found out that they weren't averse to wearing the kit.

After some deep discussion the students told us they didn't like carrying their kit around, most didn't have lockers to store it in and they simply didn't like getting changed.

Solution: Wear your kit to school on PE Days.
I completed the school wellbeing scorecard and completed an adapted version of the Warwick–Edinburgh Mental Wellbeing Scale survey so that we could track the impact of the programme.

Implementation
The findings of the discussion were taken to the head of the school who agreed that year 11 could now wear their kit to school on PE days taking away the need to change into PE kit in the changing rooms.

This obviously isn't a new situation for many, as many schools adopted this during Covid, however, our setting had reverted back to old ways. This simple change meant that the students in the discussion group felt a sense of belonging and a sense of being listened to, knowing that they were able to drive change for the better.

Before allowing the year 11s to come in their kit we surveyed their feelings. 70% of the year group said it was something they wanted to do, 24% said they had no strong feelings towards the change and 6% said they did not want this change to happen.

Impact
From that day onwards there has rarely been a student in year 11 without their kit on PE days. Students were given very specific boundaries to abide by. Their choice was either wear your PE kit to school, or change as normal, but you must be in your kit for lessons.

If wearing their kit it must be the school PE t-shirt and/or the school PE hoodie along with long bottoms. (This was especially important from a safeguarding point of view for students travelling across the city centre either before or after school).
If they still had the school leggings or tracksuit bottoms they were allowed to wear these, or black leggings could be an alternative. They could then change into the PE skort/shorts if they wanted to once at school. This has led to more engagement, more enjoyment and longer lessons due to most not needing to get changed.

Before they left for the summer we surveyed students again. This time 83% of the year group said it was something they wanted to do, 12% said they had no strong feelings towards the change and 5% still said they did not want this change to happen. That meant that 95% of the students supported the change, and we are working with the 5%

CHAPTER 10 - CREATING PSYCHOLOGICAL SAFETY

to explore their reasons for a no reply to break down more barriers.

To review the impact of the programme, I re-visited the adapted version of our Short Warwick–Edinburgh Mental Wellbeing scale survey for the perceptions of our children's progress of their mental wellbeing. The results showed great improvement in all areas.

Figure 19:

	Belvedere **Pre** RISE Up intervention	Belvedere **Post** RISE Up intervention
'They've been feeling optimistic about the future'	Some of the time	Often
'They've been feeling useful'	Some of the time	Often
'They've been feeling relaxed'	Rarely	Some of the time
'They've been dealing with problems well'	Some of the time	Often
'They've been thinking clearly'	Rarely	Often
'They've been feeling close to other people'	Some of the time	Often
'They've been able to make their own mind up about things'	Some of the time	Often
'They've been feeling able to manage their own wellbeing'	Rarely	Often
What year group are your target group in?	11	11
What are your biggest challenges for your target group at the moment?	Engagement	
What challenges has RISE Up intervention helped improve for your target group?	Attendance, behaviour, engagement, SEND, most vulnerable children	

I also completed the school wellbeing scorecard again. Our score increased to 92% from 53%, showing an improvement of 39% from a good starting point.

Figure 20:
Pre intervention:

Figure 21:
Post intervention:

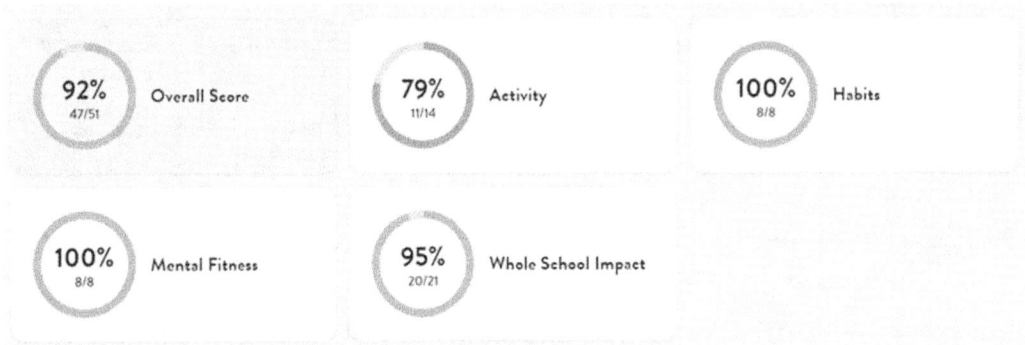

Moving forward

Our Year 11s are hopefully pathing the way for this simple change to be rolled out throughout the Academy. Younger students have been intrigued as to why the older students are allowed to wear their kit and we have made it clear that this is a trial and if they can act as role models and wear the school PE kit around school with pride, we will look to roll this out to other years next academic year.

It has also given us the chance to talk about hygiene and exercise; if they have worked hard and sweated during the lesson pupils have the option to change into their uniform as before or a change of PE top.

We have talked about different types of deodorants, sprays, creams, bars, and roll-ons and discussed why it is important to keep ourselves and clothes clean after exercise. These types of conversations would never have taken place before we built these more positive relationships with the students.

As the project was successful we decided to trial this with the younger year groups during our final few weeks and it continued to be a huge hit. We are exploring how to implement this across the whole school in the new academic term.

After further student voice regarding the kit, we have a new kit on sale from September for all students to purchase should they wish to. We now have a choice of top, one fitted with *a V neck, and one straight with a round neck, a choice of bottoms including shorts, skorts, leggings and tracksuit pants, as well as a ¼ zip top and a rain jacket.*

Students can wear any combination of this kit at any time of the year for any lessons. This is to reduce the anxiety around wearing PE kit, supporting students who need to keep themselves covered up for religious reasons and those who don't wish to wear a traditional "female" kit whilst remaining smart and keeping that sense of belonging to our school community. Feedback has told us that 82% of students across the school are happy with the changes which is positive to hear.'

Empowering physical education through trauma-informed practices: unlocking resilience and inclusion

We will now look at the evidence base behind trauma-informed practices within Physical Education. Physical Education (PE) is more than just exercise; it is an opportunity to support students' holistic development. However, the impact of trauma on students can hinder their ability to fully engage and thrive in PE.

Recognising the transformative potential of trauma-aware pedagogies, several research articles shed light on the importance of trauma-informed practices in the PE setting. We highlight their key findings, uncovering the power of trauma-informed approaches in creating a safe and inclusive environment for all students.

"Co-creating strategies for enacting trauma-aware pedagogies with pre-service physical education teachers" by Dr. Thomas Quarmby et al.

Imagine a PE class where small fouls escalate into physical conflict, students refuse to be part of a team, and adhering to game rules becomes a struggle. This article reveals that without understanding the effects of trauma, teachers often resort to punitive responses, worsening the situation for trauma-affected students.

The study emphasises the critical need to equip pre-service physical educators with trauma-aware practices to better support the learning and development of trauma-affected youth.

Forward thinking universities like Bath Spa University and UEA are incorporating this into their current PGCE Physical Education courses.

"It's more about building trust: Physical education teachers' experiences with trauma-informed practices" by Douglas W. Ellison and Jennifer Walton-Fisette.

Step into the world of physical education teachers who have embraced trauma-informed practices. Through in-depth interviews, these educators share their experiences and unveil four dimensions of trauma-informed strategies.

They create safe spaces both physically and emotionally, cultivate positive relationships with students, foster student responsibility, and guide them toward self-regulation. These dimensions, aligned with fostering resilient learners, showcase the transformative potential of trauma-informed practices even in the absence of extensive training.

"Fostering Resilient Learners by Implementing Trauma-Informed and Socially Just Practices" by Jennifer L. Walton-Fisette.

Unleashing resilience and fostering inclusivity are at the core of trauma-informed and socially- just practices. This article reveals that by understanding trauma's impact on students' lives and integrating strategies to promote safety, trust, and emotional regulation, educators can create an equitable learning environment.

Embracing a whole-school approach, ongoing professional development, and cultivating strong relationships with students are essential in effectively implementing trauma-informed and socially-just practices.

"Preparing the Next Generation of Health and Physical Educators through Trauma-Informed Programs" by Douglas Ellison, Tammy Wynard, Jennifer L. Walton-Fisette, and Sarah Benes.

The future of PE lies in trauma-informed programs that empower educators to address trauma effectively. This article emphasises the significance of integrating trauma-informed practices into teacher preparation programs. It explores strategies such as incorporating trauma-related content into coursework, providing experiential learning opportunities, and promoting self-reflection and self-care. Collaboration and creating supportive learning environments emerge as crucial factors in equipping future educators.

In summary, embarking on a journey towards trauma-informed practices in Physical Education holds tremendous promise. It empowers us to create safe and inclusive spaces, build positive relationships, nurture student responsibility and self-regulation, and address trauma-related challenges head-on.

By embracing trauma-informed approaches, Physical Education becomes a catalyst for resilience, unlocking students' potential and ensuring their overall wellbeing and academic success. Together, we can pave the way for an engaging, empowering, and trauma-informed PE experience for all students.

PE accessible to everyone
Jim Harte

It is more important than ever that PE is accessible and meaningful to all young people so that they can all reap the benefits.

Jim Harte has 39 years experience of teaching PE in Florida and making young people feel included, loved and that they belong in his lessons. Jim takes up the story:

First Who, Then What:
The question is not: "What is PE?"
The question is: "Who is PE for?"
The answer is: "Everyone."

We must think first about who PE is for, then worry about what we are going to do. The who will influence the what.

To make PE available, welcoming, and safe for everyone, there must be an acknowledgement of barriers that result in the exclusion of many from PE. Often, these barriers exist within the minds of the students themselves. They "self-exclude" because they do not see how PE is for them. They don't see a path to success, enjoyment, and fulfilment for themselves. They don't see how they are a part of PE.

In many cases, they are right to think this way. Well-meaning PE professionals can make the mistake of assuming that it is self-evident what PE should be, self-evident that it is for everyone. And they proceed accordingly.

When we acknowledge these barriers within the student's mind, we can see that it is not necessarily self-evident to the child that PE is for them. Only then can we see that our first task is to define PE in a way that is inclusive for everyone, without losing the benefits of a rigorous PE programme.

Music, themes, a story, coordinated movement:
One way to make PE for everyone is to present PE as a story, almost like an action movie but with a plot and a point – a "moral of the story". Action movies include music, a theme, often action of some kind that involves coordinated, timed movements.

Children love music, stories, movies. They can see themselves within the plot of a good story.

Why can't the PE experience take place within the context of an ongoing year-long story, one that involves music and coordinated movement? One in which the Director, the Storyteller is the PE Teacher.

A good movie can be an escape, an adventure within the mind where the movie-goer imagines themselves in the story of the movie from the quiet and safety of their movie seat.

If PE class participation can be made to feel like an exciting, year-long action story, a story that has purpose and meaning, a story that has a dignified role for everyone, a story filled with music, movement, and soaring themes, then the whole-child development and inclusion will naturally follow.

The power of positive relationships for children from low-socio economic areas
James McGinn, Liverpool School Sports Partnership

I am sure it has not gone unnoticed, particularly by those of you who work in the education and youth service sectors, that the number of young people disengaged from school seems to be increasing. Across the areas I work in (as a School Sport Partnership Manager), the issue has become prevalent. It has been noted that a significantly higher proportion of boys are disengaging from school and as such, at risk of falling behind.

Staff report that boys become discouraged, lack motivation and 'play up' very easily. In 2019, Andreas Schleicher, the Director of Education and Skills at the Organization for Economic Cooperation and Development OECD), said "talent is being wasted" because of ingrained stereotyping about social background, gender, and race (Career ambitions 'already limited by age of seven' - BBC News).

This issue is not isolated to Liverpool, the OECD also state that boys are 8% more likely than girls to say school is a "waste of time" (https://blog.innerdrive.co.uk/underachieving-boys-what-educators-can-do: accessed 10:35 9/1/21). Meaning more boys leave school with little or no qualifications and perhaps worse, an intractable mistrust of people they perceive to be in authority.

Of course there are any number of reasons young people say they don't like school; you only need a quick internet search to see this. However, for some, the sense of not fitting in, being engaged in perceived negative relationships, or not identifying with their peers who do engage in school, may dictate the need to look elsewhere to gain a sense of belonging and other needs satisfying actions. Moreover, many of these young people have experienced four or more Adverse Childhood Experience (ACEs), meaning they are already at a significant risk of poor health outcomes and the evidence of the impact of this toxic trauma is overwhelming. This can be further compounded, by what can only be described as a pervasive 'lad' culture that is all too prevalent in working class urban areas. Areas that have seen drastic cuts to public services, including youth services, which are now almost non-existent, as well as the services that tackle ACEs.

Coupled with the perceived or real lack of credible employment opportunities, some young people, albeit a minority, find engaging in illicit risk taking activities meets their financial and other needs. This risk taking behaviour is often accompanied with the carrying and use of weapons. People are all too familiar with the devastating headlines across the country. According to the Office for National Statistics (ONS), crime involving knives & bladed instruments reached a record high in England and Wales (ONS, 2019) - The ONS said police recorded 45,627 offences in the year to December 2019.

That is 7% more than in 2018, and the highest since knife crime statistics were first collected in 2010-11 . The Angel of Knives sculpture, made from more than 100,000 confiscated knives and first displayed outside the Liverpool Anglican Cathedral in 2018, is a powerful reminder of the impact engaging in illicit activities has on people's lives.

To begin to truly understand the causes of their disaffection and perhaps the appeal of a 'surrogate' lifestyle beyond the traditional social conventions, I believe it is vital to start with the source – the young people themselves. To gain this insight, I facilitated a consultation group with 20 boys aged 12 to 14 years old. The boys were identified as those responsible for the majority of disruption throughout school, regularly on a daily basis, with a significant proportion also known in the wider community for their 'anti-social behaviour'. Behaviour which has seen them involved with, (as perpetrator and/or victim) or at risk of, serious youth violence and being particularly vulnerable to gang culture.

Due to a lack of trust in people perceived to be in 'authority', the boys were reluctant to open up to discuss their issues – instead making comments such as, "what's the point of this?", "are you a grass? [sic]" "nothing changes anyway" and "no one ever listens". After some cajoling, 'banter' and honesty the boys finally started opening up. They expressed feelings of frustration, depression, were worried about bullying, 'straighteners' [sic] (organised fights used to settle disputes), stress, body image and money. However, the one issue that came up over and over was anger and not being able to control it, especially when feeling frustrated by school and often perceived austere teaching methods. This anger and frustration would often lead to confrontation with teachers and/or their peers, with minor issues quickly becoming major concerns that would often carry over into the community.

The question was how could school help? What could school do to help alleviate these concerns?

Many of the boys could feel when their emotions were starting to get the better of them and suggested the need to be able to access immediate "time outs" and "go somewhere to calm down". The 'somewhere' they describe was a safe, non-judgemental place that would enable them to gain control. The majority for the group suggesting this place should have opportunities to be physical, with combat sport type activities (pads, punch bag, fitness) being the most frequently requested activity. One boy, however, was fervently against doing extra physical activity!

It is well known that the martial arts have a strong ethos of developing life characteristics such as discipline, courtesy, resilience, self-motivation, perseverance, integrity, emotional regulation and with an expressed desire for combat sports, the utilisation of martial arts seemed to be a vital inclusion within the design of an intervention. However, by

understanding the effect the ACEs have in contributing to the issues, it was clear that engagement in martial arts alone wouldn't be enough. Therefore, I used the Youth Endowment Fund toolkit which outlines the types of programme that have the best chance of producing habitual behaviour change. Sports programmes and mentoring are considered as impactful interventions to prevent and reduce youth offending. Essentially, the decision was clear – we needed a sport (martial arts) based mentoring programme.
That framework is William Glasser's (1998) Choice Theory. Choice theory is a psychological approach that suggests that humans have the power to control their own feelings and actions and that they should avoid trying to control others. It is based on the idea that all behaviour is driven by five basic needs: survival, love and belonging, fun, freedom, and power. As previously mentioned needs, which are being met by the 'surrogate' lifestyle! I say surrogate, as for some, the people they associate with, in this lifestyle, can become more of a family to them than their biological / parental groups.

Choice Theory also proposes that people have a 'quality world', which are people, things, and activities that are most important and satisfying to them and by understanding these, the hope is that the intervention group can choose pro-social behaviours that are more effective and satisfying for themselves and others. In addition, Choice Theory also addresses how to build and maintain positive relationships.

For me, this is the most important and perhaps overlooked aspect in developing pro-social behaviours. That is, if the socialisation of the young in question would have included the seven positive habits for relationships as opposed to the seven deadly habits they may have developed a robust resilience. This resilience may have minimised the impact of any ACEs, so they did not have such a negative impact on their lives. And if more people understood the power that positive relationships have, I am sure there would be significantly fewer societal issues for us to deal with.

TIME TO RISE UP

Figure 22:

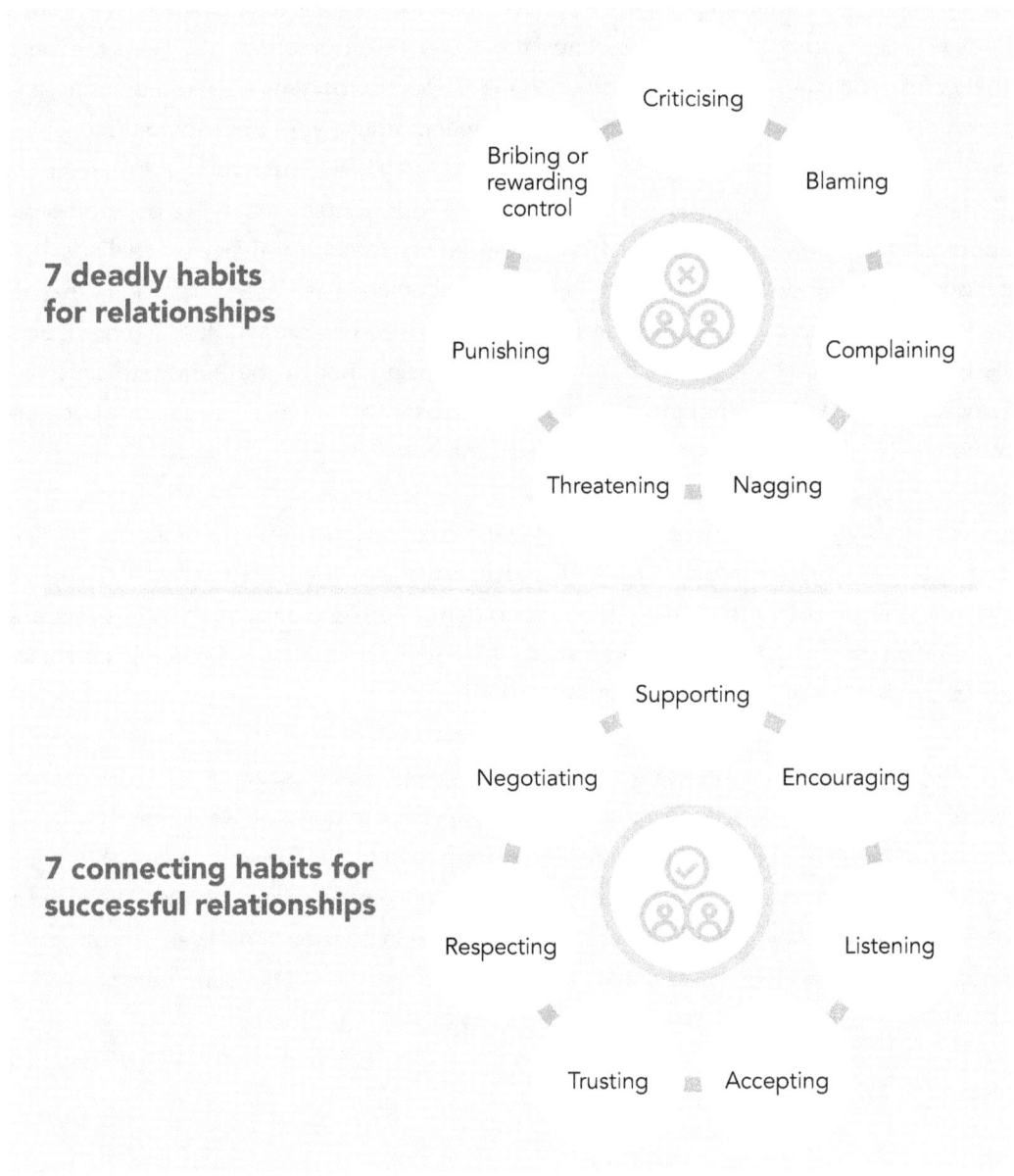

7 deadly habits for relationships

7 connecting habits for successful relationships

More and more forward thinking schools are introducing coaching models to provide opportunities for children to be listened to. Alice Smith School in Malaysia is a great example of this approach.

GROW coaching model
Richard Stockings, Deputy Head at Alice Smith School

The PERMA Model was developed by Positive Psychology pioneer Martin Seligman. PERMA stands for five elements or components: Positive emotions, Engagement, Relationships, Meaning, and Accomplishments.[1]

The place of coaching within the PERMA framework has been hugely impactful in supporting students to flourish. The focus on building resilience and developing problem solving skills through a coaching model has helped many students develop a life skill that can be accessed beyond their educational experience to support their wellbeing.

Training staff and students in how to coach and how to receive coaching has been at the heart of a deliberate and bespoke wellness curriculum in both international schools that I have worked in. Utilising a strengths based approach and evolving the GROW model, students are given a structure to understand and work through challenges as they emerge.

Our GROW model stands for:
- **G   Goal**
  What is the goal you want to achieve?
- **R   Reality**
  What is your current situation at the moment?
- **O   Opportunities/options**
  What are the opportunities/options available to you?
- **W   Way forward**
  Which option is best to select to move forward towards your goal?

Creating clear systems of referral have been important in ensuring coaching conversations are both timely and needed.

The philosophy of coaching has to be upheld by ensuring students feel both supported but also an active part of the process and that they have not just been selected because something is going wrong. It is therefore vital that students have agency in this process and can identify the type of challenges that resonate for them.

Many different models exist but I feel strongly that we need to equip coaches with the confidence and knowledge to hold conversations that can focus on subject specific issues as well as the social emotional challenges that often impact on learning. That said, teachers need well-structured training in order to feel confident in managing meetings so that they do not become counselling sessions which they are not trained to deliver.

Coaching structures can also permeate into conversations with parents and the language of coaching can be embedded into the culture of a school. Rather than offering solutions the coaching language offers opportunities to explore challenges and different approaches to solving them. Skilful questioning asks all stakeholders to think about different ways of looking at a problem and examines how we have been successful in overcoming such hurdles in the past. Creating clear steps with accountability and follow up creates action for change and a direction and confidence to make things happen.

With young people this can lead to empowerment as they often leave conversations with clear outcomes and feel positive about having the trust and safe space that a coach can provide. The relationships that this then builds in a school setting are hugely important in developing positive relationships and can quickly permeate a culture where adults and students work together to tackle challenges that we face on a daily basis.

If done well, coaching can become a key catalyst for developing the values and behaviours that will allow students to feel both physically and psychologically safe, to ensure that risks are taken, and challenges are a normal part of life and not a barrier to learning.

[1] https://positivepsychology.com/positive-psychology-workplace-labor-of-love/

Taking Action
Dan Vincent

As a disillusioned mainstream teacher and SENCO, Dan Vincent, took action and set up his own brilliant SEMH school. He gives his expert perspective here on what he has witnessed for children excluded from mainstream settings:

The positive impact of sport and physical education has long been shared and shouted from the roof tops by teachers, sports coaches, sports professionals, and the medical world. What if I was to make such a bold statement as to say sport and physical activity not only have positive mental and physical health benefits but it's the difference between achieving real social mobility and the continued suppression of those most excluded from society. It could be argued that the importance of sport and physical activity is, by no means of exaggeration, life changing.

In 2018, as a disillusioned mainstream teacher and SENCO, I started the journey of opening up our own school for those young people who the mainstream system does not fit. Please note the importance of the system not fitting the young person and not vice versa. We wanted to create an education system that was built on mutual trust/respect, that celebrated the unique qualities of an individual and that ensured young people felt safe, secure, and therefore ready to learn. The school fell under the bracket of supporting children/young people with Social, Emotional and Mental Health challenges (SEMH). I preferred to use the phrase temporary barriers to learning as opposed to challenges. Within this broad term, children and young people would be referred to us who had either high levels of social anxiety and may have been long term school refusers and also those young people who have experienced permanent exclusion from their mainstream setting.

Although, without doubt, and I carry the testaments with pride, the school made a huge difference to many children and their families, I still struggled with the balance of keeping the majority of the school population safe whilst not giving up on the young people displaying the most distressed behaviour, protected their fear with aggression and were experiencing/ experienced a significant number of Adverse Childhood Experiences (ACEs). These young people had already experienced the feeling of exclusion. They aren't ready for formal education. Right now, they just need to feel safe. To not have to carry the knife in their pocket for the journey to school. To not worry if Mum or Dad are going to be alive when they get home due to relapse. To know they have a bed to sleep in that night. Sadly, all of the above are common issues facing many young people in our schools, every day.

Although we have to keep the whole school population safe, the uncomfortable impact of permanent exclusions on the life chances for those children is something that deserves further discussion. Data gathered by the Government report into Education, children's social care and offending (2022) found that 59% of children who had ever been permanently excluded from school were also cautioned or sentenced for an offence. According to research led by Beyond Youth Custody some headline stats provide an insight into the *impact of ACE's. It was recorded that 91% of violent youth offenders experienced abuse or loss. Fewer than 1% of all children in England are in the care system yet looked after children make up 33% of boys and 61% of girls in custody. In 2012/2013 the Government spent £224 million on the provision of secure accommodation for children and yet 68% of children released from custody re-offended within a year (BYC 2015).*

As sports professionals we are, by nature problem solvers. As a situation unfolds in a match, you manage it, you problem solve. The game plan may change but you rise to it. Young people who need help, often gravitate to those who can solve problems with them. The importance of our community coaches to those most experiencing exclusion in our society is paramount. I watch in awe as the community boxing club can engage the most dis-engaged. How the football coaches can channel the aggression to assertiveness in a game situation. I worry that if a young person is excluded from school, then loses their place on the team due to "poor behaviour" the next option is exploitation, crime, punishment and therefore poorer life chances and choices. A Trauma aware approached should be embedded throughout our communities.

I know this next statement is a pipe dream but let's imagine we could persuade Governments and inspectorates to see settings and children as individual and unique without a formula to govern what "good" looks like. Imagine we adopt a holistic, as well as a strategic approach to funding earlier interventions. Imagine if the cost to health was reduced due to less drug, alcohol, and mental health pandemics. Imagine if the cost to the punitive system was reduced and therefore imagine if subsequent future employment chances were now improved, taking the reliance from the benefits system away. Imagine If we could provide the nurture a child needs when they are most distressed. Imagine if we looked at Education, Health, and Care collectively as the EHCP should do. Imagine if the EHCP really did improve the life chances of the most excluded, the most at risk of abuse and the most distressed. I believe sport and physical activity practitioners are on the front line of the battle for real social mobility and "levelling up" and I hope that with enough imagination we can make sure that every young person can utilise the skills we teach through sport and transfer these skills into a hopeful and bright future.

Chapter 11 – Connect before correct

"Whatever affects one directly, affects all indirectly."
Martin Luther King Jr.

As time has passed since lockdown we have had more and more reports of an increase in behaviours that challenge us from students, on social media channels such as Twitter, and in our conversations with fellow front line teachers. I estimate that I have spoken to teachers from over 50 different schools up and down the country in a range of settings and not one colleague has told me that behaviour and engagement has improved post Covid compared to pre Covid.

Many children who were fine before Covid are now struggling, and those who were struggling before Covid are now in a much worse place. We can't sanction our way out of this situation, it will only push teachers and children further and further away from each other with devastating impacts for our society.

It is not your fault if you are rigorously following the school sanction policy and it is continuing to make behaviour management in your classroom tougher and tougher. It's natural to fall back to something that gives us control and makes us feel safe, but the reality is that it is doing the opposite.

It encourages children to be hypervigilant and look for trouble and conflict with you. This puts you on edge as you can sense it coming and the inevitable conflicts keep coming and coming.

You are spending more and more time on phone calls home and restorative conversations, and it is starting to impact your own mental wellbeing. You gradually drift further and further away from the children you are meant to be inspiring and the visions you had of yourself, as a teacher, when you embarked on teacher training. You start to dread certain lessons, certain days and then it becomes every day because of the inevitable conflict that is coming your way.

That is the problem with the prevalent default mode of behaviour management in our schools and it can lead to blocked care.

Isn't this a book about mental health?

You may say, 'hang on', this is a book about mental health, why are we talking about behaviour but the two are interlinked.

A survey by the Children and Young People's Mental Health Coalition (CYPMHC, 2022) in Summer 2022 has found that both children and parents are unhappy with how behaviour is being managed in schools in England. As part of an inquiry into behaviour and mental health in schools, the Coalition asked young people, parents, and professionals their views on approaches to behaviour management and mental health in schools, and how they can be improved, via an open call for evidence.

Survey respondents strongly agreed that behaviour is linked to young people's mental health, but that current responses to behaviour in school do not reflect this and are not working. 79% of young people who responded to the call for evidence and 87% of parents and carers agreed that a young person's behaviour is linked to their mental health. However, only 21% of young people and 7% of parents felt that schools are responsive to young people's mental health needs when dealing with behavioural issues.

Professionals responding to the survey had more mixed views. This included teachers, headteachers, mental health practitioners and representatives from the Voluntary and Community Sector. While 32% of professionals responding said that schools are responsive to young people's mental health needs when dealing with behavioural issues, 46% disagreed.

When asked about the effectiveness of behaviour management techniques used in schools, over half of young people (59%) who responded said they were not effective in improving behaviour. 80% of parents and carers and 56% of professionals also stated that behaviour management techniques used by schools are not effective.

The inquiry is exploring the links between mental health and behaviour, how current school policies on behaviour affect young people and their families, and what schools can do to improve both behaviour and mental health. This follows widespread concern about the increased use of punitive approaches, such as the use of exclusion and removal rooms to improve behaviour in schools. The rise in the use of punitive approaches is set against a backdrop of growing mental health need among children and young people, with one in six children and young people aged 6 to 16 experiencing a mental health problem in 2021, compared to one in nine in 2017.

Sir Norman Lamb, Chair of the Children and Young People's Mental Health Coalition, said: *'We must not forget that children and young people's mental health and wellbeing is more important than ever. Our preliminary findings suggest that whilst young people are aware that behaviour is often linked to their mental health, they do not believe that current behaviour policies are effective.*

"We share the ambition of government to create supportive, safe, and inclusive school environments that enable and facilitate learning. The call for evidence has captured wide-ranging views on the topic of behaviour and mental health in schools, and we are keen to understand all viewpoints throughout the inquiry. We want to inform government policies and school practices that boost children's mental health and behaviour for everyone's benefit.'

"Our approach to behaviour needs to be more sophisticated than in the past. To simply respond to bad behaviour by punishing the child often completely fails to understand that that child's behaviour may be driven by awful experiences that that child might have had at home or in their neighbourhood. I am a strong believer in the value of creating a disciplined and learning culture at school, but I strongly object to the approach of some in our education system who believe that the answer is to exclude from school (either formally or informally) the most difficult children, too often leaving them on the scrap heap. This might solve the problem for the school, but it creates a far greater one for society and utterly fails that young person. Amongst those permanently excluded from school, children with special needs, including mental ill health and autism, are significantly overrepresented. What sort of society is it which turns its back on children who are most in need of help and support?"

As a frontline teacher, I didn't disagree with the findings, but I wanted CYPMHC to provide alternative solutions. Large schools are incredibly challenging to manage, and I have great empathy for senior leaders who take on this thankless task. It is far from easy.

I first started thinking about solutions in May 2022, when Sir Norman mentioned it to me at the Norfolk County Council RISE Up media launch. Until then, I hadn't given it that much thought, I just thought that was the way it is in large secondary schools, but it did make me curious.

I started looking deeper. The same students were in the same exit rooms day after day, nothing was improving, in fact it was getting worse and worse in terms of frequency and severity of 'offending'.

One day I was on duty and a real Jack the lad 14 year old broke down in tears to me. It was very out of character for him, but he was distraught. The issue was that he was in the isolation room again for the latest offence. He was devastated as he explained to me how 'shit' it made him feel and how it impacted his mental health. That conversation really struck me and made me re-evaluate my opinion of isolation rooms.

I saw this post on LinkedIn by Education consultant, Steve Sallis, and it resonated with me:

'IF A CHILD DOES NOT KNOW HOW TO READ, we teach…

IF A CHILD DOES NOT KNOW HOW TO RIDE A BIKE, we teach,

IF A CHILD DOES NOT KNOW HOW TO LEARN, we teach,

IF A CHILD DOES NOT KNOW HOW TO BEHAVE, we PUNISH…'

In fact we punish, punish a bit more, then up the punishment. If the penny hasn't dropped yet, we keep increasing the punishment to the point that the child feels so full of shame, that there is no longer any point, and they feel like they don't belong in our school. If they still haven't worked it out yet, we get rid of them and pass on the problem to someone else, doing so much damage to their mental health in the process.

This may be an oversimplified viewpoint of an incredibly complex situation and there are some fantastic behavioural leaders across the country, but there is no doubting that behaviour and mental health are interlinked for both children and their teachers' wellbeing.

The need for punishment

As a teacher, it's not uncommon to see children misbehaving in the classroom. Whether it's talking out of turn, disrupting other students, or failing to complete homework, it can be frustrating and disruptive to the learning environment. In response, many teachers feel the need to punish students for their behaviour, in the hopes of correcting the behaviour and maintaining control in the classroom.

However, it's important to consider why we feel the need to punish children in the first place. Often, punishment is seen as a way to teach children a lesson and discourage them from engaging in the same behaviour in the future. However, research suggests that punishment may not be the most effective way to address problem behaviour in children and may have negative effects on their mental wellbeing.

One reason for this is that punishment can create a sense of shame and embarrassment in children, which can be damaging to their self-esteem and sense of self-worth. Instead of feeling motivated to change their behaviour, children may become resentful or rebellious, which can further exacerbate the problem.

Furthermore, punishment can create a power dynamic between teachers and students, in which teachers hold all the control and students feel powerless. This can be particularly damaging for children who have experienced trauma or neglect, as it can trigger feelings of helplessness and anxiety.

This might be controversial but think about the message you are sending out when you put a seating plan in place straight away. Rarely do we do that when people walk in to a room to attend a conference session, but it has become so automatic in secondary schools.

Right from the very start you are communicating to your class that you do not trust your young people and triggering their social defence system. I prefer to say, 'I want to treat you like young adults, you can sit where you want but I expect you to try your best and to listen in silence when I or a classmate is talking to the class. If you do that you get to stay with your friends, if you don't I will have to put in a seating plan, but I really don't want to. Let me trust you.' I was rarely let down by the class.

A different world

It is really hard to describe the difference in many young people in schools pre and post Covid, unless you were on the front line dealing with it every day. I will use a football analogy to explain the social defensiveness for many children in a post Covid world, after the honeymoon had worn off.

Imagine an even game between two sides playing - a teacher on one side and children on the other side. In an ideal world both would have spells attacking and defending or bouncing ideas off each other, so the game would be end to end with both utilising the social engagement side and it would be enjoyable to watch.

In a post Covid world many students who were going end to end then retreated into a low block, and the teacher would have to work really hard to draw them out to have the same success. Many who were in a low block pre Covid, decided to park the bus and became very defiant, and it was a real challenge for teachers to draw anything out from these young people.

Those children who were parking the bus before, now didn't leave the changing room and nationally we are struggling massively with attendance figures. I have seen evidence of attendance figures across many parts of the country that are heartbreaking. In one school, I have come across, attendance is at 51% for the year. Behind the story are 1000s of children missing out on an education and the wider social benefits of attending school. We have to find ways to make school more engaging and make young people feel welcomed and that they belong in our schools.

The scale of it is immense and can feel overwhelming. I released a blog on disengagement in PE in January 2023, and it became the most popular blog I had released. It clearly hit a nerve within the PE teaching community, with 10 times as many views as my usual weekly blog.

Strategies that mainly worked for the majority, no longer work in many settings. Brilliant teachers who have successfully taught young people for many years are left scratching their heads and feeling like failures, when everything they have ever done is being questioned and challenged by some of their youngsters.

In the summer term of 2022, that experience was certainly the case for me when many of the young people I was working with were struggling with intergenerational trauma, trauma from Covid, additional individual trauma, and also trauma caused by wider instability in the school to create significant behavioural challenges. I had to look for new solutions as my traditional strategies were just not working.

Incidentally, my behaviour management strategies have always been one of my biggest strengths, as a teacher over the previous 18 years. I have also been trained pre-Covid by the government's behaviour tsar in England. Those strategies worked for me pre-Covid, but they just weren't working anymore in the chaos of a post Covid world and were actually driving children further and further away from me. From my experiences, it was clear that we are not going to sanction our way out of this situation. There needs to be more than choices and consequences.

Trauma taking its toll

I was using a 'Choices and Consequences' policy, employed by the whole school and it wasn't working for me as it had done pre-pandemic.

I would get short term results by following the process and eventually removing the child from the class, but by this time everyone in the class had been impacted in a negative way affecting their learning, and theirs and my wellbeing.

Despite restorative conversations taking place, in some of the lessons that followed, the same child often reoffended as we didn't quite trust each other, and the cycle continued and deepened. I was dealing with the surface problem rather than showing empathy and looking deeper.

The sanctions that followed, such as isolation rooms, were potentially retraumatising these young people, and the whole process was disengaging them from their learning and leading to them resenting their teachers, school and ultimately their education.

I was pulling my hair out with frustration at the situation. I had never been so committed to improving my children's mental wellbeing but all I was doing was making the situation worse!

Forgetting our basics

Many trusts have become so formulaic and standardised with their behaviour policies, and the challenge has become so overwhelming and disheartening, that it has led to many of us teachers forgetting the key ways we build outstanding relationships. When we have these fantastic relationships, it negates much of the need for behaviour management systems, because children feel safe and want to be in our lessons.

Many of us build good relationships naturally, but as the strains and stresses of the job take its toll, we may do less and less of it. As I started to struggle, I started looking around at the teachers who had the best of the relationships in my school. It was interesting that they were very often, very different from the teachers who were perceived to be the best teachers in the school. In fact, some of them weren't even teachers, but they were brilliant at making children feel safe. Some of the best for building relationships were actually teaching assistants and when I dug deeper and asked them about what they were doing and why they were successful, they often had a primary background.

When I dropped my 6 year old daughter off at primary school, I would watch her teachers closely and the way they interacted with her. Many were outstanding at building rapport and really demonstrating a sense of awe and wonder about learning and being at school, that maybe some of us secondary schools teachers in challenging situations have lost. I am really trying to pick my words carefully as I do not want to offend anyone, and it is very often not the teachers' fault. Teaching is bloody hard, and the external pressures make it the hardest, I think, it has ever been. However, I think this would be a fair criticism of where I was in that summer term of 2022 and I could see it in many of my colleagues, not just within my school but in others I visited.

Try this: Relationships

Have a look around at the teachers with the best student relationships in your school.

1. What are they doing that you could borrow?
2. Have a conversation with the teacher or teaching assistant and ask them how they do it and why.

What if?

As teachers and leaders, it's natural to want to control challenging behaviour using a behaviourist approach, when we ourselves feel defensive in situations. However, while this may bring short-term control, in the long term, it can further alienate children who are already struggling, causing them to disengage from education and feel like they don't belong in school. This can create a ripple effect throughout the class and school, making it uncomfortable for everyone involved and increasing episodes of challenging behaviour.

To make all children feel like they belong in school, we need to do more. One great example of this is Dave McPartlin, the headteacher at Flakefleet Primary School, who inspires his students to dream big and engages their social systems to create a positive school environment. By doing so, he has won over parents and created a cohesive team between children, parents, and teachers to help each child reach their full potential.

It's important to remember that schools should be places of inspiration and learning, not cold institutions focused solely on control. By fostering empathy and understanding, we can create inspirational environments that encourages engagement and a sense of belonging. So, imagine the difference it would make to your entire school if you and your colleagues, children, and parents were all operating from the social engagement system more often.

Hunting for solutions

As I went hunting for solutions, the good news is that there is one and we can re-find that magic connection with our young people. Even better, it can be taught, so we can train our teachers to transform relationships again.

Following strategies I came across; I created a 5 step model. This resulted in reducing the number of students I sent out from my classes in one term by 95% and led to transformed relationships, greater student/staff wellbeing and children thriving in their academic progress.

Before I start on the 5 step model, I have to say that you may need to drastically alter your mindset, so you need to be open minded and prepared to change.

As Summer term progressed in 2022, it was abundantly clear that my existing strategies were no longer working. It was making me miserable, and I was willing to do anything to get back to enjoying my teaching again. But as Paul Dix says, when the adult changes everything changes...

Figure 23:

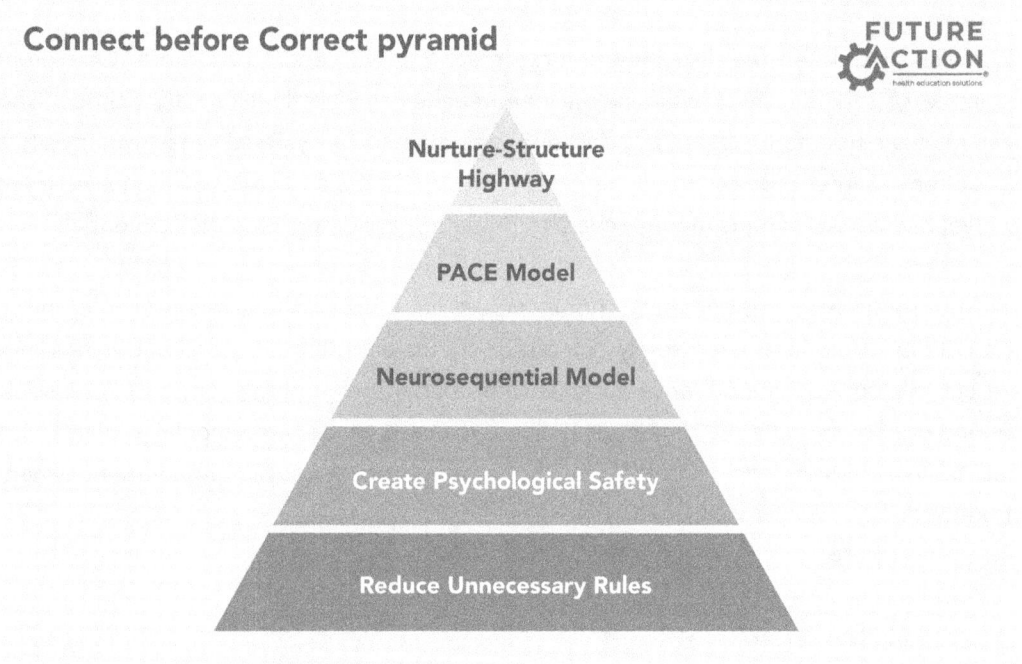

Culling unnecessary rules

The first step was to cull any unnecessary rules. There is a Sir Alex Ferguson's phrase that goes along the lines 'that he did not need to go looking for trouble, because trouble would always find him as a manager.' and as teachers many of us can relate to that in a post lockdown education world. That's why culling unnecessary rules is beneficial. I reviewed the department rules and got rid of any unnecessary ones to reduce the chances of conflict. If there was going to be conflict, I wanted it to be over something that mattered.

We had a rule that children had to take their school shoes off to keep the dance floor clean. This meant my meet and greet would involve looking at children's feet and challenging those who refused to take their shoes off.

CHAPTER 11 - CONNECT BEFORE CORRECT

It was an unnecessary rule that triggered their social defence system. I was getting fed up and annoyed with the constant whinging about why they had to take their shoes off and it was getting the lessons off to a bad start on a regular basis. In September 2022, we culled the rule so we could get lessons off to a better start. It made a significant difference to us.

In an ideal world, we would have kept the rule to protect the floor. The positive impact was minimal, but the negative impact was huge and trashing all our great work in building high quality relationships in the previous years. Children who previously had been good as gold, were kicking off and it was getting worse and worse as the weeks went by. Getting rid of that rule was huge for transforming behaviour and getting lessons off to a great start. I estimate that by getting rid of one unnecessary rule and ramping up the psychological safety cues, we reduced send outs by 75% the following term.

Consider this...

- Are there any unnecessary rules that your department has that you could cull to reduce the potential for conflict?
- What rules are in place that they do not understand?
- Even better, ask them what rules do they not understand why they are in place.

In my work as a consultant, I often host student panels with the agreement of the department I am supporting, and I ask this question about rules. The answers I get are fascinating and lead to informative discussions with the team I am supporting. I was working with a school who had a group of approximately 30% of their students disengaged in PE. The rule that was winding up their children, was that they hated lining up outside the changing rooms before going in for PE. The department were adamant that they wanted to keep the rule, so their next piece of work was to communicate why the rule is in place and monitor whether the effort/reward ratio is beneficial in the coming weeks.

In a post lockdown education world, everything is up for questioning by young people. Just like us adults, children have had a lot of time to think over the lockdowns and question why they do certain things. I have had more concepts questioned about my teaching methods in the last 2 years than in the previous 17. The days of compliance for the sake of it are over, particularly in low socio-economic areas, and we need to adapt accordingly and be sure that the rules we have in place are meaningful.

The second step in the model is to drastically up the psychological safety cues, through face-voice-body, as explained earlier in the previous chapter.

The third step was to apply 3 models in sequence, to de-escalate situations and deal with them effectively, without lowering standards. The first model I applied was the Neurosequential model created by Doctor Bruce Perry (2006).

The Neurosequential model

The Neurosequential model is a framework for understanding brain development and creating interventions for individuals who have experienced trauma or other adverse experiences. The model is based on the idea that the brain develops in a sequential and hierarchical manner, with lower-level brain functions developing before higher-level functions.

Figure 24:

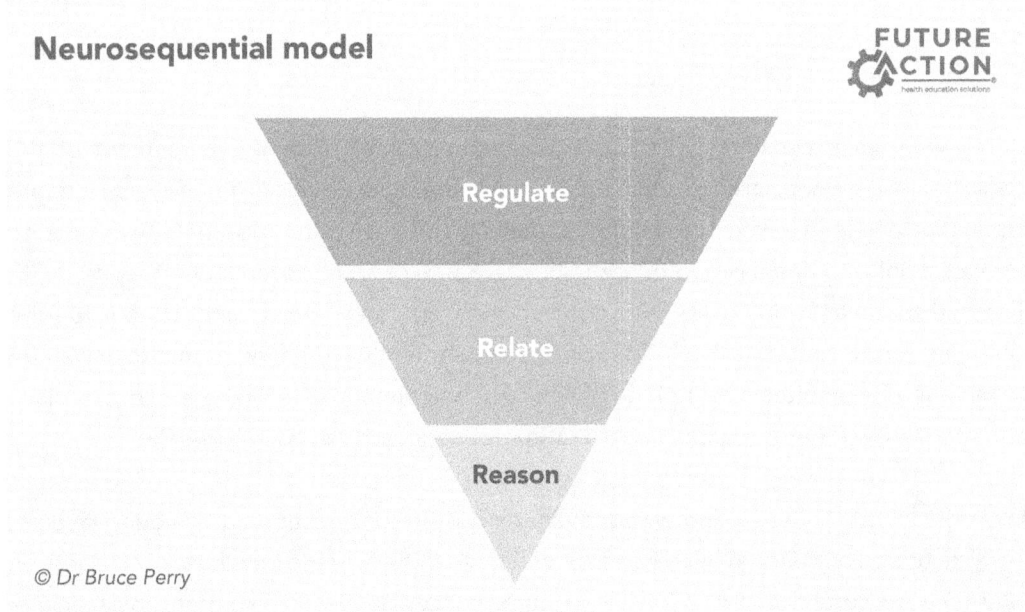

© Dr Bruce Perry

A simple way of thinking about the model and how I explain it to colleagues is:

Imagine that your brain is like a house with different rooms, each representing different parts of your brain that do different things. The first floor is the basic part of your brain that controls things like breathing, heart rate, and sleeping. The second floor is where your emotions live, like feeling happy, sad, angry, or scared. The third floor is where you do your thinking and problem-solving.

Now imagine that the rooms on each floor have to be built in a specific order, from the bottom up. That means that the basic part of your brain has to be built first, and then the emotional part, and then the thinking part.

Sometimes, when bad things happen - like a traumatic experience - it can affect the way your brain grows and develops. For example, if you experience a lot of stress or trauma when you're young, it can affect the way your brain builds the rooms on each floor. This can make it harder for you to manage your emotions, or to think things through. The good news is that with the right kind of help and support, a person's brain can still grow and develop in a healthy way.

The neurosequential model helped me understand how a child's brain works, and helped stop me getting frustrated when a child didn't respond straight away, as I wanted. This was because their body wasn't in a position to access the parts of their brain required to respond in the way I requested. By understanding how the child's brain works, it gave me greater patience, and I understood the steps that were required to get the outcomes we wanted.

Firstly, I had to help the child to 'regulate' to calm their fight/flight/freeze response. A walk to the school allotment was great for this. Also, finding some exercise for them to do to regulate and take their stress and frustration out in a safe and controlled way, or leaving the conversation until later in the day. Any form of mobilisation such as a walk together down the corridor used to be great for this.

I then needed to 'relate' and connect with the child through an attuned and sensitive relationship. I would distract children by talking about an aspect of their life outside of the school, such as a sibling or their favourite football team/tv show/computer game etc, or by pointing out something in nature that I had noticed looking out the window. Once we were relating to each other, I could then move to the 'reason' stage.

Thirdly, I needed to 'reason' with the child using empathetic statements to support them to reflect, learn, remember, articulate, and help them become more self-assured.

Previously, I was heading straight to the 'reasoning' part of their brain, focusing on my expectations of learning, and this was not working for children who were dysregulated and feeling disconnected from others. The result was inevitably failure and frustration for both myself and the child.

The PACE model

I then used Doctor Dan Hughes' PACE model (2007) as the next stage. PACE is a way of thinking, feeling, communicating, and behaving, that aims to make the child feel safe, by activating their social engagement system.

Figure 25:

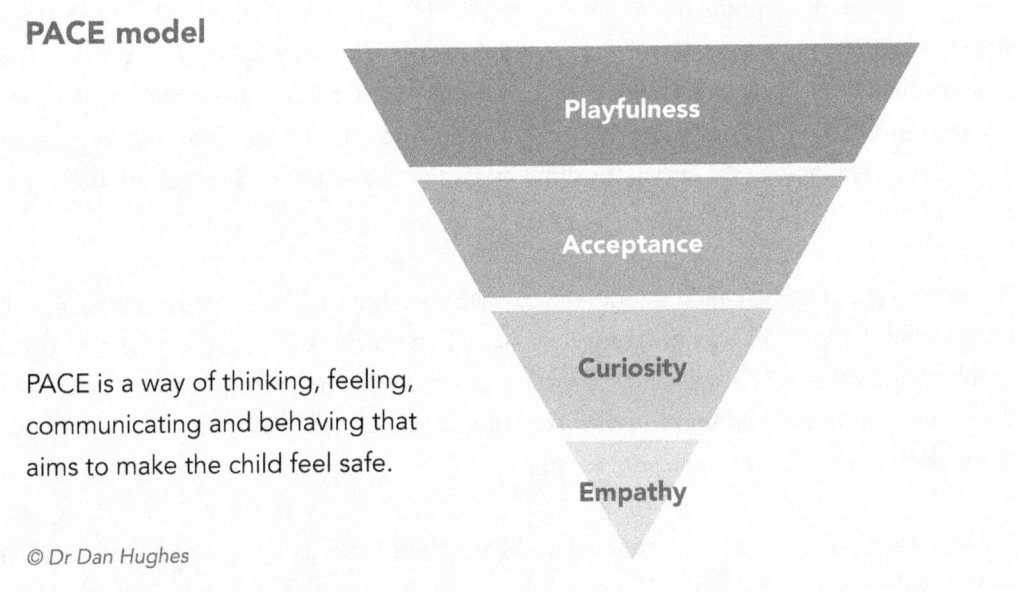

Dr. Dan Hughes' PACE model is a therapeutic approach, used to build positive relationships and create a secure attachment between caregivers and children, especially those who have experienced trauma or neglect.

PACE stands for:
- **Playfulness:** Being playful in interactions with the child, using humour and creativity to lighten the mood and create a positive atmosphere.
- **Acceptance:** Accepting the child for who they are, including their emotions, behaviours, and experiences, without judgement or criticism.
- **Curiosity:** Showing interest and curiosity about the child's experiences, feelings, and thoughts, in order to better understand and empathise with them.
- **Empathy:** Understanding and sharing the child's emotions, validating their experiences, and offering support and comfort.

Let's explore this in more detail.

Playfulness

Sometimes, playfulness is useful for diffusing situations by de-escalating them rather than ramping them up. It is not banter, but it lightens the mood and triggers the child's social engagement system, so that they can access the part of their brain to make better decisions. It is not always appropriate to use but it can be great for the right situation.

I was on-call one day when a group of girls were truanting and refusing to follow a colleague's instructions, one girl in particular was stressing out about her eye lashes. I made a light hearted quip about my eye lash treatment regime, it made her, and my colleague smile and we managed to diffuse the situation and get the girls feeling psychologically safe and back on track with their learning.

It was an important intervention, the young lady had been suffering massively from grief, following the bereavement of a sibling, and it opened the door to the start of a closer relationship rooted in acceptance and empathy, that made her feel psychologically safer in school. In the days and weeks that followed, I would regularly check in with her to check she was OK. Sometimes, that would be verbally, other times a simple thumbs up from across the room. I was trying to offer as many safety cues to reassure her and help keep her on track.

Dan Hughes states that it should be noted that Playfulness is a very small part of the PACE model and is not required at all sometimes if the situation does not warrant it. Knowledge of our children and the quality of our relationships is crucial to recognising when to implement it, and that was definitely my experience of using the concept.

Acceptance

Accepting was critical for me as children's poor behaviour and my lack of control over it in the summer term was having a real impact on my own wellbeing. I accepted the children's behaviour for what it was, and was curious why, rather than taking it as a personal slight. It took away my need to win the behaviour battle and significantly reduced my personal frustrations. Earlier on in my career, I definitely felt the need to 'Win' the behaviour battle and it can end up escalating in severe situations and piling shame on the child, so that they feel that they don't belong in my classroom. In hindsight, I would like to go back and change that about my career in teaching.

It enabled me to have greater empathy and look deeper at the causes, rather than wondering why they were trashing my lesson and triggering my own social defence system. It was a gamechanger and improved my wellbeing straight away.

Try this:
Practise the pause

This is a great technique to use when dealing with behaviour that we find challenging, especially if we are dysregulated ourselves.

1. Practise the pause. Pause before judging. Pause before assuming. Pause before accusing. Pause whenever you're about to react harshly, and you'll avoid doing and saying things you'll regret later. (Deschene, 2016)

2. Take a deep breath in and out before responding. That gap is our time to choose whether we respond with curiosity and empathy or we potentially retraumatise young people.

Curiosity and empathy

Being curious helped me look deeper and walk a mile in my young people's shoes rather than purely from my perspective of what outcomes I wanted for my department and school. I looked deeper at the issues my young people faced, what they had been through and what was triggering this challenging behaviour.

It resulted in greater patience from me, improved body language and a calmer tone which got better results. I invested in our relationships and the things that mattered to them, I was emotionally available to them, and this reduced the frequency and severity of the behaviour incidents that followed in the coming weeks and months.

I developed greater empathy for my most challenging young people. I stopped trying to fix everyone's problems and just listened. As teachers, we love to fix people's problems, but sometimes problems are so big that we can't fix them and that is ok. I couldn't fix the girl's grief who lost her loved one, but I could let her know that I was here for her when she wanted to talk, I was thinking about her, and I cared about her. She later told our school counsellor how much that meant to her to know a teacher cared.

Some of the way some of my colleagues managed her behaviour left me saddened. If I was trying to process what she was going through then I would have definitely struggled to function appropriately as well.

Often, as teachers we do not know what is going on outside of school in our students' lives, but we do know that so many of our young people are currently struggling in school with their wellbeing, attendance, engagement, and behaviour in a post lockdown education world. It's best to err on the side of caution, show empathy, talk to the child, and key staff who know their background before jumping in with both feet, all guns blazing.

It's amazing to think how many times we can diffuse tricky behavioural situations, simply by asking 'You don't seem yourself today, is everything ok, I am happy to listen?'

Sometimes, children that need love the most, ask for it in the most challenging of ways so It is important to understand that some children who may exhibit behaviours that challenge us in the classroom may be seeking attention and love in the only way they know how. This may have helped them get what they needed in the past but may no longer be serving them.

Children who have experienced trauma or neglect, or who are dealing with difficult home situations, may not have had positive experiences with adults and may not know how to express their emotional needs in a healthy way. In these cases, it's important for us to approach these children with empathy and understanding, and to recognise that their challenging behaviour may be a cry for help.

Aren't trauma informed behaviour policies too wishy washy?

Some critics argue that trauma informed behaviour management strategies encourage lower standards and are hard to implement with large numbers of children, for example in secondary school settings, where you could have schools with well over 1000 young people.

The solution for me was using the Nurture-Structure Highway as a way of getting the right balance. The Nurture-Structure Highway, developed by Jean Isley-Clarke (2017), is a framework for understanding the interaction between a child's environment and their development. The framework suggests that a child's development is influenced by two main factors: nurture and structure.

Nurture refers to the emotional support and care that a child receives from their caregivers, including love, affection, and attention. This can include physical touch, verbal praise, and quality time spent together. Nurture is important for a child's emotional development and wellbeing.

Structure, on the other hand, refers to the routines, rules, and boundaries that provide a sense of safety and security for a child. This can include things like regular meal times, consistent routines, and clear expectations for behaviour. Structure is important for a child's sense of stability and ability to learn and grow.

According to the Nurture-Structure Highway framework, these two factors are interconnected and work together to support a child's development. A lack of nurture or structure can lead to developmental delays, behaviour problems, and other issues.

The motorway

Think of a motorway with 3 lanes. On the inside lane we have nurture and on the outside lane we have structure. We want to stay in the middle lane, we definitely do not want to be in the field either side of the motorway. I have experienced both in education and it is not pretty.

Figure 26:

Nurture - Structure Highway

Does not mean low expectations

© Jean Illsley Clarke

Structure is important because when we structure routines, systems, and teaching strategies to create the right conditions, it enables students to be successful. For example, calm and orderly routines around changing, consistent, predictable structures to lesson content, all build trust and reduce the potential for dysregulation. This maximises opportunities to build relationships so that young people can thrive.

However, we don't want to veer so far over to structure that routines are so heavily fixed that there is no leeway for individual situations, leading to the young person feeling psychologically unsafe, restricted, and alone. On the other hand, we don't want to veer so far over to the other side of nurture that there is no level of challenge to misbehaviour and the young person thinks they can do whatever they want without consequence, as that is not going to do them any favours, especially when they go into wider society.

By using my understanding of the Neurosequential model, I would have conversations with a young person when they were in the right headspace, to have the greatest impact moving forward without retraumatising them, to make sure I got the balance right. As we experimented, we found that the highway balance depended on the class, the individuals, and their experiences of trauma. Some groups needed more structure, some needed more nurture to get the balance right.

No one knows your young people better than you so the challenge for you is to find that right level for your individual students, classes, and school.

Outcomes on individual students and class as a whole

By placing relationships first, and connecting before correcting, my relationships with all children I teach have been transformed. In particular, my most challenging young people feel psychologically safer, so they are calmer. This creates an enhanced environment in which all young people can learn and thrive. Not one person suffered from implementing this model.

My most challenging young people were happier & healthier, and their behaviour improved significantly over a period of time. There were of course still behavioural issues now and again.

Working with children who have suffered from trauma is never straightforward, but our children were more engaged in their learning, leading to a dramatic increase in progress, and my own wellbeing improved considerably. Lessons became fun again, my children were happier, and I felt like I was a good teacher again.

As teachers, we are in constant battle around the effective use of time. I hated having restorative conversations with children and parents, it was the last thing I wanted to do at the end of a busy day, I would much rather be running clubs and fixtures, supporting colleagues, and thinking about how I could improve the department.

Previously, it felt like I'd be punished three times when dealing with behaviours that challenged me. Once, when the child wrecked my lesson, secondly, having to take time from my day to have the restorative conversation with the child and thirdly, when I had to call the parent to give them the bad news.

Instead, I choose to invest my time up front in being emotionally available and investing in relationships with my most challenging children. Rapidly, it saved me time, particularly within a lesson and at the back end of the day. My vocation became a lot more enjoyable in the process.

I want to finish this chapter with a quote to ponder on. It's more relevant than ever.

> "Kids who are loved at home come to school to learn, and
> kids who aren't, come to school to be loved."
> *Nicholas A. Ferroni*

Consider experimenting with these strategies, you won't regret it and your young people, particularly your most challenging students, will thank you for it.

Chapter summary

- Since the lockdowns and school closures due to the COVID-19 pandemic, there have been reports of changes in children's behaviour in schools. Some children have exhibited increased anxiety, depression, and emotional distress, while others have struggled with socialisation and communication skills. There have also been reports of increased aggression and disruptive behaviour in some children. These changes in behaviour may be due to the disruption of daily routines, lack of social interaction and support, and the stress of the pandemic on families and children. Schools need to adapt to these changes as traditional methods are not as effective in many settings.
- A 5 step model helped address these issues and help students adjust to the new normal.
- Psychological safety cues refer to verbal and nonverbal signals that create a sense of safety, trust, and respect in social interactions. When these cues are present in a lesson, it triggers the social engagement system enabling individuals to feel more comfortable sharing their thoughts and ideas, taking risks, and collaborating with others. This leads to a more productive and innovative learning environment.
- Reduce unnecessary rules to decrease the chances of conflict.
- The Neurosequential Model is an approach to understanding and addressing the impact of early life experiences on brain development and function. The model emphasises the importance of considering a child's developmental history, current functioning, and specific needs when designing interventions. The approach involves

assessing the child's strengths and challenges using a neurodevelopmental framework and providing interventions that are matched to the child's developmental level and needs.
- The PACE model, is a therapeutic approach that aims to build positive relationships and create a secure attachment between caregivers and children, especially those who have experienced trauma or neglect. By being playful, accepting, curious, and empathetic towards the child, caregivers can create a safe and nurturing environment that helps the child develop trust and build positive relationships. The PACE model is based on attachment theory and is particularly effective for children who have experienced trauma or neglect.
- The Nurture-Structure Highway is a framework that emphasises the interplay between the emotional support and care (nurture) and the routines, rules, and boundaries (structure) that a child receives from their environment. These two factors work together to support a child's healthy development and wellbeing, and a lack of either can lead to developmental delays, behaviour problems, and other issues. The framework highlights the importance of creating a nurturing and structured environment for children in order to help them thrive.

Critical questions

1. Who are the best teachers in your school for building relationships?

2. Are there any unnecessary rules in your schools and departments?

3. What would your young people say if you asked them about any unnecessary rules?

4. Do you feel the need to win the behaviour battle?

Chapter references

- CYPMHC (2022). *School behaviour policies are ineffective in creating change, according to findings from a new survey.* [online] CYPMHC. Available at: https://cypmhc.org.uk/school-behaviour-policies-are-ineffective-in-creating-change-according-to-findings-from-a-new-survey/.
- Perry, B. D. (2006). Applying principles of neurodevelopment to clinical work with maltreated and traumatized children: The neurosequential model of therapeutics. In N. Boyd Webb (Ed.), Working with traumatized youth in child welfare (pp. 27-52). New York, NY: Guilford Press.
- Hughes, D. (2007). Attachment-focused family therapy. New York: W.W. Norton & Company.
- Deschene, L. (2016). *Practice the Pause.* [online] Tiny Buddha. Available at: https://tinybuddha.com/fun-and-inspiring/practice-the-pause/.
- Isley-Clarke, J. (2017). The Nurture-Structure Highway: Building Strong Foundations for Early Learning. New York: Routledge.

Additional insights

Connecting before correcting
Simon Scarborough

Simon Scarborough is currently Head of PE at Crispin School. Simon is an Education Consultant for PF Scholar and is a former SENCO and Assistant Principal. Simon leads the way for promoting belonging in PE through his outstanding work on embracing gender diversity and equity.

'Reading a post from Neil's LinkedIn account recently, prompted some deep reflection of my relationships with a wide range of students over the last 20 years.

When I embarked on my teaching career in 2001, I was not aware of the concept of adverse childhood experiences and the potential impact that trauma can have on a young person. I quickly realised the importance of building strong relationships with students in and around the classroom and became aware of the nuance and complexities that this entails. I would look on in awe at experienced staff that would be able to work with students presenting with challenging and sometimes extreme behaviours; providing the necessary support to work through the trickiest of situations.

Quite often, but not exclusively, these staff were tutors, Heads of Year / House and / or PE teachers. Neil's principle of "connect before correct " really resonated with me and prompted my reflection… and then the penny dropped. Yes, these staff had experience, but what I now come to realise is that the key to their success was that they knew the child to such an extent that they had a deeper understanding of their needs and had developed a level of trust that allowed them to support the child when they were at their most vulnerable.

Perhaps the nature of being a tutor; having daily interactions, enabling a more personalised approach to tutor sessions, allows staff to develop a stronger relationship with their tutees. Once this deeper connection has been made, the students are more likely to accept help from and follow the instructions of the tutor. This has certainly been the case with many of the more complex students I have tutored in my career.

I have also noticed that PE staff (both within my own departments and beyond) often have a similar relationship with students. This can be through effective tutoring, but perhaps it is because of the unique nature of the subject and extracurricular activities. I have heard fellow professionals over the years say, "it's easy for you [PE teachers], all students love PE". I think we all know that this is not true and quite the opposite for many. It is the approach that PE teachers take with their students, even those that lack the confidence to engage, that allows them to develop and strengthen their relationships.

Different schools have different approaches to their extra-curricular programmes. I have seen history teachers with band equipment in the back of their classroom (where he would play with students at lunch and after school). I have seen Technology teachers run bike maintenance workshops, Geography teachers running environment clubs, English teachers leading LGBTQ+ activities, Science teachers running cross fit clubs for Key Stage 4 girls. Regardless of their subject, any member of staff can invest in connecting with students on this level in an environment beyond the classroom. However, anyone working in schools will know the wide and varied demands of the job do not always allow us to directly invest as much time as we would like in the children in our care.

I have worked in and with a number of schools that have had a wide range of behaviour policies. Regardless of the policies, there remains a consistent theme; that is the tension between the need to consistently apply the clear and sometimes rigid systems and routines versus the flexibility for staff to apply their professional discretion in situations involving students with varying needs. Whilst having clear and consistently applied boundaries can help all children, this can be problematic when staff are required to uphold the school rules. Where staff are required to challenge students, this can trigger conflict and confrontation, risking an escalation, rather than a de-escalation of a situation. Using the "connect before correct" method, a simple restructuring of a conversation, can make all the difference. Recently, I approached a student that did not have the correct uniform (with whom I had several previous encounters with that did not go well!).

"Sir, I know what you are going to say…" she pre-empted.

"What might that be"? I responded.

"Do I have a note for my hoody".

"Actually, I was going to ask if you had a nice weekend as I remember said that you were going to stay at your Dad's new house".

"Oh!"

The comment took her completely off-guard. The defences came down and after a pleasant chat about the weekend, the uniform issue was resolved easily, quickly and without the escalation seen previously.

The best leaders I have worked with have the knowledge and skill to be able to uphold high expectations, whilst maintaining a level of compassion and respect for the students.

Looking back over my career, there have been specific events in various roles that have allowed me to develop a deeper empathy and understanding of what some young people have experienced in their lives and the impact this can have on their daily lives. In my first year of teaching, I attended a "Team Around the Child" Multi Agency meeting in my role as a Year 7 Tutor. Nothing could have prepared me for the exposure to the child's trauma that they were experiencing and verbal and physical violence that occurred in the meeting. In my first year as a senior leader, I found myself chairing similar Team Around the Child Multi Agency meetings. By this stage in my career, I was all too familiar with the dire circumstances that so many young people find themselves in.

When I became a Special Educational Needs and Disabilities Coordinator (SENCO), I was also the Designated Teacher for Looked After Children. I was privileged to have spent an increased amount of time working with and supporting students and their families of children with complex needs (including adopted children with attachment disorder). It was humbling to build such close relationships with the families and getting to know first-hand what their lived experiences are like. I was left in no doubt that if staff had the full history of the students that I was supporting, that they would, without question, be more compassionate in their approach and be more tolerant of the challenging behaviours that were sometimes being presented.'

The Action Hero Teacher
Karl Pupe

COVID-19 has changed classroom management forever and we must change with it. We are living in harrowing times. A 2021 Guardian report stated there has been a 70% rise in demand for children's mental health services in the UK because of the COVID-19 pandemic & subsequent lockdowns[1].

Devastatingly, this has negatively impacted students who struggle with Social, Emotional & Mental Health (SEMH) challenges who already are 99% less likely to keep up academically with their peers[2].

Classroom management post-COVID-19 is as much about the health & wellbeing of your students as it is about helping them make the grade.

The 'toeing-the-line-no-excuses' approach to behaviour management is potentially catastrophic to our more vulnerable learners and Global Majority learners.

We as educators must accept that 'one-size-DOES-NOT-fit-all.' If we are not even attempting to understand your students' most complex needs, we are doing them a disservice.

Why the way we teach SEMH students matter
When dealing with children that Social, Emotional & Mental Health needs (SEMH) one of your most difficult tasks is not getting them to learn but helping them improve their self-worth & helping them recognise & sustain a healthy self-image.

This often gets overlooked, but this is absolutely critical to their long term success. Some issues could extend from the home environment that the child was raised in. Children that come from challenging/dysfunctional families often have not had their basic needs met which can cause traumas that arrest their development. In order to cope in such frightening environments, they develop defence mechanisms like lashing out, zoning out, avoidance behaviours like walking away from you when you are talking to them etc. Because they have not been given the tools to differentiate & process their emotions, these defence-mechanisms or what I call 'mind programs' can run deep into their adulthood with dire consequences.

Some children from the moment that they were born, were told that they are 'good for nothing' & they would 'never make anything out of their lives' - how on Earth can we expect them to achieve when they have that message ringing in their minds all day?

No, I'm not asking you to be psychotherapists or counsellors - we as teachers should leave it to the professionals as they have been equipped with specialised skills that can help deal with our vulnerable kids' mental health needs.

But what I am asking you to do is to be a good human.
Care about those kids. Catch them doing the right things. Ask them how their day was. Correct them when they cross boundaries but do it with the spirit of helping them improve themselves rather than just making them feel bad.

What you don't realise is for some of these kids you may be the only positive adult that they have in their life. & they may never even say it to you. Where their caregivers have failed, you have now become their 'positive object' & your words, kindness & actions will echo throughout their lives.

I know that some of our rascals can be a handful (weren't we all?) But I want you to think about that the next time little Tommy changes the Microsoft Teams setting to German! You make a difference.

[1] https://www.theguardian.com/society/2021/feb/27/doctors-fear-new-child-mental-health-crisis-in-uk-made-worse-by-covid
[2] https://www.highspeedtraining.co.uk/hub/how-to-support-semh-in-schools/#:~:text=99%25%20of%20children%20with%20SEMH,a%20diagnosis%20of%20SEMH%20needs

Chapter 12 – Time to play

"Play is the exultation of the possible."
Martin Buber

In the final chapter of this section, we will look at the importance of play wrapped in care to mental wellbeing before concluding with some key things that you need to know when implementing a trauma informed approach in schools.

Over the last year or so we have seen the importance of play rise in profile. For many years, PE teachers and important PE organisations, such as the Youth Sport Trust (YST) and the association of Physical Education (AfPE), talked about PESSPA (Physical Education, School Sport, Physical Activity). However, play has become more and more visible. For example the title for the 2023 YST Conference was 'The power of PE, sport and play to improve mental health'.

Physical Education, School Sport, and Physical Activity are related terms in the context of promoting physical fitness and wellbeing, they each have distinct meanings and characteristics:

1. **Physical Education (PE):** Refers to structured educational programmes designed to promote physical fitness, skill development, and knowledge about physical activity and health. PE typically takes place within the school curriculum and is delivered by trained teachers. It may involve a range of activities such as sports, gymnastics, dance, and fitness training, and is typically assessed through formal evaluation methods. (Association for Physical Education .n.d.)

2. **School Sport:** Refers to organised sports programmes that take place within a school setting, typically as extracurricular activities. School sport programmes are often run by teachers or coaches and may involve inter-school competitions or tournaments. They may focus on a specific sport or a range of sports, depending on the resources and interests of the school and students involved. (Youth Sport Trust, n.d.)

3. **Physical Activity:** Refers to any bodily movement that results in energy expenditure, including activities that are part of daily life (such as walking or cycling to school) as well as structured exercise programmes. Physical activity is important for overall health and wellbeing and can include a wide range of activities, such as recreational sports, dance, fitness classes, and outdoor activities. (World Health Organisation, 2022)

So where does play fit in?

Play is defined *'as a spontaneous or organised activity that is engaged in for enjoyment, pleasure, and personal satisfaction, and involves active engagement and imaginative or creative thinking.'* Pellegrini & Boydston (2019)

Play is crucial for various aspects of human development and wellbeing, especially during childhood but also in adulthood. Here are several reasons why play is so important:

1. **Cognitive Development:** Play helps develop cognitive skills such as problem-solving, creativity, imagination, and critical thinking. It encourages experimentation and exploration, allowing individuals to learn and adapt to new situations.

2. **Social Development:** Play promotes social interaction and cooperation. It helps children learn to share, take turns, negotiate, and resolve conflicts. It strengthens social bonds and fosters a sense of community.

3. **Emotional Development:** Play allows individuals to express and regulate their emotions. It can be a safe outlet for processing difficult emotions and learning to cope with stress and anxiety.

4. **Physical Development:** Physical play contributes to the development of gross and fine motor skills. It promotes physical fitness and overall health.

5. **Creativity and Imagination:** Play encourages creativity and imaginative thinking. Whether it's through storytelling, drawing, building, or pretend play, individuals can explore new ideas and possibilities.

6. **Stress Reduction:** Play can serve as a stress reliever by diverting attention from worries and providing a sense of joy and relaxation. Engaging in enjoyable activities can reduce cortisol levels.

7. **Learning through Experience:** Play provides opportunities for hands-on learning. Whether it's through structured educational games or unstructured free play, individuals can gain practical knowledge and life skills.

8. **Problem-Solving:** Play often involves challenges and obstacles that require problem-solving. This helps individuals develop strategies for overcoming difficulties, which can be applicable to real-life situations.

9. **Bonding and Relationships:** Play strengthens bonds between children and their caregivers, as well as between peers and friends.

10. **Lifelong Enjoyment:** Developing a positive attitude towards play in childhood can lead to a lifelong appreciation for leisure activities, hobbies, and recreation. This can contribute to a more balanced and fulfilling life.

11. **Cultural and Social Learning:** Play often incorporates elements of culture and society, allowing individuals to learn about their environment, traditions, and societal norms.

Play is not just a frivolous activity; it serves as a fundamental aspect of human development and wellbeing. It helps individuals learn, grow, and thrive physically, mentally, emotionally, and socially. Incorporating play into one's life can have numerous positive effects on overall health and happiness. However, we are dealing with a generation of children who have missed out on two years of play and the associated benefits through the pandemic.

In this chapter we are going to explore the role of play in supporting our children's mental health and the work of Jaak Panksepp, his concept of 'affective neuroscience,' and his seven systems. Play is one of the seven systems and a balance of them underpins mental health. An imbalance of the systems underpins mental ill-health. Let's find out more.

Jaak Panksepp and balancing the 7 Systems Seesaw

Jaak Panksepp was a prominent Estonian American neuroscientist and psychologist. He was best known for his ground-breaking research on the emotional systems of the brain, particularly the study of animal emotions and the origins of human emotions.

Panksepp developed the concept of 'affective neuroscience,' which explores the neural mechanisms underlying emotional experiences. He identified seven core emotional systems in mammals: SEEKING, RAGE, FEAR, LUST, CARE, PANIC/GRIEF, and PLAY. His work demonstrated that these systems are present across different species, including humans, and are fundamental to our emotional experiences.

Panksepp's research (1998) has had a significant impact on the field of psychology, and his work is considered foundational to the understanding of emotions, motivation, and affective disorders. Panksepp's 7 systems refer to the seven primary emotional systems that are believed to be present in all mammals, including humans. These systems are identified based on their underlying neural circuitry and associated behavioural patterns.

Here's a simplified explanation of each system:

RAGE system

This system is responsible for our response to frustration or blocked goals. It can lead to aggressive or confrontational behaviour when we feel that our goals are being thwarted. This system is associated with the release of adrenaline and other stress hormones. The RAGE system is a complex set of neural circuits that are responsible for triggering aggressive and defensive behaviour. When activated, it can lead to feelings of anger, frustration, and a desire to protect oneself or others.

FEAR system

This system is responsible for our response to perceived threats or danger. It activates the fight or flight response, preparing our body to respond to a potential threat. This system is associated with the release of stress hormones such as cortisol and adrenaline. The FEAR system is a set of neural circuits that are responsible for the perception of danger and the activation of the fight-or-flight response. When activated, it can lead to feelings of fear, anxiety, and panic.

GRIEF system

This system is responsible for our response to loss or separation. It can lead to feelings of sadness, despair, and withdrawal when we experience the loss of someone or something that we care about. This system is associated with changes in the levels of neurotransmitters such as serotonin and dopamine. It plays a crucial role in teenagers' emotional responses to significant life events, such as the loss of a loved one or the breakup of a relationship.

CARE system

This system is responsible for our nurturing and caregiving behaviour. It is activated when we feel empathy or compassion for others, particularly those who are vulnerable or in need of help. This system is associated with the release of oxytocin, a hormone that is associated with social bonding and trust. It plays a crucial role in adolescents' development as they form relationships with peers, family members, and other important figures in their lives.

SEEKING system

This system is responsible for our motivation to explore and seek out rewards. It drives us to pursue things that we find pleasurable or rewarding, such as food, social interaction, or engaging in activities that we enjoy. This system is closely tied to the release of dopamine in the brain, which is associated with feelings of pleasure and reward. The SEEKING system is a motivational system that is responsible for exploratory behaviour, curiosity, and the search for resources. It drives individuals to seek out new experiences, to learn, and to grow.

PLAY system

This system is responsible for our enjoyment of play and social interaction. It drives us to engage in playful behaviour with others, which can help to build social bonds and promote learning and development. This system is associated with the release of endorphins, which are associated with feelings of pleasure and reward. The PLAY system is a set of neural circuits that are responsible for social bonding, exploration, and the development of social skills.

LUST system

This system is responsible for our sexual desire and behaviour. It drives us to seek out sexual partners and engage in sexual activity. This system is associated with the release of sex hormones such as testosterone and oestrogen.

For an individual to be mentally healthy, Panksepp believed that these seven emotional systems need to be balanced. This means that each system should be functioning in a way that is appropriate for the individual's current situation and environment, and that none of the systems should be dominating or suppressed to the point of causing harm.

Figure 27:

Panksepp's 7 Systems

A balance of the 7 systems underpins mental health.
An imbalance of the systems underpins mental ill-health.

Rage
Fear
Panic / Grief

Lust

Care
Seeking
PLAY

Over-active
Under-active
Optimally activated

© Jaak Panksepp

Consider this...
Think about your most challenging young people in your class, are you starting to notice any areas of the 7 systems that are overactive or underactive?

Blocked trust

Blocked trust refers to a situation where a person has difficulty establishing trust with others, due to past experiences of trauma or abuse. In trauma-informed practice, blocked trust in a state of Rage, Fear or Panic/Grief is an understandable response to trauma.

Individuals who have experienced trauma may have difficulty trusting others because they may have been betrayed or let down in the past. This can lead to a pattern of avoiding close relationships, being hypervigilant or suspicious of others, and having difficulty establishing a sense of safety with others.

In trauma-informed practice, it is important to be aware of the impact of trauma on a person's ability to trust, and to approach relationships with empathy, patience, and understanding. Practitioners should strive to create a safe and supportive environment that allows individuals to gradually develop trust at their own pace.

To support individuals with blocked trust, trauma-informed practice may involve techniques such as:

- building rapport,
- providing clear communication,
- respecting boundaries,
- and offering choices.

It is also important to acknowledge and validate the individual's experiences of trauma, and to support their efforts to develop self-care and coping strategies to manage their symptoms.

Emotional states become personality traits

Dr. Bruce Perry is a renowned psychiatrist and researcher who has extensively studied the impact of early childhood experiences on brain development and mental health. According to Dr. Perry (2006), the emotional states experienced by a child during their early years can have a lasting impact on their personality traits.

Children are born with a range of emotional states, such as joy, sadness, fear, anger, and disgust. These emotions are part of the natural human experience, and it is normal for children to experience a wide range of emotions as they grow and develop. However, if a child experiences prolonged or extreme emotional states, it can lead to the development of certain personality traits.

For example, if a child experiences prolonged fear or anxiety, they may develop a personality trait of being overly cautious or anxious. Similarly, if a child experiences prolonged anger or frustration, they may develop a personality trait of being easily agitated or quick to anger. The emotional states experienced by a child can also impact their ability to regulate their emotions. If a child experiences extreme emotions on a regular basis, they may struggle to regulate their emotions effectively, which can lead to difficulties with social interactions and relationships. Post lockdown I was struck by the sadness in some of my young people's emotional states and it became a motivating factor for me to learn about trauma-informed practice.

It is important to note that personality traits are not set in stone, and with the right support and interventions, children can learn to regulate their emotions and develop more positive personality traits. This is why it is crucial for us to support children in developing healthy emotional regulation skills from a young age.

Consider this...

What personality traits do you want the young people in your school to develop?

The importance of play wrapped in care

Since Covid, many children's opportunities to play have been more limited than before. As behaviour has declined, we have seen a trend from schools to reduce lunch and break times, to minimise the opportunities for misbehaviour. But are we missing a vital trick to help co-regulate our children, improving their mental wellbeing and outcomes in the process?

Consider this...
1. How long do your children get to play at school recreation times?
2. Has this increased, decreased or stayed the same since lockdown?

Play, in relation to mental wellbeing, first came onto my agenda at the YST National Conference in 2022. Dame Rachel De Souza, the Children's Commissioner, presented her findings on 'The Big Ask' where over half a million children, aged 4 to 18, answered questions about the topics most important to them to help them recover from the effects of Covid.

I noted with interest that young people wanted to:
- Receive support in places where they feel safe such as schools.
- Re-establish closer relationships with their friends.
- The opportunity to play.

The next day I was teaching outdoor adventure activities to a group of tricky and demotivated year 9s, so I decided to experiment. We had a lovely wood that we normally used for orienteering, so I said to the group that I didn't mind what they did for the lesson as long as they played, moved around, were safe and included everyone who wanted to play with them.

I said I would walk around the woods for health and check in with each group as I walked by, and that any child who didn't want to play could walk and talk with me. The results were excellent for that one off lesson. Smiles returned to their faces for the first time in a while and they were creative with the ideas they used to play.

As lessons progressed, I gave children more and more freedom with little interaction, but the novelty wore off. It wasn't as effective, and it appeared that the distance had returned between the class and myself. It wasn't until later on when I learned about Panksepp's 7 systems that I realised I missed out on something important.

Opportunities to play need to be wrapped in care. When play is accompanied by nurturing and supportive relationships with caregivers, it can have a profound impact on a child's emotional and social development. When children engage in play that is wrapped in care, they feel safe and supported, which allows them to explore and take risks without fear of judgement or rejection. This, in turn, helps children develop important social and emotional skills.

For example, when a child engages in play with a caregiver who is attentive and responsive, they learn to regulate their emotions and develop a sense of trust and safety in their relationships. This, in turn, can help them build resilience and cope with stress in healthy ways.

We can play a crucial role in promoting play that is wrapped in care by:
1. **Building strong relationships with students:** By establishing caring and supportive relationships with our students, we can create an environment that fosters trust and safety, which is essential for play.
2. **Encouraging cooperative play:** We can encourage children to engage in cooperative play activities that involve sharing, turn-taking, and problem-solving. Outdoor Adventure Activities is great for this.
3. **Using positive reinforcement:** We can use positive reinforcement to encourage positive behaviours during play, such as praising children for their efforts or sharing.
4. **Modelling appropriate play behaviours:** We can model appropriate play behaviours, such as taking turns and showing empathy, to help children learn how to interact with others in healthy ways.

Opportunities for schools

Schools can play a crucial role in promoting play outside the classroom. By creating a psychologically safe and supportive environment that encourages play, schools can help children develop the skills they need to thrive in school and beyond. Some ways schools can promote play include:

1. **Providing a variety of play equipment:** Adults can provide a range of equipment that encourage different types of play, such as skipping ropes, balls, and art supplies.
2. **Allowing time for free play:** Schools can incorporate free play time into the daily schedule, allowing children to choose how they want to play and who they want to play with. I have noticed with interest that my daughter's primary school often does this to help children self-regulate in the afternoon.
3. **Encouraging imaginative play:** Lunchtime Supervisors and student leaders can be trained to promote imaginative play by providing props/equipment and encouraging children to use their imagination to create their own stories, games, and scenarios.
4. **Facilitating social play:** Lunchtime Supervisors and student leaders can encourage children to play together and help them develop social skills, such as sharing and taking turns.

I had a 15 year old child who mentioned to our internal counsellor that he really struggled to self-regulate but playing basketball really helped him to calm down. Our brilliant counsellor let me know and we organised so that he could collect a basketball from me each break time so he could play on our outside court.

It provided me with a great opportunity to check in with him each day, to reassure him that he was psychologically safe and to occasionally play with him. It gave him a chance to self-regulate so that he was more successful in school and also gave him the additional responsibility of taking care of the ball and returning it each day, so that it was available the following day. It really didn't take much effort from me to provide the equipment, but it provided a lifeline for this young man, who had experienced multiple ACEs and was struggling in and out of school.

Pankepp believed that the systems were like muscles. The more we use them, the more they become part of our personality. He found that positive experiences that activate these systems, such as engaging in play or receiving nurturing and support from an adult, can become part of a person's personality and shape how they interact with others throughout their lives. Conversely, a lack of positive experiences in these systems can lead to difficulties developing social and emotional skills.

So how do we go about creating the conditions for this to occur? I believe PE teachers are expertly placed within schools to encourage play wrapped in care.

Warm ups are ideal times in lessons for children to create games using the STEP approach. Allocating a Space, a Task, some Equipment, and a certain number of People to children to create their own games, allows children to be creative and play.

When discussing this with Simon Scarborough, we both mentioned how often children come up with fantastic games to warm themselves up ready for the main part of the lesson. As a side note, it also frees up the teacher to take a step back and monitor what is going on and set up for the rest of the lesson.

Alternatively, games like hats and bowls, the bean game, stuck in the mud, skipping rope games, and Mega tag can be used to great effect to stimulate play wrapped in care. My colleague, Josh Larner, introduced Megatag to a Year 8 group who were a bit of a handful, and it had a transformational impact. The group loved the freedom of play to start the lesson and it helped Mr Larner show he cared about the group. The lessons got off to fantastic starts and it helped the rest of the lesson flow nicely, building excellent relationships in the process. It wasn't long before the rest of the PE team were borrowing his great idea to have the same impact with our classes.

Try this: Mega tag

1. Set up a space, it could be whole sports hall or a coned off grid on a field, depending on the size of your group.
2. Everyone can tag anyone.
3. They can tag anyone by making contact at the shoulder or below.
4. The person who is tagged has to sit down.
5. The person sitting down can only be freed once the person who tagged them has been tagged by someone else.
6. Play!

- *Safety* - Emphasise the importance of everyone looking where they are going and being aware of peers.

Finally, we can train our sports leaders to facilitate active play during lunchtimes, by providing appropriate equipment and giving them the skills and knowledge to play games with younger students. We need to make sure we are on hand to supervise and support where necessary, but it is a way that everyone benefits. Young children get the benefits of play wrapped in care, sports leaders develop vital leadership skills and get the buzz of helping their younger peers, and we get additional support for lunchtime clubs.

Figure 28:

Play becomes healing

Play becomes healing

Play is an essential part of childhood and is a natural way for children to learn, explore, and develop their social and emotional skills. Play allows children to express themselves freely, develop their creativity, and learn how to interact with others in a positive and constructive way.

But play can also have powerful healing effects on children's mental wellbeing. When children experience trauma, stress, or other negative experiences, play can provide a safe and nurturing space for them to process their emotions, develop coping skills, and heal from their experiences.

This is because play allows children to express their emotions in a non-threatening way, giving them a sense of control and empowerment over their feelings. Through play, children can explore their experiences and feelings, learn how to regulate their emotions, and develop a sense of resilience and adaptability.

As teachers, it is important we recognise the healing power of play and to create a psychologically safe and supportive environment for our children to engage in play. This can involve:

1. **Providing opportunities for unstructured play:** which allows them to explore and express themselves freely.
2. **Incorporating play into the curriculum:** through games, role-playing, or other playful activities that promote social and emotional learning.
3. **Encouraging creative expression:** through art, music, or storytelling, which can provide a therapeutic outlet for their emotions.
4. **Providing emotional support:** as children engage in play, help, and guide them to process their emotions and develop healthy coping strategies.

In concluding the first half of the chapter, play can be a powerful healing tool for children's mental wellbeing. By providing opportunities for children to engage in play and creating a safe and supportive environment, we can help children process their emotions, develop coping skills, and build resilience in the face of adversity.

Recovery

"Fall seven times, stand up eight."
Japanese proverb

Since starting the Diploma in September 2022 and placing relationships first, I was amazed at the benefits which came very quickly. My relationships with all children I taught had been transformed but particularly my most challenging young people as they felt psychologically safer, so they were calmer.

They became happier and healthier, and their behaviour improved significantly in my lessons. Children became more engaged in their learning which led to an increase in progress. My most challenging students in exam PE increased their predicted grade by 2.5. My classes became happy places again which helped my own wellbeing considerably. I felt like I could teach effectively again and despite the challenges that were still going on politically with the school, being in the classroom working with brilliant young people became a sanctuary for me, once again. In this final part of the chapter, we are going to wrap up trauma informed practice with some key things that you need to know.

The teenage brain

The teenage years are a time of significant brain development and change. This development can impact a teenager's behaviour, including their interactions with adults. It's common for teenagers to push away from us during this stage of development. It's important we understand this behaviour and approach teenagers with empathy and understanding.

During adolescence, the prefrontal cortex of the brain, which is responsible for decision-making, impulse control, and planning, is still developing. This can lead to a teenager's behaviour being driven by emotions rather than logic, making it harder for them to understand and navigate their own emotions and the emotions of others. Teenagers are also exploring their own identity and independence, which can lead to a desire to separate from adults and establish their own sense of autonomy. This desire for independence can manifest in a variety of ways, including pushing away from adults and resisting authority. It's important we recognise that teenagers' behaviour is not a reflection of their character or personality, but rather a result of their brain development and desire for independence.

We need to approach teenagers with empathy, understanding, and respect, while also providing appropriate boundaries and structure.

One way to approach teenagers is to acknowledge and validate their emotions and experiences. This can be done by actively listening to them, providing a safe space for them to express their feelings, and acknowledging their autonomy and independence. Building positive relationships with teenagers can also help to mitigate their desire to push away from adults.

Mattering matters

Feeling like you matter is crucial for anyone's mental wellbeing, especially children. When children feel like they matter, they are more likely to feel a sense of belonging, develop positive relationships with peers and teachers, and have a more positive outlook on their education. We can play a crucial role in creating school environments where children feel like they matter. Trauma-informed practice can be a powerful tool in achieving this.

We can create school environments where children feel like they matter by using a strengths-based approach. A strengths-based approach focuses on identifying and building on the strengths and positive qualities of students, rather than focusing on their deficits or weaknesses. When teachers recognise and celebrate the unique strengths and talents of each student, they help them to feel valued and important.

Another important aspect of creating school environments, where children feel like they matter, is to promote a sense of autonomy and choice. When children feel like they have some control over their environment and their learning, they are more likely to feel like they matter. Trauma-informed practice emphasises the importance of providing opportunities for choice and control.

Finally, creating a school environment where children feel like they matter, involves fostering a culture of care and support. Trauma-informed practice emphasises the importance of creating a safe and supportive learning environment that promotes emotional safety, social connectedness, and academic success. We can foster a culture of care by providing support for students who are struggling, acknowledging, and validating their emotions and experiences, and providing opportunities for healing and growth.

The rollercoaster of recovery

Recovering from trauma is a complex and often non-linear process. It's important for us to understand that the journey towards healing is not a straight line, but rather a rollercoaster with ups and downs along the way. This understanding can help us to support young people who have experienced trauma, with empathy and compassion. It's important we recognise that recovery from trauma is a unique process that varies from child to child. What works for one child may not work for another, and the journey towards healing is often unpredictable.

Figure 29:

The rollercoaster ride is a normal part of the recovery process and should be expected. That was certainly my experience. Weeks would go by where children were making fantastic progress and then we'd have a setback, where they would test boundaries to see if they could really trust me. We need to expect these tests, as it can be demoralising when we put so much effort into supporting our most vulnerable children, to have it thrown back in our faces.

By recognising that recovery from trauma is non-linear, we can adjust our expectations and support our students in a more empathetic and compassionate manner. This means being patient and flexible, providing additional support when needed, and celebrating even small successes along the way. We need to understand that recovery from trauma is a long-term process. It's not something that can be achieved overnight or through a quick fix. It requires a commitment to ongoing support and understanding, and a willingness to adjust our approaches as needed.

Not all students will recover

It is our goal to create a safe and supportive learning environment for all students, particularly those who have experienced trauma. While trauma-informed practice can be a powerful tool in promoting students' mental wellbeing, it's important to recognise that not all students will fully recover from their trauma. However, this does not mean that we should give up on them or that we have failed as educators. It simply means that we need to adjust our expectations and continue to do our best to support them.

We recognise that the effects of trauma can be long-lasting and may impact students' academic, social, and emotional functioning for many years. While some students may experience significant improvement with appropriate interventions, others may continue to struggle with the effects of trauma throughout their lives.

It's important we approach each student with compassion, empathy, and an understanding of their unique experiences and needs. By using a trauma-informed approach, we can create a safe and supportive learning environment that promotes healing, growth, and academic success. Schools can provide students with access to appropriate resources and support, such as mental health professionals or community organisations, that can help them to continue to heal and grow outside of the classroom.

We are not responsible for "fixing" students or their trauma. Our role is to support and empower them, and to provide them with the tools and resources they need to succeed. We can do this by continuing to educate ourselves about trauma and its impact, advocating for policies and programmes that support students who have experienced trauma, and promoting a culture of care and support in our schools.

Ultimately, not all students will recover from trauma, and that is okay. What matters is that we continue to try our best to support them, to create a safe and supportive learning environment, and to provide them with the resources and tools they need to succeed. By doing so, we can help them to lead fulfilling and meaningful lives, despite the challenges they may face.

Prioritising self-care

Implementing trauma-informed practice can be a challenging endeavour for us and our schools. One of the key hurdles lies in questioning the effectiveness of existing practices and what has historically been deemed successful. We may have relied on certain methods and strategies for years, and to shift towards a trauma-informed approach means acknowledging that these approaches may not have fully met the needs of our young people. This introspection can be uncomfortable and even disconcerting, as it challenges long-held beliefs and practices.

Furthermore, embracing trauma-informed practice necessitates change, and change is rarely a seamless process. It often involves stepping out of our comfort zone and venturing into uncharted territory. This can provoke resistance or hesitation, as we grapple with uncertainty and the fear of the unknown. At times, it may feel like progress is slow, or even like taking one step forward and two steps back. The journey towards trauma-informed practice can be filled with setbacks and setbacks can be disheartening. However, it's essential to understand that these challenges are part of the process of growth and transformation.

Implementing trauma-informed practice requires a commitment to delving deeper into interactions and issues that may have been previously addressed at a surface level. It demands a willingness to explore the underlying causes of behaviour and difficulties experienced by individuals. While this depth of understanding can be time-consuming initially, it ultimately saves time in the long run.

Self-care is important, we need to put on our own oxygen masks first. Working with students who have experienced trauma can be emotionally challenging, so it's important that we prioritise our own self-care. This may include seeking support from colleagues or mental health professionals or engaging in other self-care activities outlined earlier in the book. By addressing the root causes of challenges, we can develop more effective interventions and strategies, leading to improved outcomes for all of us. In essence, the effort invested in trauma-informed practice can yield substantial dividends.

Bringing our colleagues along on the journey to trauma informed

Trauma-informed practice is an approach that emphasises understanding the impact of trauma on individuals and adapting our practices to better support them. A trauma-informed approach recognises that behaviour is a symptom of underlying trauma and requires a shift in mindset from "What's wrong with you?" to "What happened to you?"

When we ask, "What's wrong with you?" We are making an assumption that the behaviour is intentional, and that the child is simply choosing to misbehave. This approach can lead to punitive measures and a focus on changing the child's behaviour, without addressing the underlying trauma that may be driving it. On the other hand, when we ask, "What happened to you?" We are acknowledging that the child's behaviour is a response to a traumatic experience, and that their behaviour is a coping mechanism.

This shift in mindset requires us to move away from a deficit-based model of thinking and towards a strengths-based approach. Instead of viewing children through the lens of their behaviour, we need to see them as complex individuals with a range of experiences, strengths, and challenges. This approach allows us to focus on building positive relationships, creating a safe and supportive learning environment, and providing opportunities for healing and growth.

In a trauma-informed classroom, the teacher takes on the role of a supportive ally rather than an authoritarian figure. This means taking a non-judgemental approach to behaviour and being open to hearing the child's perspective. It also means recognising the impact of trauma on the child's ability to learn and adapting teaching practices to better support them.

One important aspect of a trauma-informed approach is the recognition that trauma affects individuals in different ways. Some children may become withdrawn or anxious, while others may become aggressive or act out. It's important to understand that these behaviours are not a result of a child's character or personality, but rather a reflection of their experience of trauma.

Implementing trauma-informed practice requires a commitment to ongoing learning and growth. We must be willing to reflect on our own biases and assumptions, and to seek out resources and training to deepen our understanding of trauma and its impact. Collaboration with other educators, mental health professionals, and community organisations can be a valuable part of a trauma-informed approach.

We need to lose that desire to 'punish' children for their misbehaviour. Some of our colleagues will struggle with that, as that is all they have ever known in their own teaching journey, and in their own education experience before that. In my conversations with head teachers, who have implemented a trauma informed approach, this has been one of the biggest challenges they face.

We need to give serious thought to how we 'sell' a trauma informed approach to sceptical colleagues, so we can bring as many of our colleagues along with us to create meaningful change. I believe looking at the evidence base and presenting the facts from the ACE studies is the starting point. Showcasing stories such as Ian Wright's and Mr Pigden are also incredibly powerful to secure buy-in, but ultimately this approach might not be for every educator.

Trauma-informed practice can sometimes be an intimidating concept, for teachers who are not familiar with it. As a result, it may be helpful to simplify the language and focus on the core principles:
1. Prioritise relationships
2. Understand the unique needs of students who have experienced trauma
3. Provide appropriate support and interventions to help students succeed

Figure 30:

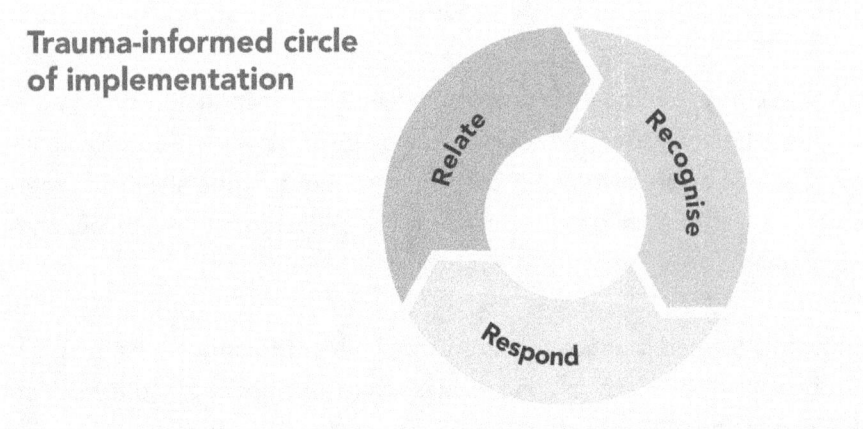

Trauma-informed circle of implementation

Staff training and advocacy for trauma-informed policies are essential components of promoting trauma-informed practice in schools. By incorporating trauma-informed principles into school-wide programmes and policies, we can create a more supportive and inclusive learning environment that promotes healing and growth for all. It would be fantastic to see more schools developing 'Relationship' policies to steer staff to better outcomes.

By simplifying the language and focusing on the core principles of trauma-informed practice, we can reduce the fear factor and create a more supportive and inclusive learning environment for all students and staff.

Benefitting all

When we invest in building positive relationships with our most challenging young people, the benefits ripple through the entire school community. By prioritising relationships and creating a safe and supportive learning environment for all students, we can reduce the need for discipline and create a more positive learning environment. This means that classrooms are calmer, teachers are happier, and students are more engaged and motivated to learn.

In a trauma-informed school, every student is recognised as an individual with unique needs and experiences. Teachers and staff are trained to recognise the signs of trauma and to respond with empathy and understanding. This means that even students who have not experienced trauma can benefit from a more compassionate and understanding approach to education.

When we invest in relationships with our most challenging young people, we create a sense of safety and belonging that benefits the entire school community. By taking the time to understand their experiences and needs, we can provide the appropriate support and interventions that help them to succeed academically and socially.

This approach has practical benefits. By reducing the need for discipline and creating a more positive learning environment, teachers can spend more time focusing on inspiring and learning rather than managing behaviour. When I implemented a trauma informed approach within my classroom, every single child benefitted. My relationship with each of my most challenging students either improved or stayed the same, none regressed. This led to calmer classrooms which permeated a feeling of greater psychological safety across the room. I was happier as my lessons were no longer being disrupted. We had more fun together, more of us were in the social engagement system and we worked together as a team to help each other thrive. I was also more emotionally available for my colleagues so I could support them more effectively simply by listening, really listening, without trying to fix everything.

We need an "army" of trauma-informed practitioners throughout our schools, including front line teachers, counsellors, social workers, and senior leaders who can work together to create a comprehensive support system that meets the diverse needs of our young people. By investing in this network of trauma-informed practitioners, we can create a safer and more supportive learning environment for all of our students. This approach is essential in creating a school environment that fosters healing, mental wellbeing, growth, and resilience in the face of adversity. Without it, we are teaching young people with our hands tied behind our backs.

Chapter summary

- Play is an essential part of childhood development, as it allows children to learn, explore, and develop their social, emotional, cognitive, and physical skills in a natural and enjoyable way.
- Dr. Jaak Panksepp's research on emotional systems identified seven basic emotional systems in the brain, which are associated with specific behaviours and emotions. Understanding these emotional systems can provide insights into how emotions and behaviour are interconnected and can inform strategies for promoting mental wellbeing and emotional development in children.
- Play that is wrapped in care is a critical aspect of children's mental wellbeing. By creating a safe and nurturing environment that promotes play, teachers can help children develop important social and emotional skills that will serve them throughout their lives. Teachers play a crucial role in promoting play that is wrapped in care, and by doing so, they can help their students thrive both in and out of the classroom. Our children need more play wrapped in care in a post Covid education world.
- Teenagers' brain development and desire for independence can lead to pushing away from adults. As teachers, we need to approach teenagers with empathy and understanding while also providing appropriate boundaries and structure.
- Mattering matters for all of us, and trauma-informed practice can help us to create

- school environments, where children feel like they matter.
- Recovering from trauma is a non-linear process that is unique to each child. It's important for us to recognise that there will be ups and downs along the way, and to adjust our expectations and support accordingly. By providing a safe and supportive learning environment, celebrating successes, and being patient and flexible, we can help our students on their journey towards healing and recovery.
- When we adopt a trauma-informed model of education, every single child benefits, from the most challenging student in alternative provision to the star pupil who breezes through school life. By investing in relationships with our most challenging young people, we create a safer and more supportive learning environment that benefits the entire school community.
- Taking trauma-informed practice from the classroom to the wider school community can have a powerful impact on the wellbeing of all students. We need an army of trauma-informed practitioners to help young people recover and thrive in education.

Critical questions

1. How are you ensuring that your most vulnerable children feel like they matter in your classroom?

2. What do your children say when you ask them what their perfect school looks like?

3. How can you ensure buy-in from colleagues to support a whole-school trauma informed approach?

4. How can you take trauma-informed practice from your classroom to your wider school to have a greater impact?

BOOK BONUS
Try the Enhancing Engagement scorecard to complete a 2 minute audit of your Trauma Informed PE provision.
https://bit.ly/PEScore

TIME TO RISE UP

Chapter references

- Association for Physical Education. (n.d.). What is PE? AfPE. https://www.afpe.org.uk/physical-education/what-is-pe/
- Youth Sport Trust. (n.d.). School sport. https://www.youthsporttrust.org/school-sport
- World Health Organization (2022). Physical Activity. [online] World Health Organization. Available at: https://www.who.int/news-room/fact-sheets/detail/physical-activity.
- Pellegrini, A. D., & Boydston, C. R. (2019). The nature of play. In P. J. Pellegrini (Ed.), Oxford handbook of the development of play (pp. 3-16). Oxford University Press.
- Panksepp, J. (1998). Affective neuroscience: The foundations of human and animal emotions. New York: Oxford University Press.
- Perry, B. D. (2006). Applying principles of neurodevelopment to clinical work with maltreated and traumatized children: The neurosequential model of therapeutics. In N. Boyd Webb (Ed.), Working with traumatized youth in child welfare (pp. 27-52). New York, NY: Guilford Press.
- Scarborough, S., & Durden-Myers, E. (2022) PE Scholar Gender equality online learning course.

Additional insights

Nurturing mental wellbeing through play: The Finnish Aapproach
In the quest for an ideal education system that not only imparts knowledge but also fosters holistic development, Finland has emerged as a global leader. Known for its exceptional education system, Finland recognises the profound impact of play on children's mental wellbeing and overall development. This section explores how the Finnish education system prioritises play and its connection to nurturing mental wellbeing.

Play-based learning: A foundation for growth
Play holds a central role in the early childhood education landscape in Finland. From the earliest years, Finnish educators understand that play is not merely a pastime but a powerful tool for learning and personal growth. The Finnish National Curriculum for Early Childhood Education and Care places significant emphasis on play-based learning, acknowledging its vital role in stimulating curiosity, developing social skills, problem-solving abilities, and fostering creativity.

Creating engaging play environments

Finnish teachers recognise the importance of creating stimulating play environments that support children's natural inclination to explore and learn. They are trained to design interactive and engaging spaces that encourage imaginative play and active participation. These environments allow children to develop their unique strengths and interests while promoting collaboration and social interaction.

The role of play in mental wellbeing

Finland's education system acknowledges that mental wellbeing is an essential component of overall development. By integrating play into the curriculum, Finnish educators aim to promote positive mental health among students. Play provides an outlet for self-expression, emotional regulation, and stress relief, allowing children to develop resilience and coping strategies. Through play, children can engage in imaginative scenarios, express their emotions, and work through challenging situations, fostering emotional intelligence and self-awareness.

Student-centred learning: Empowering students

Beyond the early years, Finland's commitment to student-centred learning continues to prioritise mental wellbeing. By encouraging active participation, project-based learning, and practical experiences, Finnish schools create an environment that promotes autonomy and intrinsic motivation. Students are given the opportunity to explore their interests, collaborate with peers, and develop a sense of ownership over their learning journey. This approach helps cultivate a positive mindset, confidence, and a sense of purpose, all crucial elements for maintaining mental wellbeing.

Equity and wellbeing: A harmonious connection

Finland's education system places a strong emphasis on equity, striving to provide equal educational opportunities for all students. This commitment to inclusivity extends to promoting mental wellbeing. By ensuring a supportive and inclusive learning environment for every student, regardless of their background, Finland aims to minimise achievement gaps and enhance overall mental health and happiness among its student population.

The Finnish education system stands as a shining example of how the integration of play and a student-centred approach can contribute to nurturing mental wellbeing. By recognising the importance of play in early childhood education and extending its principles throughout the system, Finland demonstrates that learning and mental health are inseparable. Through play-based learning and an emphasis on student autonomy, Finland equips its students with the necessary skills and tools to thrive academically, socially, and emotionally, setting a precedent for educational systems worldwide.

5As of Allyship for trauma-informed practice

Simon Scarborough and Dr Liz Durden-Myers from PE Scholar created a brilliant 5As approach to allyship regarding gender equality and the same 5As can be implemented for trauma-informed practice.

Here are 5As of allyship that can help promote trauma-informed practice in our classrooms:

1. Acceptance
Is the foundation of allyship. It involves acknowledging and accepting each student as a unique individual with their own experiences, needs, and strengths. This means avoiding judgement or assumptions, and instead creating a culture of respect and inclusivity in the classroom.

2. Awareness
Involves understanding the impact of trauma on children's mental wellbeing. This means being aware of the signs and symptoms of trauma, as well as the different ways that trauma can manifest in behaviour, emotions, and academic performance. With this awareness, teachers can respond to students with compassion and empathy, and provide appropriate support.

3. Activities
Are a key part of creating a trauma-informed classroom. They can help promote social-emotional learning, build resilience, and provide a sense of safety and belonging. Activities can include our own body language to create psychological safety, mindfulness exercises, group discussions, journalling, art therapy, and physical activities that promote self-expression and self-awareness.

4. Adjustments

Involve making adaptations to the classroom environment and teaching methods to better support students with trauma. This can include changes to the physical environment, such as providing a calm and comfortable space or sanctuaries for students to retreat to, or adjustments to teaching methods, such as allowing for more flexibility and choice in assignments and activities.

5. Advocacy

Involves speaking up for and supporting students who have experienced trauma. This can include advocating for their needs within the school system such as reducing unnecessary rules, connecting them with appropriate resources and support, and working to address systemic issues that contribute to trauma, such as poverty or discrimination.

By incorporating these 5As of allyship into our teaching practice, we can help create a supportive and inclusive classroom environment that promotes trauma-informed practice and supports children's mental wellbeing.

Consider this...
In which of these 5 areas are you strongest? Which of the 5 areas could you develop further?

Part 4:
Moving Forward Together

Chapter 13 – Creating whole school impact

"Be the change you wish to see in the world."
Mahatma Gandhi

Back at the start of the book, I mentioned that my ambition during my PGCE was to become a Director of Sport. After being a Head of PE for 5 years at my previous school, I knew how to lead a PE department, but I didn't know how to create a whole school impact. Hopefully this chapter gives you a guide of how you can do that through bringing your entire school community together to improve the mental wellbeing of your young people and colleagues.

In this chapter we will explore how we can take the early intervention strategies and trauma informed practice, outlined in parts two and three, to create a whole school impact that sends positive ripples through our communities.

I wanted to create an ethos of the whole school being 'One Big Inclusive Team' including children, parents, staff, and the wider community/peers so that everyone was pulling in the same direction.

Figure 31:

One big team...

The vision was to aspire towards everyone feeling psychologically safe, supported, and able to contribute. Children, and transforming their wellbeing outcomes, were absolutely at the heart of the vision, supported by a triangle of teachers, parents and the wider community, but we were all interconnected and everyone needed to play their part and support each other. It was a big vision but that was the intent.

Within my own school and schools I work with, there are over 11 different ways we have applied these concepts. They include:
1. Within PE lessons
2. Within RSHE lessons
3. In school clubs
4. During Enrichment days
5. During Form times
6. Cross curricular opportunities
7. Student Voice
8. Staff wellbeing programmes
9. Social media content to improve the wellbeing of the whole school community
10. Sport Sanctuaries

We are going to explore each in more detail and share case studies to give you some ideas and inspiration.

Consider this...

As I go through the different ways we approached it, consider what might suit your setting. With the exception of each parent/carer, no one knows your students and their needs and your local context better than you as teachers.

1. What would be the easy wins to implement quickly?
2. What might you be able to implement in the mid-term?
3. Who are the staff in your setting who might be willing and able to support you?

Within PE

As a Director of Sport, I was always going to start in PE. The subject naturally provides great opportunities for PE teachers to have whole school impact through the ability to create and provide physical activity opportunities. We have access to facilities, time, and equipment that other subject teachers just don't have.

PE teachers often have good relationships with many of their young people which facilitates having conversations around their mental wellbeing. Many young people will enjoy being in their PE lessons, so their social engagement system is already engaged and the equipment, be it a football, a dance sequence or fitness equipment, works well as a 3rd object to open up a conversation and to go deeper.

Our programme started in May 2020 as the first lockdown was used to test the resources with key worker children, focusing on mindfulness alongside a rigorous personalised circuit training programme.

From September 2020, all Key Stage 3 groups and some Key Stage 4 groups studied Building Mental Fitness alongside a differentiated yoga programme, as part of the school's recovery curriculum. As time moved on, pupils were offered a wider range of activities, depending on their individual needs for mental health benefits and this is where I started to create the 4 RISE categories.

We experimented with repetitive exercises, used stress busters in the fitness suite, and inclusive team sports such as dance shows, rugby, netball, and football to give students that social aspect that team sports are so great for. By giving students greater choice over the activity, we saw students demonstrate greater effort, engagement, and progress.

We used the mental health continuum, outlined in chapter 4, as a strong start activity and that helped us identify young people who were struggling with their mental health but sneaking under the radar.

We then looked at the Mental Fitness Pyramid, each of the healthy habits, and how to access the 4 happiness chemicals, for 10 minutes at the start of each lesson, before taking part in vigorous physical activity. These have been discussed in chapter 5 and 6.

The programme evolved with an optional Key Stage 4 group of disengaged students covering the content during walking for health in core PE. It was fantastic to see the group's openness to discuss their own mental health grow and create a culture of peer support so young people knew they were not battling their mental health issues on their own.

The impact of the programme was dramatic, with 94% of students who had completed the unit believing that they "feel more equipped to manage their mental health now and in the future with the skills they had been taught".

The programme was a major contributing factor to the school being awarded the AfPE quality mark with Distinction. Chair of AfPE, Mike Crichton, cited the school's "Highly effective links between Physical Education, School Sport, Physical Activity and wellbeing, including a very innovative approach to Covid19 recovery since lock down", as one of the reasons why the school was successful.

As students struggled more and more with the impact of Covid and all the changes within my school, we had to lean further on this area of activity to create meaningful PE for our young people as a traditional model was just not working, turning many off being physically active.

We used early intervention mental wellbeing programmes to engage those young people who felt disengaged in physical education. By focusing on their mental wellbeing, it was a great way of reducing the feeling of threat and being unsafe by taking the focus away from skills and performance and tapping into areas where a young person may be struggling in their life.

Mental wellbeing programmes in PE are a great opportunity to draw more young people to feel included in this vital subject for long term wellbeing. Actor, Jonah Hill, has talked about his childhood and how he hated physical activity, as it was always propositioned as a way to manage his weight issues and it made him feel rubbish about himself. He wished that physical activity had been sold to him as a way to make him feel happier and healthier instead.

We know that PE engages certain sporty types of children; we know there is a section of young people who love PE to help them get and stay in shape physically; and there are some who love the leadership opportunities and the chance to socialise with friends and that is great! The challenge is how we can engage more and more young people.

I want all young people to love being physically active. This subject has given me so much across my life, the friendships I have developed, my health, life skills, a career and living; I even met my wife and had my two precious children through PE. I want to share that gift with as many young people as I can so that they can also benefit.

What if we tried using PE to target those students, who have traditionally been disengaged, with how physical activity can benefit how they feel and their general happiness? I think this is an opportunity that we can take as a community of committed PE professionals, to make a whole school impact across our schools, our communities and across the country.

Where do wellbeing programmes fit in with the national curriculum?

According to the Department for Education (2013), the national curriculum for physical education aims to ensure that all pupils:
1. Develop competence to excel in a broad range of physical activities
2. Are physically active for sustained periods of time
3. Engage in competitive sports and activities
4. Lead healthy, active lives.

Teaching mental wellbeing within PE is well within the national curriculum in England: PE programmes of study under the 4th aim.

It would be great to see Ofsted PE subject leads give greater emphasis to this though. From my discussions with many PE colleagues and their own student voice surveys, students and staff want more emphasis on the link between physical activity and mental wellbeing and less on a more traditional PE model focusing on skills, knowledge and tactics and rules. There seems to be a disparity between the two viewpoints, especially in low socio-economic areas, and makes us question whether Ofsted are in touch with how some schools have evolved in a post Covid education world to meet the needs of their young people. I also appreciate that many PE colleagues are very nervous of mental health falling into PE's responsibility, so I hope this book reassures colleagues and helps them move forward with more confidence.

What could a wellbeing PE lesson look like?

This is one way I used a lesson in the fitness suite to teach the link between physical activity and mental wellbeing incorporating trauma informed principles.

Strong start

I used to meet and greet my class by being mindful of my face, voice, and body so that all children felt psychologically safe by triggering their social engagement system. To do this, I made sure I was smiling and welcomed each child to the classroom with a high 5 or fist bump.

I started the lesson by using the mental health continuum so that I checked in with where each member of my class was on that particular day, depending on their individual situation and circumstances. I did this within 3 minutes, by explaining the four categories on the continuum between thriving at one extreme, to struggling and ill at the opposite end. I asked children to bow their heads, close their eyes and put their hand up when I mentioned criteria that matched how they were feeling that day. I would make a mental note to check in during the lesson with those who were starting to struggle or were struggling and ill.

Depending on the conversation, I would refer to our internal specialist counsellor, safeguarding team or I would let the child know that I'm here for them any time they would like to talk as an emotionally available adult. I would recommend that any students who were struggling and ill should make an appointment to see their doctor.

Intro to RISE

I would then explain the following 4 different categories of activities that boost mental wellbeing in a variety of ways. Children could use the treadmills, cross trainers, bikes, and rowing machines for their repeaters. For inclusive teams within the fitness suite, children buddied up with a partner and help motivate each other at the same time as checking for safe technique. They would often develop a close bond as they trained each other.

Stress busting activities such as our boxing mannequin 'BOB' and weight training were great ways to release that tension in a safe and controlled way, improve their vagal tone and widen their window of tolerance. Energising activities would be skipping or bodyweight exercises such as press ups.

I would let my young people know that they had an exit ticket challenge: to tell me the name of the category they enjoyed the most, what specific activity they completed from the category and how it improved their mental wellbeing. This would give them some thinking time to plan their answer.

Time to RISE
Children would then have the rest of the lesson to work out independently with a training partner depending on their individual needs. I would often work out alongside them to act as a role model and then explain how it had helped my own mental wellbeing. Working out alongside my young people provided a great opportunity to have individual conversations with those students who were struggling without their peers noticing.

Exit ticket
We would complete the plenary, checking progress against learning outcomes before finishing with our exit ticket task. The exit ticket cements learning and gave me a chance to check in with every student, check their understanding and praise their effort being mindful of using my face, voice, and body. This approach helped to convey that they are psychologically safe with me and that I am an emotionally available adult to them. Eye contact, a high 5, a smile and a compliment is a great way to do this. The exit ticket task also creates a great opportunity to develop their oracy by encouraging them to plan their answer and communicating in detail without prompting from me.

Our children found this lesson highly enjoyable. Kieran, a student in year nine said "I really enjoy our RISE Up lessons. We learn how to improve our mental wellbeing and have a lot of freedom to choose how we do this in a safe, non-threatening environment. It has really helped me improve my behaviour around school. I really look forward to these lessons."

Adaption
If you haven't got a fitness suite, this lesson can be adapted for a sports hall or field by creating a circuit that involves body weight exercises, such as press ups and triceps dips. Include stations that involve repeatable activities such as running, walking, shuttle runs or skipping.

Transforming outcomes

This case study shows how early intervention programmes can transform wellbeing, engagement, behaviour, and progress in PE.

Case Study
King's Leadership Academy Liverpool - Creating Meaningful PE

King's Leadership Academy Liverpool is a coeducational secondary school and sixth form located in Dingle, Liverpool. King's Liverpool is a non-selective school with 'grammar school' experiences and culture. They are one of four schools I partnered with as part of our 'Liverpool RISE Up' Trauma Informed PE pilot programme in collaboration with the brilliant team at the Liverpool School Sports Partnership.

They have done a fantastic job of implementing the programme to create 'meaningful PE' experiences for a group of disengaged Year 8 girls. Brilliant PE teacher, Polly Crawley, and Inspirational Trust PE Lead teacher, Louise Mansell, talk us through their intent for the RISE Up programme, how they implemented it, and its impact on their young people.

Intent
Our intent for our 'Rise Up' programme was to improve the mindset and behaviour of one of our (shared) female Y8 classes (consisting of 18 students) through a variety of inclusive activities and lessons catered towards their personal preferences and centred around mental wellbeing and the positive impact that physical activity can have on young people. Mindset and Meaningful PE

We ultimately wanted to provide our students in this class with a more positive mindset towards PE and physical activity, different 'self-care' strategies regarding mental wellbeing, and the knowledge to be able to lead healthy active lifestyles both during and after they have left school. Many students within this class held very negative attitudes towards PE and often displayed inappropriate behaviours towards each other which sometimes resulted in disruptive arguments and even physical altercations.

Breaking down barriers
It was also evident that a lot of our students unfortunately struggled with issues regarding their self-image, physical ability, and confidence, which became particularly apparent when asking them to get changed into their kit or when asking them to engage and

participate within activities. We wanted to break down these personal barriers and negative mindsets, and instead, provide them with the knowledge required for them to self-regulate their emotions, improve their self-esteem so that they could be kinder not only to their peers, but to themselves - while simultaneously demonstrating to them how PE can be a psychologically safe and beneficial environment for them to thrive in.

We completed an adapted version of the Warwick–Edinburgh Mental Wellbeing Scale survey and the school wellbeing scorecard so that we could track the impact of the programme. We scored 53% back in March 2023. It was a good starting point, but we wanted to do more for the young people that we serve.

Implementation

We first implemented the programme by allowing the students involved to wear their PE kits to school on days where they had PE. We identified the 'changing' aspect of our lessons to be a problem for these students and decided that this would not only increase lesson time but also assist with their self-confidence and body image concerns. Immediately, this had a positive effect on the start of lessons and removed any arguments surrounding getting changed or forgetting kit. We then used their timetabled PE lessons to implement the programme, combining both practical and theory lessons.

Some of our practical lessons, inspired by the programme's intent, included yoga, nature walks, an active Easter egg hunt with prizes, and a session based around OCD, hygiene, and healthy nutrition, where we made fruit smoothies, (making a huge mess in the process), and then cleaned up together as a team.

Our theory lessons involved group discussions and a 'no judgement' environment where we shared ideas on mental wellbeing strategies and explored topics such as self-esteem, body image, and mental health – all with an underlying link to sport and physical activity. When first implementing the programme to our school, we discussed it with our Headteacher who made it clear that budgeting could be provided to enable us to offer trips and / or prizes to the students completing it, so this is something we aim to follow up towards the end of the year.

Impact

Overall, the programme has had a definite positive impact on the majority of the students in our Year 8 class, and the general attitude towards our lessons is significantly more optimistic than it was previously. We no longer have struggles or arguments regarding PE kits, and it is often that students will express their excitement or enjoyment for these lessons, despite having demonstrated negative mindsets in the past, which has been very gratifying for us to witness. Students have also begun to showcase a far greater understanding of mental health and wellbeing, and an awareness of the various coping strategies associated with this.

Since commencing the programme in March, we have witnessed a significant improvement to the overall behaviour and attitude of the students in this class, and it has become clear that the students involved have adopted a greater sense of respect and collaboration for each other.

This is something they lacked as a majority at the start of the year. The graph below demonstrates the considerable drop in negative behaviour events for this class in PE (alone) since the start of the year.

Figure 32:

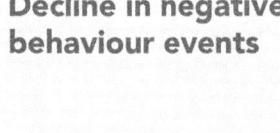
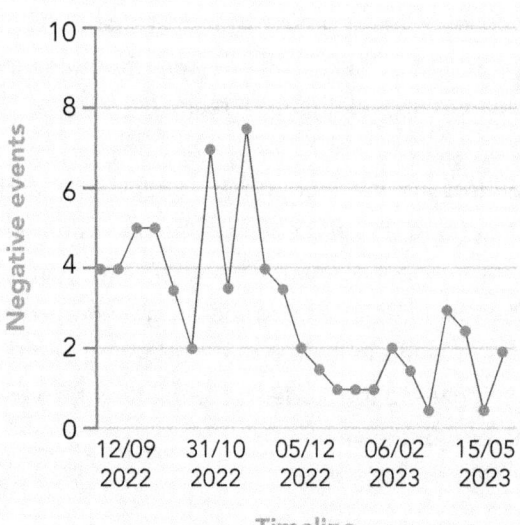

Since commencing the programme in March, our highest number of behaviour events in a lesson has been 3, whereas our previous highest number of events in one lesson was 7.5. From our class of 18, only two students have failed to respond to the programme as of yet and continue to demonstrate reluctance and negativity towards it. Despite our efforts, we are still yet to witness a constructive change in their attitudes and will continue to monitor this throughout the remainder of the programme. We won't give up on them and will do our best to create an environment that will eventually help them feel psychologically safe in PE.

Student voice

We presented our students involved with a questionnaire in order to gather a greater impression of their opinions on the programme. We have identified some key quotes taken from these:

What have you enjoyed most about the programme / lessons so far?
"I enjoyed doing yoga"
"The yoga and smoothies"
"When we did yoga it was fun and relaxing"
"Getting to understand people"

Do you feel more positive towards PE lessons, and if so why?
"Yes I do, I like it because now if someone says 'you can't' I don't believe them"
"Yes I do, if you want to do it just do it, don't listen to what people say"
"Yes, I feel more excited for it and it's more fun"
"I feel more better in PE and more happy"
"I feel more confident"

Has being able to wear your PE kit to school made you feel better around PE and getting changed, if so why?
"It's easier to do and faster"
"It's more comfortable"
"We don't waste time during PE lessons and get better exercise"

Using their answers, we re-visited our adapted Short Warwick–Edinburgh Mental Wellbeing scale survey for the perceptions of our children's progress of their mental wellbeing. The results showed that each of the 7 areas had improved from the lowest possible score to the highest.

Figure 33:	Kings **Pre** RISE Up intervention	Kings **Post** RISE Up intervention
'They've been feeling optimistic about the future'	None of the time	Often
'They've been feeling useful'	None of the time	Often
'They've been feeling relaxed'	None of the time	Often
'They've been dealing with problems well'	None of the time	Often
'They've been thinking clearly'	None of the time	Often
'They've been feeling close to other people'	None of the time	Often
'They've been able to make their own mind up about things'	None of the time	Often
'They've been feeling able to manage their own wellbeing'	None of the time	Often
What are your biggest challenges for your target group at the moment?	Attendance, attainment, behaviour, engagement, mental health, personal development	
What challenges has RISE Up intervention helped improve for your target group?	Attendance, attainment, behaviour, engagement, mental health, personal development	

We also completed the school wellbeing scorecard again. Our score increased to 88%, showing an improvement of 35%.

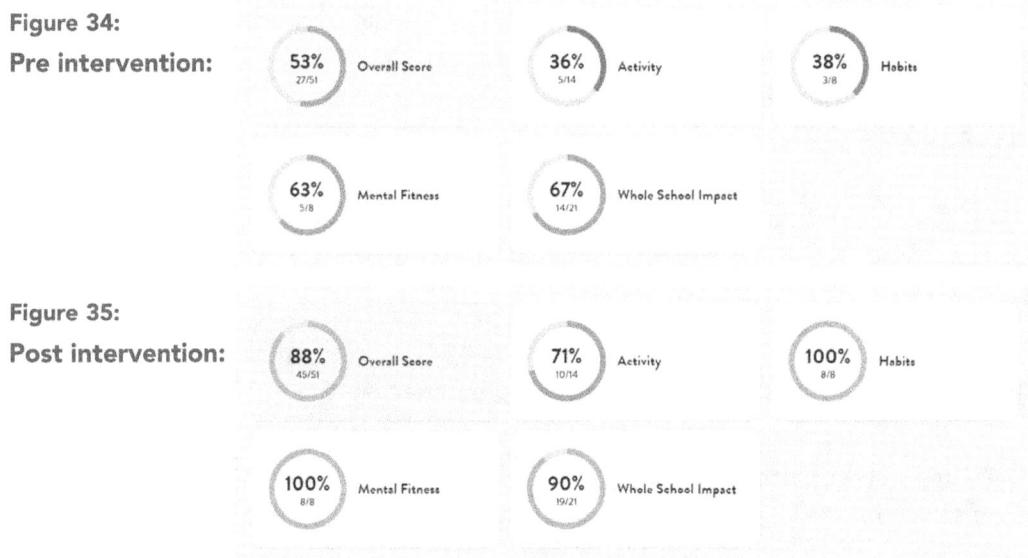

Figure 34:
Pre intervention:

Figure 35:
Post intervention:

Moving forward
This programme will certainly impact our work moving forward as it has provided us with a newly adapted, more progressive approach that centres heavily around mental health and wellbeing and less on purely just sport and skill-based PE. This new approach to our lessons recognises the importance of holistic development and ultimately creates a more inclusive and supportive environment for our students. We now practise the acknowledgement that physical fitness is just one aspect of overall wellbeing, and mental and emotional health are equally significant.

By integrating mindfulness and relaxation techniques, promoting emotional regulation, and providing mental health education as part of this programme, we can address the diverse needs of our students more accurately, but also contribute positively to productivity within PE settings and create a more fulfilling experience for students that will in time, improve their attitude towards these lessons. Having witnessed success from this one cohort, we will definitely seek to incorporate the programme into other classes, with the overarching aim of implementing it officially across our four 'Trust' schools.

Within RSHE and personal development lessons
We know that it is now statutory for schools to teach the link between physical activity and mental wellbeing (Department For Education, 2019) and this provides the opportunity for RSHE leads to collaborate with PE teachers to create meaningful programmes for each individual school setting. RSHE leads can understand from PE teachers what activity areas children in your school are passionate about and make lessons more meaningful and appropriate for children's individual needs.

I applied to lead RSHE in my school so I could have greater ownership over the RSHE curriculum and create meaningful action around early intervention programmes, mental wellbeing, and financial literacy to give children the resources and greater opportunity and choice in the future to transform their life chances. All year groups were taught the link between physical activity and mental wellbeing and year 8 students covered this in RSHE to reinforce the importance of proactive self-care strategies that they had also been taught in PE to build in opportunities for retrieval practice.

We should also be using our knowledge of Adverse Childhood Experiences, the importance of relationships, and Swarbricks 8 dimensions of wellbeing to inform our pupil premium policy and provision.

Try this:
The 8 Dimensions of wellness

The '8 Dimensions' model has been used to craft a highly effective framework for the pursuit of wellness. In no particular order, these dimensions are: **Physical, Spiritual, Social, Intellectual, Emotional/Mental, Occupational, Environmental, Financial.**

Figure 36:

Environmental
Good health by occupying pleasant, stimulating environments that support well-being

Emotional
Coping effectively with life and creating satisfying relationships

Financial
Satisfaction with current and future financial situation

Intellectual
Recognizing creative abilities and finding ways to expand knowledge and skills

Wellness

Spiritual
Expanding our sense of purpose and meaning in life

Physical
Recognizing the need for physical activity, diet, sleep and nutrition

Occupational
Personal satisfaction and enrichment derived from one's work

Social
Developing a sense of connection, belonging, and a well-developed support system.

Adapted from Swarbrick, M. (2006). A Wellness Approach: Psychiatric Rehabilitation Journal, 29(4), 311-314.

The model prominently features adjacent dimensions overlapping to convey the idea that all dimensions are connected and reliant on one another. When teaching the model, Dr. Swarbrick discusses how each dimension can impact one another, both positive and negative.

The most successful aspect of this model is that it is strength focused, building on people's daily habits and routines, to build and strengthen new habits. People often identify key activities they do each day, for example, physical activity which helps in multiple dimensions including physical, emotional, and social.

 **Try this:**

1. Rank the 8 dimensions in order of how important they are to you from 1-8, 1 being the most important.
2. Plan one best action you could do to improve your most important dimension.
3. Take action by doing.
4. Go back to step 2 and repeat with a new dimension or action.

During form times

Within form group activities, I created weekly content as part of Mindful Mondays, Wellness Wednesdays, and Physical Fridays to create and reinforce healthy habits throughout the school. This was a great way to recap on key concepts and reintroduce them on a weekly basis. I would use these slides that I would share with form tutors to highlight key strategies and people in the school who could support their mental wellbeing, such as our brilliant internal specialist counsellor. This also supported national campaigns around mental health.

Case Study
Sancroft

Harleston Sancroft Academy is the only Church of England All Through School in Norfolk. Sitting at the very heart of the Harleston community, it provides an excellent education in a nurturing, family environment. They have done a brilliant job of implementing the RISE Up programme within their form time programme to boost the mental wellbeing of their young people.

Molly Harris spearheaded the programme by completing our online training, setting the vision for the Academy, and adapting the RISE Up resources to meet the needs of Sancroft students for her team of form tutors. Tutors deliver fortnightly activities on a Monday afternoon covering a range of early intervention wellbeing topics such as mental fitness, healthy habits and accessing the happiness chemicals.

Lewis Disbury is a PE Teacher and form tutor who delivers the RISE Up activities to his vertical tutoring group. Lewis said *'I really enjoy delivering the activities with my form. It is a great opportunity to discuss all things wellbeing with my tutees, it has prompted some brilliant conversations, and it helps me show the young people in my form that I care about them. The activities are useful for promoting conversations, breaking the stigma in discussing mental health and helping our young people realise that it is ok to not be ok.*

Our young people particularly benefitted from understanding the link between physical activity and mental wellbeing, and how different activities help our young people manage their mental wellbeing. We have now added the programme to some of our PE lessons as well to incorporate physical activity to boost our children's wellbeing, and to ensure PE is meaningful for all our young people.'

Executive Headteacher, Rob Connelly, said *'As a community we have benefitted greatly from the ongoing work and support offered by the Rise Up programme so that all members of our community are supported to experience 'Life In All Its Fullness'. We are acutely aware of the ongoing and ever-changing pressures and challenges faced by children and the wider community, and we have a shared responsibility to provide support, both within, and beyond the classroom because people matter.'*

Social media content to improve the wellbeing of the whole school community

We would then use the Mindful Mondays, Wellness Wednesdays, Physical Fridays content to create simple social media posts so that our parents and wider community could access the activities and use them as a prompt to take part in a healthy habit. We would encourage families to be physically active together and we developed a link with family support groups and charities to promote and provide our facilities so that our families could exercise together in organised sessions fully funded by charities.

In school clubs

We created RISE Up clubs where students could come to exercise in a safe, inclusive environment. We had a fantastic enrichment programme every Thursday afternoon. The aim of the programme was to develop our children's cultural capital through a host of inspirational opportunities in a whole range of activities and trips. These included trips to theatres, museums and the UEA, which we were next door to. From a sporting point of view it enabled us to offer a greater range of curriculum opportunities, such as learn to swim, learn to ski, boxing, roller skating and outdoor adventure activities, such as forest school and our school allotment.

We would use RISE Up clubs to develop our children's mental wellbeing through a range of physical activities, such as walking for health or using our fitness suite or school woods. The fitness suite clubs became particularly valued by our young people and became the second most popular of the clubs we offered in school, behind football. We ended up with RISE Up clubs 4 lunchtimes and 1 afterschool per week, including a girls only session for more vulnerable girls who felt psychologically safer working out within their own gender. Without intention, this place became a sports sanctuary for our children.

Sport sanctuaries

Vicci Wells (2020), Head of Sport at the Youth Sport Trust, defines a sports sanctuary as: 'places or activities that are intentionally designed to use physical movement as a way of calming, replenishing or reawakening the senses, generating positive engagement and wellbeing.'

For my children, going for a walk to the allotment and back when they were dysregulated, and having a chat was a sanctuary for them. For others it was the fitness suite, and for some students it was borrowing a basketball or a football and going outside to escape their troubles, to regulate themselves so that they could get through the rest of their day. For other children I know that the school allotment or the art room was their place of sanctuary during the school day.

Consider this...

- Where is your sanctuary?
- Are there any areas you could utilise in your school to explore potentially creating sanctuaries for your young people and staff?

Student voice

Getting your students involved and giving you critical feedback to improve your provision can be incredibly powerful. When discussing my programme with Lee Sullivan, he gave me the idea about using student voice to shape wider impacts. My sports council helped shape designs for creating a sports sanctuary. You can use councils, pupil surveys, informal discussions, or student panels to give you the information you need to identify what they want and need. Also, what rules they consider unnecessary, to reduce opportunities for conflict to avoid triggering the social defence system. Older student sports leaders can facilitate active play sessions for younger students so both age groups benefit from the experience.

Active play and active travel

We covered the importance of play in chapter 12 but by creating opportunities for children to take part in active play during social times, it gives children a chance to regulate, have some fun and have brain breaks. Active play can be structured by lunchtime supervisors, older sports leaders, or through unstructured play.

Just as we can encourage and facilitate active play, we can do the same with active travel. The World Health Organization (2022) recommends that children and adolescents aged 5-17 should engage in at least 60 minutes of moderate to vigorous physical activity daily.

We encouraged this in my school by rewarding children with a house point if they walked, biked, or scooted to school each half term. We would administer this when we would assess children in PE at the end of each half term. It was an easy way to encourage children to take part in repeaters to widen their window of tolerance.

Enrichment days

Schools can use enrichment days to be proactive and target specific groups to boost the mental wellbeing of their young people in a fun and engaging way. We worked in partnership with a local secondary school to set up an enrichment day to target some of our girls in Year 9.

Intent
The brilliant Head of PE at Fakenham Academy, Mrs Dewson, was challenged by her Trust to create a pilot event with another school so she approached me. It quickly became clear that a traditional competition day would be unbalanced and demotivating for some of our young people who we wanted to engage. We were keen to create an event where everyone thrived so agreed on an event to boost the mental wellbeing of Year 9 girls, through physical activity and teach them some useful strategies for later in life.

Implementation
In December 2022, we welcomed 15 Year 9 students from Fakenham Academy to join our 15 Year 9 girls for the RISE Up Drop Down day.

All students were given a white t-shirt to make them feel included, valued, and connected as being part of one big team rather than 2 separate schools and in preparation for the colour run at the end of the day.

Inclusive teams
The day started with a netball festival to promote the benefits of being part of an 'Inclusive Team'. Mrs Dewson mixed the teams up so the young people played in their preferred position with a mix of classmates and girls from the other school.

This was a positive event to start the day, as the girls had to mix if they wanted their team to be successful, and it helped to break down any initial nervousness around new people. The girls were brilliant in making everyone feel included and this helped them release oxytocin so that they felt connected and loved.

Building confidence
Our girls then did a session on building a foundation of confidence in a range of areas in their lives, to help protect them during the rollercoaster of daily life. Our young people identified what they were good at in a range of areas such as subjects they excel at, hobbies

they are good at, characteristics they display in life and roles they play such as a brilliant daughter, sister, or friend. The aim was to develop the holistic confidence of our young people rather than just focusing on one aspect. We then explored positive affirmations as a way of building that confidence long after the enrichment day had passed.

Fitness suite fun
We then had time for some fitness suite fun where they took part in various 'Repeaters' and 'Stress Busters' to push away any stress and frustration in a safe and controlled way to widen their window of tolerance and help them feel calmer and more relaxed. This was particularly engaging for Fakenham students who do not usually have access to a fitness suite, so this was also a good way for them to try a new activity to inspire our young people. The punching mannequin 'Bob' was a firm favourite with the girls and got plenty of attention as our young people released their stress and tension in a safe and controlled way.

Colour run
The RISE Up mental wellbeing day finished with an exciting colour run so students could take part in an 'Energiser' & have lots of fun together.

The girls did 5 laps of the route giving them ample opportunities to be sprayed with powdered paint. They could run, walk, or cartwheel their way through the 3km route but the most important factor was that they had fun and connected with their friends while they did it.

We worked hard to create a supportive environment where the girls felt cared for, so that they could then seek and play. There were lots of happiness chemicals whizzing around and it was an activity that our young people loved to take part in.

Impact
At the end of the event, all young people were encouraged to complete a short survey so we could monitor the impact. The enrichment day got lots of 5 star ratings and we got some great feedback from our young people.

These were some of the great quotes from the girls about their day:
- 'That was the most fun I've had in ages!'
- 'It has helped me feel less stressed and more confident.
- 'It made me feel included'
- 'I felt closer to my friends, and we all had a laugh'
- 'It helped my mental wellbeing massively'

The final word
The final word goes to Mrs Dewson, the brilliant Head of PE at Fakenham Academy 'We all had such a great day. The girls thoroughly enjoyed themselves and loved the t-shirts. Both schools interacted fantastically with one another, working really well together throughout the day to boost their wellbeing.'
Enrichment days could be used for targeting specific groups such as your Pupil Premium students to maximise impact.

Consider this...

Which students would you target in your school for an enrichment day?

Staff wellbeing programmes
With the uncertainty created by Covid 19, there was an increase in staff wellbeing issues, so a dedicated staff programme was created on google classroom. This enabled staff to benefit from pre-recorded videos explaining the strategies in a way that staff could access confidentially at a time and place that was convenient for them.

Over lockdown we created staff fitness challenges, to build a supportive active community. Our head teacher was kind enough to donate prizes for the weekly raffle for those who took part. My colleague, Chris Taylor, did a brilliant job of promoting and creating opportunities for staff to take part in RISE Up physical activities after school. This occurred, during staff sports Fridays once we returned as a way to destress after a busy week.

I adapted an image I saw from a hospital, around a going home checklist, to create posters for each staff workroom. I wanted to try to foster a culture of staff looking out for each other and being kind to ourselves, as teaching can be a brutal world.

TIME TO RISE UP

The checklist contained the following:

Figure 37:

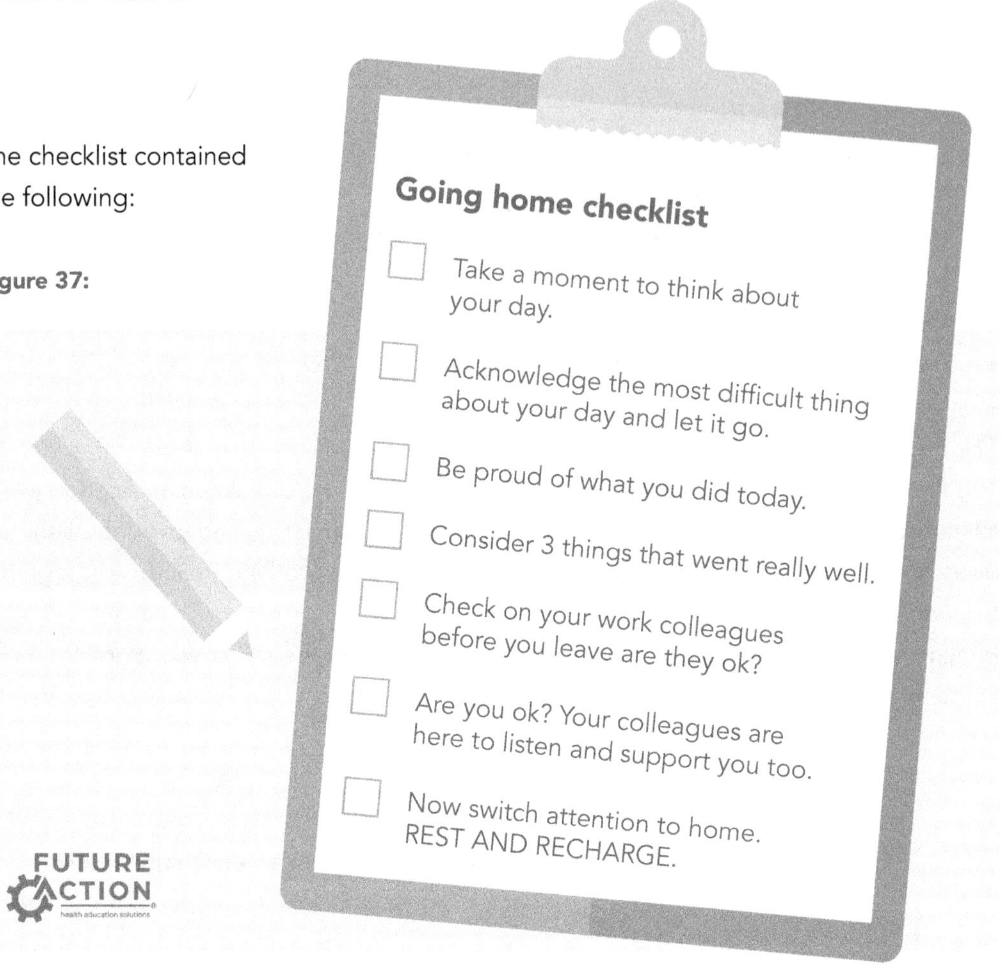

Going home checklist

☐ Take a moment to think about your day.

☐ Acknowledge the most difficult thing about your day and let it go.

☐ Be proud of what you did today.

☐ Consider 3 things that went really well.

☐ Check on your work colleagues before you leave are they ok?

☐ Are you ok? Your colleagues are here to listen and support you too.

☐ Now switch attention to home. REST AND RECHARGE.

FUTURE ACTION
health education solutions

There is so much work still to be done around teacher wellbeing, so we can make sure our teachers are able to put on their oxygen masks first. As a country we are getting it badly wrong at the moment, and the next generations of children will suffer.

Cross curricular opportunities

Our strategies around early intervention programmes can be implemented in so many subjects and give so many teachers a chance to work as a team and contribute if they wish.

It could include sessions such as:
- Mindful colouring in, in Art.
- Journalling club led by English teachers.
- Food technology teachers can lead on nutrition and hydration.
- Science teachers can explain the biology behind the healthy habits to young people or our understanding of neuroscience and mental health.

We talked about inclusive teams earlier in terms of physical activity, but that can be wider than physical education. They can be in:

- School productions: Participation in school plays, musicals, and other performances can build self-esteem, boost creativity, and promote a sense of community.
- Chess clubs: can be a great way to develop problem-solving skills and build self-esteem and self-confidence.
- Nature clubs: can provide opportunities for children to explore their environment and learn about the importance of conservation, which can be a great way to reduce stress and promote mental wellbeing.
- Form group, year group, or whole-school team: Collaborative activities that build a sense of belonging and teamwork, like class debates, science fairs, and school-wide community service projects can provide children with a sense of connection with their peers. They can boost self-esteem and increase feelings of self-worth releasing oxytocin so that they feel loved and that they belong within their school community.

Belonging matters to us as human beings and if our young people don't find it at school, they will find it in unhealthy ways, such as gangs or in internet groups locked in their bedrooms unable to socialise in person.

In conclusion, Middle leaders and class teachers can drive whole school impact and take some of the pressure off senior mental health leads, personal development leads and senior leaders. It can be great for proving your ability to have a wider impact outside your subject area and help your career development in the process.

Chapter summary

- Early interventions strategies can be used in multiple ways across a school setting to amplify impact for young people and their families.
- We want all people within our school communities to feel psychologically safe, supported, and able to contribute.
- We create one big team to include as many people as possible, as human connection is vital, and children will find it in unhealthy ways if we can't provide it.

Critical questions

1. Where do you currently teach early intervention strategies in your school setting?

2. Where is your personal sport sanctuary?

3. Are there any areas you could utilise in your school to explore, potentially creating sanctuaries for your young people and staff?

4. How could you work with colleagues to create cross-curricular opportunities?

5. What support would they need so that they can contribute?

Chapter references

- Department of Education (2013). National Curriculum in England: Physical Education Programmes of Study. [online] GOV.UK. Available at: https://www.gov.uk/government/publications/national-curriculum-in-england-physical-education-programmes-of-study/national-curriculum-in-england-physical-education-programmes-of-study.
- Department For Education (2019). Relationships Education, Relationships and Sex Education (RSE) and Health Education. [online] GOV.UK. Available at: https://assets.publishing.service.gov.uk/government/uploads/system/uploads/attachment_data/file/1090195/Relationships_Education_RSE_and_Health_Education.pdf.
- Wells, V. (2020). Sport Sanctuaries – does your school have one? [online] Barry Carpenter Education. Available at: https://barrycarpentereducation.com/2020/11/16/sport-sanctuaries-does-your-school-have-one/ [Accessed 2 Oct. 2023].
- World Health Organization (2022). Physical Activity. [online] World Health Organization. Available at: https://www.who.int/news-room/fact-sheets/detail/physical-activity.
- Future Action. (2023). Case Study: King's Leadership Academy Liverpool. Future Action. Available at: https://www.futureaction.net/post/case-study-king-s-leadership-academy-liverpool [Accessed 1 June 2024].

> **BOOK BONUS**
> Try the school wellbeing scorecard to complete a 3 minute audit of your existing provision. **https://bit.ly/FASWS**

Additional insights

Inspirational teacher educator, Will Swaithes, from PE Scholar explores the role of wellbeing programmes within PE here:

Back in 2008 I was experimenting with ways to hook more learners into PE and to provide more meaningful and relevant learning gains. I wanted more than just accurate replication of skills and outwitting opponents to be the value add for all young people from PE but that seemed to account for at least 90% of curriculum time and anything else seemed more luck than strategic intent. The QCA's Personal, Learning and Thinking (PLTS) Framework became a great way for me to hook all learners and one that, as an AST, I supported many other schools and subjects to explore and implement. The S.E.C.R.I.T life skills we looked to embed within our curriculum to discuss, explore and consider transference to other areas of life were:

- Self-managers
- Effective participants
- Creative thinkers
- Reflective learners
- Independent enquirers
- Team workers

Figure 38:

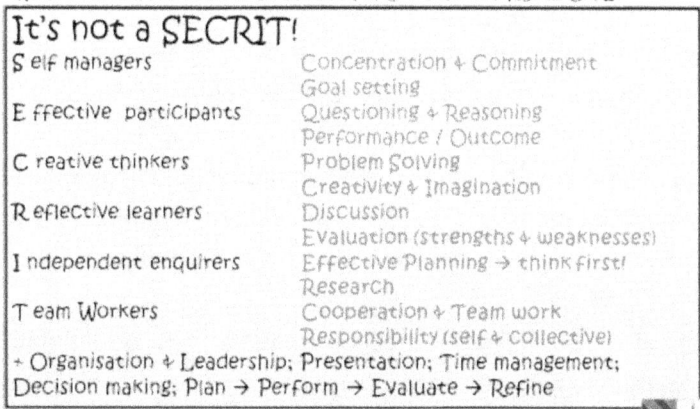

Whilst the jury is definitely still out on whether these life skills can be developed in PE and 'taken beyond the gym', I remain a firm believer that they are incredibly useful skills to explicitly learn about in and through PE. If you want to read more I recommend A Qualitative Investigation of Teachers' Experiences of Life Skills Development in Physical Education (Cronin et al., 2022) and the work of Don Hellison on Teaching Personal and Social Responsibility (TPSR). More recently I have stopped talking about S.E.C.R.I.T skills and tend to talk more about the P.R.I.C.E.L.E.S.S skills that a rich PE experience can promote and support.

Figure 39:

Whilst we definitely do not want to change the number one focus of PE from improving movement skills and confidence, I can see direct and obvious links between this and:

1. The PE national curriculum which "should provide opportunities for pupils to become physically confident in a way which supports their health and fitness. Opportunities to compete in sport and other activities build character and help to embed values such as fairness and respect".
2. Ofsted's personal development strand of inspection that focuses on "SMSC, Fundamental British Values, careers guidance, healthy living, citizenship, equality and diversity and preparation for the next stage" of education or employment.

3. The Relationships Education, Relationships and Sex Education and Health Education (RSHE) statutory guidance that has required all schools to deliver against since 2021. As part of my work for Youth Sport Trust I created and shared the following mapping document which highlights just how many of these important areas could and should be taught through PE:

Figure 40:

RSHE in PE

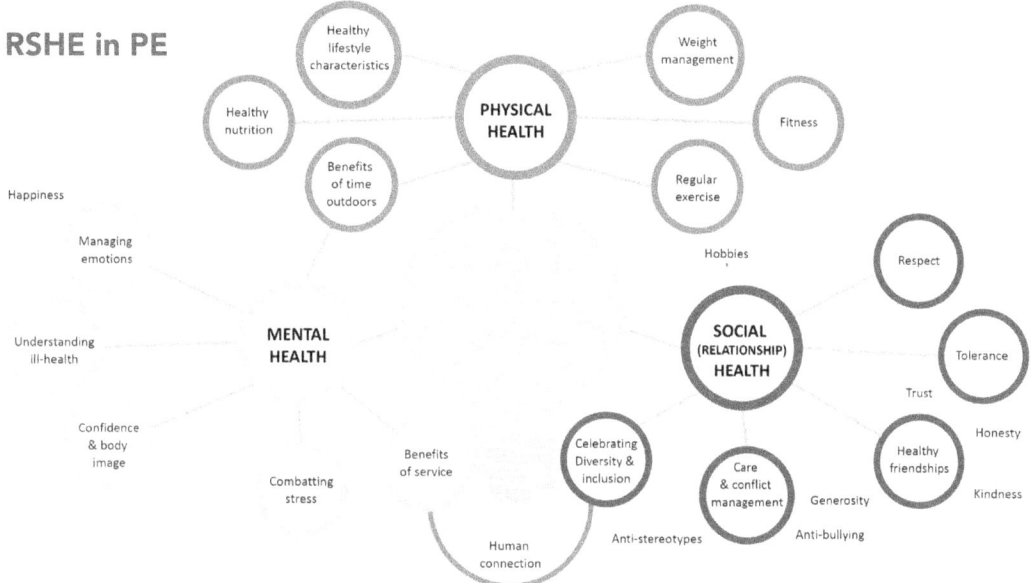

4. Our quest for more physical literacy informed PE provision

For anyone thinking about ways to provide that extra value add for all young people I would encourage you to consider the following reflective questions:
1. What is the most valuable learning you can give all students from PE?
2. What would most students currently say is the purpose of PE and how well does this match with your intent?
3. How can you retain maximal minutes moving in PE but still contribute to improved mental/ emotional and social wellbeing?
4. How can your ethos, your hidden curriculum, your displays, your use of changing times, assemblies and tutor time contribute towards an attitudinal shift amongst staff and students?
5. How will you know if what you are doing is having an impact?'

Lee Sullivan is Head of PE at Upton Court Grammar School, the author of 'Is PE in Crisis' and the co-creator of the 'Concept Curriculum'. Lee explores meaningful PE and how we help young people build a lifelong relationship with physical activity, so that when they are older they have the tools to manage and maintain their physical, social, and mental well-being:

'One key aim for PE teachers must be to prepare all students for an active life through physical education. The current and most dominant traditional form of PE delivery is sport-technique and performance focused and is failing to meet this aim. It is not an appropriate model to be meaningful for all learners. In fact, it is often creating a negative self-identity towards physical activity. This approach can often be criticised for being exclusionary and elitist in nature.

After many years of teaching PE and realising my ambition as a Head of Department, I found myself questioning my own future within education. I had lessons taken away and given to more 'academic subjects', I was seeing the same 'sporty' students at every extra-curricular club and our own student voice surveys told us that a proportion of students were either not enjoying PE or did not see the value in it. We realised that when a curriculum is obsessed with performance and proficiency, inevitably those not in the elite group will fail, which in this subject's case can have disastrous long-term ramifications.

To genuinely nurture physical literacy, we must understand the future impact that our students' experiences in PE might have. When referring to individuals who show little to no motivation in later life to engage in physical activity, Margaret Whitehead stated that "establishing and maintaining physical literacy is highly dependent on experiences which individuals have encountered in respect of their involvement with physical activity". The messages we have been inadvertently sending to students about their ability or competence have left many believing they are not 'sporty' or are no good at PE. James Clear states in his book, Atomic Habits: '"To change your behaviour for good, you need to start believing new things about yourself." I have seen a change in students' relationships with physical activity because of conceptual learning.

If students have had negative experiences in PE, physical activity, or sport when they come to our lesson, the damage may already have been done. We take a more proactive approach when planning our curriculum, methods of delivery, assessment, and lessons to ensure that the needs of our students are put first and that we are continually building *a strong relationship with our subject. We must realise that as PE teachers, we are not the final destination for our students. Instead, we are a vital component in their physical education journey.*

Therefore, I created the Concept Curriculum. A Concept-driven approach to curriculum design is one that moves away from subject-specific content and instead emphasises "big ideas" that span multiple subject areas. (Erickson, 2008). The purpose of the Concept Curriculum was not to create better communicators, stronger leaders, or more resilient students. Though I hope this may happen. The purpose of the Concept Curriculum was to provide an inclusive hook for those students that had not previously been engaged through the sport-driven focus of a PE lesson. It was to provide a positive experience within PE so that students will build a strong positive relationship with physical activity, develop confidence and competence, and continue to reap the benefits of long-term engagement for the rest of their lives.

Stephanie Beni and Tim Fletcher's work into Meaningful PE (2022) found that when young people could recognise the importance of what they were learning and make connections to life outside of the situation – either in the present or future – they came to see their experiences as meaningful. Conversely, when students continually experienced failure, they would see the subject as meaningless. This is what a concept curriculum is aiming to do. Shift the learning of the lesson from one that is skill specific, that for most are irrelevant and unachievable, to one which is inclusive, relevant, and meaningful for every learner. We should strive to create a positive PE experience for all, not just those that consider themselves 'sporty'. We should reward attitude and progress over performance and ability. We should aim to genuinely nurture physical literacy and build a lifelong relationship with physical activity, so that when students are older they have the tools to manage and maintain their physical, social, and mental wellbeing.'

Whereabouts on the PE scheme of learning does wellbeing programmes fit?

Our need was so great in my school that I wanted to target all students regardless of key stage to be as proactive as we could be in supporting our young people, preferably before problems emerged. Schools I supported would use my resources in a variety of ways, some would target all students, some key stage 2, some key stage 3, and some would target key stage 4. The key aspect was that teachers had agency to implement in a way that best suited their schools and children's needs.

Case Study

Hethersett Academy is a coeducational secondary school located in the village of Hethersett in Norfolk, UK. They were one of the first schools I worked in partnership with. Their brilliant Head of PE, Nick Austin, and Sarah Alothman, talk us through the journey they have been on to transform the life chances of their young people through RISE Up:

Background

At the start of the first lockdown in March 2020 we found time to complete extra reading in academic research and department blogs on the various PE curriculum offered at different schools. We started to focus on how key stage 4 could be improved.

Building upon the work from Sport England (2015), with particular reference to the six youth personalities, the final product was that we designed a curriculum that groups students on personality.

Source: Sport England, 2015. https://sportengland-production-files.s3.eu-west-2.amazonaws.com/s3fs-public/youth-insight_under-the-skin.pdf?VersionId=Rhi.oCS5QHjLCQfUtGBn6F7eXg9qDyX1 (Accessed on 15/9/23)

At the end of KS3 students opt for one of the following routes for study in their next school year.
- Health and Wellbeing
- Sport Education
- Social Cohesion
- Technical Development (Multi Activity)

With the effects of lockdown having an obvious impact on everyone's mental wellbeing we felt PE was perfectly placed to help ensure our students had knowledge of strategies to build their mental fitness. Two of our department then completed the training in preparation to deliver the RISE Up module from Sep 2021. This would be placed in the Health and Wellbeing route.

Delivery

The RISE Up course has been taught for 1 weekly 60 minute lesson to each of year 9, 10 and 11 since the start of the 21/22 academic year. Students working through a RISE Up booklet. We feel this has led to an increased number of students enjoying lessons and gaining a better appreciation of mental wellbeing as a part of a meaningful learning experience.

Student feedback

From an even spread of respondents in year 9, 10 and 11 we found the following:

Figure 41:
Student feedback

Positive response	Question topic	Negative response
69.3%	Enjoyment of lessons	3.8%
73.1%	Appropriate lesson topics	7.6%
42.6%	Development of strategies	6.4%
60.4%	Interest of theory	8.4%
26.9%	Improved wellbeing	1.5%
36.2%	Increased activity time	14.9%

With this data from the first cycle of the module on the curriculum we were really excited for how we could grow it to help students develop further. The overwhelming majority of students had positive and/or neutral experiences so far and this improved as our teaching became better in this module.

Case Study - The Academy of St Francis Assisi
Enhancing Engagement through extra-curricular clubs

The Academy of St Francis Assisi (ASFA) is a coeducational joint-faith Roman Catholic and Church of England secondary school in Liverpool and is part of the All Saints Multi Academy Trust. They are one of the four fantastic schools I partnered with as part of our 'RISE Up Liverpool' Trauma Informed PE pilot programme.

Inspirational PE teacher, Polly Johnson, will talk us through their intent for the RISE Up programme, how they implemented it, and its impact on their young people.

Intent
'Physical Education can positively shape the lives of our young and impressionable students by giving them a sense of belonging and self-worth. At St Francis of Assisi we believe the key to breaking down barriers is within Physical Education and positive reinforcement.

During the 6-week programme we ran at our school, twenty two students with multiple needs and abilities engaged in our 'RISE UP' project P. The students were initially selected due to behavioural issues, mental health struggles or lack of engagement in PE. We wanted to support this group of young people so that they felt psychologically safe in our school and that they belonged, to improve outcomes for them. I completed an adapted version of the Warwick–Edinburgh Mental Wellbeing Scale survey before we started and student questionnaires so that I could track the impact of the programme.

Implementation
The students initially gathered together and were given the roles of Rise up leaders. Each student was given a T shirt and we held weekly meetings and activities for the students to lead. This gave them a sense of belonging and straight away broke down some of their walls as they had been specifically chosen as leaders, for some of them this was a breath of fresh air as usually, they would be summoned to the teacher's office for other reasons.

Week 1: All students met wearing their T Shirts. I completed a questionnaire about the likes and dislikes of school life for them individually. It immediately became apparent that it was not only PE that many of them were disengaged. I asked them their likes and dislikes and we agreed to meet up at lunch time that week. The questionnaire hit on some common denominators for all students who are in different year groups. Some of these common denominators were 'school is too loud' 'I don't like the teachers' 'It's hard to make friends' 'I care what people think of me' 'I'm too unfit to do PE'.

That Wednesday I took the students down to the assembly hall and together we completed 20 minutes of yoga and a 10-minute meditation session focussing on breathing. The students really enjoyed the quiet and safe space that we created. To my surprise all the students fully engaged in this. This self-help trauma informed approach was something that they could do in their own time to help improve their mental wellbeing.

Week 2: The next week I wanted to focus on the students' mental wellbeing, so I decided to run a cross curricular activity with food technology. The students researched the health benefits of certain fruits and made and named their own smoothies. The students then handed out samples of these smoothies to students in year 7 and year 8 at break time. This is when my ' break through' with the group happened. As they had had fun with me, felt safe with me and now had a sense of belonging I could see their body language and attitudes begin to shift and become more positive. Giving out the smoothies also created a buzz as other students now wanted a T-shirt and wanted to be part of the Rise Up programme.

Week 3: This week we had a picnic in the park. All of the students brought in something to share. We discussed how we were feeling in school and how our week was going so far. We made friendship bracelets out of loom bands and as a random act of kindness gifted them to someone else. After this activity to my surprise the students had all arranged to meet up again that night to 'hang out' together.

Week 4: In week 4 we met up after school. I had a very important task for the students to do this week and they sorted out food and clothes parcels for less advantaged people with our chaplain and The Whitechapel centre. When we do something nice for someone else, we release one of our happiness chemicals, oxytocin, which makes us feel loved.

Week 5: This week the students participated in 'The Big Dig' on one of our school's drop down days. The Rise up crew led a gardening project to help improve our school's environment. As the students' confidence was now growing, they each led other students giving instructions to them about what they needed to do. They were in groups of 4 and each had a section of our school gardens to oversee. It was a great opportunity for our young people to experience biophilia. This was by far the most rewarding and happiest I had seen them, and I again had students asking me to be a part of the Rise up team.

Week 6: This week I wanted to finish with something that would push the team out of their comfort zone. It was year 6 transition day and as avid leaders they would now be responsible for leading the PE sessions with the year 6s. Each member was briefed on the rules of Dodgeball, and each given a specific role. The students led the sessions all day giving clear and concise instructions to the year 6 students and ran the Dodgeball tournament with confidence.

Impact

At the end of the last day the students completed another questionnaire about school life and the difference was astonishing. The students felt happier coming to school (especially on a Monday for Rise Up) they felt more confident. They had all become friends and more importantly knew who and where to go to feel safe. Using their answers, I re-visited the adapted version of the Warwick–Edinburgh Mental Wellbeing scale survey for the perceptions of our children's progress of their mental wellbeing. I was delighted with their progress as all aspects improved following our programme.

Figure 42:

	ASFA **Pre** RISE Up intervention	ASFA **Post** RISE Up intervention
'They've been feeling optimistic about the future'	Rarely	Some of the time
'They've been feeling useful'	Rarely	Often
'They've been feeling relaxed'	None of the time	All of the time
'They've been dealing with problems well'	None of the time	Some of the time
'They've been thinking clearly'	Rarely	Often
'They've been feeling close to other people'	Some of the time	Often
'They've been able to make their own mind up about things'	Rarely	Often
'They've been feeling able to manage their own wellbeing'	None of the time	Often
What are your biggest challenges for your target group at the moment?	Attendance, behaviour, engagement, mental health	
What challenges has RISE Up intervention helped improve for your target group?	Engagement, mental health, personal development, SEND, Supporting our most vulnerable children	

Next steps
The students are now eagerly waiting to continue this programme into September. The students now have a non-judgemental safe space and are more active and confident thanks to this project.

Sport sanctuaries
Vicci Wells, Head of Sport at the Youth Sport Trust, tells us more about sports sanctuaries

'Every child had their own unique, personal, lived-in experience during the Covid-19 pandemic. All experienced losses to their routines, structures, friendships, opportunities, and freedoms. The result was that as pupils returned to schools, they were in very different places than when they left. Educators asked, 'how could our school be that place where learners feel supported, listened to, and able to flourish once again'? For 'an anxious child 'is not in a place to learn effectively' (Carpenter 2020)[1].

Simply defined, sport sanctuaries[2] are places or activities that are intentionally designed to use physical movement as a way of calming, replenishing, or reawakening the senses, generating positive engagement and wellbeing. The Oxford Dictionary defines a sanctuary as a 'safe space'. This aligns to the biophilia hypothesis, which can reduce stress, improve cognitive function, and enhance mood and creativity. As Professor John Ratey[3] highlights 'Physical activity is crucial to the way we think and feel…it can be the cue for the building blocks of learning in the brain, it affects mood, anxiety and attention, and guards against stress' . Therefore, we have to find ways that enable young people to self-regulate their mood, re-build resilience and feel good about themselves. Physical activity, and its positive correlation to our mental health, offers this at all levels.

As educators, we are all interested in the question 'how does this child learn?' and sport sanctuaries are a fantastic way of providing safe spaces, intentional movement activities and approaches to consider, when stimulating or retaining pupil engagement.

Riverside School in Northern Ireland were keen to measure whether sport sanctuaries would have an impact on individual learners' engagement in the classroom. They co-created with pupils' Sports Sanctuaries and evolved the concept to introduce sensory sanctuaries. Their sanctuary includes green space outdoors, and areas of the classroom intentionally designed to draw upon a range of senses through individual activities, all pupil led. Pupils have a voice and a choice in what their sanctuary is and are supported by teachers.

Physical activities on offer range from press ups against a wall to stimulate proprioceptive senses, through to repetitive target games for the vestibular sense. Pupils are set individual physical skill targets alongside a sensory/behaviour target, such as 'to improve balance and reduce calling out in class'.

The impact (collated via happiness audits, focus groups, collaborative practice and using the engagement model as a form of assessment) highlighted that when a sanctuary was accessed by learners, before or mid-way through a lesson, there was a direct increase in pupil engagement. Through implementing a whole school approach there has been a positive impact on the wider ethos of the entire school community.

With engagement being considered the most important predictor of successful outcomes for children and young people (Wolke 2013), then the introduction of physical activity- through a sport sanctuary- can ensure that young people are happier, healthier, engaged, and ready to learn.'

Sources:
- [1] Carpenter & Carpenter, The Recovery Curriculum https://barrycarpentereducation.com/2020/04/23/the-recovery-curriculum/ April 2020
- [2] Wells, V https://barrycarpentereducation.com/2020/11/16/sport-sanctuaries-does-your-school-have-one/ November 2020 and https://www.youthsporttrust.org/resources/inclusion/sport-sanctuaries
- [3] John J. Ratey, Spark: The Revolutionary New Science of Exercise and the Brain 2010

Here are some Top tips for teachers who are just starting on a journey of setting up a sports sanctuary from Riverside Special Schools Head of Department, Laura McAuley, and Vice Principal Shona McCann:

1. Prioritise the voice of stakeholders and place them at the centre of your project. It is important to have a deep understanding of your learners. Take the time to observe their behaviours when they are most engaged and when they face challenges. By gaining insight into their needs and preferences, you can tailor the sensory sanctuaries to better support them. Remember that pupil voice is paramount throughout the entire process of planning and implementation. Actively involve them, ensuring their opinions are heard and valued. Our learners participated in happiness audits to identify their sensory preferences, which played a pivotal role in shaping their individual sanctuaries.
2. Sanctuaries can be created with items that don't necessarily require a large budget. In fact, our essentials list for setting up your own sanctuary consists of minimalistic and classroom cupboard items such as bubbles, shredded paper, ribbons, and various auditory stimuli.
3. Gain the support and commitment of your staff team since they will be responsible for implementing the project and working directly with the learners. By involving a small group of enthusiastic staff members who share a passion for the project, you can establish a foundation for success. We achieved this by creating a shared vision and initiating discussions with our staff, seeking their thoughts on what they believed a sanctuary should be.
4. You will experience days where it feels like Sensory and Sports Sanctuaries aren't working for your children and young people, but it is important to remember that everyone has moments of inner peace and calm. It is up to us as educators to persevere and continue to listen to what they are trying to communicate to us. It is a process of trial and error and exploration; the outcomes and benefits to individual learners are worth persevering for.

Chapter 14 - Creating cultural change, changing the narrative

'I realised if you can change a classroom, you can change a community, and if you change enough communities you can change the world.'
Erin Gruwell

In recent years, there has been a growing recognition of the importance of mental wellbeing in children's lives. This chapter delves into the transformative power of cultural change, exploring how we can play a pivotal role in changing the narrative around children's mental health and breaking the stigma associated with it. Through education, awareness, advocacy, and collaboration, we can create a cultural shift that prioritises the mental wellbeing of every child, ultimately empowering them to thrive emotionally and succeed academically.

Creating cultural change for children's mental wellbeing

As teachers, we have a profound impact on shaping the lives of children. Beyond imparting academic knowledge, we also play a crucial role in supporting their mental wellbeing. One powerful approach to making a lasting impact is by creating cultural change. By fostering a culture that prioritises children's mental health, we can create an environment where they feel safe, supported, and empowered. In this section, we will explore the steps we can take to initiate and drive cultural change for the betterment of children's mental wellbeing.

Defining the goals

To begin, it is important to clearly define the goals of cultural change. Let us reflect on the specific aspects of children's mental wellbeing that we wish to address, whether it is reducing stigma, promoting emotional resilience, fostering positive self-esteem, or improving access to mental health resources. By establishing clear objectives, we can focus our efforts and measure progress effectively.

Raising awareness

Education and awareness are foundational to initiating cultural change. Let us start by raising awareness among our colleagues, parents, and the broader community about the importance of children's mental wellbeing. Let us organise workshops, seminars, and informational campaigns to share knowledge on common challenges, signs of distress, and the benefits of early intervention. Utilise social media platforms and collaborate with mental health professionals to disseminate information widely.

Engaging with stakeholders

Collaboration is key to creating meaningful change. Let us engage with key stakeholders such as politicians, the NHS, charities, parents, fellow educators, administrators, and community leaders. Let us build relationships, share information, and work together to advocate for mental health support within educational institutions and community organisations. By fostering partnerships, we can mobilise a collective effort towards supporting children's mental wellbeing. In researching this book I have met with some fantastic therapists who have little awareness of pockets of best practice in schools and visa-versa. There is a great opportunity for collaboration to improve outcomes for young people.

Fostering dialogue and open communication

Let us create spaces within our classrooms and schools where open dialogue about mental health is encouraged. Let us foster an environment where children feel safe to express their feelings and concerns without judgement. Let us facilitate discussions that explore emotions, coping strategies, and self-care techniques. Provide training for parents and colleagues on how to address mental health issues effectively. By promoting open communication, we create an atmosphere of understanding and support.

Leading by example

As educators, we are role models for our students. Leading by example is a powerful way to create cultural change. Let us demonstrate positive mental health practices ourselves, such as practising self-care, showing healthy coping mechanisms, and expressing emotions in a constructive manner. Let us encourage self-expression and teach students the importance of seeking help when needed. Our actions will inspire and empower them to prioritise their own mental wellbeing.

Mobilising communities
Let us extend our reach beyond the classroom by mobilising community organisations, mental health professionals, and advocacy groups that focus on children's mental wellbeing. Let us collaborate on initiatives such as awareness campaigns, support groups, and workshops to reach a wider audience and maximise impact. By joining forces, we can create a collective voice for change.

Implementing policy changes
Let us advocate for policies that prioritise children's mental health within educational systems and healthcare services. Let us engage with policymakers and decision-makers to push for the inclusion of mental health education in school curricula and the allocation of resources for mental health support services. By influencing policy changes, we can institutionalise the importance of children's mental wellbeing.

Embracing diversity and inclusion
Let us recognise and address the unique needs and experiences of all children, including those from diverse backgrounds. Let us promote inclusivity and cultural sensitivity in mental health services and programmes. Let us create an environment that celebrates diversity and provides support that is accessible and relevant to every child.

A common language
How might our lives be enriched if society collectively embraced a commitment to enhancing mental wellbeing through self-care practices? What if our primary emphasis shifted from addressing mental illnesses to prioritising the normalisation of self-care strategies, much like our dedication to physical fitness? We don't wait for children to face obesity before offering support, yet there seems to be a delay in providing assistance for mental health issues. Imagine a world where we champion the cultivation of positive mental wellbeing strategies as a means of promotion and prevention.

Wouldn't it be incredible if we could create similar cultural change around our mental wellbeing for all people regardless of age? To get to that point there are a number of things we need to achieve. Firstly, we need to create a common language around discussing mental health.

Dr Catherine Wheatley explores five key definitions for creating a common language: mental wellbeing, mental health, mental illness, mental health prevention and resilience.

Mental health, mental illness and mental wellbeing
Dr Catherine Wheatley
What do we mean when we talk about mental health and wellbeing? Sometimes these terms are used interchangeably or inappropriately, causing confusion, and creating barriers to providing the most effective support for young people.

A common and consistent language of mental health is vital if teachers are to communicate effectively with students, colleagues, and parents, and create lasting cultural change. Here, then, are some ways to think and talk about mental health and wellbeing, and how to support them, as a guide to your practice.

Mental health
Good mental health means being able to think, feel, relate, and behave in ways that allow us to live our lives well: it refers to our social, emotional, and psychological selves. Generally, when we talk about 'mental health', we are emphasising the importance of maintaining this positive state, but it is also important to recognise that mental health exists on a continuum. Our mental health is influenced by different factors including life experiences, relationships and how we process our thoughts and feelings. When we experience everyday challenges, we may feel anxious, angry, or low. Usually, we can manage these feelings ourselves, or with help from family or friends. Sometimes these feelings persist for weeks or months, or they become severe enough that they stop us from living our daily lives. We may not be able to manage this mental distress without clinical help.

Mental illness
Mental illness refers to diagnosable disorders that affect our thoughts, feelings, and behaviours, causing significant distress, and preventing us from living our lives well. Mental illnesses include clinical conditions such as depression, anxiety disorders, bipolar disorder, schizophrenia, and others. It is important to approach mental illness with sensitivity, understanding, and respect, avoiding stigmatising language or judgements.

Mental wellbeing
Very simply, mental wellbeing involves feeling and functioning positively in the world: it is a state of feeling good about ourselves and the way we are living our lives. Positive wellbeing promotes mental health and can protect against disorders. Staying active, connecting with other people, learning new skills, helping others and being 'in the moment' can all enhance the way we feel and function in the world. Sport and physical activity are great ways to do all these things!

Mental health prevention
Mental health prevention programmes focus on reducing social, emotional, and psychological risks and promoting protective factors: everyone can benefit from them. Elements might include teaching mental health awareness, self-management, relationship skills and coping strategies.

Resilience
Resilience is the ability to cope with, adapt to and recover from life's stresses and setbacks. Some people are resilient by nature, and there are coping strategies that we can learn. But it's important to remember that some sources of stress – such as being a carer or living far away from family - are beyond a young person's control. These can make building resilience more difficult.

Applying the definitions in different contexts
In our educational settings, we should use the term "mental wellbeing" when discussing strategies for promoting emotional resilience, stress management, and positive coping mechanisms. Let's emphasise the importance of building strong mental wellbeing as a foundation for positive mental health.

When addressing the broader concept of psychological wellbeing, the term "mental health" is more appropriate, highlighting the significance of emotional and social wellbeing.

In instances where specific mental health conditions are being discussed, such as providing support for individuals with diagnosed disorders, the term "mental illness" should be used, promoting understanding, empathy, and appropriate interventions. We should rely on clinicians to guide us in supporting young people who are grappling with mental illness.

By using a common language and understanding these definitions, we can effectively communicate with students, parents, and colleagues, fostering a shared understanding of mental health and promoting an environment of empathy, support, and wellbeing.

Breaking the stigma: promoting open conversations and empathy

Breaking the stigma surrounding mental health is crucial in creating a supportive and inclusive environment for children's mental wellbeing. Stigma perpetuates silence, shame, and misconceptions, hindering individuals from seeking help and support. As frontline teachers, we have a unique role in challenging these harmful perceptions and fostering open conversations about mental health. In this section, we will delve into effective strategies for breaking the stigma, promoting empathy, and creating a culture of understanding and acceptance.

Understanding stigma and its impact

Before we can address stigma, it is important to understand its nature and its impact on individuals' mental health. Stigma arises from stereotypes, prejudice, and discrimination, and can be deeply ingrained in society's attitudes and beliefs. It leads to fear, shame, and the marginalisation of individuals with mental health challenges. By recognising the harmful consequences of stigma, we can actively work to dismantle it.

Promoting education and awareness

Education and awareness are essential in breaking the stigma around mental health. By increasing our own knowledge about mental health conditions, treatment options, and recovery journeys, we can challenge misconceptions and provide accurate information to others. Take advantage of professional development opportunities, workshops, and resources to deepen your understanding of mental health. Share this knowledge with colleagues, parents, and the wider community to dispel myths and foster empathy.

Normalising conversations

One of the most effective ways to break the stigma is by normalising conversations about mental health. Create a safe and supportive environment within your classroom or school where students feel comfortable discussing their emotions, experiences, and concerns openly. Encourage open dialogue about mental health and actively listen without judgement. By demonstrating empathy and understanding, you provide a space for students to share their struggles and seek support.

Challenging language and stereotypes
Language plays a significant role in perpetuating stigma. Encourage the use of person-first language when discussing mental health, emphasising that individuals are not defined by their conditions. Avoid derogatory terms and labels that further stigmatise individuals. Teach students to recognise and challenge stereotypes, replacing them with accurate and empathetic understanding.

Engaging families and the wider community
Breaking the stigma requires a collective effort involving families and the wider community. Collaborate with parents, community organisations, mental health professionals, and local leaders to create a united front against stigma. We can organise or take part in events, workshops, and awareness campaigns that promote understanding, empathy, and de-stigmatisation. By engaging the wider community, we create a network of support that reinforces the importance of mental health.

Breaking the stigma surrounding mental health is an essential step in creating a culture that supports children's mental wellbeing. By promoting education, normalising conversations, sharing personal stories, and fostering empathy, we can challenge misconceptions and stereotypes. Together with families and the wider community, we can build a society that embraces mental health, supports those in need, and enables all children to thrive emotionally and academically.

Using role models to break stigma
Consider sharing your own experiences with mental health challenges if you feel comfortable or invite guest speakers who have overcome such challenges to speak to your students. Hearing personal stories fosters connection, empathy, and understanding, showing that mental health struggles are common, and that seeking help is a sign of strength. I appreciate that not everyone will feel comfortable doing this so an alternative is to talk about role models and their experiences of mental wellbeing/health/illness so that children can empathise and identify with them.

CHAPTER 14 - CREATING CULTURAL CHANGE, CHANGING THE NARRATIVE

One of the most powerful lessons was when I used celebrities who my young people looked up to, to break the stigma. It was noticeable that our young people were engaged, passionate about the topic, and willing to contribute more than usual.

In summer 2023 it was great to see Paddy Pimblett from UFC encouraging men to talk to someone if they are struggling with their mental health after his friend died by suicide on the eve of his UFC London clash with American Jordan Leavitt.

After submitting Leavitt, Pimblett revealed the news about his friend and urging men to speak more openly about their mental health.

"That speech was just something that came from my heart; I didn't plan none of it, it just came out," Pimblett says. "I wanted to dedicate the fight to Ricky, and then I started talking and it all just came out. I couldn't help it. I think that was because I had it all bottled up inside me."

"More men going out and speaking and getting things off their chests, that means more to me than any victory in a cage ever will, lad," Pimblett says. "Winning in the Octagon does mean a lot to me, but people telling me that they haven't killed themselves – because of something I've said – and things along them lines, it means more than any win will ever mean to me, to be honest."

"We've had thousands of messages – not just me; my manager, my coach – off different people and organisations. I want to thank every single person for every one of them messages." (Yahoo Life, 2022)

There are a whole host of different celebrities, such as Lady Gaga, Sam Fender, Prince William, Prince Harry, and film star Jonah Hill, who have broached the subject over the last few years and should be applauded for it.

TIME TO RISE UP

What do Ben Stokes, Simone Biles and Naomi Osaka all have in common?

They are all amazing elite sport performers, and all took a break from elite sport in 2022 to prioritise their mental health.

These three champions are some of the toughest competitors around and have overcome huge challenges in their personal and professional lives. If they can suffer from mental health issues then it is clear that everyone can suffer too at some point in their lives depending on their situation and circumstances.

The trick to having impact with young people when using this technique is to use someone who they know and can relate to.

If the children in front of you have no interest in the sport then find a celebrity who they are interested in who has discussed mental health. Spiderman actor Tom Holland, Selena Gomez, Ed Sheeran, Camilla Cabello, and Demi Lovato have all spoken about the damage social media has had on their mental health.

When using sporting celebrities try to tailor the sport star to the type of celebrity that group of children look up to. If they're into gymnastics then Simone Biles is a great model, Naomi Osaka for tennis, Ben Stokes for cricket or Tyson Fury for boxing. Raheem Sterling has spoken in the past about how mindfulness has helped him, and rugby player Siya Kohlisi has talked about it so there is a wide range of supporting celebrities who can be used.

Figure 43:
Mental health Olympics

© Lalo Alcaraz

CHAPTER 14 - CREATING CULTURAL CHANGE, CHANGING THE NARRATIVE

Star	Sport	Reason
Simone Biles	Gymnastics	Pulled out of Olympic event to protect her mental health.
Naomi Osaka	Tennis	Had a break from tennis to protect her mental health.
Ben Stokes	Cricket	Had a break from cricket to protect his mental health following the bereavement of his father.
Tyson Fury	Boxing	Recovered from depression to become world champion.
Paddy Pimblett	UFC	Encouraged people to talk to someone if they are struggling with their mental health after the death of his friend.
Siya Kolisi	Rugby	It's ok to not be ok following social media racist abuse.
Raheem Sterling	Football	Using meditation to break the cycle of negative thoughts.

Consider this...
1. Which celebrities might resonate with your young people and help dismantle the stigma surrounding conversations about mental health?
2. How at ease would you be sharing their narrative and then transitioning into a discussion about the stigma associated with talking about mental health?

In conclusion, the examples of people speaking out about their mental health challenges serve as powerful catalysts for breaking the stigma. Their stories have sparked important conversations and increased understanding and empathy. However, to create a truly transformative impact, we must shift the paradigm and focus on mental wellbeing.

Shifting perspectives and embracing a positive narrative

As educators on the frontlines, we possess the capacity to revolutionise the broader discourse on mental health. By redirecting our attention toward enhancing mental wellbeing and arming young people with the tools they need to thrive, we have the power to reshape the often-negative dialogue that surrounds mental health. The time has come to redefine our approach, viewing mental wellbeing as a life-enriching asset rather than exclusively concentrating on addressing mental illnesses when they emerge.

In this section, we will delve into the significance of nurturing mental wellbeing and how even minor adjustments to one's lifestyle can exert a profound influence on the lives of our students. By embracing this perspective, we can take the lead in promoting mental wellness and enabling our students to flourish.

Historically, conversations about mental health have primarily revolved around addressing mental illnesses once they have surfaced. However, a fundamental shift in perspective is imperative, with a focus on optimising mental wellbeing from a preventative and proactive vantage point. By reframing our approach and accentuating the importance of mental wellbeing, we can alter the prevailing negative narrative surrounding mental health and underscore its potential for transformation.

Optimising mental wellbeing
Rather than solely addressing mental health issues, let us prioritise strategies that promote mental wellbeing. By incorporating daily practices that support emotional resilience, stress management, self-care, and healthy coping mechanisms, we empower students to navigate life's challenges with confidence and positivity.

Holistic approach
Promote a holistic view of mental wellbeing, acknowledging the interconnectedness of physical, emotional, and social aspects of a student's life. Encourage healthy lifestyles encompassing exercise, nutrition, restful sleep, and positive social connections. By addressing these factors, we lay a strong foundation for overall mental wellbeing.

Strength-based approaches
Focus on identifying and nurturing the strengths and talents of our students. By shifting the narrative from a deficit-based model to a strengths-based one, we foster resilience, self-

esteem, and a sense of purpose. Encourage students to explore their passions, develop their skills, and engage in activities that bring them joy and fulfilment.

Building resilience and coping skills
Equip our students with the tools and strategies to navigate challenges and setbacks. We explicitly teach them effective problem-solving skills, emotional regulation techniques, and stress management practices. By instilling resilience and coping skills, we empower students to face adversity and bounce back stronger. We need a 'taught not caught' approach so we are not leaving it to chance.

Promoting open dialogue
Create a safe and supportive environment that encourages open dialogue around mental health. Foster a non-judgemental space where students feel comfortable discussing their emotions, experiences, and concerns.

Collaborative partnerships
Engage in collaborative partnerships with mental health professionals, parents, and the wider community. By working together, we can pool resources, share knowledge, and develop comprehensive support systems that address the diverse needs of our students. This collaborative effort amplifies the positive impact we can have on their mental wellbeing.

By shifting our focus to optimising mental wellbeing and fostering a positive narrative, we have the power to transform the lives of our students. Through small adjustments to their lifestyle and a proactive approach, we can empower them to thrive and embrace their full potential.

Let us seize this opportunity to redefine the conversation around mental health, placing mental wellbeing at the forefront and inspiring a generation of resilient, confident, and emotionally healthy individuals.

In conclusion, changing the narrative around mental health requires a fundamental shift in our collective mindset. Instead of solely addressing mental illness, we must prioritise mental wellbeing as a proactive and preventive approach. By promoting mental wellbeing, we empower individuals to build emotional resilience, practise self-care, and lead fulfilling lives.

This paradigm shift necessitates a cultural change that permeates every aspect of society, including our educational institutions, workplaces, and communities. By fostering a culture that prioritises mental health, we create an environment where individuals feel safe, supported, and empowered to seek help and support when needed.

To drive this cultural change, we must embrace a common language that normalises discussions about mental health. By using inclusive and non-stigmatising terminology, we can foster open dialogue and encourage individuals to share their experiences without fear of judgement or discrimination.

We, as active participants in this transformation, play a pivotal role. By incorporating mental health education into our interactions, creating safe spaces for conversations, and modelling positive mental health practices, we can instil a culture of mental wellbeing in our respective domains. This includes teaching emotional intelligence, resilience-building skills, and self-care strategies that empower individuals to navigate life's challenges with confidence.

Breaking the stigma surrounding mental health requires a comprehensive approach that encompasses personal narratives, cultural change, a common language, and a paradigm shift towards prioritising mental wellbeing. Let us continue to amplify the voices of people who bravely share their stories, while actively working towards a society that values and supports mental health. Together, we can create a future where mental wellbeing is cherished, stigma is eradicated, and individuals are empowered to live their lives to the fullest.

Chapter summary

- By actively engaging in cultural change, we can reshape the way society views and addresses children's mental health.
- We need to change the narrative by focusing on positives of wellbeing rather than the negatives.
- Creating a safe and open dialogue within classrooms and schools encourages students to express their emotions and concerns without judgment.
- Leading by example as educators inspires students to prioritise their own mental wellbeing through positive mental health practices.
- We need to emphasise the importance of a common language for discussing mental health, exploring definitions of mental wellbeing, mental health, and mental illness to foster understanding and support.
- By using a shared language we can effectively communicate and promote empathy, prioritise positive mental health, address specific conditions, and create an environment that supports children's mental wellbeing.
- Breaking the stigma around mental health involves highlighting role models who have openly discussed their own mental health struggles and emphasising the importance of seeking help.

Critical questions

1. Do you feel cultural change is necessary?

2. Do you and your staff use shared language in appropriate contexts?

3. Do you and your staff feel confident discussing mental health with your children?

Chapter references

- Yahoo Life. (2022). Paddy Pimblett: Helping combat mental-health issues 'means more than any win'. [online] Available at: https://www.yahoo.com/lifestyle/paddy-pimblett-helping-combat-mental-101031017.html?fr=sycsrp_catchall [Accessed 2 Oct. 2023].

Chapter 15 - Celebrating success

"Success is not just about what you accomplish in your life; it's about what you inspire others to do."
Unknown source

As teachers, we have the power to shape the lives of our students in profound ways. Celebrating success is one powerful tool we can use to help our students feel valued, empowered, and motivated to continue growing and learning.

When we celebrate success, we acknowledge the hard work and effort that our students put into achieving their goals. This recognition can be incredibly validating and empowering, helping students feel seen and heard in a world that can often feel overwhelming and isolating. By celebrating success, we also help students build resilience and grit, developing the mindset that they can overcome challenges and achieve their dreams with hard work and determination.

In this penultimate chapter, we will explore the many different ways you can celebrate success with your students, from simple acts of recognition and praise to more formal ceremonies and events. We'll also discuss the benefits of celebrating success for both your students and yourself as an educator, exploring the ways in which this practice can help you build stronger, more positive relationships with your students and create a more supportive, uplifting learning environment.

With the tools and strategies in this book, you'll be able to create a classroom culture that values and celebrates success, supporting the mental health and wellbeing of your students and colleagues in meaningful ways. So let's dive in and explore the power of celebrating success in developing children's mental health!

Mental health heroes

One of the ways we celebrated our students' success was to present our young people with 'Mental Health Hero' certificates, to celebrate their engagement, at the end of a unit in physical education. We wanted them to know how much we valued their efforts to transform their wellbeing.

On the back of the certificates we printed our self-care menu. This meant children could refer to it if they ever felt low in their bedroom and the certificate caught their eye. It could act as a prompt for them to take action to start to move them in the right direction towards feeling better.

We also included helplines, on the back, to external services so they had a way out if they were in crisis. I don't know if it had an impact, but I wanted to do everything I possibly could to prevent the unthinkable for our young people.

Sports awards evening

We would have an annual sports awards evening with a range of categories to recognise and celebrate our children's achievements in various activities. We celebrated our students' sporting successes, but it was far more than that, we celebrated effort and attitude, leadership, and health.

We created a new category called 'Wellbeing Warriors', for children who went above and beyond to create and sustain healthy habits to transform their mental wellbeing. It was a great way to celebrate students who maybe hadn't thrived in PE previously, but had won in their own unique way and, at the same time, provide role models for children across the school.

Success breeds motivation

Success is a powerful motivator, especially for teenagers. When young people feel that they are succeeding and making progress towards their goals, they are more likely to be motivated to continue working hard and striving for success. This is particularly important when it comes to mental health, as motivation is a key factor in helping teenagers build resilience and develop the coping skills they need to navigate life's challenges.

One reason why success comes before motivation, is that experiencing success helps to build confidence and self-efficacy, which in turn motivates teenagers to continue working towards their goals.

Success can help to establish positive habits and routines, which can lead to further success and motivation. When young people experience success in a particular area, they are more likely to continue engaging in activities that support that success, building positive habits and routines that support their mental health and wellbeing.

By recognising our children's achievements, we can help to build students' confidence and motivation, setting them on a path towards greater success.

Impact celebrating success has on our relationships

Celebrating our children's success is not only important for their mental health and wellbeing, but it can also bring us closer together and help develop stronger relationships. When we take the time to acknowledge and celebrate our children's achievements, we show them that we value and support them, which can strengthen the bond between teacher and student or parent and child.

Celebrating our children's success can lead to greater feelings of warmth and closeness in the parent-child relationship. When parents celebrate their children's success, it can help to build positive emotions and memories that can be drawn upon during times of stress or conflict. It can also lead to greater feelings of gratitude and positivity in the parent-child relationship. When parents take the time to recognise and appreciate their children's accomplishments, it can help to foster a sense of mutual respect and understanding.

The benefits of celebrating success extend to our teacher-student relationship. According to a 2019 study published in the Journal of School Psychology, teachers who took the time to celebrate their students' success had stronger relationships with those students and were better able to support their social-emotional development. (Kuklinski, M. R., Weinstein, R. S., & Cochran-Smith, M., 2019)

In researching this book, I came across a great teacher down in Sussex, called Joe Goldberg. Each night before he leaves school, he quickly calls 5 sets of parents/carers to mention a good thing their child has done that day. What a great habit to celebrate our students' success and to deliver ripples of positivity throughout our wider school community. Each call is going to improve the mood of the parent whatever they have had to deal with that day and bring the parent-child relationships closer that evening.

Mr Goldberg's view is that if he calls 5 sets of parents every day, over the course of the academic year he will reach every student in the school. The resulting impact is that Mr Goldberg has incredible relationships with his young people as they know he sees them and celebrates their success. It then makes the tougher conversations a lot easier. Mattering matters to us all so let's celebrate our students when they get it right.

 **Try this:**

Ripples of positivity

1. Identify 3 students who have done a kind act for someone else, demonstrated resilience or worked hard on a brilliant piece of work.
2. Call their parents/carers to let them know with a quick call to spread ripples of positivity.

We can also hold celebration events to bring our children closer together, helping them develop a greater sense of belonging and the opportunity to build relationships with young people from other schools.

Case Study
Celebrating 'Liverpool RISE Up'
We held a celebration event for the 'Liverpool RISE Up' programme, at Childwall Academy in collaboration with the Liverpool School Sports Partnership. This event brought together children from Belvedere Academy, Kings Leadership School Liverpool and the Academy of St Francis of Assisi for a day filled with physical activities and plenty of fun.

Young people participated in four RISE physical activities, each designed to promote the link between physical activity and mental wellbeing. The day started with a high-energy session of Raving 'Fit.' Young people danced and created their own motifs, setting a lively tone for the day ahead. Inclusivity then took centre stage with Kinball, an activity designed to foster a strong sense of belonging among all participants, through teamwork and cooperation.

Young people had the chance to enjoy Fitness Suite activities aimed at relieving stress and expanding their window of tolerance. Repeater and Stress Buster Activities were on the menu, providing a relaxing yet challenging experience. We hosted confidence-building activities inspired by the remarkable story of Liverpool's own 'Meatball Molly' McCann, a local hero and inspiration to many.

The day culminated in a joyous colour run, where young people and staff celebrated their achievements and formed deeper connections with each other. This colourful event was a fitting finale, emphasising fun, connection, and belonging as we dodged the rain! We loved the comments and smiles from all the young people and teachers throughout the day.

We celebrated the incredible achievements of our partner schools, their young people, and the Liverpool School Sports Partnership. Together, they've achieved remarkable results for their young people, making a positive impact on their lives and futures. Their whole school plans moving forward are incredibly exciting.

Celebrating our colleagues

It is important to celebrate staff who complete training in supporting students with their mental wellbeing. By recognising our colleagues' efforts and hard work, we create a culture of support and recognition that promotes mental health and wellbeing.

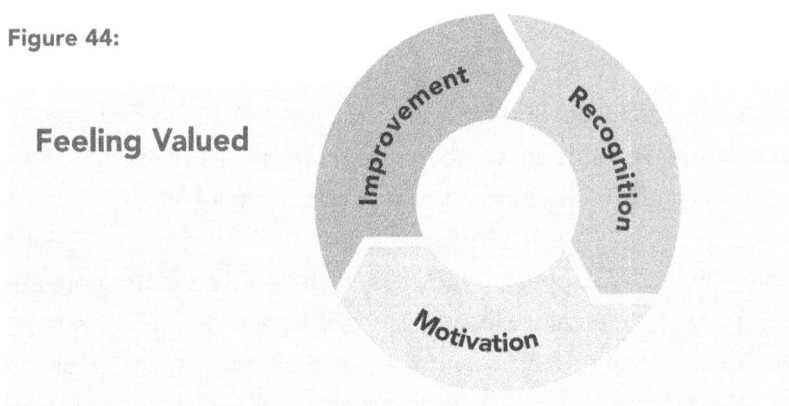

Figure 44:

Feeling Valued

One of the most significant benefits of celebrating staff who complete training in supporting students with their mental wellbeing, is recognition and motivation. Recognising staff's hard work and dedication motivates them to continue to improve their skills and knowledge in this area, which ultimately benefits students. This recognition also makes staff feel valued and appreciated, leading to higher levels of job satisfaction and retention.

It sends a message that mental health is essential and valued, and the organisation is committed to supporting the mental health of its students and staff. This, in turn, creates a safe and supportive environment where staff and students can feel comfortable discussing mental health concerns and seeking help.

Celebrating staff who complete training in supporting students with their mental wellbeing leads to better outcomes for students. When staff are trained in supporting students' mental wellbeing, they are better equipped to identify and support students who may be struggling with mental health issues. This, in turn, leads to improved academic and social outcomes for students, who receive the support they need to manage their mental health and succeed in school.

Furthermore, celebrating staff who complete this training can increase staff confidence in their ability to support students who are struggling with mental health issues. This confidence can lead to improved relationships between staff and students, as well as increased job satisfaction and retention. Staff who feel confident in their ability to support students with their mental health needs are more likely to feel satisfied with their jobs and remain in the education field long-term.

To celebrate staff who complete their training in this field, schools can hold recognition ceremonies, share success stories, provide ongoing support, and encourage self-care practices. Holding events to recognise staff who have completed mental health training, such as certificate presentation ceremonies or celebratory lunches, shows appreciation for their hard work and dedication. Sharing success stories of staff who have successfully supported students with their mental health needs, inspires and motivates others to continue their training.

As we developed a training programme for colleagues, we had the programme accredited by the CPD Certification Service and presented personalised certificates to all colleagues who had completed the training to recognise their efforts. We created case studies to celebrate colleagues who had gone above and beyond to transform the mental wellbeing of their young people to inspire additional colleagues.

We now build communities of teachers who are passionate about transforming the mental wellbeing of their young people so that they can connect, support, and learn from each other. A great example of this is the brilliant group of PE teachers who were part of the 'Liverpool RISE Up' pilot programme.

Overall, celebrating staff who complete training in supporting students with their mental wellbeing is important for promoting a positive culture around mental health, improving outcomes for students, and increasing staff confidence in their ability to support students with their mental health needs.

Consider this...
How would you like to be recognised to motivate you to transform mental wellbeing outcomes for your young people?

Celebrating school success

As children's mental health has declined, parents have become increasingly concerned about what schools are doing to support their children.

Youth Sport Trust research carried out in February 2021 among UK parents of school age children found that pupil wellbeing is the top factor for parents when choosing a secondary school (65%) ahead of location (62%), culture and ethos of the staff (59%), facilities (57%), OFSTED rating (57%) and exam results (48%). For primary schools, pupil wellbeing was the second most important factor behind location.

The research, conducted by YouGov, surveyed over 1,100 UK parents with children aged 18 and under. The study found that two-thirds of parents would have liked more information on what schools were doing to support their children's mental wellbeing. The study also highlighted the importance of physical education (PE) and school sport in promoting children's wellbeing, with 81% of parents believing that cuts to PE, sport, and break time in schools would have a negative impact on their children's wellbeing.

By celebrating the work your school is doing around mental wellbeing, it can help bring parents on side with the school, defusing parental conflict and aiding everyone working together for the benefit of the child.

Not only is prioritising wellbeing the right thing to promote for our young people, but it provides an opportunity for schools to increase their school roll and ultimately their school budgets by promoting the great work you do around wellbeing.

Schools can celebrate the great work they do around mental wellbeing in a number of ways:
- Apply for externally verified wellbeing awards: use the award to publicise the school's work to the wider community.
- Share success stories: how the school supported those students who overcame mental health challenges on their journey.
- Organise events: such as Mental Health Awareness Week, where students can participate in activities and workshops that promote positive mental health.
- Highlight mental health resources for students: such as counselling services, peer support groups, and self-help resources.
- Involve parents and the community: organising mental health events, workshops, and seminars that educate parents and community members on how to support students with mental health challenges.
- Recognise staff contributions: from those who have made significant contributions to mental health initiatives in the school. This can be done through awards, certificates, or public recognition.

Overall, celebrating the great work done around mental wellbeing in schools can help to reduce stigma, promote positive mental health, encourage more students to seek support when needed, and help with parental satisfaction with the school.

Parents Case Study
A mother's story

In Chapter 13, we showcased the brilliant work of Mr Austin, Miss Alothman and the Hethersett Physical Education department in implementing an early intervention programme through their Key Stage 4 curriculum.

Hethersett Academy was one of the first schools I worked with. They have been on a fantastic journey and were rewarded with a thoroughly deserved 'Outstanding' inspection from Ofsted in 2022.

I revisited Hethersett Academy to explore the impact of their early intervention programme, through the eyes of one of their parents and the impact it has had on her daughter.

The parent is also a Social, Emotional & Mental Health (SEMH) counsellor in another great school I partner with, so is incredibly well placed to talk about the impact of the programme. Mum takes up the story here:

Adolescence, Social media, and a mother's fears
As a mother, I always worried about the impact adolescence would have on my daughter; it is a very challenging time of life for anyone, with many developmental and physical changes. The expectations and norms displayed on social media have always been a huge concern for me. I have always ensured that my children are aware of the impact social media plays on mental health.

Impact of the pandemic
My daughter went from being a young girl to a teenager during the pandemic; this meant that she developed a new sense of self in isolation to her peers. She was not used to socialising with others in the outside world in her newly developed 'teenage self'.

As a result she became anxious, insecure, and struggled with regulation. She struggled with her sleep and spent hours in front of her computer completing home learning or on her phone interacting with others. She became demotivated and was reluctant to exercise.

Transformation
For a period following lockdown, my daughter felt very insecure in PE. She was consistently commenting on how insecure she was of her body, how she felt different to her peers, and

how others would body shame one another. This caused her to become highly anxious on the days she had PE lessons.

I was not aware that my daughter had started the 'RISE Up' Early Intervention Programme but had noticed a huge change in her wanting to take part in her PE lesson. I then noticed a change in her outlook, self-awareness, and confidence.

Feeling positive
I asked her if there was anything that had changed, and she spoke about the impact the PE Programme was having on her wellbeing and mental health.

My daughter felt really positive about taking part in the programme, and she was pleased that her friends were taking part. This facilitated the process in terms of the ability for her and her peers to embed the programme and skills learnt into their daily lives.

Engagement in PE
It had been requested that my daughter be taken out of PE to take part in an academic intervention, however, she requested that she was not removed from PE. She felt that this would have an impact on her mental health. She was able to describe all the benefits of the Early Intervention Programme provided and how it had a positive emotional and physical impact on her.

Positive changes
Since my daughter took part in the 'RISE Up' Programme, she is able to positively influence those around her with regards to the confidence she has in herself, and the impact social media has on this.

She takes part in journalling and mindfulness regularly. She has set personal goals for herself both mentally and physically. She is now able to advocate for herself and others in terms of what mental and physical health entails and tries to lead a balanced lifestyle.

This has had a positive impact on our relationship as the programme has facilitated her ability to communicate her worries to me, and we are then able to problem solve together.

This is how my daughter summarised the impact of the programme:

"Becoming a teenager during lockdown was so hard, I always compared myself to people on social media because I spent so much time on my phone. After the programme I feel more able to focus on my mental wellbeing and how important physical health is. I know myself so much better than before. I also like to help my friends feel more positive about themselves and also feel comfortable asking my PE teachers for a bit of support when I am feeling down"

Feeling grateful for the school

I was really grateful that she had the opportunity to take part in the programme. As a counsellor myself, we know that school-based mental health interventions can have a significant impact on various student-level outcomes and reduce pressure on downstream services such as Child and Adolescent Mental Health Services (CAMHS). I was pleased to hear that this was a universal programme in PE and that students were learning and developing these crucial life-skills. I would definitely like to see more programmes like these in all schools.

Schools making a difference

School-based universal programmes enable young people to receive support and develop self-care skills.

Schools are able to provide early identification and intervention of a mental health need in young people, in a protected and familiar context, without needing to self-refer or be externally referred to mental health services.

Understanding what works is important in the assigning and delivery of effective interventions, so that young people's mental health and wellbeing are enhanced, their long-term outcomes are improved, and strain on downstream services is reduced.

As a parent, I think it is important to make use of the potential of schools to provide effective early interventions to improve the mental health of young people. It certainly helped my daughter.

In conclusion

Celebrating success is an essential aspect of promoting mental wellbeing in schools. It is important to acknowledge and celebrate the achievements of our students, colleagues, and school community as a whole. This not only boosts morale and motivation, but also fosters a positive school culture that values and recognises the efforts and contributions of everyone involved.

Celebrating success can take many forms, from acknowledging academic achievements to recognising personal milestones and acts of kindness. It is essential to create a culture of celebration that is inclusive and supportive, where all students and staff feel valued and recognised.

By celebrating success, we can create a sense of belonging and pride in our school community, which in turn can have a positive impact on mental wellbeing. Celebrating success can also help to build resilience and promote a growth mindset, as students and staff are encouraged to learn from their successes and failures.

Promoting mental wellbeing in schools requires a holistic approach that encompasses all aspects of school life. Celebrating success is an essential part of this approach, as it helps to create a positive school culture that values and recognises the efforts and contributions of all. By celebrating success, we can help to boost morale and motivation, foster resilience and promote a growth mindset, and ultimately support the mental wellbeing of our students, colleagues, and school community.

Chapter summary

- Celebrating our children's success is an important way to strengthen relationships and develop tighter bonds between parents and children, or teachers and students. By taking the time to recognise and appreciate our children's accomplishments, we can help to build positive emotions, memories, and experiences that can benefit us all in the long run.
- Celebrating staff who complete training in supporting students with their mental wellbeing is vital in promoting a positive culture around mental health, improving outcomes for students, and increasing staff confidence in their ability to support students with their mental health needs.
- Celebrating the great work done around mental wellbeing in schools can help to reduce stigma, promote positive mental health, encourage more students to seek support when needed, and increase numbers on roll and ultimately the school budget so other areas of the school can be invested in.

Critical questions

1. How are you celebrating your children who are making a commitment to transform their wellbeing?

2. Are there 3 students you can identify who have done something positive that you can call their parents/carers to celebrate tomorrow?

3. Does your school do anything to celebrate your colleagues who are prioritising children's mental wellbeing?

4. Does your school promote what it is doing about transforming mental wellbeing to your wider community?

Chapter references
- Kuklinski, M. R., Weinstein, R. S., & Cochran-Smith, M. (2019). Teachers' beliefs and behaviours regarding the celebration of student success: An exploratory study. *Journal of School Psychology*, 75, pp.123–137.
- Youth Sport Trust. (2021). Parents want wellbeing prioritised in schools as pandemic hits home. Youth Sport Trust. https://www.youthsporttrust.org/news/parents-want-wellbeing-prioritised-schools-pandemic-hits-home

Chapter 16 - Time to RISE Up

"Every new beginning comes from some other beginning's end."
 Seneca

As we reach the final chapter of this book, it is important to reflect on the scale of the problem we face when it comes to children's mental wellbeing. There are many factors that have contributed to this current situation, including the damaging effects of social media, the impact of lockdowns, intergenerational trauma, poverty, racial injustice, the cost of living crisis, the Ukraine-Russia war, and academic pressures.

Despite these challenges, it is important to recognise that schools have a critical role to play in promoting children's mental wellbeing. We have explored two contrasting scenarios: "Heaven," where children are equipped with the skills they need to flourish and transform their mental wellbeing, and "Hell," where families and communities are devastated by intergenerational trauma and the cycle of daily life struggles. As we move forward, it is crucial that we prioritise the development of skills that can equip our children for the challenges of the 21st century so that our young people can move forward with hope.

Despite an incredibly dedicated workforce consisting of exceptional teachers and leaders, many schools are struggling to provide students with the necessary tools and resources to develop these skills. This highlights the need for systemic change and a collective effort to support children's mental wellbeing. By working together, we can create a brighter future for our children and for society as a whole.

As Sir Ken Robinson (2006) so elegantly argues in his Ted Talk on 'Do schools kill creativity?' Intelligence is diverse, dynamic, and distinct. We have to rethink the fundamental principles on which we're educating our children. Our task is to educate the whole child so they can face their future.

Skills for the future

As the world becomes increasingly complex and interconnected, it is important that our schools equip children with the skills they need to thrive in the future. While there are many skills that could be considered essential for success in the 21st century, some of the most important for me, include in no particular order:

- Ability to Manage Their Mental Wellbeing
- Emotional Intelligence and the Ability to Build Relationships
- Physical Literacy
- Numeracy
- Literacy
- Financial Literacy and the Ability to Create Value
- Technological Literacy to Adapt to Emerging Technologies
- Creativity
- Growth Mindset
- Adaptability
- Problem-solving
- Critical thinking

Consider this...
Would you add any qualities that you would like your children to have as they enter adulthood?

We need a system that is flexible to the requirements of each child, rather than children being flexible around the needs of the system. We need greater choice so that young people can choose a pathway that inspires them and develops a lifelong love of learning. Special schools such as the Wherry School in Norfolk have demonstrated that this is possible by striking a superb balance between a formal and informal curriculum.

We can't keep sleepwalking around this issue, we need to take action to reform our school curriculums, to create positive change for the sake of our young people. It is time to prioritise the development of skills and qualities that will help our children succeed in the future, and to ensure that all children have access to the resources and support they need to thrive. By taking action now, we can create a brighter future for our children and for society as a whole.

So what action do we need to take?
I believe from the evidence base and my experiences and conversations with teaching colleagues across the country, that the impact of Covid has fundamentally changed many of our children, making teaching harder than it has ever been. Many children are now increasingly hypervigilant and feeling unsafe in their classrooms triggering the fight, flight, fright response. This is leading to increased behavioural problems, disengagement, and poor attendance.

We have to adapt to our young people in front of us, to create psychological safety first, so that they can thrive, and we can thrive as teachers. Without adapting to our young people, our role is going to get harder and harder, resulting in more and more excellent colleagues leaving the profession to the point where we will be struggling for teachers to teach our children.

The secret formula for transformational teachers
To become a transformational teacher and improve our children's mental wellbeing in a post-lockdown education world, I believe we need to focus on the following formula:

Outstanding relationships +
Early Intervention Strategies +
Opportunities for Physical Activity and Play =
A Transformational Teacher for Mental Wellbeing

Let's explore each aspect of this formula in more detail.

Outstanding relationships

Outstanding relationships are at the heart of promoting children's mental wellbeing in schools. As teachers, we have a unique opportunity to build positive relationships with our students that can create a safe and supportive learning environment. Here are some key aspects of outstanding relationships that we can focus on:

- Understanding the importance of psychological safety cues: These cues can be conveyed through our facial expressions, tone of voice, and body language. Understanding how to use safety cues effectively can help students feel psychologically safe, supported, and able to contribute to class and society. By increasing and exaggerating our safety cues we can indicate safety and support to all our students.

- Building a sense of belonging: Belonging is a basic human need, and it is essential for promoting children's mental wellbeing. Teachers can help all students feel a sense of belonging by creating a positive classroom culture, celebrating diversity, and providing opportunities for social connection and collaboration.

- Be emotionally available: creating a safe and supportive learning environment where students feel comfortable sharing their thoughts and feelings with us. It requires us to be present and engaged with our students, actively listening to their concerns, and showing empathy and understanding. To be emotionally available, we need to cultivate our own emotional intelligence, which involves being aware of our own emotions, managing them effectively, and being able to recognise and respond to the emotions of others. We can create opportunities for children to express their emotions through activities like journalling, group discussions, and role-playing.

- Creating a positive classroom culture: creating an environment where all students feel safe, supported, and respected. This can be achieved by setting clear expectations, promoting positive behaviour which does not retraumatise our most vulnerable children, providing opportunities for student voice and choice, and celebrating student success.

- Being flexible and adaptable: We should be able to adapt our teaching approach to meet the needs of individual students. This may involve using different teaching methods, providing additional support, or making accommodations for students with special needs, such as those who have suffered from adverse childhood experiences.

By focusing on these key aspects of outstanding relationships, we can create a safe and supportive learning environment that promotes children's mental wellbeing. Students who feel psychologically safe, supported, and respected are more likely to be engaged, motivated, happier, and successful in their learning.

In order to support colleagues who wanted to move in this direction but maybe didn't have the confidence or knowledge of how, I created the 7 step 'Recover Roadmap' with an accompanying teacher training course. The aim of the programme is to show colleagues how they can explicitly develop their craft to focus on relationships so that they can transform outcomes for their young people.

Figure 45:

The Recover Roadmap

A 7 step process to guide teachers how to implement trauma informed practice in Physical Education to transform relationships, wellbeing, engagement, behaviour & progress within 90 days, and children's life chances in the long term.

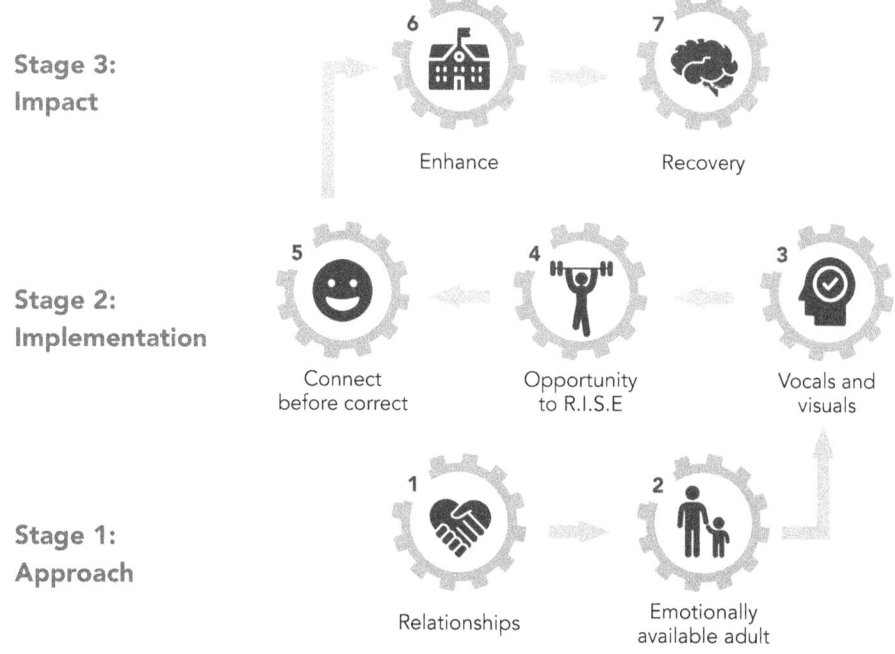

Early intervention strategies

Early intervention strategies are essential for promoting children's mental wellbeing in schools. By teaching young people a range of self-care strategies, teachers can equip them with the skills to manage their mental health long after they have left school.

Earlier in part two we discovered some key aspects of early intervention strategies that we can focus on:

- **Healthy habits:** We can promote healthy habits, such as regular exercise, practising mindfulness, healthy eating and drinking, and adequate sleep, to help students manage their mental health. Encouraging students to develop a routine that includes these healthy habits can improve their overall wellbeing and help them feel more in control of their lives.
- **Balancing social media usage:** Social media can have both positive and negative effects on mental health. We can educate students about the potential risks of social media and provide guidance on how to use it in a healthy and balanced way. This can include setting limits on screen time, encouraging face-to-face interactions, and promoting mindfulness practices.
- **Accessing the 4 happiness chemicals:** Dopamine, oxytocin, serotonin, and endorphins. We can teach students how to access these chemicals in healthy ways to improve their mental wellbeing when they are feeling low. This can include activities such as exercise, socialising, helping others, and pursuing hobbies.
- **Building self-confidence and self-kindness:** improve students' mental wellbeing by promoting a positive self-image and reducing negative self-talk. We can encourage students to focus on their strengths and practise self-compassion.
- **Using worries as a positive to reduce anxiety:** Worries are a natural part of life, but they can become overwhelming and lead to anxiety. We can teach students how to reframe worries as positive opportunities for growth and development. This can involve teaching students problem-solving skills and encouraging them to focus on solutions rather than dwelling on problems.
- **Raising aspirations and achieving goals:** Setting and achieving goals can give students a sense of purpose and direction, which can improve their mental wellbeing. We can help students set realistic and achievable goals and provide support and encouragement along the way.

CHAPTER 16 - TIME TO RISE UP

By focusing on these key early intervention strategies, we can create healthier, happier young people and reduce the burden on specialist support services such as the NHS and CAMHS.

In order to support colleagues who wanted to move in this direction but maybe didn't have the confidence or knowledge of how, I created the 9 step 'RISE Up Roadmap' with an accompanying teacher training course. The aim of the programme is to guide colleagues to reduce their students' anxiety, build their confidence and create sustainable early intervention programmes within their schools.

Figure 46:

The RISE Up Roadmap

A proven step by step process that guides innovative teachers to reduce student's anxiety, build their confidence and create a sustainable early intervention wellbeing programme within 90 days.

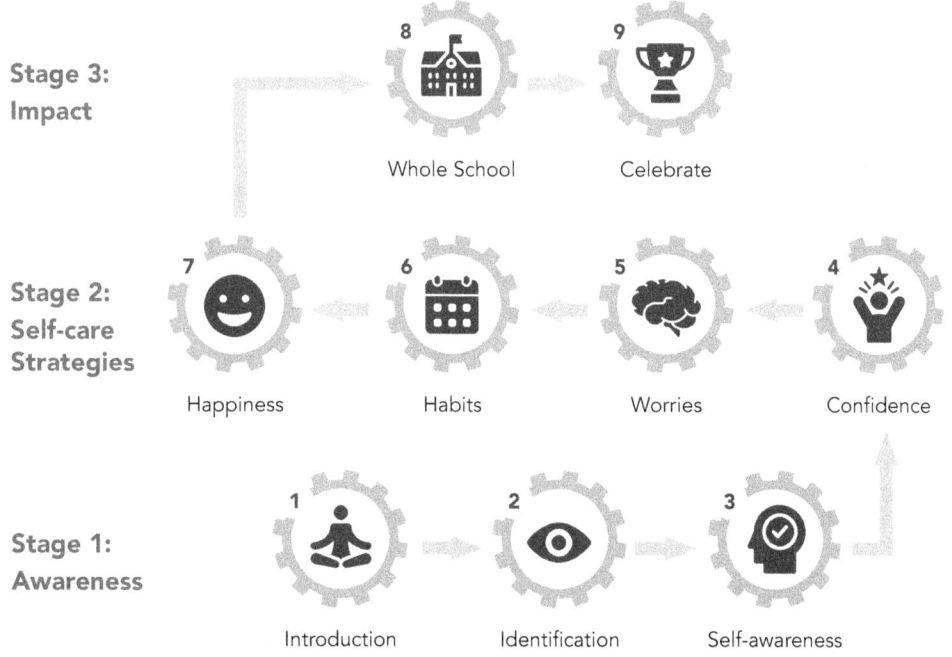

Opportunities for physical activity and play

Opportunities for physical activity are essential for promoting children's mental wellbeing in schools. Teaching children about the link between physical activity and mental wellbeing can help them understand how physical activity can be used as a tool for self-regulation. Providing opportunities for physical activity that suit students' needs can help them feel calmer, grounded, and more confident.

Here are some key aspects of opportunities for physical activity that teachers can focus on:

- **Creating safe spaces:** We can create safe spaces where students can engage in physical activity without fear of judgement or bullying. This can involve promoting positive attitudes towards physical activity, and providing a range of activities that cater to different interests and abilities.

- **Providing variety:** Offering a variety of physical activities can help students find activities that they enjoy and that are appropriate for their individual needs. This can include both formal and informal activities such as repetitive activities like running, walking, or swimming, team sports, individual sports, outdoor adventure activities, weight training, martial arts, dance, and yoga.

- **Creating a sense of belonging:** Physical activity can create a sense of belonging and foster positive relationships among students. We can encourage students to work together as an inclusive team, celebrate each other's successes, and promote a positive attitude towards physical activity. Reducing the feeling of threat and creating psychological safety is key for this to occur.

- **Encouraging active travel:** Walking or cycling to school, can promote physical activity and mental wellbeing. We can work with parents and local authorities to create safe routes for students to walk, scoot or cycle to school, and reward those young people who do.

- **Integrating physical activity into the wider curriculum:** Helps students to understand the importance of physical activity and mental wellbeing. This can involve incorporating physical activity into lessons and form times, providing breaks for physical activity during the day, or offering physical activity as part of homework assignments.

- **Creating opportunities to play:** Opportunities for both supervised and unsupervised play are crucial for promoting children's mental wellbeing in schools. Supervised play wrapped in care provides a structured and safe environment where children can develop their social skills and learn new skills under the guidance and support of adults. Unsupervised play, on the other hand, allows children to explore and play independently, developing their creativity, imagination, and resilience. Providing opportunities for both types of play can help children develop a positive attitude towards play, build their social skills, and promote their emotional and cognitive development, which are important for academic success and personal growth.

By focusing on these key aspects of opportunities for physical activity and play, we can create a positive and supportive learning environment that promotes children's mental wellbeing. Students who engage in physical activity regularly are more likely to feel calmer, more grounded, and more confident, which can help them succeed in their academic and personal lives.

When we combine all three aspects of the formula we can be a transformational teacher for children's mental wellbeing, both now, and long after our children have left our care.

Figure 47:

The Formula:

| Outstanding Relationships | | Early Intervention Wellbeing Programmes | | Physical Activity and Play |

 A Transformational Teacher in a Post Lockdown Education World

Everyone has a role to play to create this transformation

From teachers, senior leaders, parents, government, Ofsted, Initial Teacher Trainers, training providers and children, everyone has a role to play to enable this vision to occur. So what do we need from each key stakeholder?

What do we need from frontline teachers?
In order to care for others, we must first ensure that we are taking care of ourselves. We must prioritise our own mental wellbeing in order to be in a position to care for our students.

We need to embrace trauma-informed principles and adapt our existing practices to create a safe and supportive learning environment for all students. We need to be prepared to undertake training to understand the evidence base and what is at stake for our children and wider society.

When dealing with behaviour that challenges us, it is important to look beyond the surface behaviour and address the root cause of the young person's behaviour. This requires a deep understanding of trauma and its impact on our children's mental wellbeing. We need to create a sense of belonging within our classrooms and extracurricular programmes by prioritising relationships and creating a psychologically safe environment that triggers our children's social engagement systems.

We must be mindful of our own biases and avoid re-traumatising children with our judgements. This means approaching each child with compassion and understanding and providing the necessary support and resources to help them overcome their challenges.

Physical activity is also a crucial component of promoting our children's mental wellbeing. We should provide opportunities for children to move and engage in physical activity throughout the day, both in and outside of the classroom.

By prioritising our own mental wellbeing, embracing trauma-informed principles, and creating a safe and supportive learning environment, we can help promote the mental wellbeing of our students. By providing opportunities for physical activity, we can also help our children develop the skills and tools they need to manage their own mental health and wellbeing, both now and in the future.

What do we need from senior leaders?
To effectively promote the mental wellbeing of our students, senior leaders in schools must play a key role.

Just like frontline teachers, in order to care for others, we must first ensure that senior leaders are taking care of themselves. They should prioritise their own mental wellbeing in order to be in a position to care for their colleagues and students.

Senior leaders must prioritise staff wellbeing by ensuring that teachers feel psychologically safe, supported, and able to contribute to the school community. This means taking action to reduce excessive staff workload, providing resources and support for staff to manage their own mental wellbeing, and creating a positive working environment that enables teachers to thrive.

We need senior leaders to budget for and provide training and support on trauma-informed principles and ensure that they themselves understand these principles. Our senior leaders need to provide appropriate time for staff to complete this training without it becoming another additional task for frontline teachers to complete.

Senior leaders should also introduce whole school relationship policies that promote positive relationships between staff and students and review existing behaviour policies. This can include practices such as restorative justice, with appropriate staff training, so that it is actioned effectively, which prioritises repairing harm and building relationships rather than punishment. Too often restorative conversations are not as effective as they should be due to a lack of effective staff training.

The best senior leaders will target triggering the social engagement system, which is crucial for promoting positive mental health in both staff and students. They will also reward teachers who prioritise building positive relationships with their students and promoting a sense of belonging in the classroom.

Creating a "one big team" ethos is important for promoting a sense of belonging between all staff, children, and parents. By creating a positive and inclusive school community, senior leaders can support the mental wellbeing of all members of their community.

Finally, senior leaders should support families, as and when possible, and build relationships with parents to create a supportive network. This can enable us to lean on parents for support when required and work together to promote positive mental health and wellbeing for our young people.

What do we need from the Government?
To effectively promote the mental wellbeing of our students, we need support from the government.

First and foremost, we need less judgement and fair funding for schools. This means ensuring that schools are funded equitably so that all schools have access to the resources and support they need to thrive.

The government must pursue evidence-based policies that promote positive mental health and wellbeing. This includes funding trauma-informed training for teachers and ensuring that teachers are equipped with the necessary skills to support students who have experienced trauma.

We need fair pay for teachers and fully funded schools, so that teachers are adequately compensated for their vital work and schools have the resources they need to support their students. We need our teachers to feel valued, and fair pay is a vital part of looking after their own wellbeing so that teachers can take care of our children.

The government should continue to invest in internal school counsellors and mental health support teams to help young people make sense of their stories. This will enable students to access support more quickly and easily and promote positive mental health outcomes for all students.

We need governments across the world to put pressure on social media companies to create change in their policies around children and harmful content.

Finally, the government should invest in specialist support services, such as Child and Adolescent Mental Health Services (CAMHS), so that children in crisis receive the support they need in a timely and effective manner. This will enable children to access specialist support when required and ensure that all children have the opportunity to thrive both in and outside of the classroom.

What do we need from Ofsted?
To effectively promote the mental wellbeing of our senior leaders and students, we need support from Ofsted. Ofsted should take a more supportive approach to school improvement, rather than triggering the social defence system of our school leaders, which trickles down and impacts the rest of the school. Often, this results in teachers being asked to complete tasks to protect senior leaders in the event of an inspection, rather than investing time in relationships with our young people. We need Ofsted to work collaboratively with school leaders to celebrate strengths and identify areas for improvement.

By taking a more supportive approach, Ofsted can help to create a positive and inclusive school culture that promotes positive mental health and wellbeing for all members of the school community but particularly our senior leaders. This will enable senior leaders to better support their students and frontline staff and provide a safe and supportive learning environment where our children can thrive. We owe our brilliant leaders like Paul Collin, Rob Connelly, Rachel Quick, Rae Snape, and Dave McPartlin this duty of care.

What do we need from social media companies?
To effectively promote the mental wellbeing of our young people, we need support from social media companies. Social media has become an integral part of young people's lives and can have both positive and negative impacts on their mental health and wellbeing.

Social media companies must take responsibility for limiting children's access to harmful content and promoting positive mental health and wellbeing. This means implementing age verification processes and ensuring that harmful content is not accessible to children and young people.

In addition, social media companies should prioritise promoting positive mental health and wellbeing by providing resources and support to their users. This can include creating educational resources and promoting mental health campaigns, as well as funding and providing access to mental health support services for those in need.

By taking responsibility for the impact of their platforms on young people's mental health, social media companies can help to create a safer and more positive online environment for all users. This will enable young people to access the benefits of social media while minimising the potential harms and promote mental wellbeing for all.

What do we need from parents/carers?
Parents and carers play a vital role in promoting positive mental health and wellbeing for their children, both at home and in the wider community.

Parents and carers should prioritise building positive relationships with their children, creating a safe and supportive home environment where children feel valued, loved, and heard. This means taking the time to listen to their children, validating their feelings, and providing emotional support when needed.

In addition, parents and carers should prioritise promoting healthy habits and lifestyles, including regular exercise, healthy eating, and adequate sleep. They should also be mindful of their children's use of technology and social media and ensure that they are accessing appropriate content and using these platforms in a healthy and balanced way.

Parents and carers should work collaboratively with schools and other professionals to promote positive mental health and wellbeing for their children. This means taking an active interest in their child's education and mental health, attending parent-teacher meetings, and seeking support when needed.

We need to be mindful as teachers that some parents had a difficult time navigating their own school experiences, so we need to up our psychological safety cues to create an environment where these parents feel comfortable and that they belong in our schools, so we can all work as a team for the benefit of the child.

By working together with schools and other professionals, parents and carers can create a supportive network for their children and promote positive mental health and wellbeing for all.

This will enable young people to thrive both at home and in the wider community and ensure that they have the support and resources they need to reach their full potential.

What do we need from children?
To effectively promote the mental wellbeing of our young people, we need support from children themselves. Children play an important role in promoting their own mental health and wellbeing, as well as that of their peers.

Children can prioritise their mental health and wellbeing by engaging in activities that promote positive mental health outcomes, such as taking part in physical activity, creative pursuits, and spending time with friends and family. They can practise self-care techniques, such as mindfulness and meditation, to manage stress and build emotional resilience.

Children should also be encouraged to seek help when they need it, whether from trusted adults, such as parents or teachers, or from professional support services, such as school counsellors or mental health professionals.

In addition, children can play a role in promoting positive mental health and wellbeing for their peers by showing kindness and empathy, and by creating a positive and inclusive school culture where everyone feels valued and respected.

By taking an active role in promoting their own mental health and wellbeing, and that of their peers, children can help to create a safe and supportive learning environment where everyone has the opportunity to thrive. This will enable them to reach their full potential and achieve success both in and outside of the classroom.

What do we need from Initial Teacher Training providers?
We need Initial Teacher Training providers to teach the new generation of teachers about trauma-informed practice. These providers can equip teachers with the knowledge and skills to recognise and respond to the effects of trauma on students' academic and personal lives to create generational change.

Innovative universities like Bath Spa University and the University of East Anglia are already leading the way in this area with their PGCE PE programmes. These programmes provide students with the opportunity to develop an understanding of trauma-informed practice and the skills required to put this into action in their future classrooms.

What do we need from training providers?
To meet the needs of frontline teachers, CPD training providers should focus on the following:

- **Time-efficient training:** Teachers are busy professionals, and their time is valuable. Training providers should offer training that is concise, targeted, and effective, allowing teachers to learn the skills they need in a time-efficient manner.

- **Accessible training:** Teachers should be able to access training easily and conveniently, whether through online courses, in-person workshops, or other methods. The training should be available at a time and place that is convenient for the teacher.

- **Relevant skills based on evidence:** The training should focus on implementing skills in practice that they need to make a real impact in their classrooms.

- **Best practice:** The training should draw on best practices from the field, incorporating the latest research and insights from experienced educators. Teachers should have the opportunity to learn from their peers and share their own experiences.

- **Supportive community:** Teachers should feel supported and valued as they participate in training. This might include opportunities to connect with other teachers, share resources, and collaborate on projects. Creating a community of practice can help teachers feel less isolated and more empowered in their work.

Overall, training providers should focus on delivering high-quality, relevant training that is accessible, time-efficient, and supportive of teacher learning and growth. By doing so, they can help teachers become more effective and make a real difference in the lives of children.

This case study highlights how we can train our teachers en masse whilst giving them the agency to implement wellbeing programmes in a way that best suits their setting and young people.

Case Study
Norfolk County Council RISE Up

In April 2022, Norfolk County Council used some of the Department of Education 'Wellbeing in Education' grant to commission the 'RISE Up' programme. The 'RISE Up' programme guides teachers to reduce students' anxiety, build their confidence and create sustainable early intervention wellbeing programmes within 90 days. The programme was designed to offer a toolbox of self-care strategies and physical activities to support young people to manage their mental wellbeing. I provided bespoke support after staff completed the online training, so the programme was adapted to each specific school's needs.

Norfolk County Council was motivated to commission the RISE Up programme after young people across the county consistently highlighted mental health and wellbeing as the issue they were most concerned about. More consistently providing early intervention strategies and learning, and identifying those young people who need help earlier, are both key to improving support.

RISE Up can be used in a range of curriculum areas, offering strategies to manage the mental wellbeing of young people. The programme has three aims:

1. To identify individual young people struggling with their mental health and direct them to the specialist support they need as early as possible.

2. To provide young people with a range of self-care strategies to protect and build their mental wellbeing to transform their life chances and reduce the pressure on upstream services.

3. To teach the link between physical activity and mental wellbeing.

The programme has a clear emerging and emerged evidence base and there has been fantastic buy-in at the secondary level, enabling Norfolk County Council to build a community of like-minded colleagues who can transform the mental wellbeing of young people over the coming years. This is especially important for relationship building and managed moves. Norfolk County Council is moving towards a consistency of approach across settings, so programmes like these are really important.

62 out of 76 Norfolk Secondary and Special schools participated in the programme, with over 350 teachers and support staff accessing the training. Over 10,000 young people in Norfolk have benefitted from the programme. 93% of young people reported that their ability to manage their wellbeing improved after completing the programme.

RISE Up has received positive feedback from young people. Lily, 14, said: "I notice that the teachers pay so much attention to everybody - not a day goes by where I'm not asked how I am about five times. You really feel cared about."

Sam, 13, said: "My mental health has gone from really low to the highest level it has ever been. I've realised that I can turn my problems into solutions for my future. The 'RISE Up' unit has helped me in many ways such as building my confidence and my self-esteem. Now my body knows that it can go further than I ever expected and my confidence about my mental health is higher than ever before."

RISE Up received many 5-star reviews from teachers who found the programme important for integrating wellbeing and health into their curriculum and pedagogy. The programme has empowered teachers with the knowledge they need to help improve their students' mental health.

In conclusion
The RISE Up programme has been successful in supporting young people to manage their mental wellbeing in Norfolk. The programme's focus on early intervention strategies and learning, and identifying those young people who need help earlier, has been important in improving support.

Our partnership with Norfolk County Council has helped to build a community of like-minded colleagues who can transform the mental wellbeing of young people over the coming years. The positive feedback from young people and teachers is a testament to the programme's success in empowering young people and providing teachers with the knowledge and skills they need to support their students' mental health.

This case study is evidence that we can provide appropriate training for teachers on a large scale so that they have the skills needed to impact young people's mental wellbeing. It is a cost effective method when compared with the amount of money required to provide treatment for a year in CAMHS. More importantly, it is far more beneficial to both the individual and wider society to create young people with the skills they need to flourish in life rather than having to fix an adult who is struggling later on.

The benefits for our young people

Creating more transformational teachers in a post-Covid education world can bring about various benefits that can positively impact students' lives in the short and long term.

One of the immediate benefits is the transformation of relationships between teachers and students. Transformational teachers are those who create meaningful and personal connections with their students, and this can lead to improved behaviour, engagement, and attendance, which will ultimately result in improved learning, progress, and academic attainment.

Transformational teachers can help break the cycle of childhood trauma in the long term. Childhood trauma can have a lasting impact on a person's life, leading to mental health problems, substance abuse, and other negative outcomes. By building outstanding relationships with our children, transformational teachers can create a safe and supportive environment that can help mitigate the effects of childhood trauma, potentially extending the quality and quantity of life for some.

Another short-term benefit of having transformational teachers is the early intervention skills they possess. These skills can help reduce anxiety and build confidence in children, which can improve their overall wellbeing and academic performance. In the long term, this can give many young people the life skills to manage their mental wellbeing long after they have left school, whatever the world throws at them and however the world develops.

Lastly, transformational teachers can promote physical activity among their students, which can have both short and long-term benefits. Physical activity has been shown to improve mental health and wellbeing, increase self-esteem, and reduce stress and anxiety. Additionally, it can help young people feel healthier, happier, calmer, a sense of belonging, loved and connected, and feel alive and energised.

Time to RISE Up together

If we can all work together as one big team, we can collaborate to create an inclusive society that we are proud of, for all our young people. By working together, we can help create a world where every young person feels supported, valued, and empowered to reach their full potential.

Collaboration is crucial to achieving this goal. We must work together to share our knowledge and expertise, to learn from one another, and to support each other in our efforts to improve the lives of young people. By pooling our resources, we can create more effective interventions, programmes, and policies that truly make a difference.

Creating an inclusive society is not just a moral imperative - it is a matter of saving lives and helping young people thrive in the future. Mental health challenges, social isolation, and discrimination can all have devastating effects on young people's wellbeing and future prospects. But by working together to create a supportive, inclusive environment, we can help young people overcome these challenges and build a brighter future.

It is time to RISE Up and take action. We must come together as a community and commit to creating a world where every young person feels supported, valued, and empowered to reach their full potential. By working together, we can create a better future for all young people - one where mental health is a top priority, inclusion is the norm, and every young person has the opportunity to thrive.

Are you ready to RISE UP?

Chapter summary

- To become a transformational teacher and improve our children's mental wellbeing in a post-COVID education world, we need to focus on the following formula: Outstanding relationships + Early Intervention Strategies + Opportunities for Physical Activity = Transformational Teacher for Mental Wellbeing.
- To create transformational teachers we need all stakeholders to come together such as frontline teachers, senior leaders, the government, Ofsted, parents, children, social media companies, training providers to form One Big Team.
- Creating more transformational teachers in a post-Covid education world can bring about numerous benefits, including transformed relationships, improved academic performance, breaking the cycle of childhood trauma, building life skills, and promoting physical activity. These benefits can positively impact students' lives both in the short and long term and help them navigate the challenges of an ever-changing world.
- It is time to RISE Up and take action. We must come together as a community and commit to creating a world where every young person feels supported, valued, and empowered to reach their full potential. By working together, we can create a better future for all young people.

Critical questions

1. How can you contribute to improve mental wellbeing outcomes for young people so that we can RISE Up together?

2. What training and support do you need to feel psychologically safe, supported, and able to contribute?

Chapter references

- Sir Ken Robinson (2006). Do schools kill creativity? | Sir Ken Robinson. YouTube. Available at: https://www.youtube.com/watch?v=iG9CE55wbtY.

www.ingramcontent.com/pod-product-compliance
Lightning Source LLC
Chambersburg PA
CBHW082020300426
44117CB00015B/2290